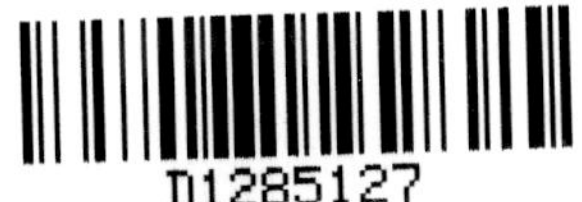

Women's Rites, Women's Mysteries

Praise for Women's Rites, Women's Mysteries

Women's Rites, Women's Mysteries is a well-written, thoughtful, and useful book that can help women with important passages in our lives, as well as with everyday life. The book is well grounded in research and analysis. Ruth Barrett provides a level of insight seldom found in books of this genre.

—Riane Eisler, best-selling author of *The Chalice and the Blade* and *Sacred Pleasure*

Ruth Barrett brings her many years of experience in teaching and priestessing in the Dianic tradition to this book. Her thoughtfulness, intelligence, and depth of understanding make it a valuable resource and will open a new perspective for many Pagans.

—Starhawk, best-selling author of *The Spiral Dance* and *The Fifth Sacred Thing*

Ruth Barrett has given us the missing link between a good and the great ritual. Millions of women are interested in goddess worship today, in personal or communal activities. There are many books to learn from, but Ruth Barrett has given us the depth and reasons why. She reframes the knowledge once again for the new generation, as we must for webbing the Goddess back into herstory. Ruth has thoughtfully deepened and filled the rest of the Dianic sacred script.

—Zsuzsanna Budapest, best-selling author of *The Holy Book of Women's Mysteries* and *Summoning the Fates*

Ruth Barrett's wise words open the door to a greater connection with spirit through ritual. This book will be of aid and interest to any woman who wishes to deepen her understanding of this aspect of the spiritual search.

—Patricia Monaghan, author of *The Book of Goddesses and Heroines* and *Seasons of the Witch*

Even though this book was written for women, its lessons can be applied in any ritual context. Ruth Barrett challenges the reader to think about the process of creating rituals. This is no "cookbook." Ruth covers many angles that are missing in previous books on ritual and fills in important details that other authors leave out. Definitely the best book on creating rituals that I have read.

—Kerr Cuhulain, author of *The Wiccan Warrior* and *Full Contact Magick*

Ruth is a great priestess. It is wonderful to have some of her vast experience captured on pages at last. With this book she has brought the Dianic tradition forward, clarified its Goddess-centered premise, developed its thealogy, and provided strong material for ritual building. Women will use this book and the world will change. Most importantly, she has emphasized sisterhood and shared power; the soul of our movement.

—Shekhinah Mountainwater, author of *Ariadne's Thread*

Women's Rites, Women's Mysteries by Ruth Rhiannon Barrett, high priestess *emerita* of the Los Angeles Circle of Aradia, is the best book anyone, female or male, who has anything to do with rituals is going to find. Drawing on more than twenty-five years of practical experience in constructing and facilitating private and public rituals for large and small groups, Ruth speaks from her heart when she tells us how to do the work. This book addresses numerous issues of vital importance to all Pagans . . . *Women's Rites* is one of the most useful books you'll ever find on how to construct and facilitate a ritual. Whether you're a hidebound Gardnerian or a hidden Myjestic or an adventuresome eclectic, whether you're male or female, whether you do rituals every time the moon changes or just find a public Samhain ritual to attend—this is the book you need to be reading before you attend or participate in any ritual. As the thousands of women who have attended Circle of Aradia's public rituals for twenty years can attest, Ruth is a superb ritualist. She knows how to construct and lead a ritual that will be meaningful to everyone in the room. She knows how to move the energy and keep people's attention. If you have anything to do with ritual, buy this book and read it carefully. You won't find better, more practical information anywhere else.

—*Sagewoman Magazine* review, 2005

Women's Rites, Women's Mysteries is at out one of the most useful books ever written on ritual. The writing is very clear, the concepts are very understandable and the directions are concise and easy to follow. The rituals are adaptable for individual work or for group workings. Meditations are provided, as well as follow-up for after the ritual, for personal reflection on what you did or did not achieve. If you ever want to engage in ritual—public or private—buy this book!

—*The Beltane Papers* review, Issue #39, 2006

Ruth is a fabulous teacher and knows more about ritual than any priestess I've ever met.

—Wendy Griffin, Academic Dean Emerita of Cherry Hill Seminary.

Ruth
Barrett

Women's Rites, Women's Mysteries

Intuitive Ritual Creation

Tidal Time Publishing, LLC
Mason, Michigan

Third edition, 2018, Tidal Time Publishing, LLC
(First edition ©2004 AuthorHouse)
(Second Edition, 2007, Llewellyn Publications)

Interior and cover design by Steuben Press
Cover art by Nancy Chien-Eriksen, "Diana, Goddess of the Hunt"
(airbrushed acrylic on canvas)
Interior illustrations on pages by Jane E. Ward
Crossed Labrys illustration by Shen Womack-Smith; beardedragyns.org

Library of Congress Cataloging-in-Publication Data
Barrett, Ruth, 1954
Women's rites, women's mysteries: intuitive ritual creation / Ruth Barrett. —3rd ed.
Includes bibliographical references and index.
ISBN -13: 978-0-9971467-1-4
ISBN -10: 0997146710
1. Women—Religious life. 2. Rites and ceremonies. 3. Spiritual life.
4. Goddess religion. 5. Feminism.
Library of Congress Control Number: 2018905537

Tidal Time Publishing, LLC
P.O. Box 709
Mason, Michigan 48854

www.tidaltimepublishing.com
Printed in the United States of America

Contents

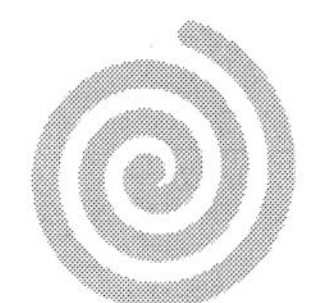

Acknowledgments

To my teachers:

She who first called me, and she who answered the call.

Shekhinah Mountainwater (of blessed memory), my first goddess teacher, who introduced me to magical sisterhood in the moon hut in the woods. Thank you for the singing magic and for teaching me the profound power of myth as living stories of the present. Thank you for overlaying the goddess year and Women's Mysteries and inspiring me to integrate these themes more consciously into Dianic seasonal rituals.

Zsuzsanna Budapest, who ordained me to continue the Dianic tradition she started in Los Angeles in 1971.

Windsong, who introduced me to magic of the elements from Celtic craft. Thank you for your teachings and your generous heart.

Kay Gardner (of blessed memory), for believing in me more than I believed in myself. You will always live in my heart.

Deena Metzger, in whose writing classes in the late 1980s I began to learn freedom of flight through imagination. Thank you for sharing your visionary ways and the power of words.

My parents, Florence (of blessed memory) and Mike Bienenfeld, who lovingly raised our family within the rich traditions of Reconstructionist Judaism, providing my brothers and me with a model of integrated spirituality for daily life. Thank you for embodying spiritual leadership and an unending dedication to community. Thank you both for teaching me that it is a divine duty for human beings to evolve religion and make it relevant to the times we are living in. Thanks to the brilliant inspiration of Rabbi Mordecai Kaplan, who said, "The ancient authorities are entitled to a vote, but not a veto."[1]

My beloved daughter, Amanda, light of my life, who taught me that

[1] Kaplan, *Not So Random Thoughts*, 263.

I could love another human being beyond anything I believed myself capable of. Thank you for the blessed gift of mothering such a brilliant, talented, and beautiful spirit.

Falcon, my beloved life companion, magical partner, and teacher, for sharing my commitment to bringing ritual partnership teachings forward to women. Thank you for sitting by my side to edit numerous drafts of this book, adding your suggestions, wisdom, and multisensory perceptions to the content. Thank you for journeying with me to an ever-deepening magic.

The Dianic women's community and Circle of Aradia in Los Angeles, for granting me the highest honor possible by allowing me to serve you from 1980–2000, and especially the many dedicated women who participated over the years in the ritual facilitator's circle for Circle of Aradia's community seasonal rituals. Thanks to all of my students everywhere who came through my classes in Dianic tradition in the early years. Your participation helped me to clarify these teachings, and to become a better teacher through your brilliant questions and commitment to transforming your lives through the power of ritual. My thanks to HP Cerridwyn RoseLabrys for your commitment to our tradition and by holding center so beautifully at Circle of Aradia.

To Nan Brooks, Pat Devin, Wendy Griffin, Rae Atira-Soncea (of blessed memory), Patricia Monaghan (of blessed memory), Kasi Moondeer, and Gretchen Lawler for their inspiring conversations and ideas to this book.

To Karen Cayer whose personal support and help with all things internet has been a blessing in my life.

To the women of The Spiral Door Women's Mystery School of Magick and Ritual Arts senior support staff and teachers – Nicki Harris, Sara Macaluso, Jaymie Homan, and Tracie Jones. You have restored my faith in the power of women to stand in integrity in this world, even when it isn't easy. To my current students everywhere, thank you for blessing me to be a beginner again, to grow and deepen in both my learning and teaching to the present moment. Together, with open minds and hearts, we learn to shape chaos and human needs into works of great power and beauty.

About This New Edition

I am so excited to be re-publishing *Women's Rites, Women's Mysteries* through my own publishing company, Tidal Time Publishing, LLC. I've had the opportunity to make updates, substantial additions (including an updated expanded index), and revisions to this book since its 2007 publication with Llewellyn. This 3rd edition also re-integrates material on the Guardian Priestess that was including in the 1st edition, but by my choice at the time, not included in the Llewellyn edition.

Since this book's original publication in 2004, exclusively female-centered rituals and even the right for women to gather have been under increased attack and eliminated by so-called progressives and transgender activists as being "non-inclusive". The foundation of the Dianic tradition has always been exclusively for and about natal women and girls, and not about males or males who identify as women. Gender identity is not about or akin to biological sex, and transgender ideology dismisses biology, girlhood, and sex-based oppression as completely irrelevant to being a woman. Dianic rituals have always been about restoring reverence to the female body, celebrating female biology, autonomy, agency, and addressing ways to counter and heal from sex-based oppression and violence. I am one of many working for liberation from gender stereotypes that limit and oppress humanity, while recognizing and seeking ways to honor the sacred in our biological differences.

The definition of "feminism" that I refer to throughout this book remains steadfast to the eradication of the dominator model of power in our lives, institutions and our world. Feminist issues include sexism, pay inequity, safe housing, healthcare, domestic violence, the pornography epidemic, human trafficking, reproductive autonomy, sexual violence, environmental issues, sustainability, and much more.

Invocation

Goddess Mother of the Earth,
Your belly swells to give Life birth.
Womb from which all things must pass,
Mother of bone, and rock, and grass.
By blood and root, and bud and skin,
We call on You to enter in,
By branch and stem, by seed and flower,
Bless us with Your loving power!

Goddess Diana, Holy Mother,
Antlered Huntress of the Night,
As You are our sacred will,
Guide our arrows into flight!
Protector of all living things,
You, the strength of woman-soul,
Take our passion and our will,
To heal and mend the world whole!
Blessed be!

Introduction

From earliest times across cultures, women have created, facilitated, and participated in ceremonies and rituals that are sex-based and separate from those of males. The practice of female-only ritual was not born from a rejection of the male sex but rather from understanding and honoring women's unique biological rites of passage and the ways in which our female bodies inform our diverse life experiences. The purpose of this book is to guide women through the creation and facilitation of rituals for their life passages and personal experiences from the goddess and female-centered spiritual perspective of Dianic Witchcraft.

There are physical and psychological experiences and rites of passage common to all women's lives, crossing the boundaries of age, class, culture, race, ability, sexual orientation, and religion. This book was written to empower women by asserting that we, as the physical embodiment of the Goddess (She who is the life force present in all things), are sacred, and our rites of passage are sacred occasions worthy of ritualizing.

My intention in this book is to teach you how to *think* like a ritualist. By working with the practices in this book, you will move through a process that empowers you to identify your needs and helps you to fulfill them for yourself. As you grow in your own personal process, you may also choose to assist others in accessing their own intuitive creativity through ritual making. This book is specifically not a didactic ritual "cookbook." Though books containing specific rituals tell you exactly what to do, they rarely explain the reason or motivation behind a given enactment or symbol, leaving you with only a superficial understanding of the rituals. In simply following a recipe, you are less likely to develop the inner tools needed to create meaningful rituals on your own.

I've been teaching magic and ritual making for almost forty years, and in that time I've consistently found that while women have a great hunger for ritual to reflect the events in their lives, they often do not know how to begin. For many, the very thought of creating meaningful ritual is too intimidating. Out of societal conditioning, women often wait for others to take the lead or simply suppress their own needs, desires, and dreams to varying degrees. Consequently, we lead lives that too often are physically, emotionally, and spiritually unfulfilled. Because daily life has become so increasingly trivialized and superficial, it is all the more critical that women challenge themselves to make meaning in their own lives and in the lives of others. We are the women we've been waiting for.

My first teacher of goddess spirituality was Shekhinah Mountainwater (of blessed memory), a founding mother of the goddess movement. I met Shekhinah in 1972 and studied with her weekly in 1975 and 1976. When my studies formally began, there were no feminist or goddess-centered spirituality books in print. In 1976, Zsuzsanna Budapest, widely considered the mother of contemporary Dianic Wiccan tradition, published *The Feminist Book of Lights and Shadows*. This early work was incorporated into *The Holy Book of Women's Mysteries* and included ancient women's festivals rediscovered by the research of Jane Harrison. This pioneering book drew many women to feminist and Goddess-centered Witchcraft. I met Z that same year and was eventually initiated into her coven, the Susan B. Anthony Coven #1.

Four years later, at Hallowmas 1980, I was ordained as a High Priestess by Z, and she passed on to me her Los Angeles ministry. For the next twenty years I served as High Priestess to the local Dianic community, teaching and facilitating ritual. I eventually co-founded Circle of Aradia, which remains the longest-lived Dianic community in the United States. I was the second woman Z ordained as a High Priestess, the first being visionary musician Kay Gardner (of blessed memory).

Being twenty-five years old at the time of my ordination, and a new mother of a daughter, the responsibility of taking on Z's ministry felt enormous. How was I to build on Z's teachings and her largely improvisational approach to ritual? It was apparent to me early on that a majority of the women coming to the Craft through the feminist movement lacked a common magical foundation. I was concerned that this lack would compromise our ability to be as magically effective as we could be, despite our great passion to make changes in our lives and in the world. I began to develop and build a sound, consistent magical foundation and practice that I could teach my students and community, who could then pass on their knowledge and skills to future generations of Dianic Witches. To accomplish this, I explored both within and outside of the goddess spirituality movement, seeking knowledge from other Wiccan and Craft family traditions. I began to incorporate and apply these magical practices into a Dianic context. I also brought my own numerous contributions to the content of the tradition through my music, creativity, sensibilities, and inspiration from the Goddess, as I was empowered to do. Z was proud of the successes I had in fleshing out and evolving the tradition that she revived, and even more so in my ability to teach it and effectively pass it on.

In 2000, like Z before me, I ordained a new High Priestess for Circle of Aradia and moved to Wisconsin where I lived and taught until 2013. In Wisconsin my work was focused on developing and co-teaching a clergy training program for Dianic women with my life companion, Falcon River. This collaboration resulted in the Spiral Door Women's Mystery School of Magick and Ritual Arts, and the co-founding of Temple of Diana, Inc., a federally recognized Dianic temple. I returned to southern California for four years to help with my mother's care until her passing in 2016. After my mother's death, Falcon and I returned to the Midwest, and now reside in the state of Michigan where I continue to teach local classes and workshops in magic and ritual arts at women's festivals and conferences throughout the United States and abroad.

I wrote *Women's Rites, Women's Mysteries* to be used as a guide and resource for individuals and groups, both beginners and experienced ritualists alike.

Years of working with women individually and in groups has helped me to develop a clear, step-by-step process for teaching the components of effective ritual-making for any occasion or life-cycle event. These steps are included in chapters on how to develop a ritual's purpose and theme, learn energetic preparation, and create an appropriate ritual structure. Other chapters provide guidance in writing invocations, in-depth facilitation guidelines for small and large groups, and methods for constructive evaluation and ongoing improvement of rituals.

Drawing heavily on Shekhinah Mountainwater's influence and teachings from my early days of goddess studies, I integrated and evolved a deeper concept of a woman's wheel of the year into the cycle of Women's Mysteries for Dianic rituals. In chapter 9, "The Year Is a Dancing Woman," you will find an explanation of nature's seasonal holidays as they correspond to and overlap with female life-cycle events.

The concluding chapters on ritual facilitation as spiritual service and on the role of the Priestess, with focus on the service of the Ritual Priestess and the Guardian Priestess, offer my perspectives from experiences in contemporary spiritual service in Dianic Wiccan circles. In the appendices I have included substantial Dianic herstory, cosmology, and ample doses of personal opinion from my experience as an elder of this tradition.

If you are a woman who is new to women's ritual—even if your spiritual or religious affiliation currently lies outside a goddess and female-centered perspective—I welcome and invite you to drink from the well of creative inspiration as you begin to integrate ritual-making into your life. If you are among the thousands of women who are already practicing Dianic Witchcraft or another form of goddess-centered spirituality, I invite you to expand and deepen your skills in the area of ritual making and facilitation for yourself and others. It is my intention to clarify, expand, and deepen your knowledge of commonly discussed magical concepts by presenting information often omitted in other sources.

It is my hope that by celebrating Women's Mysteries and ritualizing other life-cycle events, women can heal from the internal and external oppression that estranges body from mind to participate more fully in their lives and communities. I have done my best to give you what I have learned, created, and hold sacred. Through the rituals we create and share, may we enter the Mysteries of female embodiment with wonder and awe, always expanding the possibility for deeper meaning in the daily sacredness of being alive.

In Her service,
Ruth Rhiannon Barrett

chapter 1

THE POWER OF WOMEN'S RITUAL

The invited guests arrive to the heartbeat of a drum. A circle forms as women begin to sing a chant whose words praise the sacred Crone, the Goddess in Her third aspect of maturity and deepening wisdom, as well as the woman being honored tonight as she crosses the threshold into her elderhood.

She is changing, she is changing,
her river now runs underground
Time of deepening, time of deepening,
the years of bleeding are all done
Inward journey, inward journey, final secrets to be sung
Name her river "Wise Blood" in celebration.[2]

Led by a procession of singing women, Kay enters the room dressed in colorful robes. She invokes her ancestors, calling the spirits who have guided her in her life as a woman and musician. The facilitating priestess explains to the guests how, in women's rituals, every age is honored and each transition marked as one passes into another stage of being. This ritual tonight honors Kay as an elder who formally enters a new stage of life as a wise woman.

Kay lights seven of the eight candles that represent the Fibonacci series,[3] sharing a memory, image, or some wisdom from every stage of

---

[2] Ila Suzanne, "Menopause Chant," in *Ouroborous: Seasons of Life*, an oratorio composed by Kay Gardner (Ladyslipper Records, 1994).

[3] The Fibonacci sequence, named after Leonardo Pisano Fibonacci (1170–1250), is a number sequence in which each number is the sum of the two preceding numbers. This sequence appears in different areas of mathematics and science.

her life. Her daughter presents her with a symbol of her mother-line, linking the generations one to another. Kay plays her flute, improvising from Spirit, letting divine inspiration come through her music. While speaking aloud her future visions and wishes for the Fates to weave, Kay lifts two chalices in her hands, pouring water back and forth between them, symbolizing the flow between her manifested art and creativity. She speaks her commitment to herself as an elder and to the aspects of cronehood she will celebrate. Lifting the full chalice to her lips, Kay drinks in her commitments, making the magic a part of her internally. She then punctuates the magic externally by lighting the eighth candle, symbolizing the manifestation of creativity in her next stage of life. As another chant begins, Kay gives thanks for the many gifts of her life.[4]

...

Kay's croning ritual is only one beautiful example of how a woman's life cycle may be celebrated.

The Dianic Tradition, Women-Only Ritual and Female Sovereign Space

The widespread distribution of author and feminist activist Zsuzsanna Budapest's *The Holy Book of Women's Mysteries* (originally published in 1976 as *The Feminist Book of Lights and Shadows*) on its publication in 1989 initiated a surge of interest in women's personal and group ritual from a feminist and goddess-centered perspective. Z's books defined the foundations of what she called Dianic Witchcraft as "feminist spirituality."

The Dianic Wiccan tradition is a goddess and female-centered, earth-centered, feminist denomination of the Wiccan religion (also known as Witchcraft), revived and inspired by Z Budapest in the early 1970s. A visionary by nature, Z realized that what later was named the second wave feminist movement, needed a spiritual foundation. She knew that through goddess-centered ritual, women would be able to connect with,

[4] Adapted from a croning ritual created by Kay Gardner and the author in December 1996.

honor, and heal the deepest parts of themselves, bringing their inner strength and wisdom to conscious awareness. This still remains true today. As women create and participate in ritual with other women, we are empowered by witnessing and supporting one another in our path of healing. Participating in women's ritual allows us to evaluate, validate, and honor the physical crossroads and emotional transitions of our lives.

From the beginning of the goddess movement to the present, women have been increasingly drawn to Z Budapest's branch of Dianic tradition for its feminist values, its exclusively female participants and its emphasis on Women's Mysteries. With the exception of Shekhinah Mountainwater's teachings, Z Budapest's Dianic tradition was the only Women's Mystery tradition available for women to tend to their individual souls.

The Dianic tradition is distinguished by its exclusive focus on the Goddess in its cosmology, magical and ritual practices, and exclusively female-centered rituals enacted in what I call "female sovereign space". "Sovereignty" meaning "having independent authority, the right to govern itself, unlimited power or authority, possessed of supreme power, enjoying autonomy."[5] I posit that female sovereignty and female sovereign spaces are necessary for women to truly become free and heal from our generational inheritance of sex-based oppression and gender stereotypes.

The spiritual focus and ritual practices of Dianic tradition are practiced with, for, and about the female experience of living within a patriarchal society, and the many ways that our female bodies inform our life experiences. Feminist consciousness, values, and visions are often interwoven into the ritual content. As my beloved friend, author Patricia Monaghan (of blessed memory), said in her keynote speech at a Daughters of Diana Gathering[6], "Our practice is oracular, our heritage is feminist." Dianic tradition's Goddess-centered cosmology, ethics, eclectic practices

---

[5] All definitions are from the Merriam-Webster Dictionary.

[6] Daughters of Diana Gathering is an annual conference produced by Temple of Diana, Inc. www.templeofdiana.org.

and rituals are primarily shaped and inspired by fragments of ancient Goddess worship, folklore, the legacy of our feminist foremothers, our ancient and contemporary oracular heritage of divination, and some adaptations from other Wiccan traditions. Dianic tradition's female sovereign rites herald back to ancient times in which priestesses chose to dedicate themselves exclusively to a specific goddess and to serve women through that devotion. Women choosing a female-centered and goddess-focused ritual practice are actually reclaiming an ancient heritage of their foremothers.

The heart of the Dianic Wiccan tradition is honoring what we call, Women's Mysteries: the five blood mysteries of our birth, menarche, giving birth/lactation, menopause, and death. Contemporary Dianic rites of Women's Mysteries also include other essential physical, emotional, and psychic passages that only women can experience by being a natal-born female living in a patriarchal culture. As a feminist Wiccan tradition, the Dianic tradition speaks to how becoming conscious about how growing up in a largely female hating culture affects our daily lives, and our feelings about *being* female.

Dianic rituals celebrate the mythic cycle of the Goddess in the earth's seasonal cycles of birth, death, and regeneration, corresponding and overlapping with every woman and girl's own life-cycle transitions. Therefore, Dianics honor the Goddess in every woman through our seasonal ritual celebrations. Our rites mark life passages and celebrate women's ability to create life, sustain and protect life, and return to the Goddess in death.

Dianic seasonal themes are not based on an exclusively heterosexual fertility cycle, as other Wiccan traditions are, and therefore inclusive of lesbian sexual orientation. From the beginning of its contemporary practice, the Dianic Wiccan tradition has also inspired rituals that are intended to help women heal from, and counter the effects of, misogynistic, patriarchal social institutions and religions.

Women embody the Goddess as Creatrix. Physically, we embody the power of the Goddess in Her capacity to create and sustain life. Our wombs are the living metaphor of Her creative potential and thus are the very source of our creative power. Even if a woman has had a hysterectomy, the power of her womb will continue to carry within her the energetic potential of its creativity. Inspired by ancient mythic cosmology of the Goddess, wherein She draws Herself out of Herself in the original act of creation, many women embrace the metaphor of spiritually giving birth to themselves and each other. Within Dianic Wiccan rites, the focus is on each woman's own experience, opinions, ideas, and feelings, and not those of her spouse, lover, family, or friends. Within Dianic circles, women have the opportunity to discover their true selves, apart from the constraints of patriarchal culture. I have often seen women go through an adjustment period, having never before considered prioritizing or focusing on their own thoughts, feelings, and ideas.

In earlier times, women's exclusive gatherings were recognized as being vital for the good of the greater community. Z Budapest describes how in pre-patriarchal times,

> women's mysteries were concerned with the natural cycles of life, and rituals were designed for specific purposes: to insure good weather conditions for crops, to promote good health among the people, to guard against disease and pestilence, and to maintain good fortune for the entire community by conscious reinforcement of the practice of keeping women in contact with each other as manifestations of the Goddess.[7]

There are contemporary feminist reasons why it is empowering for women to spend time in female sovereign space. In her book *Fugitive Information*, feminist writer Kay Leigh Hagan writes that

---

[7] Budapest, *The Holy Book of Women's Mysteries*, 55–56.

> relief from constant exposure to men and male needs is necessary for a woman to perceive the depth of her innate female power, which she is conditioned to ignore, deny, destroy, or sacrifice. Time spent alone and in consciously constructed women-only space allows a woman to explore aspects of herself that cannot surface in the company of men.[8]

By prioritizing female-sovereign spaces, whether in ritual or daily life, many women are able to find their center and explore their own truths. Baby girls are born through and into the unfolding mysteries of womanhood. The circle of womanhood is the very circle of life itself, for it is upon our sacred womb blood, the generative gift that is passed from mother to daughter, that human life depends. While all human beings celebrate this mystery, standing humbled by the enormity of it, only women can fully embody the experience.

The word *mystery* is defined as

> something that has not been, or cannot be, explained; hence, something beyond human comprehension; 2. A profound secret; an enigma; 3. Rites, practices, or doctrine revealed only to initiates; 4. Profound and inexplicable quality or character; 5. A secret religious rite to which none but duly initiated worshippers were admitted.[9]

Caitlin and John Matthews, Celtic scholars of the Western mystery tradition, say that the word *mystery* comes from the Greek *myein*, meaning "to keep silent."[10] The Western mystery tradition refers to a body of esoteric teaching and knowledge, a system of magical technique and

---

[8] Hagan, *Fugitive Information*, 68.

[9] *Webster's New Collegiate Dictionary*, 557.

[10] Matthews, *The Western Way*, Vol. I, 37.

belief that practitioners maintain dates back to the beginning of time; the "foretime" in which our ancestors first began to explore the inner realms of existence. This tradition is called "Western" to distinguish it clearly from the Eastern and Oriental systems.[11] Although the Western mystery tradition does not identify itself as part of Wicca, its teachings have had a great influence on modern Witchcraft. In the Western mystery tradition,

> mysteries are gateways, thresholds between this world and the Other, the meeting place of gods and people. As symbolic verities, they appear removed from the mundane world, difficult for the uninitiated to approach: from the viewpoint of the Otherworld, mysteries are a language in which spiritual concepts can be communicated and stored.[12]

According to the Matthews, "the real secret about the mysteries is that they cannot be communicated by one being to another," and "while keys and guidelines to this knowledge can be given, *the actual knowledge is revealed to the initiate by personal experience and revelatory realization*"[13] (italics added). Mysteries are experiences wherein specific wisdom is deeply embedded. To use a familiar saying, you can lead a horse to water, but you cannot make it drink. Ah, but you *can* make it thirsty! The work of a priestess or ritual facilitator is to make a woman thirsty for the mystery that only she can open herself to experiencing. While the ritualist can create the possibility of mystery, each recipient herself must step over the threshold alone. Whether a woman is new to the Goddess or a long-time practitioner, if she approaches the threshold of mystery with the open mind of an initiate, she allows herself greater possibility of entering and experiencing the mystery.

---

[11] Ibid., 2.
[12] Ibid., 36.
[13] Ibid., 37.

Mystery is truth-that-can-be-known only through personal experience. However, similar to something hidden that is revealed as layers of veils are lifted, the truth becomes clearer, yet it often still remains just out of reach, awesome, elusive, and enigmatic. Like a snake shedding her skin, consciousness reveals, unfolds, and expands with each experience of mystery. One stands in its presence, awestruck and grateful for the gift of living. This knowing cannot be captured or compartmentalized, so while we can have access to the knowledge inherent in the Mystery of our woman's body, its totality is always just out of our reach. By experiencing our own body as sacred, natural, beautiful, and whole, we are able to access all the resources within the body of the Goddess since we are a reflection of Her. Women's Mysteries honor and celebrate our rites of life—an organic, natural, and unfolding process. Women's rites reclaim what is naturally our own: our bodies, our wisdom, our intuition, and our power.

The word *ritual*, from the Sanskrit *r'tu*, is "any act of magic toward a purpose." *Rita* means "a proper course"; *ri*, meaning birth, is the root of *red*, pronounced "reed" in Old English. *R'tu* means "menstrual," suggesting that ritual began as an act of recognizing menarche.[14] In Dianic ritual, we initiate each other into the circle of women from cradle to grave. We initiate ourselves and assist others in accessing the knowledge and innate power of creation that is our female birthright. We feed each other the fruit from the Tree of Knowledge, the Apple of Wisdom, symbol of female wisdom and the mysteries of creation. When we take our power as women to initiate ourselves into the five blood mysteries, we are taking the conscious initiative to evolve ourselves beyond our patriarchal cultural and religious inheritance rather than allowing our evolution to be defined by others.

---

[14] Translations from Grahn, *Blood, Bread, and Roses*, 5.

Sex And Gender

Given that the Dianic tradition is based in the experience of being female-embodied, I want to make clear the difference between the words "sex" and "gender". The words *sex* and *gender* are not equivalent words, and not at all interchangeable. *Sex* is the word that refers to the body, a set of biological attributes in humans and animals; our physicality internally and externally. Sexual anatomical and physiological features come from DNA—the chromosomes and genes that are present in every cell of an organism. In terms of biology, a woman is an adult human female and a girl is a pre-pubescent human female.

In contrast, *gender* is a socially-agreed-upon mental concept which puts human characteristics into strict gender categories, and decides which characteristics are assigned to each sex. Most of us can easily name these so-called "natural" qualities ascribed to males or females, attributes like strength, gentleness, and so on, and commonly referred to as "masculinity" and "femininity". These qualities, however, are universal human qualities inherent in males *and* females. When these human characteristics become gendered and enforced, we have set limitations on our humanity. Those who insist that enforced gender stereotypes are "natural" and based on biological sex, are asserting their belief that females and males are incapable of the full range of human expression. Deviations to social stereotypes are condemned as unnatural and considered dangerous to the culture. Gender socialization influences how people perceive themselves and each other, how they act and interact, and how power and resources are distributed in society. It becomes obvious that gender stereotypes are a tool of patriarchy when these supposed natural qualities have to be enforced.

The Dianic tradition rejects patriarchal gender stereotypes for girls and women, boys and men, and wants liberation from all patriarchal limitations of human expression, while celebrating the sacred bodies we have.

The Dianic tradition is not about the male body, male life passages, socialization and cultural experiences: those are Men's Mysteries. For males, the natural processes and transitions of the female body are simply outside their experience, no matter how much they might think they understand or empathize with women they have known. Conversely, women can never truly understand what males experience through their own unique biology or how those experiences might inform their lives. It is for this simple reason that males, or males who gender-identify as women, are not included as participants in the Dianic tradition. Some Dianic women also participate with their male partners or children at other times and in other Wiccan denominations. It would be as disrespectful to men's unique needs and experiences in celebrating their embodied Mysteries if women insisted on inclusion, as it is for men seeking inclusion in rituals of women's embodied Mysteries. Our Mysteries are simply not about them. It is my hope that eventually there will be as much understanding and support for exclusively female spiritual experiences as there are for those experiences exclusively for our beloved sons, brothers, and male partners.

Dualism and Gender Stereotypes

Dianic tradition differentiates from other Wiccan denominations whose cosmology and magical practices are based on a male/female duality and worship of the Goddess and the God, her male consort. Dianic rituals and practice focus exclusively on the Goddess as the original source of creation, the Primal Matrix. In the Dianic tradition, unlike other Wiccan paths, the seasonal year is not divided into male and female halves or based specifically on the heterosexual fertility cycle. Instead, seasonal holy days focus on the mythic cycles of the Goddess alone as she eternally transforms herself throughout the year. Her eternal seasonal dance of transformation becomes a metaphor for the cycle of women's lives.

In the Dianic tradition, the Goddess has always been inclusive of the God. Just as a mother creates, contains, and births both male and female from her body, the Goddess gives birth to both variations of Herself from Her womb. The God, however, cannot do the same for Her. In males there is no counterpart to the womb, and so Dianic celebrations of women's blood mysteries are simply not about the God, nor the specifically male experience. Although the God is not invoked in Dianic rituals, nor is there any specifically male imagery on the altar, He is always present as a part of Her totality. Choosing not to specifically invoke the God is not a denial of what is actually male in nature, or half the human race. Dianics simply do not focus on Him as separate from His mother, His creator and beloved.

A popular and widely accepted concept is that every person contains a male and female "side", with prescribed characteristics for each gender. Dianic tradition rejects this concept, as it serves only to perpetuate a divine and secular heterosexism. In other Wiccan traditions, the Goddess and the God have assigned gendered characteristics attributable to Their divine sex. It's hard to ignore how much these gendered "divine" characteristics are similar to the gender stereotypes enforced by the dominant culture already discussed. Consider questioning the source of these ascribed "natural" characteristics and enforced dualities by asking, "Who made this up?" and "Whose cause does this advance?" Historically, "natural" male traits that are valued in male-dominated cultures are considered "good." Traits less valued by the patriarchal culture are designated feminine and considered inferior, sometimes to the point of being declared evil.[15]

Enforced gender stereotypes ultimately disempower everyone. In a patriarchal culture, characteristics shared by all human beings such as loving and nurturing are not considered "natural" male characteristics, and strength and courage are not considered "natural" female characteristics. When I gave birth to my daughter by natural childbirth, I

[15] A historically glaring example of this extreme attitude was the *Malleus Maleficarum* (The Witches' Hammer), published in the fifteenth century by inquisitors Kramer and Sprenger. This sadistic manual was responsible for the deaths of suspected European witches.

experienced myself both physically and mentally more powerful then than at any other time in my life. Since strength and power are stereotypically gendered to males, does this imply that my "male" side birthed my baby? If a man is sensitive, loving, and nurturing, are we to say that his "inner feminine" has kicked in? Dualism reinforces the assumption that males are not naturally capable of gentleness, compassion, and receptivity. How absurd! The human traits of strength and gentleness are traits that all people need to be in balance within themselves. Teaching children that these gendered traits belong to only one sex or another perpetuates dualistic thinking and keeps males and females in adversarial opposition, inhibiting our capacity to become whole human beings. These arbitrary separations are oppressive to both sexes, limiting us in our thinking and behavior about who we are as individuals and what we are capable of being or becoming. Riane Eisler, author and activist, promotes the return of a partnership society:

> There are traits stereotypically labeled masculine that are in fact excellent human traits for both women and men. These are traits that both women and men can (and, if permitted, do) share: for example, assertiveness or the capacity to say what one wants rather than feeling one has to manipulate or placate, as powerless or dominated people are taught they must do. And, as many men are today also learning through both the men's and partnership movements, there are traits stereotypically labeled feminine, such as empathy and nurturing, that men, too, can find and, if permitted, do share—and above all, that these traits do not make a human being less of a man, but rather more so.[16]

By extension, then, wouldn't this thinking limit the nature of the gods

[16] Hagan, *Women Respond to the Men's Movement*, 52.

and goddesses? Surely they are as capable as we of great power, gentleness, compassion, and destruction. It's also hard to ignore the overarching emphasis in other Craft traditions on the young, sexy and fertile goddess with her lover, the young, lusty and always virile god. Let us not reinforce gender stereotypes on the deities we purport to honor.

In the past forty years, there have been many challenges to sexism, with some positive changes made. Most of you reading this book lead different lives and have many more choices available to you than did your mothers. However, while there have been some very real changes in the law and in the quality of life for some women and their children, the work of bringing down the patriarchal system is far from over. Girls still learn to hate themselves and their bodies when the ideal of patriarchal femininity as "natural" is reflected in every TV commercial and program. The majority of girls and women who don't measure up to this artificial standard of "femininity" spend their time (and often considerable resources) dealing personally with institutionalized sexism, in an effort to "fix" themselves to conform. Those girls and women who don't attempt or choose to conform to these standards have to deal with the fallout of being different. They are often bullied by their peers, called "unnatural", "lesbian", or assumed to be lesbian, often with little support for just being their non-conforming selves.

Males are still raised to see women as "other." One of the worst names you can call a little boy (after "faggot" or "gay"), is "girl." However, males are naturally born to identify with women. As a baby boy suckles from his mother's breast, he doesn't know that there is a difference between them: they are one. Later, the patriarchal institutions of family, culture, and/or religion take that baby boy away and teaches him "other-ness." Thereafter, his life is spent in proving how different he is from his mother and other females, and in distancing himself from what she represents within his own self. He learns to minimize her, degrade her, and rank himself above her. He must become everything that girls and women are not supposed to be according to patriarchal definitions of feminine traits and behaviors. He is supported and rewarded daily for doing so by our male-dominated patriarchal culture and more specifically through the institutionalized power dynamics of sexism.

Boys who are reluctant to separate completely from their mothers are often ridiculed, oppressed, and tortured with words ("mama's boy," "sissy," "fag," "soft male"[17]), threats, and sometimes blows. They are even murdered by their peers for not measuring up. The terrible irony of this cultural travesty is that when boys become young men, they are somehow supposed to love women.

Patriarchal culture continues to disempower our sons, inhibiting their ability to have true, loving, and intimate connections with women, both emotionally and sexually. This disempowerment also affects our sons' ability to have close relationships with other men. Some men can become allies to women as adults through hard work, vigilance, and, very likely, suffering. To truly love women, males must give up their male privilege and reject the dominant cultural values that institutionalize male supremacy. For a man to become a feminist ally involves a process of self-transformation, speaking and acting against the diverse purveyors of violence against women and girls. He must be willing to give up his male privilege that has been handed to him since birth. Men who choose to become true allies of women are outlaws from the "boys' club" and this places themselves at great risk. Becoming a male who truly loves and respects women takes greater courage than any patriarchal-defined act.

Dianic witches envision a world where *all* human beings are whole unto themselves. This does not mean that the self is isolated. Instead, the goal of living is to feel complete within oneself, not looking for completion through another person. This process takes work. Patriarchal romance perpetuates the belief that people are incomplete and must walk around in misery as half a person searching for their other half. Wouldn't relationships be healthier if each person in an intimate relationship

---

[17] A term used by Robert Bly in *Iron John*, 2.

strove for personal wholeness and sought out a partner who was also whole? Striving for wholeness within ourselves means nothing less than rejecting the false assumptions that somehow our brains exist disconnected from our bodies, our hearts from our spirits, and our psyches from our emotions.

Healing the Body/Mind Split

To celebrate Women's Mysteries is to reclaim and to make sacred our journey through the five blood Mysteries of womanhood: our birth, menarche, giving birth, menopause, and death.[18] Although the blood Mysteries are natural, physiological occurrences, these passages have been ignored, discounted, and shamed by a cultural denial of women's uterine blood and by oppressive, male-dominated religions. Many women do not even realize that we are being robbed of the opportunity for profound spiritual connection through the reverent celebration of our bodies' changes.

Under patriarchy, women are not permitted to live our womb-cycles consciously. We are forced by culture, religion, and economics to adopt an artificial structure for our lives; limiting and denying how we experience menstruation, pregnancy, birth, and menopause physically, emotionally, and psychically. In our patriarchal culture, the natural cycles of womb blood are defined as unclean, polluting, and shameful, if they are recognized at all. In other cultures and times when women menstruated they would take themselves away from their daily routines and expectations to immerse themselves in their menstrual experience.[19] Fearing the power of women's blood, male-dominated cultures and religions have denied women this essential honoring of our cyclic nature or have reframed women's seclusion as necessary due to their "unclean"

---

[18] Males also experience the first and last Mystery - of being born from his mother's womb, and returning to the Great Mother in death.

[19] There are numerous books and resources on menstruation traditions and taboos for further reading.

nature during this time. Mothers teach daughters to hide the evidence of their monthly cycle. After years of keeping this secret, most women experience menopause in silence, depression, and isolation. In breaking this pattern of lies and secrets, women are returning to the celebration of uniquely female biological passages. For women reclaiming our ancient goddess heritage and birthright, these transitions become the most sacred and spiritual part of our lives.

It is not convenient to be female in patriarchy. Time itself is measured according to male productivity, schedules, and sensibilities. Fitting into a linear workweek is simply not compatible with the lunar-based cycles of women's bodies. We become angry with ourselves for being female because it poses problems for us living in patriarchy. Every woman, and every female animal that has ever lived, bleeds according to her own cycle. This is part of the essence of being female. We bleed in accordance with the cycle of the moon; our inner tides ebb and flow. Yet many women experience this profound fact as a nuisance. Imagine what it might be like if women were supported in fully experiencing our natural cycles. What if we lived in a world where getting a spot of menstrual blood on your skirt or pants was not cause for embarrassment, humiliation, or shame? Imagine a world in which women would be supported, and even honored, for our ability to bleed regularly and copiously without becoming ill or dying—something that no man is capable of.

> The moon, almost always associated with women, is widely considered to be our special domain. This is due to the clear coincidence of the periodic cycle of the moon and the monthly hormonal cycle of women. Undeniably, they are all but identical. A most natural female affinity is thus firmly established. A common connection bound in blood. A woman's monthly blood is called, *die mond*, "the moon," by German peasants. In French, it is *le moment de la lune*.

> Native American peoples commonly refer to menstruation women as being on their "moontime." The English word, *menstruation,* means "moon change" and comes from the same Indo-European root as "moon," "month" and "measure." The Gaelic term for menstruation and calendar are the same.[20]

Before the onslaught of patriarchy, women's bodies were perceived as the very image of the Goddess, the Creatrix of All. Patriarchal thinking splintered this early, holistic understanding of the unity of body, mind, and spirit. The Christianity of the early, male-dominated church preached specifically about the evils of the flesh, of both women and nature. This doctrine set the stage for modern man's rape of the earth and socially accepted violence against women and children. Women's bodies were and are considered evil and below God, as is the physical world of matter. Patriarchal religious philosophy has preached that the earth is a "vale of tears," merely a way station before the promised joys of the afterlife. Such concepts play a large part in creating a suffering world by encouraging resigned acceptance of the miserable conditions that human beings create for themselves, other creatures, and the environment.

From the early patriarchal social systems to the present, human bodies, especially the bodies of women and children, have been property. In fact, ownership of women and their children was the original purpose of marriage. A woman did not belong to herself but to a father, husband, brother, or master. Inheritance rights changed from matrilineal (mother to daughter) inheritance to patrilineal (father to son) inheritance, reinforcing the fact that women no longer belonged to themselves. Women could be turned out of their own homes or even killed, if there was no male son or heir to succeed a dead father or husband. Women continue to suffer from the impact of the historical change from

[20] From a January 2018 blog post by urban shaman, Donna Hennes, 2018.

gynocentric (mother/woman-centered) cultures that flourished in Old Europe between 6500 and 3500 bce (surviving in Crete until 1450 bce) to andocratic (male-dominated) societies.[21]

The word *patriarchy* means "rule of the fathers" and describes the worldwide dominant political structures within which we live. I have chosen to use the word "patriarchy" in this book to describe the institutionalized, self-perpetuating political, religious, and economic system of dominance and subordination whose manifestations include racism, sexism, classism, looks-ism, homophobia, violence against women and children, and the destruction of nature. Riane Eisler, author of *The Chalice and the Blade* and *Sacred Pleasure*, describes patriarchy as a system in which "the primary principle of social organization is ranking, backed up by fear and/or force."[22] My use of the word "patriarchy" includes our attitudes, beliefs, and behavior, both conscious and unconscious, that perpetuate a culture of dominance and subordination ("power over"), in contrast with creating an egalitarian culture where power is shared, and ranking becomes obsolete. Patriarchy is the polluted water in which we all swim. The challenge for all of us in these times is to heal from internalized oppression and eradicate patriarchal institutions that harm us all and threatens to destroy all life on our planet.

I do not use the word "patriarchy" interchangeably with "men." Historically, men have been and continue to be the primary perpetrators of our dominator heritage; however, women and children also cannot help but swallow this polluted water to greater or lesser degrees. And while men continue to derive the greatest privilege from this imbalance of power, women are also responsible for its perpetuation. Everyone is affected by the dominator model of power, for it is inherent in the very fabric of our society, the cultural context of our lives.

On a personal level, patriarchy perpetuates itself through body shame, addictions, internalized self-hatred, child abuse, battering, eroticized

---

[21] Gimbutas, *The Civilization of the Goddess*, viii.

[22] Eisler, *Sacred Pleasure*, 4.

violence, pornography, and the sexual practices of sadomasochism, the eroticization of domination and subordination.

Patriarchy is the paradigm of our world, the filter through which we view and experience life as compartmentalized and disjointed, rather than whole and interdependent. Until we become aware that patriarchy is both an internal and external system, and work to heal from its effects, we will continue to think and behave out of this patriarchal paradigm. Contemporary women's rituals seek to change our consciousness from patriarchal conditioning by restoring value to women's lives and validating an egalitarian worldview based on a respectful and harmonious relationship with all people and nature.

It is impossible to calculate with certainty when the shift from a gynocentric partnership culture to a patriarchal (androcratic) dominator system precisely occurred, but this shift "gradually led women themselves to experience their bodies from a male perspective."[23] How have we as women continued to internalize and collude with patriarchal attitudes in our self-perception? To what extent does that societal shift continue to affect us personally and collectively today? The daily miracles of women's ability to create and sustain life have been so long denied to us, how can we begin to measure the depth of our loss, the absence of our birthright to recognize ourselves as reflections of the Goddess? I believe that the patriarchal legacy of ownership is the source of the disconnected feelings so many women have within their bodies. If we don't feel that we truly belong to ourselves, how can we be truly present and aware of what we feel physically and emotionally? The re-claiming and re-creation of women's rites takes the diverse and disconnected threads of our lives, reweaving them into a tapestry, a whole multicolored cloth of physical, emotional, and spiritual health.

[23] Ibid., 164.

Ritual and Women's Lives

Unlike other religious and spiritual traditions where religious experience is focused on an externalized source (a deity who exists outside of human experience), Dianic rites center on embodiment: ritualizing the female body where healing and revelatory experiences are made possible through unifying body, mind, and spirit. Intuitive movement, dancing, chanting, drumming, and sounding as part of ritual practice can achieve great meaning and facilitate healing at a deep level, especially when they are utilized with a clear understanding of the ritual's purpose. "Meaning is not in the world; it is not out there waiting to be found. Meaning is created in the interaction between the self and the other, the one and the many, the group and the natural world."[24] When the spiritual experience is embodied in the women who are participating in a ritual, a fundamental intention of Dianic tradition can be realized: to re-sanctify the female body as a manifestation of the Goddess, the source from which all things emerge and return. Lesbians and bisexual women, who may need to heal from internalized homophobia as well as the other aspects of misogyny, can experience positive transformation within a spiritual tradition that says the body of a woman who loves women is holy. Through the embodied spiritual experience of the Goddess, heterosexual women can heal from internalized misogyny and homophobia, reaching greater depths of self-love, love and appreciation for all women, compassion, and personal power.

"Having experienced something during ritual in the framework of religious meaning, we are changed when we return to the common sense world, and so is that world."[25] Although aspects of women's ritual can be experienced as therapeutic, its general purpose is to empower women to participate in their lives at a deeper, fuller level. Dianic tradition and goddess spirituality has inspired many women to exercise the power of

---

[24] Brown, "Serving the Spirits," 217.

[25] Geertz, *The Interpretation of Symbols,* from the introduction.

choice with greater clarity and to take greater responsibility for their lives and their extended communities. The very process of creating ritual supports this when a woman takes an abstract idea or issue and through the ritual-making process must choose what would physically represent the idea or issue. Doing this causes her to have to move from the abstract to keen focus as she puts her issue into a physical, symbolic form to interact with.

Rituals are symbolic enactments that facilitate change and generally occur in the context of relationship. Ritual provides a form to convey meaning to ourselves through the manipulation of symbolic objects and specific activities or actions. In short, ritual is enacting meaning. A ritual serves as a bridge to carry purposeful, symbolic meaning to the personal or collective conscious and subconscious mind. When consciously created and enacted, ritual can be transforming; linking the past, present, and future into a continuum that can be observed, felt, and learned from. By using ritual to mark our life passages, we can "connect the dots" of events in our lives to see the pattern in what may have previously felt like a random series of events. Like composting, we can transform the influences of past events that shaped our attitudes about womanhood, sexuality, love, and life, and re-weave our experiences into our lives into a new pattern.

> The rites and symbols of religion grow out of the nature of human beings and of religion. Ritual and symbol play a part in every phase of life. Many who oppose ritual in religion are the first to incorporate a great deal of it in other phases of life. Marriage, rings, clothes, pictures of loved ones, the manner of greeting old friends and of introducing new ones; all are rituals and symbols. Ritual is the language of religion.[26]

---

[26] Kabbalat Shabbat (Sabbath Evening Service), compiled by Mickey Bienenfeld, Cantor Emeritus, p. 34, 2001.

Sadly, many women describe their previous experience of religious ritual as meaningless. This response is usually derived from experiences of religious traditions that are male-centered, with little to no attention paid to the daily realities of women's lives and experiences. When women empower themselves to ritualize passages that they deem as significant and to which they can ascribe their own meaning, like a snake they shed their old skins and emerge into a new reality, a new conscious awareness. The mundane world of the previous moment becomes transformed and they are brought closer to greater understanding of the sacred. Women who create and participate in their own life-cycle rituals are saying that their lives are important, that their stories matter, and that every human life is a gift to present and future generations.

Daily rituals remind us to celebrate the sacredness of life, especially the simple things. There is a difference between ritual, an act that carries a symbolic meaning, and routine, as in acts that are done again and again with no overlay of meaning for the conscious or subconscious mind; for example, brushing your teeth "religiously" in the same manner for fifty years. However, a daily, repetitive act can become ritual if the act of brushing one's teeth is accompanied by a prayer or consciousness about the sacredness of the body. Most of us eat bread daily without thinking about how it arrived at our table. However, the eating of bread is elevated to ritual when accompanied by a blessing of thanks to the Earth Mother who is the grain and who made the grain from the earth and the water that caused it to grow. In the traditional Jewish blessing for bread, gratitude is given to the Source of Life for bringing forth bread from the earth, thus acknowledging the partnership in creation between human beings and the Creator. Saying grace over a meal enhances the meal and, therefore, is a simple type of ritual, as in this earth-based blessing before a meal: "Thanks to earth, who gave us all this food; thanks to sun, who made it ripen good. Praise and thanks to dearest earth and dearest sun."

Ritual and Spellcraft

Spellcraft always includes ritual by definition, since it is an act that carries a symbolic meaning, but not all rituals include spellcraft. For example, a spell may be included in the middle of a seasonal ritual where a circle has been cast and invocations spoken, but the spell portion itself can also be done on its own with or without a ritual container, invocations, or an altar. Spellcraft in and of itself is a ritual act that utilizes symbols, including stones, herbs, oils, and other objects, to manipulate energy with the intention of bringing about a desired result. Casting a spell usually involves gathering objects that are symbolic and imbuing them with energy. Specific energy is raised and directed through or into those objects, often accompanied by precise words of intention and feelings to frame the outcome. The energy is purposefully released and directed toward a particular goal to transform a situation or create an effect that was not there before.

Spellcraft is not only about raising and sending energy out into the environment; it can also be directed and released internally or into an object. For example, a woman working an internal spell for transformation might use her chalice or cup as the magical tool for taking qualities such as self-love or compassion into herself. The woman will perform certain ritual acts to infuse or "charge" a liquid in the chalice with the desired quality before drinking it.

Ritual and Ceremony

Although ritual often includes some level of spellcraft, from the simple to the complex, ritual may become a ceremony when done to simply, yet powerfully, mark or confirm what is formally beginning or ending. Although some people use the words "ceremony" and "ritual" interchangeably, ceremony describes a more formal act, or series of acts, often symbolic, as prescribed by law, religion, or state. Implied in the ceremonial act is strict attention to details as prescribed by the form of the ceremony itself. Ceremony generally allows little to no room for improvisation and is generally more rote, regimented, and concerned with the exact order of things: specific words that must be precisely spoken and the precision of each enactment. Common examples of ceremony would be weddings, presidential inaugurals, coronations, graduations, and many familiar religious occasions.

Ritual as a Tool

The purpose of ritual, on the other hand, is transformation. Ritual can be designed to initiate a life change or attitude, facilitate a change already in process, or name and claim a change or transformation that has already occurred. Although a ritual is likely to have a specific purpose, form, enactment, and direction of flow, an approach that combines flexibility with skill gives the ritual experience room to incorporate unforeseen inspirations and unexpected responses. There may be ritual aspects to ceremony and ceremonial aspects to ritual. It is the internal result of the experience that ultimately indicates which form is dominant on the occasion: personal transformation or merely a formal marking of an event. Like tossing a pebble into a pond, ritual has the potential to change the energetic pattern of our lives with ripples that extend out to the greater world around us.

Dianic rituals tend to flow easily and most often contain improvised sections. Although each ritual contains an understood purpose and sequence of activities, they are largely script-free, with the exception of a few ceremonies that contain a precise liturgy, such as initiations and ordinations. Creativity, inspiration, and improvisation in Dianic ritual are a way of honoring the Lady of the Wild Things who serves her instincts, intuition, and her muse. For example, rather than reciting invocations that remain the same throughout the year, Dianic invocations are sourced and created from a deep place of connection and reverence within each woman to the powers she calls and wills and, therefore, they change with the season or the ritual's purpose. Facilitators and participants alike may find themselves inspired to speak spontaneously as the Goddess moves them.

Ritual can give women a sense of connection to our ancestors and to the greater circle of women spanning centuries of history and culture. This is especially true of the blood Mysteries, where we so deeply feel the uterine blood connection from our maternal ancestors, to our grandmothers, to our own mothers, through ourselves and on to our daughters. When we celebrate a young woman's first bloods, we are linking back to our single shared African ancestor from our most ancient past, through our women-line, our women's blood. It is upon the womb blood of women that all human life depends. It is the elixir of life contained within the holy grail of the womb from which Creation herself sips.

In ritual making, symbols are the language we use to convey the messages we choose to internalize to bring about transformation. The word *symbol* means "fallen together"; a symbol is the falling together of an idea and its representation in such a way that they are henceforth inseparable.[27] One of the most significant traits distinguishing humans from other animals is the ability to symbolize. "Symbolism is so definitive a language that the message conveyed, regardless of origin or context, is perfectly clear, whether one agrees with the message or not."[28] Jungians believe that if a symbol has been around long enough, it becomes what it represents.[29] A good example of this is the swastika. Its origins as a symbol go back to the Paleolithic, and its use was widespread throughout the world as a symbol of infinity, the sun wheel, and a moon sign. The Nazis adopted the swastika in the 1930s, thinking it was a "pure Aryan" symbol. Now, in modern times, the swastika is associated with Nazism and everything their philosophy stands for. Symbols are a vehicle for human awareness; in ritual, symbols can stimulate internal and external transformation. As women working in both new and ancient ways, we use our chosen symbols such as the pentacle and cauldron to externalize our beliefs and

---

27 West, *Outward Signs*, xv. 24 Ibid.

28 Ibid., 8.

29 Redmond, *When the Drummers Were Women*.

personal processes, learning more as we go, and then internalizing and transforming again as the symbols expand and deepen our perceptions.

The aspect of human consciousness reached through meaningful symbols and ritual is called the psyche. The psyche is the part of our awareness and our being that resonates with symbols, myths, and stories. It, in turn, is connected to a larger consciousness that Jung called the collective unconsciousness. In effective ritual, both the right and left hemispheres of the brain are engaged through the simultaneous use of visual symbols, spoken words, movement, and/or rhythm. The whole person is addressed and stimulated. Potentially, the rhythms of the two brain hemispheres synchronize on the subconscious (or alpha) level of consciousness, which is the gateway between the conscious mind (beta), and deep mind (theta), creating feelings of euphoria, expanded mental powers, and intense creativity. This hemispheric synchronization may be the neurological basis for a higher state of consciousness.[30]

To be transformed through ritual, a woman must be fully present, awake, and engaged in multiple levels of awareness. She is not truly participating in ritual if she simply "buys her ticket" and watches the performance like a movie or play. She must be willing to become involved. Some people routinely use mood-altering substances to "participate" in ritual, thinking that it will help them to bypass their conscious mind and access deeper levels of consciousness. Most often, rituals in which participants ingest quantities of recreational drugs or alcohol are largely ineffective, with only rare exceptions, such as the peyote rituals of the native peoples of Mexico and Central America where there is a cultural context for the use of psychoactive plants. A serious student and practitioner of the Craft knows that one of the challenges of making magic is to develop the ability to move flexibly from one state of consciousness to another. Only when an individual is able to be fully present, both in mind and heart, without the influence of drugs or alcohol, will the ritual succeed in its intention.

---

[30] Redmond, *When the Drummers Were Women*.

In an effort to heal and change attitudes or beliefs from their past that affect their present lives, many women are creating rituals that revisit past experiences and milestones not recognized as significant at the time. There is healing in giving ourselves what we were not given, or did not know that we needed, in the past. For example, a post-menopausal woman may create or participate in a menarche ritual to help her heal from generations of familial denial of that important passage for young women. Countless times, I have witnessed the power of ritual to transcend linear time and help heal past experiences.

Witnessing in ritual space is not passive. It means actively supporting one another as we participate in meaningful acts and share in milestones of our lives. Mutual witnessing within a ritual circle is one of the elements that makes the group ritual experience so powerful. One of my students expressed an experience of witnessing as "a chance to actively support while not actively participating" as she held supportive space for another student. Group ritual experiences reinforce a sense of community and can offer a safe and loving context for individual joys and sorrows. Witnessing affirmations or promises made as part of the ritual allows us to support others' intentions as well as our own. Knowing they are being heard, many women speak words that seem to come from a wise, previously unknown part of themselves. They may feel physically powerful in a way they have never before experienced. Being witnessed also reinforces the importance of the passage, because we who participate in the ceremony affirm, by our very presence, that our lives have inherent value.

There are occasions when ritual may involve aspects of sacred theater. Enactments of goddess myths, similar to a mystery play, are sometimes included in seasonal holy day rituals as a way of passing on our traditional wisdom and conveying the meaning of the season. This type of ritual, which may appear to be performance-oriented, involves a more advanced form of symbolic magic and can be very powerful for both the women assuming the roles and those who attend. The instrumental act of role-playing the part of a goddess can give a woman information not usually accessible to her.

Another type of more advanced ritual work that may seem performance-oriented is called *aspecting*. In practicing the magical art of aspecting, a woman embodies the energetics of a specific goddess, transforming herself internally and, at times, externally to become Her. This is a much more serious ritual act than the rehearsed enactment of a mythic role in a ritual theater piece. Great care and training are needed to prepare a woman to aspect. She is not pretending to be the goddess, but, in fact, her consciousness shifts, opens to, and allows her to fully embody the energies of the goddess like an overlay, bringing Her presence into her and through her. This is not to be confused with possession by deity that occurs in other religious traditions. The woman who is aspecting should have some awareness of her own energetic shape. She has chosen to *join* (not merge), to share her consciousness and form with a goddess. She must also have the skills on how to both join and disengage safely, fully returning to her own self.

Sympathetic magic, sometimes called "folk" magic, homeopathic or imitative magic, is another art often incorporated in Dianic ritual (more on this in chapter 4). Traditional examples of this kind of magic would be dancing or leaping high into the air to encourage the crops to grow tall, or giving the first fruits off a tree to a pregnant woman to eat so the tree continues to be abundant for others.[31] When we enact things physically in ritual, the purpose of the ritual becomes more tangible to the mind and, therefore, more personally transforming. Involving the whole body in ritual engages all of the senses and gives us unique access to greater knowing beyond the cognitive level. Often disregarded, movement has its own wisdom to offer.

Ritual is a teaching tool, a way for women to teach ourselves what we need to know or become. Ritual has the potential to bring women to a deeper understanding and alignment with our true will. The Dianic

[31] Frazer, *The Golden Bough*, 32.

ritual circle becomes a conception vortex for expanding the realm of possibilities.

Life-Cycle Rituals

Any life passage or transition we experience deserves conscious attention. We internalize attitudes or beliefs about ourselves, our bodies, our sexuality, and life in general based on how we and others respond (or don't respond) to our life experiences. In the aftermath of a significant transition, we often formulate life decisions, consciously or unconsciously. These decisions influence us from our present into our future, affecting our behavior, actions, and choices. Unexamined, negative, subconscious decisions can have devastating and far-reaching effects.

An example of this might be a girl's first menstruation. Too often, this first experience is met with secrecy, embarrassment, or shame. Somewhat more positively, but less frequently, the girl's parents do their best to not make it a "big deal." Either way, the girl develops an attitude that being a woman is either dirty and shameful or that at its best it is "no big deal." This attitude follows her into womanhood, affecting her relationship with her body, her sexuality, and the physical symptoms of her monthly cycle. In other words, what we do or don't do in treating or responding to a significant life passage or transition can have an enormous effect on the rest of a woman's life.

According to medical intuitive and healer Caroline Myss, every memory, decision, and attitude carries an energetic factor or consequence. There is an energetic cost to carrying and not dealing with these negative experiences. For every negative experience we don't consciously deal with, there is a leaking of present life-force energy toward that past experience. In Myss's words, "you are in as many places as your emotional energy takes you," and using your present reservoir of energy to "finance" the past is one of the causes of susceptibility to physical illness.[32] Ritual provides an opportunity to address these memories, decisions, and attitudes energetically. It is never too late to "call your spirit back," as Myss describes it, and unplug your circuits from those experiences.

The impact of unmarked passages on our lives is impossible to comprehend fully. However, many women are creating rituals to help heal and change those past attitudes or beliefs that affect present consciousness. We are magically reaching back into the past, revisiting these experiences, making different decisions based on new awareness, and marking milestones that were not recognized as significant at the time.

There are many examples of significant passages that most women don't usually consider as occasions for ritual, among them:

* Weaning a baby
* Releasing or grieving after a miscarriage or abortion
* Becoming a grandmother
* Choosing not to become a biological mother
* Experiencing the birth of a sibling
* Starting a new career
* Becoming an adoptive parent (which may include the adopted adult or birth mother)
* Healing from an illness or accident
* Preparing to make love
* Becoming clean and sober
* Healing the "empty nest" when children leave home
* Preparing for surgery
* Forgiving oneself for past behavior
* Releasing your womb after a hysterectomy
* Releasing your breast/s after a mastectomy
* Coming out
* Divorcing or separating

---

[32] Caroline Myss, Ph.D., *Energy Anatomy* audiobook (Sounds True Recordings, 1996).

* Quitting a job
* Finding the first gray hair
* Healing from childhood abuse

Any event that a woman finds personally significant is worthy of ritual attention.

chapter 2

RITUALS IN THE BELLY OF THE BEAST

It is women who most often organize, plan, facilitate, and mark life-passage events or rituals within their cultural, religious (where allowed), and secular contexts. Generally speaking, it is women who are more interested in spirituality and who become more personally involved with group interactions, relationships, community building, and family bonding. Women accept with excitement the opportunity to create and facilitate a life-cycle event, but often we don't consider the underlying messages and who the event ultimately serves. Without this awareness, such an event is often a "junk food" ritual: an illusory feast that leaves the spirit empty.

Since it is our intention to develop conscious and meaningful ritual making, it is useful to begin by looking at some of the secular, socially sanctioned rituals from mainstream American popular culture. Let us particularly examine these familiar rituals for:

THEIR OVERT AND COVERT MESSAGES: Women may benefit from these mainstream life-cycle events, but all of us—planners, recipients, and invited guests—can also receive insidious, negative messages from them. Who ultimately benefits?

THEIR RITUALISTIC ASPECTS, BASED ON PREDICTABLE STRUCTURES AND SYMBOLS: Each event has specific elements and activities that make the occasion recognizable as a specific passage (e.g., a baby shower, wedding, graduation, etc.). An event that omitted the standard elements would feel incorrect.

THE CULTURAL CHOICES ABOUT WHAT OCCASIONS ARE CONSIDERED VALID AND IMPORTANT ENOUGH FOR CEREMONY: Although ritual occasions have been largely defined and supported by people of Western European descent, they are also widely practiced by many people of color in the United States. The exclusion of diverse racial, ethnic, and cultural influences in the standard celebrations reinforces "white" as the norm in our society.

The purpose of looking at the underside of these rituals is to demonstrate through these examples where too often female subordination and other gendered cultural conditioning is programmed unquestioningly into the content of a rite of passage. Of course, there are more egalitarian and empowering ritual variations because of changing social attitudes, however the general form and expectations for these rituals continue to be widely perpetuated with the best intentions. Therefore, no one should feel guilty, ashamed, or uncomfortable about having participated in such events. As this chapter makes clear, I've been to my share of them, too. We may regard them as meaningful, significant, even beautiful events in our lives. Yet these rituals reinforce the values of the dominant culture, which can explain the empty feeling we have when we look back on some of them.

As you read about these socially sanctioned rituals, consider how they could be reclaimed and transformed into something more personally meaningful to the recipient and attendees. Though this chapter deconstructs a small sampling of mainstream American rituals, you can examine any ritual from this perspective. In contrast to some of the ritual occasions described, I have occasionally added simple ideas or suggestions to consider as alternatives. In chapter 11, "Visioning New Rituals," I have included alternative "tastes" of other rituals to stimulate your own creativity.

The Bridal Shower

The bridal and baby showers are the only primarily women-centered secular ritual gatherings sanctioned for heterosexual women in America.

In theory, these gatherings are a wonderful opportunity for women to share experiences and wisdom with the bride-to-be or the expectant mother. But they are often a wasteland of missed opportunities for meaning, for both rituals generally focus around the superficial, the commercial, even the vulgar.

> *I remember attending* my first bridal shower, given in honor of my cousin Sally. My aunt planned the bridal shower with Sally's future mother-in-law and Sally's best friend, Annette. Following luncheon conversations regarding weight-loss diets and the latest popular movies, Sally sat surrounded by a pile of brightly decorated gifts. Annette, pen and pad in hand, took dictation. As Sally opened box after box, to the delight of the guests, Annette jotted down Sally's remarks about each gift, such as "Oh, I really needed this!" regarding the new vacuum cleaner, or, "It's so big and beautiful!" about the decorative vase. Sally had no idea that Annette would read back her exact words as a comic rendition of her honeymoon exclamations upon first gazing at her husband's penis. Most of the gifts she received were items for cleaning and cooking in the home. The only other gifts offered were sexy lingerie, given by girlfriends, that brought a huge pink blush to her face.

...

Women attending bridal showers like this one often leave feeling that women's gatherings are stupid and infantile. Why the silly games that serve only to limit women's experience of each other to that of silly children? Are we assumed to be incapable of mature and meaningful conversation?

I learned through attending many bridal showers over the years that the gifts my cousin received, the sexy lingerie and items for cleaning and cooking, were the norm. Through these symbolic gifts, Sally's friends and family were affirming the patriarchal definition of "wife," teaching Sally through the symbolism that her new role was that of a "cleaning slut."[33] The lingerie reinforced the patriarchal edict that a good wife must always be sexually available to her husband. Looking closely at the gifts, it becomes clear that they were not really for Sally at all: they were items for her future husband's care and feeding. The shower itself wasn't really about her, it was about what she was expected to become for someone else. Sally, as a woman and a person, was rendered invisible by her peers, many of whom had gone before her in losing their own identity. The ritual activities were reduced to games that kept the conversation trivial, preventing the women from actually sharing their authentic experiences of marriage and partnership. In the midst of this collective unconsciousness, an opportunity for a personally meaningful event shared with other women was lost.

Wouldn't this ritual gathering have been more meaningful if it were really about marking Sally's transition from single woman to a woman committing to a life partnership? The bridal shower could have affirmed the potential for sacred sexuality, for seeing and worshipping the divine through one another. However, this bridal shower, in its traditional pop culture form, trivialized Sally's relationship and demeaned the sacredness of sexual union within a committed relationship. What if, instead of empty games, the older women had dared to share advice and explore with each other what it was really like to love another person for the long haul? What if they had engaged in constructive conversations about how to be in healthy, long-term relationships and discussed the responsibility and maturity needed to maintain them?

Women often personalize negative feelings within themselves when the nature of their relationship changes or ends over time. They assume that

---

[33] A term coined by one of my workshop participants.

it must be their fault; that there must be some innate weakness within them if the partnership has ups and downs; that they are over-reactive, too sensitive, too dramatic, "too much."[34] A more personally meaningful bridal ritual could affirm realistic expectations of marriage and the reality that all things change, and that all relationships move in cycles like the changing phases of the moon.

The Baby Shower

> *My co-worker, Margaret,* was expecting her first child in six weeks. The previous year, she had miscarried in her second trimester. Margaret must have read every book on childbirth that she could find and listened to every birth story that friends and strangers insisted on telling her. This left her both excited and terrified as the birth date drew closer and her belly continued to expand. I had heard that Margaret's husband, Tom, had become a little more helpful around the house as her pregnancy advanced, but he'd been making jokes in public and private about how he hadn't had any sex in months and how Margaret was turning into a whale. Tom insisted on referring to their unborn baby as "him," although he told everyone that he would be fine with having a girl.
>
> Wearing her most flattering pregnancy maternity dress to hide her pregnancy and weight gain, Margaret arrived at her baby shower, which was given by her mother and a few close friends. She was greeted with hugs and kisses, while her girlfriends and female cousins delicately patted her belly and guessed at the sex of the baby. They

[34] VanArsdall, *Coming Full Circle*, 4.

> reassured Margaret that by nursing, she would lose those extra, unwanted pounds. Margaret was tired and whispered to me that she would really like to take a nap. After a lovely lunch, she looked over at the mountain of baby gifts she was expected to open in front of the group, took a deep breath, and began to open the first one. The gifts were gender-neutral baby clothes, toys, and some much-needed items such as an infant car seat, a stroller, and a crib.

...

Like the wedding shower, Margaret's baby shower was filled with infantile games and the unwrapping of gifts for the baby or its care. Instead of bawdy speculation about the honeymoon, the women obsessed over the gender of the infant. The pink and blue blankets lay in waiting as a gender-coding box. This baby shower was "traditional" in that the father was not present, communicating through his absence that Margaret would be the primary parent to care for and raise their child.

This ritual opportunity for women to support and empower Margaret in her awesome transition into the wonders, mysteries, and challenges of motherhood focused instead on a baby not yet born. Certainly most new moms need the baby gifts, but why, once again, was the woman supposedly being honored made invisible? The gifts were all for the baby, with nothing given to acknowledge or honor Margaret's rite of passage. Margaret's experience, her transition, was missing from the gathering like the center of a doughnut: the "invisible obvious."[35] Margaret's body and life experience were in transition from Maiden to Mother, yet she was not personally honored, nor was this transition articulated. Instead she was treated as though she was simply the vessel for the new life inside her. As birth-giver, Margaret would never again be the same person, and

[35] Hagan, *Fugitive Information*, 81–93.

the life growing inside her would remain a central focus for most of the remainder of her life.

From a Dianic perspective, this is an occasion for a Women's Mysteries ritual. This time offers tremendous opportunity for the psychic and physical empowerment of the mother-to-be. The focus of a Dianic ritual would be on her needs and experiences, and on assuring her that the women in her circle of friends and family would be there to support her in this life transition. Empowering rituals for expectant mothers already exist in other cultures, such as the Blessing Way of the Navaho. A ritual scenario for Entering the Circle of Mothers is included in chapter 11.

The Wedding Ceremony

The processional music had started; the nod to cue the bride was given. The moment my friend Gini had been waiting for her whole life had at last arrived. Dressed in an exquisite white satin gown, with matching shoes that badly squeezed her toes, Gini took a step forward. Her father stood just inside the chapel door and beamed as his daughter entered. "All rise," said the officiating minister. Gini's father offered his arm to his veiled daughter, who took his support and steadied herself while noticing the long length of the room she was to travel to where her beloved David was waiting. As the procession culminated at the altar, Gini's father handed his daughter over to the groom. The wedding guests watched Gini passively waiting as David lifted her veil. We listened as Gini vowed "To love, honor, and obey." It was to the new husband that the minister gave his instructions: "You may kiss the bride." The wedding

> guests threw rice as the newlyweds left the church, an old blessing for fertility and childbearing.

...

We are fortunate to live in a time when creative and egalitarian wedding ceremonies have grown in popularity. As a priestess who holds legal ministerial credentials, I have officiated at dozens of weddings for heterosexual couples, union ceremonies for same-sex couples (and legal weddings since 2008 in the U.S.A.) While rituals and ceremonies to witness and celebrate the joining of couples are occasions for great joy, we often forget that the origins of the state and/or religiously sanctioned heterosexual marriage ceremony are about the transfer of ownership of women and children to men. While a significant number of weddings are performed as a religious ceremony, the ritual elements included in Gini's wedding are also found in many secular ceremonies.

We expect to see the traditional walking of the bride down the aisle by her father or another male elder, where she is formally "given away" to the waiting groom. The origin of this ritual act is clearly an ownership exchange, where the current male owner (the father) gives the bride to her new male owner (the groom). In many cultures worldwide, this bridal exchange includes a dowry to the new husband. He is paid to take her, and the dowry usually represents the woman's worth and/or class background. In some cultural contexts, the dowry demonstrates societal reinforcement of the new marriage and provides much-needed financial support. However, the bride usually has no control over these resources: they belong to her husband.

In mainstream America, the bride's family traditionally pays for the wedding, including the formal gown and a reception. At an average cost of a wedding in 2016 at $35,329,[36] this might be viewed as the modern equivalent of the dowry. It could easily be concluded that a woman has

[36] https://www.theknot.com/content/average-wedding-cost-2016

no value in the new partnership unless she is accompanied by material goods or property that "sweeten the deal."

In my friend's wedding ceremony, Gini was veiled and it was David, the groom, who ritually lifted her veil. In cultures where the families still arrange marriages, the bride and groom often don't meet until their wedding ceremony. The lifting of the veil by the groom's parents, or by the groom, is necessary in order to verify that the woman under the veil is the one he or his parents "purchased." The wearing of the white wedding gown signifies virginity and purity, a custom that dates from the Victorian era. Another symbol represented in the veil is the hymen of the virgin bride, which, theoretically, has not been penetrated by any man prior to the wedding. David's act of lifting Gini's veil declared him to be the active partner in the sexual aspect of the marital relationship and symbolized his complete possession of her body.

One of the most significant and lasting aspects of Gini and David's marriage ceremony was Gini losing her family name. In the ceremony itself there was a lot of talk by the minister about the newlyweds "merging into one." In actuality, however, it was only Gini who did the merging, symbolized by the loss of her family name to become "Mrs. David Smith." Have you ever tried to locate an old friend after she has gotten married? It is virtually impossible to locate her unless you can find out who she married. For all intents and purposes, she has disappeared.

The tradition of name-changing has great significance to women. It not only symbolizes an utter change in personal identity, but magically speaking, it means an alteration of the very nature of the bride herself. In the traditional pronouncement of "man and wife," it is her role in life alone that changes. He remains a man, but she becomes a wife. One could also say that she has never really been herself. Even her family name before marriage reflects her mother's ownership by her father. One of the contributions of the second wave of the feminist movement was offering creative alternatives for both women and men with regard to name changes, or name merges, and ways to conduct a more egalitarian marriage ceremony.

Years ago, while conducting a marriage ceremony for a heterosexual couple, at the conclusion of the ritual I pronounced them, at their request, "partners in this lifetime, lovers in trust." The groom's best man, a born-again Christian who was very unhappy that the couple had a woman—let alone a Priestess—conducting the ceremony, began objecting angrily, "No! No! Man and wife! Man and wife!" He completely disrupted what had been, up until that point, a lovely ceremony. Instead of kissing his bride, the groom had to deal with calming down his "best" man. The importance and power of the anticipated ritual pronouncement completing the ceremony became all too clear to those present.

The Honeymoon

> *Julie and Martin,* tipsy from champagne, pulled rice from their hair and zoomed off in the car adorned for their departure with clanking cans tied to its fender. The honeymoon suite had been reserved for months. Martin picked up the keys at the hotel desk, exchanged winks and congratulations from the hotel manager, and escorted his new bride to the door of their suite. After unlocking the door, Martin picked up his bride in his arms and carried her over the threshold to the bedroom.

...

For many women, the ultimate in romantic love is the ritualized honeymoon act of the groom carrying his bride over the threshold of their home or through a bedroom door, where they will consummate their marriage. This is a ritual enactment of submission by the wife to the husband, intended, consciously or not, to set the tone for the rest of their marriage. Traditional custom does not call for the couple to take hands and walk over the threshold together to ritually consummate their married life: instead, she is both symbolically and quite literally carried as a possession, a subordinate to the dominator. He carries her to the bed where the traditional ritual of sexual consummation takes place. Here, he "takes her" in the epitome of illusion that is patriarchal erotic romance based in dominance and subordination. Sexuality in marriage is symbolically placed in the domain of the "man of the house."

The word *hymen* was the veil that covered the inner sanctum of the Goddess's temples and has its counterpart in women's bodies.[37] The ritualized lifting of the veil during the marriage ceremony and the penetration of the hymen (veil) in the virgin bride are related symbols that give symbolic ownership rights to a man over the Goddess as represented by his bride.

I think that this custom may contain the remnants of an even older, more sacred meaning of glimpsing the Goddess. Ancient statues of Isis bore the following inscription: "I am all that has been, and all that shall be, and none among mortals has hitherto taken off my veil."[38] I can only speculate that the veil of the Goddess was taboo and not to be lifted, literally or symbolically, by Her mortal worshippers as a sign of reverence and respect. To see the Goddess unveiled, naked in Her true nature, would be to go insane from gazing into the very heart of creation, as it is beyond the scope of the human mind to grasp it in its totality. To unveil Her in Her manifestation as a mortal woman, however, may have come to represent the mortal male's privilege to control the Goddess. He now owns and controls Her by owning and controlling his wife.

As a teenager, I remember gazing at the classical paintings in European museums where "The Rape of the Sabine Women" or "The Rape of Europa" were popular themes. The paintings of conquering men lifting and carrying off the women struck me as similar to the honeymoon

---

[37] Walker, *The Women's Encyclopedia of Myths and Secrets*, 407.

[38] Gage, *Woman, Church, and State*, 16.

custom. Is it possible that the honeymoon ritual has origins in rape conquests? Soldiers abducting and then forcibly marrying the conquered people is an old story in history.

In *The Golden Bough*, James Frazer speaks of a widespread custom that has survived into modern times called "racing for a bride." The bridegroom, or a group of suitors, pursues the bride through obstacles in order to capture her. Sometimes she is armed with a whip to use against those unwelcome to her, favoring the one whom she chooses with her heart.[39] Although I may not be able to prove my theory of this custom's origin, the honeymoon ritual of being lifted over the threshold remains a symbol of women surrendering to men's control.

The honeymoon, traditionally held in June, was originally a month of pairings that intentionally included a menstrual period. The old belief was that the groom contacted the source of life by making love with his bride during menstruation.[40] To create a ritual dedicated to celebrating sacred sexuality within a committed relationship, honoring, blessing, and pleasuring the body of one's life partner in the name and spirit of "She who creates through the pleasures of the body," is to reclaim our connection to the life force Herself. It is my hope that this meaning of the honeymoon will be restored and reclaimed by lovers in times to come.

Anniversaries

> *Carol and Jim* were both running late to get home from work. Carol realized at noon that she had forgotten to pick up that watch Jim had eyed at the mall, and Jim realized at 3:00 p.m. that he had forgotten to order the roses he knew Carol was expecting. Although they had been married just five years, between work and

---

[39] Frazer, *The Golden Bough*, 181.

[40] Walker, *The Women's Encyclopedia of Myths and Secrets*, 408.

raising their three-year-old son, Eric, they hadn't had much time for each other. In fact, both Carol and Jim hoped that the other had remembered to make a dinner reservation and book the baby sitter...

...

Anniversaries traditionally commemorate the transfer of ownership performed at the wedding ceremony. Typical celebrations include checking the traditional list for which gift or special stone a husband should give to his wife based on the number of years the marriage has lasted, assuming he hasn't already traded her in for a younger model. The longer she stays married to him, the more "valuable" she becomes, and so does the ritual gift. Dinner, flowers, and a card are commonplace. Stereotypically, he forgets; she cries. Lesbian and gay couples are not exempt from these patterns of expectation and forgetfulness.

An anniversary could be a wonderful ritual opportunity to evaluate the quality of your relationship over the previous year. What has been good? What needs more attention? How might you better support your partner in manifesting their dreams? This might be a time to ritually rededicate yourselves to the relationship. An annual ritual that reminds a couple of the qualities that originally brought them together and reaffirms the sacredness of their connection as lovers and life partners is life-enhancing and helps the couple to not take each other for granted. This might also be a wonderful ritual to be witnessed by your children, family, and friends.

Sweet Sixteen

In 1970, I was sixteen years old and living in Los Angeles, California. Although people often described me as a "hippie princess," I believe that I was fairly

> conventional in a time of " flower power," Vietnam War protests, fighting for the passing of the ERA, and the Women's Liberation movement. I was also reading Robert Graves' *The White Goddess* and collecting traditional folksongs from the British Isles about Otherworld beings. My parents asked me if I wanted a "sweet sixteen" party, and in those days, any excuse for a party was all right with my friends and me. My parents provided all my favorite foods and, basically, left us alone to enjoy ourselves. We played guitars until late into the night, and everybody sang Joni Mitchell and Leonard Cohen songs. I remember my "sweet sixteen" party being extra special and different from other birthday celebrations in my teens because my parents wanted to make sure it was special for me; and because of their loving support, it was.

...

Because a sixteen-year-old girl can now acquire a driver's license in the United States, this age marks the beginning of more physical mobility and independence. At this age young women in America are often given a special party by their parents that sometimes includes a ritualized, formal presentation to invited family and guests who are intended to represent "society." In wealthier segments of American society, these were called "coming out" parties. Not too long ago, this formal presentation meant that a young woman was now available to wed, and the occasion allowed her to be inspected by potential suitors. In other words, the girl was on the market. Although present-day "sweet sixteen" parties cross all class lines in the United States and in Europe, the practice likely originated in the debutante balls of the white and wealthy classes. The "young lady," dressed in light pastel colors, was expected to impress the family's guests, particularly potential suitors, with her simple elegance, grace, and good breeding.

The popular phrase "sweet sixteen and never been kissed" implies sexual ignorance, innocence, and virginity. A traditional gift from the girl's parents is a necklace with a single pearl, or a necklace of pearls, symbolizing purity and chastity. Since there are no rituals or celebrations sanctioned in American popular culture or in Western religion for a girl's first menstruation, the "sweet sixteen" party is a socially acceptable way of stating that a girl has crossed the threshold into young womanhood.

In her best-selling book *Promiscuities: The Secret Struggle for Womanhood*, Naomi Wolf explores the conflicting messages directed at young women during and since the sexual revolution and asks, "What, then, in our world, makes a woman? Who gets to decide?" Without initiation rites to help girls become women,

> the power to define our entering womanhood was bestowed upon boys and men. And they, unlike the older women in the tribes, were bound by no tradition or social pressure to consider our "becoming women" in relation to our well-being or that of the community.[41]

This is in contrast to her research, which shows that in other cultures,

> it was older women, who upheld the values of femaleness, and decided when a girl could join them in womanhood. Their decision was based on whether the girl had attained the level of wisdom and self-discipline that would benefit her, her family, and the society.... In our culture, a girl's passage through tests and rigors into womanhood is marked in the realm of body control such as dieting, but also in

---

[41] Wolf, *Promiscuities*, 138.

> the realm of sex acts and the accumulation of material possessions. Our girls move toward womanhood through the demarcations of what they can buy and own or of who wants to sleep with them.[42]

This cultural belief has serious consequences:

> Since every girl who ever grew has needed to know she has made a successful transition from girlhood to womanhood within the value system of her own culture, why should we be surprised that our levels of teenage motherhood and teenage abortion are so high; that so many teenage girls see their impregnation not as a derailing of their journey to adulthood, but as its fulfillment?[43]

Imagine instead a menstruation ritual where the young woman's mother, grandmother, other female relatives, and women elders of her community gather to celebrate her transition into womanhood. During the ritual the young woman is honored and acknowledged for her character, accomplishments, and interests. She could be encouraged to expressively dress herself, prepare a short speech, recite poetry or prose, or perform a dance that best expresses how she perceives the world. She could be supported in sharing her own dreams and aspirations.

Imagine creating a ritual for girls that might affirm

> what they already know but rarely see affirmed: that the lives they lead inside their own self-contained bodies, the skills they attain through their own concentrations and rigors, and the unique phase in their lives during which they may explore boys and eroticism at their own pace—these are

---

[42] Ibid.

[43] Ibid., 137.

magical. And they constitute the entrance point to a life cycle of a sexuality that should be held sacred.[44]

Imagine a ritual for a pubescent girl that affirms her emerging sexuality as her own, blessing her to love whom her heart chooses without the dictates of a heterosexist and classist society.

The Beauty Pageant

I must have been nine years old in the early 1960s when I saw a beauty pageant on television for the first time. I had never seen anything like it and was mesmerized. Young white women, a lot of hair spray in their perfectly coifed hairdos, paraded in swimwear, turning their bottoms to the all-male judges. They took turns singing, tossing batons, and giving speeches. At the end of the evening, one of the women was selected as the most beautiful woman in California. She cried hysterically as a shining tiara was placed on her very big hair. I watched the other contestants standing behind her, glaring through their frozen smiles. From the perspective of a prepubescent, chubby girl, I couldn't imagine ever looking even remotely like her. This started a twenty-year obsession and battle with my own body to be thinner.

...

I cannot help but believe that the origins of the beauty pageant lie in the slave markets and human auction blocks of our not-so-distant past.

---

[44] Ibid.,138.

The ritual elements contained in the modern-day beauty pageant are the parading of women, often in body-revealing swimwear, displaying their bodies and "talents" for the judges, and the crowning and presentation of a title upon one tearful young woman deemed the "fairest of them all." Women observing the pageants internalize the message that there is but one aesthetic ideal of female beauty that represents the standard for all women. Little girls want to grow up and become Miss America, or at least look like her, and in fact, beauty pageants are now also held for female infants, toddlers, and young girls. These children are made-up and sexualized to look like miniature adult women, complete with mascara, ruby-red lipstick, and "sexy" outfits.

A behind-the-scenes view of many adolescent and adult pageants reveals self-inflicted physical abuse in the form of anorexia, bulimia, painful body waxing, and plastic surgery in order to look "naturally" beautiful. The winner is judged and rewarded not for being beautiful but for how well she "does" beauty according to patriarchal standards.[45] Even if the contestant is intelligent and studying to be a neurosurgeon, she'd better look good in a bikini. The clear message to my nine-year-old self and to other young women was that patriarchal culture values the "packaging" rather than the contents. I have no suggestions for changes to improve this event. It is time to scrap this one entirely.

Birthdays

> *Ellie was turning* thirty "for the fifth time." As we all stood around the flaming, elaborately decorated birthday cake, Ellie whispered to me in confidence that she wasn't sure that she even wanted to have a birthday

[45] Noted from an early 1980s article by Nicki Craft, published in a local Santa Cruz paper. Craft interviewed protesters whose activism against the beauty pageants encouraged a highly publicized pageant to relocate. I apologize for losing the appropriate credits for this reference.

party this year; that she was "getting too old for such a celebration," and, "after all, what was there to celebrate?" Over the past few years, Ellie thought that she had gotten too fat and that her time was running out to find a husband.

We sang the birthday song in appreciation for our dear friend. Ellie listened and then spoke aloud her birthday wish. As she blew out the candles, Ellie looked around at her loving friends and, savoring the first bite of birthday cake, exclaimed, "Thank God, at least there's chocolate!"

...

Contemporary birthday rituals are still accompanied by magical rites. Although they are done out of sequence for proper magic, the basics have survived. Traditionally, at the anniversary celebration of one's birth, there is a gathering of friends and family where a special birthday cake is presented, lit with the number of candles corresponding to the number of years of life, plus one candle "to grow on." Birthday wishes are made in silence; the birthday recipient blows out the candles and must eat the first piece of cake. (In real spellcraft, this corresponds to "taking in" the well-wishes of the participants by consuming the cake.) Gifts are given to the "birthday girl," and she usually opens them in the presence of the guests.

This all sounds wonderful, and indeed it is, except for one major omission. There is an invisible someone who shares this birthday. All birthdays are also the anniversary of your mother's "birthing day." Whenever I attend a birthday party where both mother and daughter are present, I make it a point to tell the mother, "Happy Birth Day" or "Happy Labor Day." Almost without exception, she looks at me with confusion and tells me that it isn't *her* birthday, but her daughter's. I simply reply, "It is your birth day, too." The light in her face that the eventual realization brings is delightful, yet it is sad that something so obvious is denied in the most common celebration in human societies. Most mothers are far removed from the memory and conscious understanding that they were present at the birth of their child and that this was, and still is, their day too. Even women who have made conscious ritual of their birth-giving experiences overlook this important fact. Despite all the talk and politics surrounding "family values," a mother is too rarely honored, remembered, or respected.

Sadly, like my friend Ellie, women enjoy birthdays only until they reach a certain age. After the age of thirty, birthdays become a day of self-hatred or a day not counted, as exemplified by the statement, "I'm turning twenty-nine—again." Negative comments about growing older often begin much younger than thirty. The ageist message behind these comments is that a woman's value is in her youth and attractiveness according to patriarchal standards of beauty. Once past a certain age ("over the hill"), invisibility is her fate. Young women begin to lie about their age and fear their next birthday as a curse rather than as a blessed step in the process of becoming an elder who holds wisdom. Aging becomes something to feel ashamed about rather than proud of. Dying the hair to cover the gray and cosmetic surgery starting for some young women in their twenties are common remedies for the "problem" of growing older. Recently, an older woman in my community revealed she was seventy. She had always been silent about her age, even while others were being honored for crossing the threshold to cronehood. She experienced her announcement as a "coming out" experience for herself and has since begun to claim her place as an elder with pride.

Here's a suggestion to improve the birthday celebration. If your mother is alive, think of some way that you can honor her or thank her for bringing you into the world. Even if your relationship with her is difficult or estranged, think of some way to acknowledge her as the doorway for you into this life. Send a card, flowers, or a gift with the message, "I'm so glad I was born; thank you for making it possible. Happy birth day to you, too, Mom," or simply, "Happy birth day, Mom" or "Happy labor day, Mom."

Funerals

My friend Leslie was found dead on the floor of her bathroom at twenty-five years of age. She had lost her struggle with anorexia and bulimia at a time when these eating disorders went largely unrecognized and untreated by most medical professionals. She was an extraordinary and stunningly beautiful young woman who dressed in long, loose white gowns. She had the most sparkling eyes I've ever seen, and she glowed as if from some inner light. As I entered the church for her funeral, I saw at a distance an open casket in front of the podium. This was my first experience attending a non-Jewish funeral service where open caskets are not custom, thus I had never before seen a dead person, and I never expected to view the deceased's body. With much trepidation, I slowly walked up to the casket and looked down at my dear friend. I gasped aloud, as Leslie's light, so familiar to me, was completely absent from her face. I barely recognized that Leslie and her corpse were the same person I had known. After the initial shock came a strange comfort and knowing: the bright spirit that Leslie was had fled the shell of her body.

I listened to the minister talk about Leslie in the generalities of someone who didn't know her. No one from her family gave a eulogy, nor was anyone present invited to share their memories. Unlike my experiences at Jewish funerals, where everyone is invited to throw a bit of dirt on the casket as they leave the burial site, there were no ritual activities for her parents, family, and friends to participate in. I left the funeral feeling very disconnected and wondering what comfort there could possibly be for Leslie's parents.

...

Funeral practices can be quite diverse, based on everything from the religious tradition to the last wishes of the deceased. These can range from a somber and isolating service, where the life of the dead is only superficially acknowledged, to a full-blown wake or party with liquor and a brass band that plays music all night long.

In American popular culture there is often an intense fear of death and funerals. The disposal of the physical remains of the deceased is usually not the time or place for the deceased's family and community of friends to gather to deal with their loss. Instead, separate memorial services before or after the funeral are the allotted time to talk about the dead and share feelings of grief, anger at the loss, and love.

Whether death comes unexpectedly or as a result of a lengthy illness, it takes time for the shock to wear off and for reality to set in. Memorial services I've either attended or facilitated have provided great comfort and meaning for the surviving friends and family, especially when the gathering has been designed in accordance with the loved one's wishes. If the deceased was cremated, the memorial service is sometimes the place where the ashes are ritually released to the elements. Memorial services can provide a sacred container for memories to be recalled, appropriate honor to be spoken, and the healing process of mourning to begin. Growing up in Jewish tradition, I was taught that mourning is perhaps

> the ultimate liminal, or disconnected state. Outside us, the web of life has been torn. Within us, body and soul are wrestling apart. Our tradition recognizes that, while body and soul may have been severed almost instantaneously for the loved one who died, the reweaving of body and soul in the survivors—the agenda of mourning—happens in stages over weeks, months, years, and generations.[46]

Jewish law and custom take the mourner through a prescribed process of going deep into their experience and out again, beginning with *shiv'ah*, a formal period usually lasting seven days, and another at thirty days or for a full year where life-cycle festivities are to be avoided.[47]

In Wiccan and other goddess traditions, death is not separate from life, and the funerals and memorial services I've attended focused on celebrating the life and values of the deceased. Although there is no one single belief as to what happens after death, there is a general belief that the energy or spirit of the dead person transforms into something else and continues on in some form, seen or unseen. The ancestors and our beloved dead live within us and in the trees and water, in the food we eat, in our living memories, and in our hearts. The Goddess as the source of all creates us, and we all must return to Her darkness for rebirth. Still, we must let our deceased loved ones go. In several old English and Scottish ballads, and their American variants, there are stories that speak to the widespread belief that the dead feel and are disturbed by excessive grief of the living. The usual time period mentioned in the ballads is a year and a day for the living to finish with their mourning or risk a visitation by the deceased, who begs for sleep.[48]

The best resource I have come across, and have personally used for practical rituals, blessings, meditations, and liturgy on crossing over, is

[46] Orenstein, *Lifecycles,* 344.
[47] Ibid., 348.
[48] Wimberly, Folklore in the English and Scottish Ballads, 231.

The Pagan Book of Living and Dying by Starhawk, M. Macha NightMare, and The Reclaiming Collective. This beautifully written book is a blessing to have in times of need, such as preparing for the death of humans or beloved animal companions.

Acknowledging the anniversary of a death can be a meaningful and healing ritual. Lighting a twenty-four-hour candle, cooking a favorite meal of the deceased, and setting up an altar to their memory and doing some act of good in their honor are but a few possibilities.

Housewarming

> *Jane and Emily* had saved their money for years to buy their new home. Now their dream had become a reality. They invited family and friends to celebrate this accomplishment with a huge party and barbecue in their new backyard. Guests arrived with potted plants, flowers, six-packs of beer, and decorative house accents. The house tours went on all afternoon as Jane and Emily showed everyone the before and after photographs of the house and all the work they had done to transform it into their home.

...

The existing custom for a housewarming is primarily the sharing of food with friends and family in the new residence and the giving of gifts such as plants or home accessories. In expanding these ideas for more meaningful ritual, one might consider making the housewarming a "house blessing." The new residents begin by sweeping (with a new broom) the previous occupants' energy from the home, starting in the interior at the back of the house. The sweeping of energy is done through every room, gathered together, and swept out the front door and out into the street. After releasing the old energies, return to the house and purify it with incense, spring water, a burning candle, and salt, sprinkling these elements clockwise through the house beginning in the northern-most corner. Then, in each room, speak an intention or blessing as to the quality of life one wishes to have in that room. Others can add their blessings for your life in your new home. This simple ritual is fun for everyone and gives the new residents a conscious way to begin anew.

Graduation

> *"This cap looks* ridiculous!" I wailed at my parents in frustration as I tried to make the mortarboard look even remotely flattering on my head. The black gown was blisteringly hot and too short, and we were already late for the ceremony.
>
> My 1971 high-school graduation ceremony was held at the local state university's football field to accommodate the large number of graduating students and their families. The graduates entered the field chaotically and took their seats. I couldn't locate my friends for the longest time since every one of us looked alike. I also couldn't find my family in the bleachers because they were seated so far away. The class president droned a speech to inspire us to higher education and "take our place in this world," which was followed by "You'll Never Walk Alone," sung by the girl's glee club.
>
> The moment arrived when the first of several hundred of us were called by name in alphabetical order to pick up our diploma and shake hands with the school

> principal. The student entrusted to read the names off, however, had ingested LSD before the ceremony, and was thus inspired to make up special names in addition to the list he was given. Some of us graduated several times that afternoon, making it a very chaotic, entertaining event after all.

...

It is very important to acknowledge any task that takes years of dedication and commitment to complete. Graduation ceremonies are usually associated with the completion of a degree at a learning institution. The graduate usually receives cards and sometimes money. The amount of gift money sometimes corresponds with the status of the institution she graduated from. Since graduation ceremonies are usually associated with high schools, colleges, or universities, by default there is less value placed on alternative types of learning, such as non-accredited schools where learning is self-motivated through independent study and experience. This is a clear demonstration of the value that class places on one particular type of education rather than valuing alternative learning methods. We rarely receive acknowledgment, cards, or checks for graduating from the "school of life." For myself, and for many women I have known over the years, the skills and experiences we have used the most frequently, professionally and personally, were learned outside of a formalized, accredited educational system.

Although there can be much to gain in attending a university, most institutions of "higher" learning are given the stamp of approval because they adhere to patriarchal society's standards and values. Their intention is to graduate a student who will fit into and maintain the status quo. This conformity is reaffirmed and strengthened through the ritual enactment of graduates entering the graduation ceremony all together in long rows, wearing the same traditional cap and gown. The individual student is rendered anonymous. If you have ever attended a large graduation, it can be very difficult to identify your graduate in the sea of other graduates. After a plethora of boring speeches, the diplomas are given out and the graduate is tossed out into society to be "successful."

I suggest an additional ritual where the graduate invites her friends and family to share this crossroads of accomplishment. She is dressed in an outfit or costume of her choice that best symbolizes how she sees herself after accomplishing her educational goal. She prepares an altar with symbols of her life path and shares with the guests, in a focused way, the process of her learning and what she now understands about life. The graduate, her parents, and others light candles to bless and empower her as she takes her skills out into the world to make her own way.

Although the preceding examination of popular American rituals has been limited primarily to secular rites, I must also mention two religious rituals that affect many women's lives with their overt and covert messages: circumcision and baptism.

Circumcision

> *One week after* the birth of my nephew, I received the invitation to attend his *bris*. Ritual circumcision is performed on infant males in Jewish religious tradition, and the word *bris* means "covenant." This custom is so entrenched in Jewish culture that to refuse to circumcise one's son is unthinkable. I called my parents and my brother to inform them that I would not be attending the ceremony. I told them that I would not support the ritual "celebration" with my presence but would come to visit after the ceremony to see my family and my new nephew. When I arrived at the house, the *bris* ceremony was still in progress, so I entered the front door and

> went immediately to the back of the house. There, I found my sister in-law sobbing. She was in agony that her new baby boy was being subjected to this torture enforced by tradition.
>
> My nephew is a young man now, and someday I will tell him why I chose not to attend his *bris*.

...

Ritual circumcision in Judaism is performed by a *moel*, a rabbi who is specially trained to perform the *bris*. (Circumcision for "hygienic" secular reasons is also practiced routinely in most hospitals in North America.) After having attended one nephew's *bris* and boycotting the next, I can only tell you that if it had been up to the mothers of those infant sons, this custom would likely have ended centuries ago. In both circumstances, the new mothers were sobbing in the back of the house while their precious infant was having a portion of his body cut off without anesthetic.

This ritual is frequently called one of the Men's Mysteries. But, unlike the Women's Mysteries based on natural events, there is nothing natural about genital mutilation. The mystery to me is why must they insist on doing such a horrible thing to an infant! It carries a clear, although covert, message to the new mother: you have no mother-right to your son; he isn't yours but belongs instead to the father and to male religious society. The new mother is "put in her place" only days after giving birth. A Jewish mother who refuses to allow ritual circumcision would be seen as a traitor to Jewish religious tradition and an affront to her Jewish family and people.

Female genital mutilation, also misnamed "female circumcision," is practiced primarily outside the United States in Muslim and African countries, although cases in the United States have also been reported. This atrocity is also done in the name of tribal custom, religion, and tradition, and utterly destroys a woman's ability to experience sexual pleasure. Girls often become ill from infections caused by the procedure, and some die. Women's genitalia are partially or completely stripped away, rendering them incapable, in the minds of men, of infidelity (since there is no pleasure in sexuality), and therefore only capable of breeding.[49] The clear message to girls is, "Your sexuality is dangerous and uncontrollable. You have more value as a woman and are more attractive to men with your clitoris and labia removed." This mutilation is performed, often without anesthetic, primarily by women upon prepubescent girls who are forcibly held down by their mothers and other female attendants.

Both female and male genital mutilation hide atrocity under the cover of religious or cultural tradition, making it difficult for anyone outside those cultures to effectively protest these practices. Although ritual scarring, piercing, marking, tattooing, and cutting the body have been part of human religious and tribal affiliation traditions since ancient times, the enforced removal of our children's genitalia must stop. We must find other, gentler ways to accept our children into the tribe without partially or fully destroying their ability to celebrate life through sexual pleasure.

Baptism

Another religious ritual that is an affront to mother-right is baptism, practiced by many Christian denominations. An infant of either sex is ceremoniously sprinkled with or even submerged in water by a priest or minister, and the child is pronounced "reborn" through Jesus, the Holy Spirit, or the Trinity. The overt and covert message to the child's mother is that her body is unclean. For the child to be "saved" from the original sin of Eve, it must be reborn through the male god. Waters of the baptismal basin are used to cleanse the infant from the tainted blood of its mother. Tap water is accepted as more sacred than the very womb

---

[49] For further information on female genital mutilation, read Alice Walker's *Possessing the Secret of Joy* (Harcourt Brace, 1992) and *Warrior Marks* by Alice Walker, Pratibha Parmar, and Vicki Austin-Smith (Harvest Books, 1996).

blood and water of life, without which none of us—Pagan, Atheist, and Christian alike—would be here.

I can imagine the baptismal ritual adapted as an honoring of the mother and woman's uterine blood that nurtured and brought forth the infant. It could be a celebration of the birth-giving power of women and a family ritual of welcoming and blessing the newborn into community.

Moving Forward

Before we move forward into the creation of women's rituals, let us take a moment to reflect on the socially sanctioned rituals we have just examined. Some of the rituals listed are already being renovated, reclaimed, or improved to better reflect the conscious intention of the participants. Some of you may now be feeling guilty, disturbed, or angry at this critical examination, especially if you have enjoyed your participation in them or have created some of these rituals for your family and friends. My intention in focusing on the underside of these ritualized occasions—on how and why they are created and what their purpose is—is not meant to judge all of them as unnecessary or obsolete, or to call those who have participated in them ignorant or evil. The intention is to peel back the veil of illusion and to inspire you to a critical analysis of what these rituals promote and sustain in the larger society apart from the personal meanings that individuals may ascribe to them.

Before reading the next chapter, take some time to ponder the following questions. Answering these questions will provide you with valuable information about yourself that will assist you in the creation of powerful and meaningful rituals.

Make or buy a journal to be used for your ritual-making journey, and record your answers there. Keeping a journal can be a great way to begin exploring personal or group ritual. It can be a valuable tool for recording your thoughts, ideas, and feelings about your life experiences. Major life changes can be accomplished in tiny steps. Consider setting aside ten minutes a day to write. Make yourself a warm beverage, light a candle, sit down in a quiet space, and write. Don't judge it or correct it. Don't even read it. Just write. This may be your first personal ritual. Savor this communion with yourself. You may choose to have more than one notebook: one for your personal journal, the other for working specifically with the material and exercises in this book.

Questions to Ponder

1. How does ritual fit into your life now? Think about specific examples of the kind of ritual that you actually do. How often do you do them? Is that often enough?
2. What were the last two rituals that you participated in? What were the "messages" that the ritual was intended to impart?
3. What was the most meaningful ritual that you've participated in, and what actually happened in that ritual that made it meaningful to you?
4. Can you analyze the specific components or aspects that may have made that ritual so powerful for you?
5. While ritual can be powerful and profound, ritual can also be boring, tedious, and meaningless. Analyze the components of what made another ritual that you attended boring or meaningless to you.
6. If you have attended rituals where some people are participating and some people are only spectators, how has that affected your experience?
7. Ritual is a large part of practicing Dianic Wicca and other female-centered and goddess traditions. If you have attended any exclusively female rituals, what are the aspects of women's ritual that contribute to it working or not working for you? Evaluate this in terms of your own subjective experience.

Ritual of Reclamation

If you feel the need to shed uncomfortable feelings from your past participation in any of the rituals we have discussed, I suggest that you try the following ritual:

Take a few minutes to appreciate yourself for responding to your need for ritual making. Appreciate the love, kindness, good intentions, and generosity that you brought to those past occasions. Hold yourself in loving compassion and forgive yourself for anything you might regret in the aftermath of your expanding awareness. Go to your sink and wash your hands, watching the water go down the drain. Let any guilt, anger, and regrets go down the drain with the water. Dry your hands with a clean cloth. Move on to more conscious ritual making.

chapter 3

DEVELOPING THE PURPOSE

Enthusiastic inspiration is essential to good ritual. Without skill behind the inspiration, however, the end result is like the work of an aspiring artist who loves art, is drawn to create, but hasn't acquired the actual physical and mental skills to manifest what she envisions. Beginning with this chapter, you will be guided through thought processes and given tools you can use to develop skills for creating powerful and meaningful rituals.

Once you have pondered the questions at the end of the chapter 2, proceed to the following practice to begin exploring ritual's limitless possibilities.

PRACTICE: *What are your personal needs for ritual?*

In your ritual-making journal, make a list of occasions, from the mundane to the profound, for which you might consider creating ritual. Perhaps begin by listing events and transitions from your past. Add to this list as you read and gain more experience with different kinds of ritual.

Look into the past and consider how an event, experience, or passage might have deserved a ritual of some kind. It's never too late to give yourself a ritual for a past event; past events can still be healed, honored, and celebrated. Our minds do not seem to care how long ago the occasion was. In ritual space, time has little meaning or effect. The possibilities for healing and transformation are infinite.

After making a list of past occasions for rituals, begin a list of present and future events that might deserve conscious attention. Some suggestions for ritual occasions are:

* Seasonal and lunar rituals
* Conception
* Choosing not to become a biological mother
* Protection for a fetus
* Preparing for childbirth
* Easy labor
* Weaning a baby
* Baby naming
* First menstruation
* Every menstrual period
* Menstruation as sign of not being pregnant
* Miscarriage
* Afterbirth burial
* Becoming a grandmother
* The birth of a sibling
* Abortion
* Empty nest
* Giving up a child for adoption
* Adopting a child
* Moving out on one's own
* Ritual for autonomy
* Sexual healing
* Before making love
* After making love
* First chosen sexual experience
* Beginning a journey, either physical or psychological
* Starting a new career
* House blessing
* Birthdays (honoring your mother and yourself)
* Starting school
* Completion of learning something (including, but not limited to, graduation)
* Severing ties with your family
* Reconnecting with your family
* Becoming clean and sober
* Seeing or burying animals killed on the road
* Accepting your challenges
* Welcoming first or additional pet
* Receiving your first paycheck
* Starting a business
* Learning your first musical instrument
* Blessing and consecrating sacred ritual tools
* Ending an addiction
* Leaving childhood friends
* Resolving conflict
* First gray hair (or last non-gray hair)
* Starting or leaving therapy
* Marriage or hand-fasting
* Menopause
* Divorce, separation, or to end a relationship with a life-partner or friend

* Renewal of commitment of vows with a life-partner
* Two families bonding
* Dealing with your parent's divorce when you were a child
* Bringing on or hastening a change
* Resolving a relationship
* In honor of remembering (incest or other trauma)
* Healing from incest or other forms of childhood abuse
* Healing from sexual assault
* Death of a parent, friend, sibling, child, or pet
* Getting off of welfare
* Leaving a patriarchal religious tradition
* Coming out as a lesbian
* Coming out as a witch
* Opening blocked feelings
* Safely releasing rage
* Preparing for death
* Reclaiming your family
* Hysterectomy or mastectomy
* Major or minor surgery
* Ovulation
* Moving away from childhood friends
* Croning: becoming an elder
* Getting fired
* Quitting a job you hate
* Ending the work week
* Greeting the day
* Going to bed
* Leaving a dwelling
* Fueling your activism
* Joining or leaving a coven
* Taking a new name
* Getting published
* Completing a project
* Making a piece of art
* Cooking and eating holy-day foods
* Letting go of a belief that has outlived its time
* Leaving a home
* Closing up your parent's house after their deaths
* Taking care of an ill or dying parent, partner, friend, or other family member
* Recognition of one's disability

The preceding list includes specifically female experiences, many other life-cycle events, personally significant life-experiences, and transitions of body, mind, and spirit. What else would you include? Add your own ideas to this list.

Practice for Self-Awareness

This practice is an extremely powerful way to become more aware of how significant moments and life experiences continue to affect and guide you in the present, often without your conscious consent. This practice is a necessary, and important step in the personal ritual making process.

1. Take a moment to remember what you now understand to be an important experience, event, moment, or transition in your life that perhaps you or others didn't treat as significant at the time.

   Another approach is to think about an attitude, belief, or habit you have that you now recognize as hindering your quality of life. Can you recall an experience as a source point for this thinking pattern?

2. Recall what happened and how you remember feeling at the time.

   If you're wishing to ritualize a future event (like an upcoming birthday, graduation, completion of a project, etc.), notice the source of your need and any internal beliefs connected to it so that you can honor the history of the process. Our life experiences don't just happen in a place disconnected from the rest of the world, culture, family background, etc.

3. How did you internalize that experience?

   Recall and reflect now on the conscious or previously unaware decisions you made based on that experience. In retrospect, how did those decisions affect, affirm, or undermine your beliefs about life, love, yourself, or other people? What internalized messages, feelings, attitudes, or decisions from that experience continue to motivate your actions, decisions, or beliefs in the present? How much of your life force from the present continues to be spent on those decisions? What are you carrying into the present from your past? What other threads from your life are linked?

4. After examining this issue, what interpretations, decisions, or meanings do you still hold to be true? What decisions would you choose to change? What new decisions do you choose to hold? What meanings do you want to ascribe to this experience now? Record or share your answers in some way (by writing, drawing, dancing, talking, singing, etc.).

Repeat this practice often.[50] Different passages can bring you to great personal revelations. Begin to make a list of other passages or transitions you would like to create ritual around. It is not too late to create a ritual in the present that would have been healing or helpful twenty or thirty years ago. Ritual has the power to transcend time, allowing the mind and heart to heal and begin anew.

Developing the Purpose

A clear and conscious purpose is the foundation of any ritual, so we begin the process of creating a ritual with what may at first glance seem to be quite obvious questions: What is the need or reason for this ritual? What is its purpose? What do you hope to accomplish by creating and experiencing this ritual?

As obvious as these questions may sound, many women fail to arrive at a clear purpose for their rituals. Without a clear purpose, your ritual will develop like a crazy quilt, a series of random actions that lead nowhere in particular. If you are a woman who enjoys entirely spirit-led spontaneous ritual rather than planned ritual, you can still make spontaneity the ritual's purpose and create a container for a spontaneous experience.

If you think of a ritual as a journey you want to take, developing the purpose is about deciding where you want to go. It's difficult to get to

---

[50] I developed this process with Felicity Artemis Flowers from the results of a co-facilitated workshop in the mid-1980s called "Our Sacred Bloods: Introduction to Women's Mysteries."

your destination if you don't know where you're going. Whether you are creating a solitary ritual or creating a ritual with a group, it is important to eventually write out the ritual's purpose clearly and concisely. The clearly articulated purpose can be understood as the *container* for the ritual's intention. Inspired by sister ritualist Nan Brooks, I have included and expanded upon some of her key ritual-making questions to ponder and write down. Invest a generous chunk of quality time in this process. This exploration is an exercise in self-intimacy. Use these questions, as you may need to guide yourself toward clarity.

If the ritual is for someone else and you are assisting her in developing her ritual's purpose, help her to explore the questions and write down or record her responses as simply and clearly as you can. Simply ask her to tell you what she's been thinking about or feeling. Ask her if she would be comfortable if you make some notes as she shares with you. Invite her to tell you the story or background as to why she feels the need to create a ritual for herself. Allow her to speak her truth without interruption except for clarifications. Notice as she processes her feelings, metaphors, and the story, and if it sounds like she needs a different ritual than she originally thought. Follow her lead as she explores. Not all the questions may apply to her. As you listen supportively, remind yourself that this ritual is not for or about you.

What is the occasion, event, transition, passage, or experience you are thinking about making a ritual around?

Is it marking your daughter's first menstruation? Making a new career change? Preparing yourself to adopt a child? To forgive yourself for a past mistake? To help heal from the death of a loved one? A prosperity ritual? To deal with and support one another in healing from body hatred? To initiate a new cycle of creativity? To bless a new baby? To celebrate a seasonal or secular holiday? To celebrate the full, new, or dark moon?

Allow the initial process to be chaotic. I describe this state of clarifying the ritual's purpose as "creative chaos," which is more commonly known as "brainstorming." Exploring your own creative process will teach you how to shape chaos, create conscious boundaries, and discover the underlying threads of truth that will eventually become the fabric of the ritual. Sometimes ideas for enactments will occur even before a conscious purpose has been fully developed. Go ahead and note any ideas so you may return to them later, but remember that your first task is to create a consciously constructed purpose. Following this ritual-making process puts the horse before the cart.

Every person is different in how they arrive at clarity of their ritual's purpose. Some of us need to talk about our issue(s) with another person just to hear ourselves think. Others may need to draw, doodle, sculpt, move, or dance. Be curious and respectful about your ways of arriving at inner truth. Sometimes the purpose for the ritual is not revealed or clarified until a sufficient amount of processing, brainstorming, stream-of-consciousness writing, sharing, story-telling, or emotional release is done first. If you are alone, it may be helpful to journal your feelings, or use a tape recorder so that you can refer to the details later on. As you process your issue or passage, it is quite possible that your original purpose may expand, alter, or change entirely. Some women discover that they need to do a different ritual first to prepare themselves to receive the other one.

As you think about this particular event, transition, experience, passage, or holy day, what feelings arise?

Allow your feelings to surface and be acknowledged, shared, written down, or expressed. Know that there may be a range of conflicting emotions: pain, anger, joy, relief, bliss, fear, etc.

Are any of those feelings ones you want to address and/or express in your ritual?

There may be a multitude of emotions connected with the passage. Your ritual can acknowledge the fact that "we live with the contrasts because we know that no moment exists without a multitude of combinations: sorrow and joy, pain and comfort, despair and hope."[51] However, unless your intent is an extremely long ritual, you will need to select a primary emotional focus or two for the ritual. It may take longer to come to consensus about this in a group. Allow extra time for this if necessary.

Ultimately, what do you want the ritual to accomplish for you? What process do you want to initiate, support, or complete by doing this ritual? What meaning do you wish to derive or reassign?

Now that you have processed your feelings and what you want the ritual to accomplish for you, you need to distil it down to a clearly articulated phrase in the length of a sentence or two. This phrase serves as the container for your ritual's purpose. If you have taken the time to process and clarify your need for this ritual, the finalized distilled ritual purpose holds all the feelings and backstory of your need. Select words that accurately resonate with the true nature of your need. Be as precise and selective with words as you will be with the eventual ritual enactment(s).

When the core issue(s) for the ritual becomes clearer, begin to formulate the purpose into a phrase. For a solitary, personal ritual, write out a purpose beginning with the words:

"I want to (celebrate / honor / heal / release) … "

Articulate the basic need and purpose for the ritual. It may be helpful to think of this as if you are sending out an invitation to a party and you want people to be prepared properly.

EXAMPLE

You are turning fifty-nine years old, your bloods stopped three years earlier, and you would like to create a ritual about owning your wisdom

[51] Levitt, *A Night of Questions*, 36.

as an elder or wise woman. You feel conflicted about having a ritual around this passage. While you are feeling happy to have reached this age of deepening wisdom, you also feel fearful about cultural attitudes toward aging women. You have already begun to feel less attractive even as you struggle to see and embrace your maturing beauty. You would like to try to include all of your feelings if you can, but as the main focus, you want to claim yourself as a wise woman.

Once the main focus is clear, the ultimate purpose of the ritual is also clear and should be written down in a clearly stated purpose:

> "I want to celebrate my fifty-ninth birthday by ritualizing my transition into 'wise womanhood.' I want to share my personal feelings about the aging process in American youth-oriented culture, and then move into the celebration of formally becoming a wise woman in my life and in the lives of my friends, family, and community."

Do you already know that you want to include participation from others? If so, how much?

Determine what kind of participation you really want. Do you want to include the feelings and wishes of others that are present? Do you want others to actively participate—to facilitate the ritual on your behalf, to act as witnesses for you, to give some form of energetic support, or all of these?

If you are undecided at this time, skip this question and the next until you have experienced the "Going Wide" Sensory Practice in the next chapter. If you wish to include others after that practice, return to your ritual purpose and expand it to include others. If you already know that you are planning a solitary ritual without the inclusion of others, skip this and the following question entirely.

If you want your ritual to include others, then write out an expanded purpose.

(For clarity, I've underlined the words added to expand the original purpose above.)

> "I want to celebrate my fifty-ninth birthday by ritualizing my transition into 'wise womanhood.' I want to share my personal feelings about the aging process in American youth-oriented culture and have other aging women share experiences from their lives. With my sisters witnessing, I then want to move into celebrating the formally naming and claiming of myself as a wise woman in my own life, the lives of my friends, family, and community."

NOTE: There is a natural sequence to consider when developing a ritual purpose. In the sequencing of the purpose and for the eventual structuring of the ritual itself, always place any release work prior to the celebration phase of the ritual. Empty out first before you fill.

Here are two other examples of clearly developed purpose statements for passage rituals:

RACHAEL'S STATEMENT OF PURPOSE

Rachael spent five years in a live-in relationship with an alcoholic womanizer. Although the relationship ended thirteen years ago, she continues to be angry and reprimands herself for being "so young and stupid." She feels that she learned valuable lessons from the experience but has been unable to release the shame that surrounds it.

> "I want to release self-blame and constant self-berating for not living up to my present expectations of myself.

I want to forgive myself for not having the skills needed to handle the situation as I would now. Finally, I want to acknowledge what I learned from the experience and what I have taken with me into my present life that is positive.

I want the ritual to be mainly for myself. I also want some spoken participation by my women friends about some experience they have berated themselves about and how they have succeeded in forgiving themselves. In this way, I will see that I am not so alone."

DIANE'S STATEMENT OF PURPOSE

Diane has just weaned the last of her three children and does not plan on having any more. She doesn't know what it will feel like to reclaim her body for herself, having dedicated it to the service of others so intensely for so long.

> "I want to honor the power of my body that has created and sustained the lives of my children and to celebrate the return of my body to my self. I also want to hear from other invited mothers about their similar experiences."

The Importance of Metaphor in the Ritual Making Process

> *"... metaphor allows us to understand our selves and our world in ways that no other modes of thought can."*[52]

[52] Lakoff and Turner, *More than Cool Reason - A Field Guide To Poetic Metaphor*, xi.

Metaphor is a tool so ordinary that we use it unconsciously and automatically, with so little effort that we hardly notice it. It is so omnipresent: metaphor suffuses our thoughts, no matter what we are thinking about.[53] Identifying the metaphors that you use to describe your ritual's purpose can give you inspiration for ritual enactments later on. Consider Diane's statement of purpose above where she says, "I want to honor the power of my body that has created and sustained the lives of my children and to celebrate the returning of my body to myself." Diane uses the metaphor of "returning" her body to her self. Diane's choice of words describe her feelings of disconnection from her self to the degree that she wants to celebrate "returning" her self to her self. Taking this metaphor as inspiration for a ritual enactment, Diane could create an object that symbolizes the return of her body to her self and receive that object in her ritual. The object that Diane receives is a symbol that will awaken both a cognitive and energetic connection within her as she interacts with it. Diane is then *enacting the metaphor* when she receives the object as her "self" in the ritual.

The essence of metaphor is understanding and experiencing one kind of thing in terms of another.[54] Here are two other examples for utilizing metaphor as inspiration for ritual enactments. When facilitating my student Kate's personal ritual-making process, she described wanting to release her regrets over a nephew's suicide as "wishing the knot in my throat would ease." Later in her ritual, I literally handed her a rope with dozens of knots tied into it for her to untie as she cried and spoke about her regrets. In another example, my student Mary described a life transition as feeling like she was "running into walls." Later in her ritual she used the wall metaphor by asking women to hold up large sheets of cardboard with negative messages that she wrote on them. She was able to physically experience these obstacles in her ritual by cutting through or moving around the "walls".

---

[53] Ibid.

[54] Lakoff and Johnson, *Metaphors We Live By*, 5.

Things to Remember When Helping Another Woman Design Her Ritual

* Your role is to help her develop the purpose and eventual symbolism of her issue. While suggestions can be helpful, be mindful to not impose your personal agenda or what you think would be good for her to focus on. She may be challenged enough just by giving herself permission to focus on and explore her own needs. Listen to what is important to *her*.

* Find ways to support her in choosing her own experience and limits. Stay present and focused entirely on her, helping her to keep focused on the occasion.

* Consider the possible impact of a woman's age and the blood mysteries cycle. We are not disconnected from our bodies' rhythms. A woman in her forties describing interrupted sleep patterns, intense mood shifts, an emotional roller coaster ride, and being "overly sensitive" for no apparent reason may be signs for the onset of menopause. A ritual to honor the menopausal years rather than a ritual to banish feeling un-centered is a reframing that can be empowering.

* Listen for clues as she speaks, paying close attention to her needs. Take notes as you observe, hear, and feel the images, words, and emotional themes she expresses. Listen especially for the metaphors she uses to express her issue. Her metaphors may be useful for developing enactments for the ritual's core work later on.

* Listen to her with your whole body as she talks about the passage. Notice what physical sensations you are having as you listen to her. Notice her body language. Open to the possibility of subtext as she describes her feelings about the ritual. Reflect these perceptions/observations back to her as you assist her in creating her ritual's purpose. Ask if you heard her correctly by speaking her intention back to her in her own words and metaphors.

* The job of the facilitator is to be out of her process unless invited. Even if invited, limit your participation in her process. The ritual is not about you. If you feel the need to ask her a question during the process, ask yourself first if it is your own need to know, or is your question to assist her in becoming clear.

Small Group Ritual

When a ritual group or coven consisting of peers develops a specific ritual purpose, it works best if consensus can be reached. This popular kind of ritual planning is a different process than one or two women designing a ritual for their group without group process or input. In either case, to participate fully participants must be able to relate to the ritual's purpose through personal interest or curiosity. Larger group rituals that are often designed and facilitated by a smaller core group and open to the public must consider different issues than a small group ritual created by and for a circle of intimates. These issues are especially addressed in chapter 10, "Facilitation as Spiritual Service."

I strongly suggest that someone in the group be designated moderator to initiate and facilitate the group's discussion and process. Her role is to keep the group focused, keep the conversation going, and make sure that everyone's voice is heard. She may ask that women raise their hand if they wish to speak so they don't talk over each other. In an ongoing ritual circle this is a role that can rotate throughout the year. It is also helpful to designate someone as the scribe, willing to take notes that can be referred to throughout the ritual-making process.

Begin every ritual making session with a group attunement. The simple act of creating connection and coming into resonance together makes a huge difference in the process and outcome of the planning session by setting the tone for the group's process. Without this simple act, the group can take off with a bunch of spinning needs with no center point.

Come into resonance at the start of your meeting by setting the group's intention for clear communication, abundance of creativity, and an honoring of your work together. Attunement can be as simple as sitting or standing in a circle, holding hands, breathing together, and speaking a simple prayer for blessing the work you will do together. Coming into resonance can mean singing or chanting together, reading an appropriate piece of poetry, and lighting a candle while voicing the group's intentions. Magically speaking, this allows women to shed the concerns of daily routines and become present so group energy may begin to form.

When developing a purpose with a group, allow everyone's ideas and thoughts to "fall into the cauldron." If this part of the process is allowed to flow freely, the group will develop the ritual's intention more authentically. This process often takes much more time than expected. Breathe through your differences in perception as you process the issue or occasion. Creating a group ritual by consensus requires each woman to step back a little as an individual and consider herself an important part of a group vision. This requires really listening to each other and hearing what another is saying. This is the primary difference between a personal ritual that is designed for the unique needs of a specific individual and a group ritual designed for the needs of many.

Look for common threads in all the ideas brought forward. Stay focused on developing your purpose first before the temptation to jump into creating enactments, logistics, or getting too scripted. Doing otherwise can greatly impede creativity and authentic expression. Allow yourselves to be supporting and supportive. This is sometimes challenging in a group of creative women with lots of ideas, but putting the cart before the horse by making enactments fit a purpose after the fact is not usually as effective.

Encourage, but do not insist, that all members of your group participate in the creative process. Some women are natural wordsmiths and may unintentionally intimidate others who need more time to formulate ideas into words. The designated moderator may notice a woman who remains silent during a creative session. Periodically check in with her, asking,

"What do *you* think about this?" Practice leaving pauses between ideas so that women who need more time to form their ideas into words have an opportunity to share them. The bottom line is that women are more committed to a ritual working well if it represents them. Individuals in the group must feel that their voice or vision is in it.

There is a difference between holding back and holding space for yourself and others. Compare and contrast this difference. If you are a woman reluctant to step forward and participate, consider asking yourself what you *do* have a "yes" for.

If the ritual is a seasonal or lunar celebration, the ritual purpose may be more universal in nature or may focus on an area of women's mysteries appropriate to the time of year in the goddess cycle (see chapter 9). Discuss the holy day or lunar celebration and, if appropriate, its correlation with the cycle of women's lives.

The narrower the focus of the ritual, the more likely it is that only a part of the group or women's community may wish to participate. For example, a healing ritual for incest survivors may be relevant or appropriate only for those who are working on their own healing or supporting others' healing. If a ritual is planned to address intense personal issues, such as abortion, sexual assault, abuse, or domestic violence, a trained and licensed therapist should be present or should actually facilitate the ritual. Do not take women on a ritual journey if you are unskilled or unprepared to handle the possibility of an emotional or mental crisis such as a mental breakdown or an abuse flashback. In my work, I have included either the presence of a trained therapist or a therapist on call if a ritual has the potential to go beyond my skills as a ritual priestess.[55]

Eventually come into agreement around the need or purpose for the ritual, including where the group wishes the journey to take them, both individually and collectively. If the group is not completely clear,

---

[55] If you do not hold a legal ministerial credential allowing you to work in areas considered therapeutic, there may be legal liability to consider if you are providing ritual dealing with intensely specific personal issues.

continue to develop the ritual's purpose with the sub- sequent questions from the personal ritual-making process.

Once the main focus is clear, the ultimate purpose of the ritual is also clear and should be written down. For a group ritual, write out a purpose beginning with the words:

"We want to (celebrate/honor/transform/initiate)..."

EXAMPLE

Your ritual circle wants to celebrate the seasonal holiday of Imbolc, the holiday of the Celtic year that celebrates the waxing of daylight after winter's darkness. The Irish goddess Brigid, (later adopted as a Catholic saint), is traditionally associated with this day. In northern Europe, Imbolc marks the first day of spring. Traditionally, it has always been a holy day for women and is considered to be the greatest holiday of Women's Mysteries, representing the eternal renewal of the Goddess from the old hag of winter into Her youthful form again. In the Dianic tradition, this is the customary season for ritualizing themes of initiation, spiritual dedication, rededication, and renewal.

On earth's surface, the waxing light is clearly seen and the hardiest of the new shoots begin to peek out of the ground, not to blossom yet but clearly visible to sharp eyes. Six weeks after Winter Solstice, there is evidence that the earth is awakening from her winter's sleep.

Let's imagine that your ritual group wishes to celebrate the early signs of spring and rededicate themselves to their spiritual path. Women wish to do both personal and group dedications that are witnessed by everyone present. Remember that in celebrating any seasonal holiday it is important to structure the ritual so that the needs of both the individual women and the group are addressed.

EXAMPLE OF A CLEAR STATEMENT OF PURPOSE

> "We want to celebrate the holiday of Brigid, renewing ourselves spiritually as individuals and as a group. We also want to make personal dedications for the coming year that are witnessed and supported by the entire group."

Practice

Pick three diverse occasions from your life, either past, present, or future. Follow the process above and arrive at a clear and concise purpose for each occasion. In at least one occasion, include other participants. Feel free to do extensive thinking and writing before arriving at a purpose. This will help you access from within what you truly need.

If you are using this process in a ritual group, have the group pick three diverse occasions you might consider ritualizing and go through the above process to arrive at a concise purpose.

chapter 4

DEVELOPING THE THEME

By coming to a clear purpose for your ritual, you have decided on the destination for your journey. To develop your ritual's theme is to choose what vehicle of transport will take you to that destination. There are numerous ways to get there once you know where you are going.

The next step in the ritual-making process is to translate the ritual's purpose and emotional content into integrated symbolism and physical enactments that will provide a meaningful experience and, ultimately, transcend words or any ritual "props." It is important to remember that ritual is, in itself, only a tool.

> It is a means of bringing the heart, mind, body, and spirit to the smallest possible point of concentration. Everything about creating a ritual is designed to increase that concentration ... all help the mind to shift levels and work on those levels during the time of the ritual.[56]

All effective rituals engage the physical senses as gateways to different levels of consciousness within the mind. When we are awake, our mind operates on three levels or thinking states: conscious, subconscious, and unconscious. In her book *The Open Mind*, Dawna Markova, Ph.D., explores these states of consciousness and how our minds do not all think alike. Understanding mental diversity is extremely relevant to ritual making and the practice of magic.[57] Dion Fortune is famously quoted as saying,

---

[56] Ashcroft-Nowicki, *First Steps in Ritual*, 15.

[57] The quotations on this and page 58 are from Markova, *The Open Mind*, 21–29, 46.

"Magic is the art of changing consciousness at will."[58] Creating rituals with multi-sensory enactments will assist everyone participating, to move from one state of consciousness to another fluidly.

In the conscious mind-state we generate beta waves. Our conscious mind "is like the mouth of the mind that takes information in and chews it up, but doesn't swallow or digest it." Here the mind separates, ranks, analyzes, and organizes. The conscious mind is the left brain, where you are the most focused and alert, intentional, goal-oriented, and productive for tasks like balancing your check book; in this mind-state "you are most actively engaged with the outside world."

In the subconscious mind-state we generate alpha waves. Markova describes this mind- state as "our in-between state, the revolving door of our minds where the vast array of input we receive from the outer world is sorted. It is a transitional (*trance*-itional) way of thinking, for here the brain is metabolizing information and exploring options." This alpha mind-state sorts the information that the conscious mind brings in and functions as a threshold "that is both receptive and active, between our interior and exterior minds, where we are motivated into action and soothed into relaxation."

In the unconscious mind-state we generate mostly theta waves. The theta mind-state is often referred to as right-brained, visionary, spaced out, day-dreamy, or meditational. This is the most receptive and expansive mind-state, where the brain thinks in many ways at once, as if in a web, creating and carrying messages indirectly through dreams, symbols, and imagery...[It is here where the mind searches internally for] how new information fits with what you have already experienced, making new patterns from it, storing information for the long term, and dreaming new possibilities for the future.

Through ritual making, we seek to reach this state of mind for our deepest healing and transformation.

[58] Welsh born Dion Fortune (1890-1946, birth name Violet Firth) was considered to be one of the most influential figures in the birth of Modern Witchcraft.

Markova writes that each of these states of consciousness seems to use a different symbolic language for processing and expressing information, either auditory, visual, or kinesthetic. Although every person, unless severely physically disabled, processes information through all three types of input, individuals are more strongly stimulated by one type of input than another at each layer of consciousness.

For example, visual input might stimulate a woman's brain to produce beta waves, making it easy for her to learn how to do something by reading directions in a book or watching someone do something. Auditory input may either help or hinder her in connecting her thoughts, stimulating her brain to produce alpha waves, the part of the mind that sorts the information she receives. Kinesthetic input might take her into a deep theta wave trance, enabling her to change or create new patterns in her unconscious mind. Another woman's conscious mind might be most stimulated by kinesthetic activity, her subconscious activated visually, and her deep mind affected by auditory stimuli.

The most effective ritual affects the theta mind, the state in which your mind experiences the world most deeply, although you may have the least conscious awareness of this effect after the ritual. It is in the theta mind-state that new neurological patterns are created with the potential to make profound life changes.

Be very curious about how you are affected by visual, auditory, and kinesthetic stimulus. Notice what takes you into the different states of consciousness. When designing a solo ritual for yourself, you don't have consider how or if the ritual will engage others. When the ritual is created solely to meet your needs, you will naturally be designing the ritual experience according to how your own mind is organized.

However, if you are including others and want to engage everyone who participates in a ritual, express the theme of your ritual with the full range of modalities: imagery, sound, and hands-on kinesthetic activities. Keep in mind that we do not all think alike, nor do we express ourselves in the same ways. Create a ritual space that delights and entices the senses, one that will enable the participants to bring the full range of their consciousness to bear on the purpose of the ritual.

If you are working in a ritual group and have decided what the group will do for the core of the ritual work, allow for individual expression of the ritual's enactments. For example, if you are including a guided meditation in your ritual, do not insist that everyone close their eyes. Instead invite women to either close their eyes or let them rest their eyes open and unfocused. Do not insist that they sit or lie still, and invite them to either be still, or stand, or move their arms or torso while standing quietly in place. Some women in your group will need to move while speaking; others will need to be silent or still. What will take one woman into deep trance will bring another woman to full consciousness. Because each of us has her own patterns and pathways of perception, processing, and deep knowing, supporting each woman's expression allows for everyone to have an optimum ritual experience.

I highly recommend learning more about the visual, auditory, and kinesthetic modes of learning. Although it is beyond the scope of this book, such study will greatly enhance your understanding of states of consciousness and their application to ritual making.

Drawing on Markova's work, the following information may be helpful as you consider incorporating ways of developing your ritual theme to reach all who participate.

KINESTHETIC: Physical stimulus such as smelling a rose, eating a ripe peach, snuggling a puppy, sensing the energetics of a room, getting a massage, and hiking in the woods will either bring you fully present or take you into lighter or deeper states of trance. Some women use dance or swaying or rocking motions to take themselves into trance; others need to tap the rungs of the chair they are sitting in as they study a textbook so that they will remain conscious of what they are reading. For some of us touch is casual and easy, for others it is intensely personal and sacred.

To stimulate the kinesthetic channels, a ritual could include movement, touch, dance, handcrafting something, drumming, incense, and food or drink.

VISUAL: Visual stimulus such as watching a play, reading, viewing a movie, and choosing an item from the crowded shelf of a grocery store may bring a woman to full consciousness or send her into a daydream or even to sleep. A woman who responds to visual input by coming fully present connects deeply with others through eye contact. For a woman who responds to visual input by going into trance, direct eye contact can be unpleasant and even feel very invasive. Some people "feel" what they see.

To stimulate the visual channels, a ritual could give particular attention to the ambiance of the ritual's environment from the conscious use of color, lighting, candles, seasonal symbols and decorations, costume, and the appropriately decorated altar.

AUDITORY: Auditory stimuli, such as birdsong, jackhammers, harp music, your professor's lecture, or your child's cry, will take you into different states of consciousness as well. Some people think most clearly with the TV on and the stereo blasting in a crowded coffeehouse. Others need absolute silence to access their thoughts. Some people need to talk out loud to think something through. Others must be very careful of which sounds they allow themselves to hear because they literally feel sounds in their body.

To stimulate the auditory channels, a ritual could include speaking, invocation, storytelling, poetry, singing, chanting, creating or listening to music, and drumming.

In considering this information, it is important to realize that in every group ritual at any given moment, some people will be fully present, some will be in a light state of trance, and some will be off on a journey. When planning a well-prepared meal, a chef considers what foods go together—how the flavors, colors, and textures will blend together—and the final presentation of the meal. In this instance, what will complement the ritual "meal" for a total experience that feeds each participant? Consider which elements (earth, water, fire, air), seasonal aspects, and aspects of the Goddess correspond most to the purpose. Mix these ingredients carefully, considering how much of each to add to the ritual stew for optimum flavor.

"Going Wide" Sensory Practice

Pick one of the rituals for which you have written out a concise purpose and work with it in the following practice. This "Going Wide" practice will expand your perceptions and help you to access authentic intuitive and sensory information from your deep mind that you can use to externalize your ritual's theme and establish its general mood and ambiance. The abundance of information revealed by this practice will later on allow you to pluck out what is essential from what is informative and possible but not necessary to include in your ritual. Many women have also found this practice useful for accessing the inner truth in making daily life decisions. Our five physical senses of sight, smell, taste, touch, and sound correspond to the attributes of the four elements of earth, air, fire, and water, plus the presence of Spirit, the power that animates life. In addition, I have identified how each of the senses might stimulate the visual, auditory, or kinesthetic channels.

You may start in any sensory mode to begin if you are doing this "Going Wide" practice on your own. Think about the ritual's purpose. Speak it aloud and listen. Let the purpose sink deeper into the waters of your creative mind. Let images, sounds, smells, tastes, and bodily sensations rise up and float on the surface of your conscious mind. Open yourself to whatever comes. Afterwards, write down, draw, or move your body to remember and record your ideas. Share your associations with someone. If possible, ask someone to take you through this practice and tape record or scribe your responses. Depending on your answers to initial questions, not all of the questions will be applicable, so feel free to follow the trail initiated by your deep mind. You also don't have to begin in the order of sensory exploration presented here. If you run into a block, explore another sensory modality. Let the free-flowing images and sensing flow uninterrupted.

You are not likely to use all the information that arises from your deep mind, but this process helps your mind become flexible, creative, and truthful. Intuition is energetic information[59] sourced from the intelligence of your body. Honor your intuitive knowing. You can narrow down what you will actually incorporate into your ritual at a later time. Take yourself into your ritual; feel/sense, see, hear. Don't think! Let this process breathe as you breathe. Let your senses go wide. There are no limitations.

If you are facilitating someone else through the "Going Wide" practice, pay attention to how she responds to the modality you start with and follow her lead. If she seems blocked or frustrated and nothing is coming forward immediately, try another one of the senses and return to the other later. Do not confuse being blocked with needing open spaces to think or search for words uninterrupted. If this is the case, do not fill her silences with your words or questions. Be patient as she digs inside herself for buried treasures.

If she takes off with her ritual and is freely describing it to you, do not make her conform to your order of questions. Listen to her and go with where she is taking herself. However, if she starts to develop her enactments in great detail, logistics, and sequence, gently guide her back to this process with, "That sounds great. We'll get back to that a little later."

Now, take in a deep breath, sink into your ritual purpose, and begin.

Sight: Fire/Visual

Where are you? Where is the physical location? Are you indoors or outside? (Consider the pros and cons for each location later on.) What does the ritual space look like? What is there? What time of day or night

[59] Carolyn Myss, Ph.D., *Anatomy of the Spirit* (Sounds True Audio Series, 1996).

is it? What kind of lighting is present? What colors do you see? What are you wearing? Are there others present? Are they wearing specific kinds of clothing? Is there an altar? If so, what does the altar look like? What objects are on it? Is there anything else you see?

Smell: Air/Kinesthetic

Do you smell anything specific at the ritual? What scent, if any, is present? Are there spices, flowers, incense, herbs, scented oil or water, ocean breezes, forest, just the air around you, or none of these? Is there anything else you smell?

Taste: Water/Kinesthetic

Are you tasting any special foods, edible herbs, or drink as part of the ritual? If so, is it something sweet, salty, tart, or bitter? Is there a special meal or feast afterwards? Is there anything else you taste?

Touch: Earth/Kinesthetic

What does the ritual space feel like? Are you standing, sitting, or lying down? What sort of surface are you on? Are you touching or feeling something specific? Are you being touched by participants or a special person? Is there lots of space around you? What type of clothing are you feeling on your body? Are you wearing clothing at all? Are you dancing or moving in some way? Is there anything else you are touching or feeling?

Sound: Spirit/Auditory and Kinesthetic

What are you hearing in your ritual space? What sound is present? Music, song, chant? One voice or many? Do you hear particular instruments, nature sounds, ocean waves, wind? Is there recorded music, spoken words, or silence? Are you speaking or singing something? Is someone speaking something to you? Do you hear a combination of these? Is there anything else you hear?

Lastly, "Is this complete for now, or is there something else you see, feel, hear?"

PLEASE NOTE: Women often love to collaborate with others and are eager to incorporate other women's thoughts and visions into their personal ritual. Women are conditioned to include or accommodate others, so if you are guiding someone through this practice for their personal ritual, please do not lead her toward your vision. Wait until she shares her intuitive associations first, and only then ask her if she wants to hear your associations from this practice (I don't recommend offering your thoughts as a general rule). This process is not about you, and your ideas may not be what she needs. If she gets stuck somewhere in this process, quickly move her on to another sensory modality. You can return to that modality again later.

If you are using this "Going Wide" practice as part of creating a group ritual, it is useful to have someone volunteer to take the group through the process and have someone scribe what comes forward. The group facilitator holds the ritual purpose as the container for the process. Come into resonance together and ask the facilitator to state the ritual purpose. As with the personal process, let the images and sensing from the group flow uninterrupted, with no agreements, disagreements, or logistics derailing this free-flowing part of the process. Expect that there is likely to be completely different associations amongst group members, and keep the process flowing and breathing. The facilitator may or may not need to go through the sensory questions as written, and may simply guide along whatever comes up that the group sees, senses, and feels. After long pauses, the facilitator can simply ask, "Are we complete for now?" and wait momentarily before moving the process along.

Taking your ritual's purpose through this "Going Wide" practice takes you inside your future ritual *in present time*, and conjures the sensory ambiance of your ritual. Now you have a ritual container with life in it. The ritual energetics have begun to form, and your deep mind may have already begun giving you insights into enactments for the core work.

Set your notes from this practice aside for now. In the next step of the ritual-making process, you will refer to your sensory associations from the "Going Wide" practice to consider how they might be useful in creating your core ritual enactments. Soon you will review all of your notes and the ideas that have surfaced, and begin to apply them to creating the ritual environment and flushing out the content of the ritual itself. Later on you can deal with the logistics of whether an indoor or outdoor location (or a combination of both) is the most conducive for your ritual, or how your altar and the surrounding ritual space might be made to reflect the ritual's purpose.

Before developing the core enactments of your ritual, let's first explore the sensory "language" of ritual found in folk magic, and thematic categories of ritual with some ideas for how these themes might be enacted.

FOLK MAGIC: Thinking in "Things"[60]

Many ideas for ritual enactments involve some form of what Frazer termed sympathetic magic - in which objects, entities, or effects are understood to be *in sympathy* or "connected" to one another in other-than-ordinary ways. One way of generating "sympathy" (according to Frazer) is through the principle of *homeopathy,* or *imitation* - focusing on the principle of thought that "like produces like, or that an effect resembles its cause; that one can produce a desired effect by imitating it in some way". This is the intersection of ritual and spellcraft.

In folk - or vernacular - magic, the language of communication involves physical things, sensations, and objects. Vernacular magic is almost never subjective, but rather "results oriented" - aiming to effect change in the objective world. In folk magic, the language of communication is through physical things, sensations, and objects. Folk magic is not subjective, but results oriented with objective results. The tangible is the vehicle for communication between a sender and a receiver through a method of transfer in some form. For example, the concept of protection is abstract. The concept of protection is made tangible through a physical object

[60] From a brilliant spellcraft class I took with folklorist, Steve Wehmyer, PhD, in 2007, and personal conversation.

to touch, wear, or feel, that embodies, stands for, or equals the same. The wearer is both working with the symbol and the energy encoded in the object. In folk magic *the physical and the spiritual are one and the same*. Magic is the language of the senses, encoding information in our five senses. When your ritual involves symbols and enactments that are tangible and/or physically engaging, you will reach a deeper level of consciousness necessary for long-term transformation.

Types of Ritual

Most rituals can be grouped into thematic categories: creation/manifestation, release/transition/transformation, honoring, and celebration. Sometimes the ritual's purpose mutes the distinction among categories. For example, a healing ritual might include aspects of release, transformation, and creation. Wedding ceremonies include aspects of honoring and celebration. Understanding the categories of ritual can help to clarify and focus your intent.

The ideas provided here are only intended to act as a springboard for your own creativity and can't begin to exhaust the possibilities for ritual activities. Additionally, you need not be limited to only one idea per ritual. They can be mixed and matched in any way that fits the stated purpose of the ritual, as long as the sequence of activities makes sense. For a group ritual, take care not to overwhelm the participants or exhaust yourself with too many activities. Sometimes less is more. Develop the ritual theme in ways that will nourish you and the others present. Simple, meaningful activities are often far more transformational than elaborate, theatrical productions.

Each thematic category of ritual is described below, along with suggestions for ways to enact the theme. Remember that many of the enactment ideas in one category may also be appropriate in another. I have also indicated what visual, auditory, and kinesthetic modalities are stimulated by the suggested enactments. Some enactments may incorporate more than one sensory mode. For example, when only a few participants in a group ritual actually do the hands-on work, their experience is kinesthetic, while the rest of the participants experience a visual and/or auditory enactment. Remember that in a group ritual, women will always be in different states of consciousness depending on the visual, auditory, and kinesthetic stimulus being used at a given point in time.

Consider also that for some group rituals, especially those where the public is invited, not all the women attending will be involved in the ritual design process. Women who were not part of the ritual design process are therefore being asked to adapt to the symbol systems and enactments chosen for them by others, rather than by consensus. It may be necessary to inform them as to what the symbols or enactments represent and instruct them in how to work with them so that everyone can work with the same concepts in mind.

The following ideas are intended to stimulate your thoughts regarding the "core work" of your ritual.

Creation Rituals

Creation rituals are intended to bring something into physical, mental, or emotional manifestation. These are rituals in which a new cycle is set into motion or an existing cycle is renewed. Creation rituals include lunar rituals for the waxing (new to full) cycle of the moon; fertility rituals; rituals to mark entry into a new school or career; or project rituals for planting a garden, nurturing a new love relationship, or simply preparing to open to new possibilities.

IDEAS

* Create a symbolic object prior to or during the ritual. Create something that symbolizes what you are creating in your life (kinesthetic, visual).

* Bring magical gifts to support the occasion, such as altar objects that illustrate the purpose (visual).
* Enact a symbolic birthing scene or design a physical enactment depicting birth, such as going through a passageway, moving between legs, creating a tunnel with arms and passing each woman through into the "new reality" (kinesthetic, visual). Note that if you add words or sounds to kinesthetic or visual enactments, then you have added an auditory stimulus. Also note that auditory input can become visual stimulus depending on the words being used (poetry that uses metaphor triggers visual imagery).
* Mix things in a cauldron and bring out what you are manifesting (kinesthetic, visual).
* Build a story with words, each woman adding words as the story evolves (auditory).
* Nurture or plant a seed (kinesthetic, visual). Depending on the long- or short- term goal of the ritual, consider the difference between planting a redwood seed and an alfalfa seed.
* Weave yarn into a new pattern (kinesthetic, visual).
* Knot a "witch's ladder" (kinesthetic). A witch's ladder is a string or cord with a varying number of knots tied in it, and it is used similarly to a rosary or prayer beads for personal autosuggestion. You touch each knot as you speak or think a word or phrase in concentrated repetition. Note that if a chant is used while tying the knots, an auditory stimulus is added.
* Start sewing a quilt to be finished at the completion of a new project (kinesthetic, visual).
* Tie things together (kinesthetic, visual).
* Create a community or group art piece (visual, kinesthetic).
* Sweep something in a deosil (clockwise) pattern with a special

broom (kinesthetic, visual).

* Feed yourself and/or others to "ingest" the new reality with symbolic food or drink (kinesthetic).
* Dance something into yourself, into your body and psyche (kinesthetic, visual). If recorded music, live drumming, or chanting is used while dancing, an auditory stimulus is added.
* Sing together, creating and weaving sounds and/or words (auditory, visual).

Release/Transition/Transformation Rituals

Ritual themes of release, transition, or change are about letting go and allowing your mind, body, or psyche to begin an intentional process of transformation. These rituals most often initiate a process of healing, with the intention of the ritual being the release or transformation of dysfunctional or destructive behavior patterns, beliefs, and/or physical disease or injuries. Feelings of anger, despair, grief, and frustration over violence, injustice, personal, political and environmental issues can be facilitated into personal empowerment through this form of ritual.

Rituals for emotional healing initiate a process of changing patterns in the unconscious mind. Healing rituals are generally not intended or expected to be a quick fix, "just add water" remedy for the short term. Healing rituals must be followed up with conscious work while the unconscious "dis-ease" pattern is gradually transformed and integrated into a new, healthy pattern. While many of us want instant gratification, long-term change requires ongoing mindfulness.

When doing any ritual work that involves release or banishing, make sure to replace what you have released by clearly stating afterwards, within the same ritual, what will fill the void. The more specific you can be about what you are replacing, so much the better. If you are uncertain or not yet aware of what will refill the space, state positively that you open yourself to life-affirming opportunities for growth. Stating this will create a space for what will eventually manifest by declaring an affirmative intention for positive change. For example, you may state, "I release self-hatred" while burning a symbolic representation of self-hatred or performing another enactment. To complete the change, follow the statement and action of release with a clearly stated intention, such as " ... *and* I welcome in its place transformation and the possibility of experiencing compassion, healing, and love."

Release/transformation rituals include dark moon rituals (the lunar phase that precedes the visible crescent of the new moon); banishing self-hatred, racism, and violence against women and children; healing from physical or sexual abuse; rites of protection; cleansing and healing from physical illness or injury; shedding old habits or addictions that limit one's life in the present; and dissolving the effects of abusive or harmful relationships.

IDEAS

* Dissolve soil or salt in water (kinesthetic, visual).
* Sweat it out through physical movement, a sweat bath, or sauna (kinesthetic).
* Dance it out (kinesthetic, visual, auditory).
* Shout it out (auditory, kinesthetic).
* In the presence of running water, watch the water carry away something that represents what you are releasing (visual).
* Use stones to absorb negativity, then throw them into deep water or bury them deep in the ground (kinesthetic, visual). Note that water and earth elementally are not interchangeable. Consider what you are getting rid of and decide which method makes more sense for your issue. There are energetic aftereffects to your ritual action. If you throw the stone onto the ground, there is the possibility that someone else will pick it up and take in what you have left behind,

like catching a cold from someone else. Deep water prevents anyone from getting to that stone again. In traditional Witchcraft, if you bury something in fertile earth, it will grow. Anything that emerges from the earth must first go through a process of transformation. The deeper you bury it, the more complete the transformation will be before it emerges again. In either case, when you are done, turn away and do not look back.

* Remove clothing purposefully and release what it symbolizes as you remove it (kinesthetic, visual). Depending on how harmful the thing to be released is, it may be wise to burn or destroy the piece of clothing.
* Separate or pull objects from each other (kinesthetic, visual).
* Cut or tear something up (visual, kinesthetic, auditory).
* Untie symbolic objects that are connected (kinesthetic, visual).
* Flush a symbol down the toilet, being sure that what you choose to flush is ecologically sound to dispose of through this method (visual, auditory).
* Destroy an image or transform the image into something new or changed, or take an image representing the old way and change it into something new or transformed (visual, kinesthetic, possibly auditory if accompanied by words and/or sounds of the image being destroyed).
* Utilize images of transformation such as a chrysalis turning into a butterfly or a snake shedding its skin (visual).
* Burn a symbolic object (visual, auditory).
* Break a symbolic object (visual, auditory, kinesthetic).
* Give something away (kinesthetic, visual).
* Sweep widdershins (counterclockwise) with a special broom (kinesthetic, visual).

* Use a laying-on of hands to pull or push negative energy out of the body. Remember to refill the space with positive or neutral energy. Wash your hands to remove any lingering energy (kinesthetic).
* Work energy toward healing the body, mind, or heart through a variety of modalities, including herbs, spells, hugs, intensive energy projection, and release (kinesthetic, visual).
* Burn a candle to absorb negativity and another candle to return neutral energy to the environment (visual).
* Wash your hands or your body, and watch the water run down the drain (kinesthetic, visual, auditory).
* Tie a cord to a part of yourself; when it falls off, the issue is released (visual, kinesthetic).

Honoring Rituals

A ritual to honor someone or something is to acknowledge an accomplishment or a completed transition into a new station in one's life. An honoring ritual is not done during the transitional time from one state of being to another, but after having arrived at the new phase of life. Honoring rituals acknowledge the present, what is now so.

Women are often experts at giving rather than receiving. It is sometimes challenging for a woman to fully accept being the focus of loving attention and recognition. Being seen or recognized by those witnessing is a major part of honoring rituals. Emotional preparation of the recipient for such an honoring ritual may be necessary. Meditating on the occasion will help bring the honoree's consciousness into the present moment, and by centering she will come into wholeness, helping her to open fully to the experience. A pre-ritual massage or hot bath may also help the recipient open fully to receiving the ritual.

Examples of honoring rituals include cronings, graduations, anniversaries, first menses, achievement recognition ceremonies, funerals, and memorial services.

IDEAS

* Name aloud or proclaim what is now so (auditory).
* Read or recite poetry celebrating the occasion (auditory, visual).
* Share experiences, realizations, truths, and visions (auditory).
* Create a special altar with symbols of the accomplishment (visual).
* Display photographs of yourself or others (visual).
* Wear or be adorned with a special garland or crown (visual, kinesthetic).
* Receive nurturing physical attention, such as a massage (kinesthetic).
* Dance to express the emotion (kinesthetic, visual, auditory).
* Pour libations in thanks for the accomplishment (kinesthetic, visual).
* Feast on special foods (kinesthetic, visual).
* Receive a formal blessing, perhaps spoken by someone special (auditory, visual).
* Speak or write affirmations (auditory, visual).
* Give or receive special gifts, food, wishes, or blessings (auditory, visual, kinesthetic).
* Pass over a symbolic threshold (kinesthetic, visual).
* Be witnessed by others or be a witness to others as they ritualize their transitions (visual).
* Tell stories or pass along wisdom (auditory, visual).
* Decorate the person of honor (visual, kinesthetic).
* Take a new name or title (auditory).

Celebration Rituals

As with honoring rituals, the theme of celebration focuses on commemorating what is presently occurring and may also include the transitional phase of becoming. The most familiar celebration rituals are birthdays. Celebration rituals also commemorate historical events that continue to have meaning in the present. These rituals may be linked to time-honored traditions, so including an honoring of the ancestors may be appropriate at many of these rites. Through the passage of time and the cycle of the seasons, we remain connected to our ancestors. We ritualize our connection with each other in the present with an awareness of our connection to the past.

As the wheel of the year turns, we can use seasonal celebrations to help ourselves attain greater awareness of the natural world. We can learn once again to walk in step with the rest of creation and align our lives with the universal cycles of life. Other celebration rituals might include worship or acknowledgment of cosmological or celestial influences —the sun, moon, stars, or natural phenomena such as thunder, lightning, etc.[61]

In planning a seasonal ritual, listen to what the Earth is saying. Let her message suggest what you might do. You can get lots of ideas just by paying attention to Mother Nature as the great teacher. For seasonal rituals especially, look out your window; go outside; be with the body of the Earth. This is how you will understand and attune to the holiday most easily. Create your seasonal rituals to be consistent with where you actually live, and honor that place. You might also wish to research how the people who lived on the land before your people came here celebrated the seasons. This may help you to understand the seasonal message for people living in our time.

Relate the seasonal holiday to the life cycle of women, e.g., how the Maiden goddess corresponds to the season of spring. Be certain, in choosing and relating such symbolism, that the women attending the

---

[61] Hope, *The Psychology of Ritual*, 7.

ritual can relate to it. If you draw inspiration but not relevant focus from ancient sources or liturgy, the ritual may become merely an entertainment. Although a ritual based on ancient Greek mythologies about Persephone and Demeter may be an interesting experience, if participants are not able to relate personally to the theme or symbolism, the ritual may fail to provide meaning.

IDEAS

* Write a poem or song of praise for the celebration (auditory, visual).
* Invoke your ancestors (auditory, visual).
* Have a guided meditation or visualization (auditory, visual).
* Take a hike or circle outdoors (kinesthetic, visual).
* Perform a moving meditation, dance, or repetitive gestures (kinesthetic, visual, auditory).
* Dress in clothing that reflects the colors or mood of the season (visual, kinesthetic).
* Tell stories or myths appropriate to the season (auditory).
* Create a ritual tool to use that is seasonally appropriate (kinesthetic, visual).
* Give gifts, wishes, or seasonal blessings (auditory, visual, kinesthetic).
* Feed or offer drink to others; feast on special seasonal or symbolic foods (kinesthetic, visual).
* Create a seasonal altar (visual, kinesthetic).
* Do spellwork especially appropriate for the season: for example, "planting" wishes at Spring Equinox (visual, kinesthetic, auditory).
* Light candles (visual). Candles are wonderful to use for certain kinds of magic, but they may not be appropriate or necessary for all rituals or spellwork. Other forms of elemental symbols and

enactments may be more appropriate for the purpose, such as herbs, stones, and natural or created objects or images. Candles may still be desired to enhance a ritual mood, however, and their color and shape should reflect the theme and purpose of the ritual.

Ritual Theater

Sometimes rituals include the telling or acting out of a story or myth. Modern theater evolved out of ancient religious ceremony. Myths and stories may be enacted with dance, music, narrative, and song.

> Ritual, unlike theater, does not distinguish between audience and performers. All share formally and substantially the same set of beliefs and accept the same system of practices, the same sets of rituals or liturgical actions. A congregation is there to affirm the theological or cosmological order, explicit or implicit, which all hold in common, to actualize it periodically for themselves.[62]

Performance can be quite powerful when presented as an introduction to the ritual itself or included within the body of the ritual. In ritual theater presentations, facilitators and/ or priestesses become en-*actors*.

It is important to distinguish between ritual theater and particular ritual enactments, most notably *aspecting* a deity. There are skills that great actors possess that a ritual priestess should try to develop, such as the ability to project her voice and move with confidence and fluidity. This does not mean, however, that someone with acting skills will automatically make a great ritual priestess. This is particularly true when a woman has chosen to aspect the Goddess for all or part of the ritual. When a woman aspects the Goddess, she becomes a "house" for an invited deity to enter. If you are *acting* the character of the Goddess, you are not aspecting Her. The

[62] Victor Turner, "From Ritual to Theatre," *Performing Arts Journal Publications* (New York, 1982), 112.

skill of aspecting is not "Sheila Thomas starring tonight as Demeter." It is an egoless process of disappearing into a deity rather than pretending to be a deity. Aspecting is about inviting a goddess to join with you for a specific duration of time. I experience aspecting as an overlay of a goddess form where I am hold what feels like a dual consciousness. I am aware of my separate self but intimately *joined* with Her unique presence.

Living in Southern California for decades, I had the pleasure of training several priestesses who were actors by profession. The ones who thought that ritual priestessing was about superficially performing a role learned the differences over time, and some became proficient ritualists capable of embodying the Goddess in Her many forms. Women who facilitate ritual are not stars of a show, even though sometimes they may be perceived of as such, even by themselves. Women who feel shy or self-conscious about facilitating in ritual may assume that they have to be comfortable with performing and experience performance anxiety. Women's ritual is not a spectator event. While it is true that a ritual priestess must at times project a presence that is larger than life, her work is not a performance. It is a work of the spirit crafted from the heart of the Goddess. I experience this state as simultaneously being more than myself and fully myself.

It is important to realize that if you include aspects of performance in your ritual, you are separating participants from facilitators, making them an "audience" to your "show." This can remove participants from the co-created aspect of the ritual. If a performance of ritual theater is included in your rite, remember to reintegrate the "audience" as full and equal participants again as soon as the performance has been completed. Create a transition that supports the group's integration of meaning conveyed by the performance.

Developing the Core Ritual Enactments

In this chapter, you have been introduced to the ritual theme categories and have read over some ideas to stimulate what enactments you might do for your core work in your ritual. Think of a ritual enactment as *embodied action*.

Now that the intuitive look and feel of the ritual have been brought forward, what do you want to *do* in your ritual? Now it's time to go wide again with your ritual purpose, by first reading aloud or recalling your ritual purpose statement. Take a deep breath. Walk into your ritual, filling the ritual space with all of the sensory modalities that came to you in the "Going Wide" practice that brought life to the environment of your ritual.

Now, what is happening there? What are you *doing*?

Recall if any enactments are already present from the "Going Wide" practice. If so, mention them and notice if what came through in the practice, is still what you wish to do for the core work. If not, make changes or allow other ideas to arise that could enact the ritual's purpose and metaphors. Immerse yourself in the feeling of your ritual from that practice. Let your mind go wide again to what you see, feel, and hear yourself actually doing in your ritual. Write down, draw, or tape record these ideas that intuitively come to you. Remember, our minds do not all think alike, so cultivate curiosity and honor your individual process by exploring how best to access your own creativity. The more you engage in ritual-making practices, the better you will learn to have greater trust in your abilities to chose enactments appropriate to your inner meaning. Continue to record more ideas for enactments and what they mean to you.

If you are facilitating this process for someone else's personal ritual, ask her to remember her ritual's purpose, step into her sensory experience of her ritual's ambiance, and with a light touch simply guide her to her own discoveries by moving her along in her vision with *"and then..."* or *"and what happens next?"* Avoid asking her for the minute details or logistics to her enactments in this process. You can sequence before or after an enactment(s) later. Asking her for too many details will cause her to lose the creative flow and narrow her vision. Afterwards, let her use you as a sounding board or resource, as needed.

If you are creating the ritual with a group, ask someone to serve as a facilitator of the role described above. With a group of women coming up with ideas, there will be lots of great ideas to work with. Each woman in the group should try to stay unattached to her own ideas as one woman's inspiration will likely lead to another. Eventually it will become apparent what ideas the group as a whole resonates with best. I have also tried to find ways within any group ritual for women to work with their individual needs and the expression of that need. Consider the possibility of an enactment that everyone does in a similar manner with space for individual expression of the ritual theme. For example, the group might agree on a general purpose for the ritual, as in "To honor our individual winter descent and to create a group energetic web of support to carry us through the dreamtime," and make space in the ritual for individual expression of that theme instead of everyone being asked to express their personal process in exactly the same way. Some will speak, some will breathe, dance, or "move" their winter descent, while others may draw a picture that they show.

Once the core enactment(s) are created, then flesh out the rest of the details of your ritual by picking up pieces, blending, or embellishing elements from your "Going Wide" practice notes or any other ideas that have come to you since then. Then take yourself from the beginning of the ritual through to the end, similar to telling a story, and make sure that the sequence makes sense. Remember, you want to create a sequential flow of activities that will take you (and others, if it is a group ritual) on a transformational journey, not a roller coaster ride.

Facilitating Yourself in Solitary Ritual

Since every woman facilitates her own spiritual experience at her personal altar, and there is no intermediary between herself and the Goddess, a woman can facilitate her own ritual. Facilitating yourself in solitary ritual is an excellent way to learn how to be both a participant and a facilitator. Solitary ritual can be a very powerful and intimate experience. Since responsibility for the ritual rests entirely on you, including all the preparation, enactments, and outcome, there is more flexibility and room for improvisation. The time actually spent in ritual can feel more fluid, like a moving meditation or a monologue.

You may find that more time than you had expected passes between the planning phase and actually doing your ritual. This may not necessarily be avoidance of doing the ritual but time for your unconscious mind to integrate and process the ritual purpose. Be honest, and trust yourself: you will know when the time is right.

Even in solitary ritual, pre-ritual preparation is very important. It helps to ensure your deep surrender to the ritual's purpose. You may experience an intense degree of personal intimacy once your self-consciousness is alleviated through personal energetic preparation and purification of the ritual space.

A former student of mine, Barbara, facilitated herself in a ritual she designed several months following a miscarriage. She had previously done ritual only within a group setting and was hesitant about ritualizing this loss on her own. The purpose of her ritual was to let the spirit of the child go, to honor herself as a creator, to heal the pain of the loss, and to open to life again. Creating and facilitating this ritual on her own allowed her to flow with her own intuitive timing, spending hours with herself in a space of loving compassion. She described her experience as profound.

Facilitating Transitions

"You are always moving toward or away from a moment"[63]

---

[63] Wisdom from my long time friend and sound engineer Scott Fraser who passed this quote on to me from a member of the Kronos Quartet.

Ritual can be compared to composing a piece of music. Ritual facilitation, whether you are facilitating yourself or others, is the skill of knowing how to get from one part of the ritual to another purposely and smoothly. The individual parts of the ritual must have a thread that connects one action or activity to the next that makes both thematic and energetic sense. Who and how will you guide the ritual experience along, providing verbal or nonverbal signals or instructions, or simply keep the ritual on track if focus wanes or disruptions arise? Transitions can be facilitated by one woman or several. What matters is that whomever is facilitating knows what they are responsible for, and how they will work with the energy and focus of the ritual's intention with any logistics that apply (such as moving a bowl of water from an altar to carrying it around to the participants).

As you move the creative process into an appropriate structure for your ritual experience and create an outline with the sequence of your ritual's enactments, pay extra attention to how and who will take responsibility for getting you from one part of the ritual to another. Ritual facilitation skills are explored further in this book; however, in designing your ritual flow, mark transitions from one part to another with red flags that must be returned to and resolved before the ritual is enacted.

In the last pass of the ritual flow, work out the logistic and facilitation details along the way. Having to yank back and forth between the open mind necessary for creativity and the narrow mindset of logistical details (as necessary as they are), and who is going to facilitate what part of the ritual, is tiring and derails the ritual-making process. First, create; *then* figure out what and how to physically implement what you need and who will take responsibility to facilitate parts of the ritual.

The Importance of Conscious Choice

Becoming aware of why you choose to do a particular enactment takes practice and vigilance. If you don't understand the motivation or meaning for your enactment, then the ritual becomes meaningless. This is not to say that you need to fully comprehend the Mysteries intellectually, but make an effort to have an understanding, or at least an intuitive sense, of why you are doing what you're doing. Don't include a ritual enactment because you think you are supposed to or because you read about how to do it in a book. If you do not understand the purpose for your actions, how can you expect to have the needed personal connection with your ritual and create the transformation you want? Connecting personally with the purpose and theme is essential for the ritual to have its desired effect.

Practice

Pick one of your personal ritual purposes and take it into the "Going Wide" Sensory Practice. Which category(s) of ritual best describes your ritual's theme(s)? Develop the core work of your ritual and flesh out the ambient details with information from the "Going Wide" practice or new insights that you are now aware of.

chapter 5

THE RITUAL ALTAR

The ritual altar is created to visually focus your consciousness on the ritual purpose. It is the visual representation of the ritual work. The items on the altar symbolize your intention, so you must consider how the building of the altar can best represent the purpose or nature of the ritual. Carefully consider the compatibility of every component, from the color of the altar cloth and the objects to be placed on it to the ritual tools.

Whether the ritual is solitary or group, altars built from an earth-based Wiccan or goddess perspective usually contain symbols representing the four elements of air, fire, water, and earth, a symbol representing Spirit, and an image of the Goddess.

In the West, the idea that the universe is comprised of distinct types of energy originated with the Greek philosopher Empedocles (fifth century bce). According to Aristotle, Empedocles made no distinction between thought and perception, and his theory of the elements refers not to the material, chemical composition of matter, but to the way in which people can think about existence, the ways in which things are experienced. The elements explain not objective reality, but subjective reality. In this sense, the four elements are the four fundamental ways in which something, anything, can be experienced.[64]

A microcosm of both the physical and subjective universe is thus represented on the altar, providing a way for us to deepen our understanding of reality and interact with the universe. (We will discuss the elements in greater detail later in this chapter.)

---

[64] Anderson, "The Essence of Earth." He includes a footnote reference to Robert Hand's *Horoscope Symbols* (Gloucester, MA: Para Research, 1981), 184.

A cauldron placed in the center represents Spirit, the force that animates all creation and weaves it into this web called life. It is an ancient symbol of the Goddess's womb, with its powers of creation and dissolution. All these forces represented on the altar make a metaphoric statement that the powers of the physical universe are present, and that all of nature is sacred and filled with the spirit of the Goddess.

Essential to a Dianic altar is the presence of specifically designated female images or imagery representing the Goddess. Having female-specific imagery to represent the Divine on an altar is heretical in patriarchal religions. Therefore, placing Her image on an altar is an act both personal and political. In a world where almost anything else can symbolically represent the Divine Creator *except* woman, placing a female image on the altar challenges everything we have been taught. For many women, placing and seeing a physical representation of a woman in a location designated for worship is a simple but important first step in recognizing themselves as created in Her image.

The Personal Altar

In addition to symbols of the elements and the Goddess, your altar for solitary ritual might hold many personal symbols that reflect who you are. Your personal altar will change as you change. Use it as a mirror for the inner processes of your psyche, representing any aspect of yourself that you wish to focus on. You can represent aspects of yourself that you love, as well as those aspects of yourself that you are working on healing, changing, or accepting. When you externalize yourself symbolically, you gain greater clarity of your true nature and have a more tangible sense of where you are in your life.

Trust your intuition as to what needs to be on your personal altar. Your altar might include photographs, drawings, a painting or sculpture. It could include other personal objects found, created, and gifted. You might provide a small feast for your own enjoyment or as an offering to

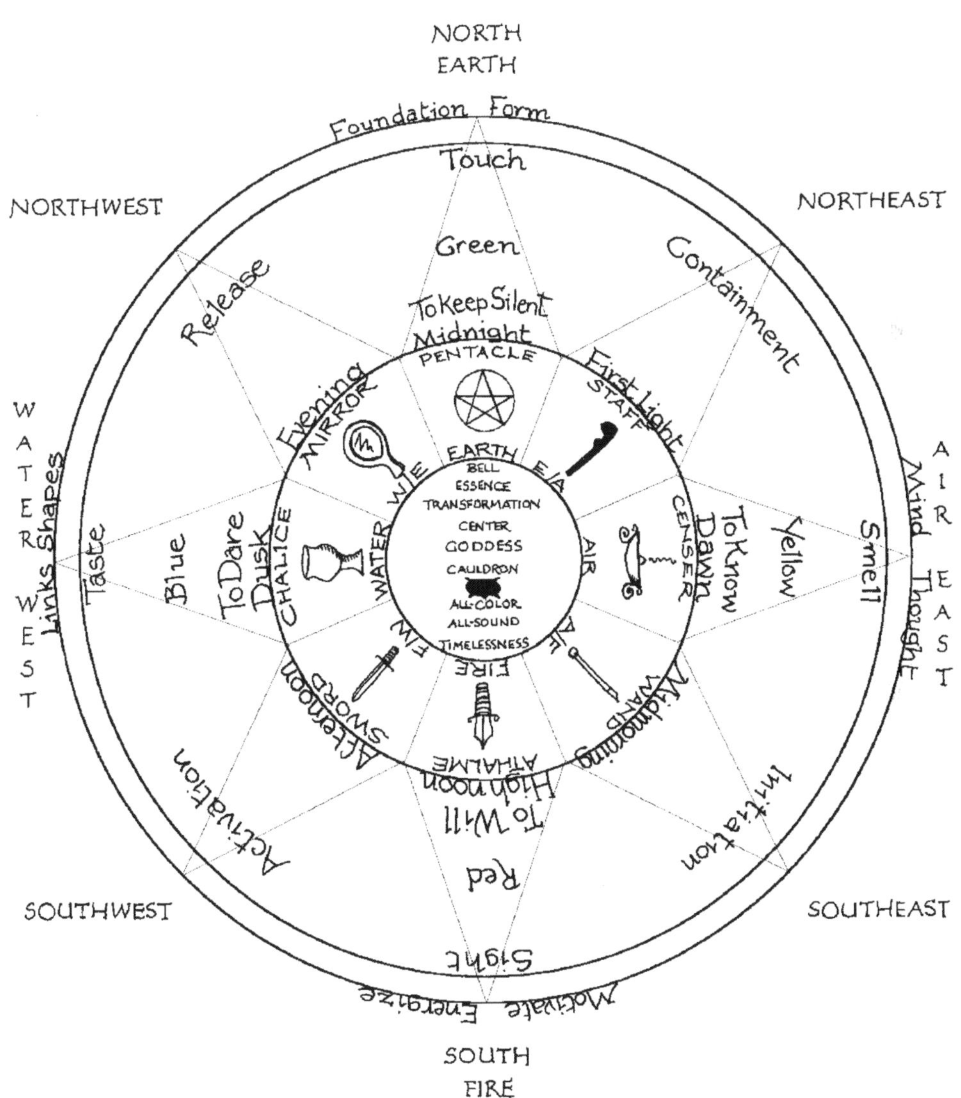

The Elemental Wheel

those in the realm of Spirit. Whatever you choose to include, an altar should be a multisensory expression of your own inner process. You might not immediately understand why you feel you must have a particular item present, but eventually, you will become conscious of its importance. As you heal, change, and transform, the symbols on your altar can be changed, transformed, or removed to reflect you as you change.

Some women change their altar every six weeks to correspond with the wheel of the year. In the goddess calendar, every six weeks there is a holiday based on the solstices, equinoxes, and cross-quarter days. You can reflect the changing of the seasons by using a different altar cloth and including different seasonal symbols. This is a wonderful way to transition into a deeper understanding of the turning of the wheel of the year.

You may also wish to include a photograph or items that link you to your ancestors, your foremothers. This act reminds us continually that our ancestors are always with us in spirit and live in us through our spiraling DNA.

Some women choose to have a single personal altar, while others create many altars with different focuses. Some altars are created outdoors and others inside the home. You might choose to have an altar for a specific goddess you are honoring. Another altar might be shared with your partner or family. Yet another altar might be for honoring your ancestors.

Choose a location for your personal altar that will be undisturbed by others. Remember that this altar is your space alone; all women should have one place in the world that is solely theirs. Although you may choose to share other altars in your home, these other altars can never take the place of your personal one.

Every woman is a priestess at her own altar, the place where she is her own highest authority. At your personal altar, you are the facilitator of your own personal spiritual experience with the Goddess. No one is going to walk in and tell you that you are "not doing it right." There is no intermediary between Her and you. You have a direct line to your own experience of the Goddess that is subjectively real and unique. This knowledge can be very empowering for some women who have seen only (usually male) priests acting as an intermediary between divinity and humankind.

The Group Altar

The obvious difference between a personal and a group altar is that a group altar is shared with others. The amount of personal items may need to be limited depending on the size of the altar and the number of women expected at the ritual. The selection of items and the creation of the altar should be as carefully discussed as the other aspects of the ritual so that the visual effect is harmonious and cohesive. If several items are brought by each woman, it may be a good idea to spread them out and mix them together in order to balance the personal energies of the objects and create a pleasing aesthetic. Of course, the elemental symbols are always included.

Some items might be placed on the altar in advance of participants arriving, or the altar might be put together by the entire group as they convene. How the altar is to be put together may be decided by the group when the ritual is planned. Does the group want the altar already prepared as women arrive? Do you want to build the altar together as a pre-ritual, preparatory activity? Do you want to make the altar building an enactment, a part of the core ritual activity? If so, have you given women an invitation to bring certain items for the altar in advance? How will you assist women in putting the altar together?

A candleholder that can hold three candles at once is often found on the altar for seasonal group rituals in the Dianic tradition, as well as on many personal Dianic altars. These candles represent the Goddess in her triple aspect of Maiden, Mother, and Crone (see appendix A). In my local community's rituals, one of these candles is always lit and dedicated to personal transformation, another for community growth and change, and the third for a global concern.

In addition to the ritual candles discussed below, I advise keeping an additional "working" candle on your altar. This is a candle that does not carry someone's personal intention in its wick. This candle can be removed from your altar to purify the ritual space (see chapter 7), and then returned. It can also be used to light other candles without having to constantly strike matches. In group rituals, a working candle allows participants to light their personal candles easily and discourages them from lighting their candle off of someone else's already-lit spell candle. You don't want to unintentionally mix someone else's spell into your own spellwork.

Setting Up Your Altar

Understanding Correspondences, Elements, Elemental Energy, and Ritual Tools

The practice of magic is primarily based on your relationship with, and understanding of, the elements. Having a working understanding of the elements is an essential component of ritual making and spellcraft. As you grow in your awareness of the natural forces of the earth, your relationship with the elements, as energies both within yourself and without, will deepen, giving you greater access to wisdom and connection with the other beings around you. Exploring the psychological and physical attributes of the elements will inform your choice of which elemental symbols and energetic correspondences are more appropriate than others to incorporate in a given ritual.

When we discuss the elements, we are not just describing states of matter but types of essential energy. Since these energies are distinct in character and attributes, they offer a consistent and verifiable link with which the subjective aspects of a ritual may be utilized to their utmost. The elements can also be described in a cause-and-effect relationship. To use a physics term, there are specific, measurable vibratory levels associated with each of the elements, yet they are also interdependent and interactive. This relationship offers a consistent frame of reference for any magical or ritual working.

For example, fire has the highest, fastest vibratory rate of all four physical elements and may be used magically for fast change. The second highest and fastest vibratory element is air, followed by water and then earth. Each of the elements also corresponds to one of our human senses of smell, touch, taste, sight, and hearing.

The ritual tools—the wand, the athame, the chalice, the pentacle, and the cauldron— correspond to the various elements, and all are extensions of our human senses and of our psyches. These tools assist us to a particular end. These tools stimulate the conscious mind and assist us in transitioning into the intuitive realm of the deep mind. Using a ritual tool is performing an act of sympathetic magic where the kinesthetic motion and the visual image create the energetic reality. Although you may not wish to utilize all of the traditional Wiccan magical tools in your rituals, it is important to understand what they are and how they can be used. Only these five most common tools will be discussed here.

Most Wiccan traditions are based on a male/female duality and ascribe a specific sex to each element and its corresponding tool. In these traditions, air and fire are the "male" elements, and thus the ritual tools associated with them are considered to be energetically "male". Water and earth and their ritual tools are sexed as female, and associated with "female" energy. Remember that Dianic tradition's cosmology and practices are not based on a gendered male/female duality; therefore, Dianic correspondences are based on aspects of the Goddess and the energetic function of the tool.

Please note that the placement of the elements in association with specific directions do vary among traditions, particularly those that identify as pre-Gardnerian and Stregheria (Italian Witchcraft). However, since the basic nature of the elements do not change (i.e., fire is warm and dry, water is cool and moist), the physical elements can inspire our subjective/magical reality by providing a consistent frame of reference that can be universally understood and worked with across varying magical traditions. Some practitioners of contemporary goddess spirituality reject any pre-existing system of placement of the elements and tools, preferring instead to create their own associations and placements. While this may be subjectively satisfying, it is magically unsound in that attempts to influence the larger social or community sphere require the use of more universally understood associations in order to have the greatest effect. This could be compared to creating an entire language that is spoken by only one person or a small group. When that person or group attempts to communicate with others, they can't be understood. Placements of the elements and their tools have been in use successfully (for hundreds of years in some cases) because they work.

Practice

Consider how you might utilize the elements of earth, water, fire, and air physically or symbolically in your ritual. In the lists of ritual enactment ideas given in the previous chapter, consider which elemental energy is being utilized. For example, lighting a candle activates the fire element; floating a written note in a stream activates water. You might also consider the seasonal and elemental focus of the ritual theme when choosing your core enactments: for example, Summer Solstice is associated with the passionate and willful element of fire. Winter Solstice is associated with the element of resting earth, Fall Equinox with the dissolving power of water, and Spring Equinox with the renewing power of air.

Practice

This practice will help you to notice the relationships between the elements and their energy; how they affect and are affected by each other; and how they are interrelated and interdependent. You may find it helpful to use pencil and paper to draw a circle. Divide it into four quarters. Draw a second, smaller circle at the center for Spirit. As this chapter's discussion proceeds, note your observations on your drawing.

While making a diagram like this can help you to organize your knowledge of the elements, it is important to also understand that in the very act of drawing lines, you may inadvertently reinforce a perception of fixed divisions between the elemental forces. The most conscious part of the human brain first compartmentalizes, focusing on separate aspects, before widening to include the perception of the whole system. This idea would be misleading and inaccurate, since we are working to understand how the forces are interconnected and not truly separate from one another For example, fire needs air to interact with and fuel (earth or air) in order to burn. You may also see similar correspondences in more than one place on your elemental wheel. Use the diagram as a tool to comprehend the whole, but do not let it become an inflexible ruler. The accompanying elemental wheel illustration in this chapter will help to convey the elements, with their corresponding tools and other associations, as a holistic, interrelated system.

In beginning to understand the nature of the four elements, know that you already possess much of this knowledge within you. In fact the reason you, and everything else around you exists is that these powers have united and been enlivened. When this happens, life happens

These correspondences should make common sense based on simple exploration of the world around you and your own life experiences of interacting with, and being affected by, the elements. Think and listen with your mind, open and feel with your body and emotions, as the elements with their specific energy and corresponding ritual tools are discussed. In Chapter 8 we will continue to develop these ideas for building an "elemental inventory" with its applications for invocation, ritual and spellwork.

Air/East

On your altar, at each cardinal point, set a votive candle to mark the symbolic home of each elemental power. Place a white votive candle in a yellow holder in the east to mark the direction of air. Yellow is the color for the element of air, the color of the new sun as it rises in the eastern sky at dawn, beginning a new day. East represents new beginnings, a new cycle. Both the sun and moon rise in the east. Casting the ritual circle begins in the northeast as the place of initiation.

Air is the element associated with the mind, intelligence, flashes of insight, clarity, awakening, mental creativity, freedom of thought, communication, inspiration, ideas, wit, humor, and the knowing that comes from connections made through the mental processes. It is the element of the spoken word, word magic (words being "shaped breath"), of music and sounding.

The power of air is the power to know. There are, of course, many types of knowing that are learned through exploring the other elements. Knowledge can come from many sources, including study, our life experiences, new perspectives, and inner revelations. As the seasons begin their transition, go outside and take in a slow deep breath. The "winds of change" carry news over great geographic distances. What do you notice when you breathe in the seasonal messages carried on the winds? What information do you know now, that you didn't know before?

An image for the air element and its correlation to the mind is that of a light bulb turning on in the brain, with an accompanying "Ah-ha!" Expressions such as "it suddenly dawned on me," "airhead," and "a new day dawning" reflect air's associations with the mind and beginning anew. Balanced aspects of air include diligence, inventiveness, and optimism. Un-centered expressions of air include cunning, misleading speech, destructive gossip, mental cruelty, and psychological instability. Intelligence and the ability to use words effectively can inspire and teach; however, when out of balance or motivated by ill intent, these same traits can be cruel.

The time of day most associated with the air element is daybreak. Dawn arises with the sense of a new slate, a new beginning. The eagle soars into the blue-white and pale yellow air of morning, seeing with clarity over wide distances. She sees an endless landscape of possibilities.

The season associated primarily with air is spring, the season of the earth's renewal, the seasonal cycle of visibly emerging life. We breathe in and exhale air every moment of our lives, and thus we are "inspired."

The physical form of air is represented by the censer, the container used to hold burning incense. When lit and used in ritual, incense has the power to stimulate, manipulate, and awaken the deep mind through our sense of smell. Our sense of smell is one of the most powerfully primal senses that we humans possess. It is a part of our natural intelligence and gives us access to memories, enhances pleasure, and supports our survival by warning us of rotten food or dangerous people. We can consciously manipulate our own minds and other's behaviors through the choice of scents that we place on our bodies and/or in our environments. In the motion of the rising smoke, we can see the air element and observe that its initial direction of flow is expansive, upward and outward, toward the future.

The primary magical tool of air is the wand. In many contemporary books on goddess Craft that draw heavily from Gerald Gardner's work, as well as in the tarot, the wooden wand has traditionally been associated with the south, the fire element, and the male principal. However ceremonial magicians commonly use the wand as a tool of air to draw runes and other sacred symbols in the air, or to summon spirits. Both ceremonial magicians and some Wiccan traditions use the wand to cast spells. In Wiccan books written by Alexandrian witches Janet and Stewart Farrar, and in Raven Grimassi's books about Italian Witchcraft, the wand is placed in the east as a tool of air, placing the athame, or ritual knife, to the south, as a tool of fire. Dianic witches are divided over placement of the athame and wand. Try both and experience what associations work more effectively for you. If you are working with a group, you will need to come to agreement on where you will place the wand and athame.

Sadly, many Dianics rarely use the wand because of its male sex-based association from other Wiccan traditions. It is far more common to see a feather being used as a tool of air, where the witch, after inviting the air element into the ritual circle, literally moves air with the motion of the feather. Isn't it time we reclaimed access to all the tools of the magical arts? Isn't it odd that we apply our feminist analysis to some issues (magical, environmental, social, global, etc.) and ignore, deny, or flat-out run from others? Branches are like hollow straws. Thus, the wand as a magical tool can be used in spellwork effectively to both draw and send energy, just as a tree branch, when attached to its trunk, draws nutrients from both the earth below and the sun above.

When I was a novice witch, I was taught that the wand's connection to the energy of fire is that "fire is latent in wood." In other words, the wood has the capacity to be fuel (as can many other things), and that sap in the wood is likened to blood, associated with the passion, temper, or the fire aspect within blood. However, I have always believed that the connection of the wand to air poses a stronger case for relationship. Wands come from tree branches that reach to and wave in the air. In fact, trees actually create oxygen through the process of photosynthesis. A simple way to observe and know about the conditions and movement of air is by observing trees and other vegetation. A storm-tossed tree gives us both a practical demonstration of the power of air and the wisdom of flexibility in a stressful situation. The song of the wind through branches, even when a tree is bare of leaves in the winter, brings the voices of our ancestors, still carried upon the wind, alive once more. Many traditional wind instruments are made of wood or reeds.

Specific trees are associated with magical attributes and used for various purposes, including wand making. Hazel, oak, alder, rowan, willow, or fruit tree wands all have different magical properties and significance, according to various magical schools and European folklore sources. It is important that the wand be straight, rather than curved, since the energy must be able to move unencumbered directly down through the wand. (The same can be said for the athame, the ritual knife.) The traditional measure of a wand is the distance from the inside crook of your elbow to the end of your middle finger on your dominant hand. Learn to use a wand before you progress to a staff.

The staff is a larger tool of the air element. Whereas the wand is a single branch, the staff represents the rooted trunk of the World Tree that connects the upper and lower worlds. The World Tree, Yggdrasil, is familiar to students of Norse mythology and is usually said to be an ash, sometimes a yew. In a Dianic context, the World Tree represents the Goddess in Her form as the Tree of Life, creator of all life and all realms. Therefore, the magical staff should be crafted from the trunk of a tree and not the branch, as the energetic properties of the different parts of the tree are quite different. Always harvest a wand or staff from a willing, live tree.

For many women, this may prove to be difficult. Urban women often do not have access to forests, and of course, it is inappropriate and illegal to cut down trees on public lands like city and state parks. Try to make contact with a rural landowner. Look for someone who may have a wooded lot that needs to be thinned. Saplings and young trees make excellent staffs. They are full of the life force and primed for growth. This is a great way to appropriately harvest a young tree whose spirit is willing to serve the Goddess as a magical staff.

Fire/South

On the southern compass point of your altar, set a white votive candle in a red holder. Red is the color of fire, of blood, and represents passionate energy and directed will. Fire is the force that energizes, activates, and motivates us to action. Fire expresses the full range of passionate emotions such as ecstatic joy, rage, sexual arousal, grief, and impassioned love. When we feel passionate, we physically get hot!

Fire is the force that illuminates; therefore, it is the human sense of sight that correlates to the element of fire. We see by the light of the sun and stars and by the sun's reflected light from the moon. It is light, or lack of it, which has the greatest effect on our emotions. People in northern climates frequently suffer from Seasonal Affective Disorder due to the lack of sunlight in winter. It is the reflected light of the sun during the full moon that causes women to ovulate and be fertile. Light is the metaphor for internal revelation and truth. We can sense physical and emotional health in a person through the light in their eyes and the glow of their skin.

The quality in humans most associated with fire is the power to will. What is the will? It is through inner illumination that we are aware of the reality of the will, which otherwise cannot be measured or proven. The simplest and most frequent way in which we discover our will is through determined action and struggle. "To will" is not the same as to want. When we make a physical or mental effort, or when we are actively wrestling with some obstacle or coping with opposing forces, we feel a specific power rising up within us. This inner energy gives us the experience of "willing."[65] Some people call this quality "gumption" or "strength of character." Magical will works in accord with precision of intention, allowing the witch who has married her will to her purpose to form and send energy toward a specific goal.

Summer Solstice is the holiday that corresponds to the height of the sun's power, as does high noon of each day. The sun is at its highest point during midday, therefore noon is the time of day associated most with the power of fire. Similarly, Summer Solstice is the time of year where the sun is at its peak in the cycle of the year.

Fire is a powerful energy, and like all the other elements, it can be in or out of balance within the self. Fire rises as it burns toward the future. Our language has many expressions that describe the passionate aspects of fire: "don't add fuel to the fire," "light a fire under it," "warm heart," and "I'm on fire for you, baby." Someone with a temper is called a "hot head," has "heated discussions," or is described as having a "short fuse." Loyalty, courage, the will to live, to fight for what you believe is right, or

---

[65] Assagioli, *The Act of Will*, 9.

to burn with passion in creating art or love are some of the life-affirming aspects of fire. Fire can rage with the intensity of a wild fire or comfort with the steady, radiating heat of a bed of coals. Fire is an energizer. Its energy prepares you for movement, and its power is the motion of action. When out of balance, fire can be a destructive force that consumes the self and others. Uncontrolled rage, cowardice, disloyalty, and the quality of thrill-seekers who blindly risk their lives and endanger others are unbalanced aspects of fire within the self.

Like all magical skills, the focused and directed will can be a tool for good or ill. The danger of untempered will is that it lacks heart and can become cruel and sometimes fatally dangerous. As Roberto Assagioli notes,

> One of the principal causes of today's disorders is the lack of love on the part of those who have will and the lack of will in those who are good and loving. This points unmistakably to the urgent need for the integration, the unification of love and will.[66]

Feminist Wiccan spiritual values affirm the need to redefine power and how it has been used over the past 5,000 years under patriarchy. In feminist ritual, we affirm our will to be free from internalized and externalized oppression. The Wiccan Rede states, "An' it harm none, do as thou wilt." The Rede is the accepted "golden rule," advising ethical conduct, governing and guiding magical workings of all kinds. The Rede further states, "Do what thou wilt shall be the whole of the law. Love is the law, Love under Will,"[67] affirming love and its power of interconnectedness, empathy, and compassion as the foundation from which the will should exercise its power. Our will must find ways to serve

---

[66] Ibid., 91.

[67] Adapted by Aleister Crowley in the 1890s. Quoted by Gerald Gardner in *Witchcraft Today*, 1954. Earliest references from the 1600s Rabelais's *Garzgantua and Pantragruel* (researched by Anna Korn).

love: our love of life, our Earth, our home, and our loved ones.

In the Dianic tradition as I teach it, the athame[68] is the ritual tool associated with the fire element and the power of transformation. Traditionally, the athame is a double-edged, black-handled ritual knife made of metal; however, athames may also be made of wood or stone. As a metal tool that conducts electricity, the athame is generally used to cast the ritual circle, temporarily separating the ritual working space from the non-ritual space. It is not necessary that the athame be sharp, since the athame is rarely used to pierce or cut anything physical and is only used energetically through motion and projection.

In its larger version, the athame becomes the double-edged ritual sword that is primarily used to cast the circle for very large gatherings or community festival rituals.[69] The athame blade (or sword) mirrors the shape of a flame. Its use can be likened to a welder's torch, which is used to apply heat to melt and shape, to cut, or to bind two edges together. The symbolism of the double edge is found in the saying "To bless, to curse, and to pierce between the worlds." Just as the waning and waxing moon of the labrys (the Cretan double-edged ax) encompasses the polar aspects of a cycle, magic also cuts both ways. The power to end is also the power to begin.

There is an old saying, "A witch who cannot hex cannot heal." I would add to this, "A witch who cannot charge her blade can neither cut nor seal" (see the consecration ritual for magical tools later in this chapter). There is huge responsibility undertaken with the practice of magic. The energy of magic is neutral. It is the will of the practitioner and her ethics that determine how that energy is directed, and to what end. Ethical use of the will means having the wisdom to understand and clearly discern when to create and when to destroy in order to create something new. Both aspects, creation and destruction, are parts of the eternal cycle of death and life, life and death.

---

[68] Also spelled "athalme" and pronounced "a-tham-ay".

[69] Some groups use the sword to cast the circle only from First Harvest through Winter Solstice, signifying the reaping and resting cycle of the year.

The athame is also used to "charge," to imbue or direct energy into an object for a specific purpose. To do this, you send energy down the blade as you touch an object to infuse it with the energy and qualities you desire. To "pierce between the worlds" has to do with the conscious directing of energy down through the tip of the blade to create doorways between the cast circle and other realms, as in the act of invocation.

When choosing a ritual knife for your athame, be certain that it has never been touched by blood. Do not use or purchase it if you are not sure. Should you wish to consecrate it with blood for your own use, use your own menstrual blood, freely given, and never blood from a poke in the finger. Be aware that if you do this, the blade will be bonded to you and can't be given to or used by another. If you are no longer bleeding, use your vaginal fluids or saliva. Because a ritual sword is often a tool used by a group, it is unwise to consecrate a ritual sword with personal fluids as you might with a personal tool.

Use the athame to energetically separate truth from lies or illusion by gesturing with the knife, cutting away from you. Use it to set limits or let go of an attitude or belief, energetically severing your connection from unhealthy behaviors that have outlived their time. Energetically cutting these things away from yourself in a ritual can powerfully affect your deep mind when your will is in alignment with the tool.

Water/West

West is the realm of water. Mark its compass point on the altar with a white votive candle in a blue holder. Water, as an element, is a linking, carrying, and shaping force. It represents creativity, adaptability, and primal intuition. Water is most often associated with human emotions that allow us to "flow into" or "merge" with another when loving, or "fill" with compassion and empathy. Without a boundary or container, water flows and meanders, following and changing the shape of the surface it travels on. In its liquid form, water's natural horizontal or downward direction of flow (depending on the container or lack of one) inspires introspection and reflection on the past. Our bodies are like full sponges; just like our Mother Earth, we are comprised of 98 percent water and only enough matter to form a fragile container. Water is the basic ingredient in blood, saliva, and cellular fluid. Women's bodies are like springs. We bleed monthly from no wound. We pour forth milk from our breasts, and honey from our yonis when making love.

When we invoke water, we invoke the Great Shape Maker; our ability as women to create. Its power is the power to dare, to have the courage to dive into the depths of our consciousness, to love and connect deeply, to create, release, transform, adapt, to shape and be shaped. Water has the power to dissolve and regenerate matter, symbolically or quite literally.

The formative power of water is to shape, dissolve, transform, move, or carry earth. Its rate of flow is what determines its power to shape and move earth. Water sustains and renews life through the nutrients it brings to the land and to our cells. As a baby forms in the womb, water shapes a woman's body and brings nutrients from the mother's cells to the space that her body has created for the formation of a new shape, a new being. Water, more than any other element, has the ability to transmute and travel through the realms of earth, air, and fire. It can become liquid, solid, or gas. Water is the habitat of our origin, the primal womb of the Goddess, where we grow and quicken in the dark primordial sea of our own mother's womb.

The nature of water as a connecting force is present in expressions such as "stream of consciousness," "going with the flow," getting "swept away," "filling up," "spilling over," and "diving in." When out of balance, we describe ourselves as "drowning," or when gullible, we appear to "swallow everything."

Autumn is the time of year associated with water. It is the time of drawing inward in preparation for winter. In autumn, hardwood trees go dormant and sap recedes into the root system. Many mammals in the Northern Hemisphere go into a state of hibernation and their hearts beat at a slower rhythm. At sunset or dusk, the sea becomes calmer, and our consciousness transitions in preparation for night and dreaming. The surface of water was the original mirror, reflecting both imagery and energy. On your personal altar in the west, place a mirror. It is here that you summon the courage to create, to see yourself as a reflection of Goddess as Creatrix. Dare to witness your own unique beauty. Dare to see yourself as She sees you.

The chalice or cup is the tool associated with the water element. Just as oceans are contained by land, water is contained by the chalice. Therefore the chalice becomes the symbol of the element it contains. Like the cauldron and its symbolism of Spirit, the chalice is a symbol of the womb, container of the life-giving waters. When a woman stands in the traditional and ancient posture for invocation, arms raised and held apart, hands upturned and open, she embodies a living chalice, a potential recipient of creativity and connection. It is a receptively active posture, opening to receive the Goddess's energy, to listen to Her wisdom and guidance.

The water element corresponds to the human sense of taste. When we drink from the chalice, we taste the blessings of life, taking in the Goddess's love. A libation, which is similar to a toast, is a prayer of thanksgiving. As the libation is spoken, the woman raises the chalice to the Goddess. She pours a little of the liquid as an offering of thanks onto the earth or altar and then drinks from the chalice. In some group rituals, usually in smaller groups, the chalice is passed deosil[70] around the circle for others to offer a libation and drink.

In magical and ritual work, the contents of the chalice as a tool of water can be used as a carrier for what you would like to, quite literally, take into yourself and make a part of you internally. For example, you might use the chalice ritually by sitting at your altar, having filled the chalice with any liquid you especially enjoy, and "charge" the liquid with self-love. To charge the contents is to imbue the liquid with that chosen intent

---

[70] Pronounced "dyash-al" in Irish and Scottish Gaelic.

and energy. When you drink it in, you're making self-love a part of you on both an energetic and cellular level.

If you wish to purify the ritual space, place a bowl of water on your altar somewhere in the west. This bowl of consecrated (blessed) or charged water can be removed for use and returned to the altar as needed. Salt water or water from a sacred well can be especially useful for purification.

Earth/North

The element of earth represents the matter of the body of Gaia, the tissue of the womb of the Great Mother Herself. Place a white votive in a green holder at the northern compass point on your altar to represent the vegetation that grows from the earth. The earth element also represents the solid matter of the human body and all the other sentient beings. The human sense that corresponds with earth is touch. We participate in life through the gift of our physical being.

Winter is the season associated with the earth element, as the earth rests from her time of growth. This is the time of the year when life goes inward in preparation for renewal. Winter is a time for spiritual reflection in preparation for rebirth. The power to keep silent is the gift of the earth element. In the silence of this pause, wisdom may be accessed, integrated, and internalized. To find knowledge, one must be willing to seek silence; to listen, look, and feel in greater depth. When we open ourselves to nature, we are humbled. With earth wisdom we learn balance. We learn when to speak and when to keep silent.

The power of earth is usually described as strength, stability, and endurance. This is, in part, an illusion. Earth is the element that is constantly being carried, acted upon, and transformed over geologic time by the other elements: water, air, and fire. We, as children of earth, are not stable or enduring. We are in a constant state of transformation from the moment of our conception to the drawing of our last breath and beyond. However, earth is the densest of the elements and thus represents the foundation of our personal character. Earth represents the positive traits of determination, perseverance, patience, reliability, prudence, and generosity.[71] We ascribe earth's enduring attributes to human characteristics when we describe someone is as "solid as a rock," "earthy," "the salt of the earth" or "dense." Interestingly enough, if you examine a common rock under magnification, it is porous. For magical purposes, the earth and all physical matter is porous. Otherwise, you would not be able to imbue objects with energy, as they would be incapable of containing or absorbing anything. When out of balance, a person with too much earth energy can become too rigid, becoming stagnant without the ability to be flexible. She may be driven to acquire material possessions to excess, beyond what she needs to live comfortably, or deny herself the pleasures of life to her detriment.

Midnight is the time of day for earth, a silence and pause before the new day begins. The north is sometimes called "the place of mystery." The sun never reaches the north and it is always out of darkness that life and new possibilities are born, where Spirit manifests into form.

Earth's barely discernable direction of flow exists in the eternal present, in slow yet constant change. Oftentimes the term "grounding" is associated with the earth element and is presented as a way to begin a ritual or magical working. Unfortunately, many people do this practice incorrectly and depress their own energy into the earth instead of reaching for the center of the earth to connect with her. The practice of "centering" is an alternative approach. Becoming centered means obtaining a state of conscious openness and balance in present time. Being centered is to be fully present and gives a woman access to the infinite resources of her deep mind. (See chapter 6 for centering practice.)

The pentacle, a five-pointed star pointing upwards and set within a circle, is the traditional altar symbol representing the direction of north, the earth element, and protection. It corresponds to the shape of the human body. The pentacle is drawn in a continuous line that symbolizes

---

71 Anderson, "The Essence of Earth," 9.

and affirms the interconnectedness of life. Just as the earth contains all four elements and is infused with Spirit, four points of the pentacle represent the elemental forces of air, fire, water, and earth. The fifth point represents Spirit, the Goddess's power that animates, weaves and binds the elemental forces together in balance, harmony, and order.

The origins of the pentacle are ancient and found worldwide, appearing as early as 525 bce on a signet ring worn by a Pythagorean sect in southern Italy.[72] Although an ancient concept in the East and West, the pentagram (the five-pointed star without the circle) did not appear in northern Europe until the latter half of the Middle Ages.

The pentagram becomes a pentacle when it is enclosed within a circle and inscribed on a disc or stone. The pentacle represents "the great round," the planet Earth herself, the great cauldron-womb of the Goddess that contains all the elements symbolic of the wholeness and oneness of life. The pentacle is a non-gendered-specific representation of All That Is. While it is debated whether the pentacle is specifically an ancient goddess symbol, we can ascribe a new meaning to it by reinterpreting it in a purely goddess context, where the circle is the Goddess's womb and all possibilities are contained within it.

Place a pentacle on your altar to represent the interconnected and interdependent body of the Earth Mother. Fresh flowers, rocks, bones, or dried herbs, as seasonally appropriate, can also be used to represent the Earth. Another traditional symbol for the Earth is salt. Salt is used primarily for purification purposes and can be placed in a dish on your altar in the north. It can be sprinkled along the perimeter of the ritual space or mixed with water to purify ritual tools or other sacred items. Salt can also be used to charge water and is the basic ingredient added to water to make it "holy water."

The pentacle as a tool of earth is used in spellwork for both manifestation and composting, just as earth nurtures life and decomposes life into

---

[72] Grimassi, *Encyclopedia of Wicca & Witchcraft*, 285.

compost to feed something new. The pentacle can be used in conjunction with the moon cycles of waxing and waning. Place a representation of what you wish to bring into form (manifestation) on the pentacle during the new to full moon cycle. Place a representation of what you wish to release/transform (compost) on the pentacle during the waning moon phase to dark moon.

Goddess/Spirit/Center Point

The center, Spirit, or goddess point on your altar is marked with a white votive candle in a clear holder to represent all colors. The Goddess is the life force. She is the power in the universe that moves through all the physical and nonphysical forms that we can feel, see, hear, and know. She is all that is, was, and ever will be. She is form and spirit combined.

Understanding Her is a challenge that is never fully realized. She cannot be confined to words or images. She is timelessness, outside of time. Her season is all seasons, as the Wheel of Life is constantly in motion. Her power is the power to change. Her nature is to transform, transmute, and shapeshift endlessly.

Desirable human qualities that are attained through being centered and balanced in your relationship with Spirit include enlightenment, wisdom, transcendence, and inner peace. Through Her, we may experience our connection to the rest of the universe. When out of balance, our sense of connection to Her is disrupted. We become depressed and isolated from our inner and outer worlds. Dealing with everyday matters of survival and mundane responsibilities can become overwhelming.

The primary symbol for the Goddess is the cauldron. It represents Her womb, the original Holy Grail from which all things emerge and to which all things return. The cauldron takes back form, decomposes it, dissolves it, and then transmutes it into something else. It is the primal chaos of creation from which all seen and unseen forms emerge. Having a cauldron at the center of your altar keeps you mindful that there is one law and that law is that all things must change.

The human sense related to Spirit is hearing. Another ritual tool commonly used to represent the Spirit point is a bell. Sound vibrations can alter consciousness, taking some of us into a state of trance. Through sound and vibration our minds can travel beyond the limitations of everyday consciousness to experience the oneness of the entire web of creation. In Wiccan tradition, this state of perception is often called "between the worlds." Listen to the sound of Tibetan bells, the enchanting strings of the harp, or the calming song of crickets on a warm summer evening, and experience the transforming power of sound vibration.

Consecration of Ritual Tools

When you consecrate your ritual tools, you formally dedicate and bless them for use in magical or ritual work. Consecrate anything that you are using to direct energy with. Remember, for any magical or ritual act, the more conscious you are of the purpose and meaning of everything that is used, the deeper and more effective the work will be. A dish of salt representing the earth element will have greater impact on the deep mind if it is ritually prepared rather than carelessly dumped out of a carton or shaker and plopped on the altar. Consecration of ritual tools such as the wand, chalice, or athame is best done in advance of any ritual preparation, and in most cases once done, it does not need to be repeated before every ritual. However, a new tool or elemental symbol ought to be purified first to neutralize it from its previous handlers before consecrating it to ritual use. If you personally made your tool from natural materials, then a purification is unnecessary prior to consecration.

Although the chalice need only be consecrated once, the liquid in the chalice must be consecrated prior to every ritual. To charge the contents of your chalice, sit with it and deepen your intention. Draw up energy from the earth; feel it coming up through the earth, into your body and up your spine. Release some out of the top of your head, and run the rest down your arms and into your hands. At the same time, draw energy down from the stars through the top of your head, down your spine and legs. Send some out of your feet, and run the rest down your arms and into your hands. Move the energy through the chalice. See/feel the chalice glowing with life force. Say aloud some words of blessing. A simple example would be, "I bless and consecrate thee, Creature of water. Let all ill be cast out and all good enter in. I bless you to aid me in the name of the Goddess."

Following is a more elaborate Dianic consecration ritual.

Consecration Ritual

For any new ritual tool, set up your altar with the physical elements represented above, and a cauldron at the center. The example below is a consecration for an athame as a tool of fire.

Light your four elemental/directional votive candles in their holders beginning with the yellow one in the east and continuing sunwise. Deepen yourself. Light your incense and candle with a blessing to the spirits of fire, saying,

> "Blessed be thou, creature of fire."

Ring your spirit bell and say,

> "Diana, Holy Mother, bless and empower this athame that I consecrate and dedicate to you and unto the arts of magic."

Touch your new athame to the cauldron, inside it and outside. Acknowledge that everything emerges from her womb, above, below, within, and without, throughout the worlds.

Proceeding deosil, introduce your new athame to the elements by passing or touching your new tool through them. Remember that this is not a purification, but an awakening that acknowledges the interrelationship between all the elements and their magical/elemental working partnership. As you introduce your new tool to each element, feel the different energies they represent.

Since the athame is a tool of fire, begin at the south. Pass your athame through the tip of the flame of your working candle.

Proceed to the west and sprinkle or anoint your athame with spring water.

Proceed to the north and lay or sprinkle salt or earth on or over your athame.

Proceed to the east and pass your athame though the incense. Let it be caressed by the smoke and scent.

Turn to the direction of the tool—in this case, the south—and say,

> "Guardian[73] of fire, bless my athame and imbue it with your power. I vow before you, in the name of the Goddess, to always use my powers wisely, in accordance with free will and for the good of all."

Once you understand the purpose of consecration, you may wish to embellish or write your own personally meaningful words. Even if you do not yet fully understand why a symbol is on the altar, create a meaning so you can have a connection to the altar as the energy center for the ritual. Plan on following up with study. Sometimes the meaning follows the action if repeated over time. It is common for women to create their own personal associations and meanings for symbols and enactments aside from, or in addition to, the more traditional spiritual meanings.

Having an understanding of, and respect for, the roots of a traditional symbol or custom gives depth to contemporary ritual-making practices. Often there are important reasons for a ritual activity being done in a specific way. Without an awareness of the motivation for an action, a ritual can become meaningless and empty and sometimes even dangerous.

---

[73] Guardians of the elemental realms are discussed in Chapter 13, under the heading, Guardians in the Craft.

If the older roots are not clearly understood, how can contemporary practice evolve with any integrity or substance? If you consider changing aspects of traditional custom, ritual, or use of a symbol, try first to gain some understanding of where it originated. From this understanding, you can adapt, ascribe new personal meaning, or choose to stop using a symbol or custom if it is deemed not salvageable. This is the challenge for women currently evolving or inventing spiritual or ritual practices.

Practice

FOR A PERSONAL RITUAL

Meditate on the ritual occasion you have been working with. Write about or draw what your altar might look like. Include any tools or other symbols that correspond to your theme. Ask yourself why those symbols and colors are appropriate for your particular ritual. Write down the meanings for yourself.

FOR A GROUP RITUAL

Think about ways of developing the ritual theme that will reach you and the majority of women present. How can the altar reflect the theme of the ritual? If it is a seasonal ritual, think of the altar as a mirror, reflecting the nature of the season. Consider the color of the altar cloth, the objects and decorations on it, and the seasonally compatible ritual tools. Write about or draw what your altar might look like, as well as any tools or other symbols that correspond to your theme. Ask yourselves why those symbols and colors are appropriate for your particular ritual. Write down, draw, or sculpt the meanings for yourselves.

chapter 6

Energetics for Ritual

Energy follows intention. It's not just what you do, but what you are thinking, feeling, or embodying while you do it. A ritual created with clear intention is more powerful and easier to facilitate. Like setting a stage, you use the intention to create and then embody the desired mood with visual, kinesthetic, and auditory stimuli that advance the ritual's theme. In Dianic Craft, this process is called "energetics." As it applies to ritual, energetics is the intentional generating or manipulation of energy so that it aligns with, supports, and carries out the ritual's theme. Having a clear purpose for the ritual is essential to creating the appropriate energetics for it. When you embody your intention you come into resonance with the ritual's purpose and generate the ambiance that can be felt by others.

Take yourself back to those moments when you were electrified by a speaker or storyteller. Recall being swept into intense feeling by a singer, musician, or dancer. Truly gifted artists are inspired by their own work as they share it with their audiences. Artists take you with them into the intention of a piece of work, drawing you into the energetics they set. Energetics for ritual works in the same way: intention accompanied by skill is everything.

Using the metaphor of planning a journey, you have reached the third step in the ritual-making process: choosing the fuel, the energy, that will move you and others through the ritual experience. A vehicle, whether a car, bus, or plane, requires a specific type of fuel. If you put diesel fuel in a sports car, the car might not move at all—it might chug along in distress, or it might blow up. The same thing can happen with your rituals. Different rituals require specific types of energetics or they, too, might stall, chug along, or blow up, leaving participants drained, empty, and unsatisfied at the ritual's conclusion. Whether planning a solitary or a group ritual, you must consciously consider the specific quality of energy you'll need to move the ritual through to its desired destination. You must also determine the best way to generate that energy and maintain it for the ritual's duration.

You are already quite experienced with energetics, although you may not realize it. You intuitively sense specific energies around you daily. You sense energy every time you meet a new person and have an immediate feeling of comfort or discomfort. You meet a friend for lunch and know, as she crosses the room toward you, that there is something terribly wrong or wonderfully right. You enter a room and suddenly feel a desire to leave or immediate ease and familiarity.

Sensing the diverse and changing energy around and within you is an important magical skill to consciously develop. As you become more sensitive to the qualities of energy around you, you can begin practicing the conscious manipulation of energy to achieve specific goals. You already manipulate energy, for instance, every time you have housework to do and don't have the energy to face it. To alter your attitude, you may purposely select music that is lively and loud. To keep yourself focused on the intention of making the housework a ritual cleansing activity, you may choose classical or spiritually inspiring music. Intuitively, we tend to select sounds that help to raise our energy level, shifting our mental attitude and physical response into increased motivation. Later, to relax, we're likely to choose music that is calm and soothing.

Consider the following: before you attend any special event, notice what starts to happen inside you when you imagine yourself at an anticipated event. By projecting yourself into the future occasion you can feel an energetic shift inside. We sometimes call this "getting in the mood," or "setting a mood", which is another way of saying that you are actually generating and aligning with the quality of energy you anticipate needing, wanting, or falling victim to during the event. You are creating a tangible energetic form from your expectation of the end result. You are projecting yourself into the future experience and creating how you expect or desire it to be.

How do you prepare for a romantic date? What do you do to get ready? Do you think about the date a lot? Do you think about how that person is going to respond to your appearance and your energy level? What are you going to talk about? Do you think about what clothing you will wear—what colors, textures, and style? Some women will prepare themselves to upbeat music, which raises their own energy in order to meet their dates at a high energy level, while others may choose quieter, more romantic music. What do you do?

What do you do when you expect to encounter someone with whom you experience anxiety or fear? Do you stall your arrival time? Avoid their eyes or physical contact? Find a way to insulate yourself from their energetic influence? If you are conscious of the need to do some protection, do you prepare energetically to affect the way you experience that encounter?

When our expectations and energetic preparation for an event don't match the event itself, the contrast can be disturbing and may require some hasty readjustment of energy. For example, knowing in advance what a movie is about helps you to energetically prepare yourself to see it. If you expect a romantic comedy and encounter a violent psychological thriller or horror film, you're forced to shift your energy, and you may feel disappointed or resentful.

Practice

Think about what you do when preparing yourself for the following events. Take your time with each example so you can feel the energy in your body adjust as you anticipate each different occasion. Pause with each one and "notice in."

* You have been invited to a fabulous New Year's Eve party with your female friends. The theme is to come as your Goddess self.

* You have to go to your spouse's or your partner's family for Thanksgiving dinner.
* A loved one has died and you are participating in the funeral.
* Your new lover has invited you to a romantic Valentine's Day dinner.
* You are going camping in a wilderness area for the first time with a small group of friends.
* You are bringing home your new puppy or kitten.

How does each of these experiences affect your mood? How does your body react? Muscle tension? Pain? Pleasure? Smells? Tastes? If you notice any energy shifts as you feel into these experiences, it means that you are coming into resonance with the occasion.

Too often, women's rituals fall drastically short in the area of considering the importance of energetics. Many women do not even consider energetics at all. Although they may still derive value from the rituals they have created or participated in, without this essential element they have no measure of comparison from which to discern the difference. As you grow in your awareness of energetics, each ritual you create or attend as a participant is an opportunity to either name the nameless "it's not happening" feeling or to acknowledge the feeling of energy moving in the ritual.

Structure your ritual so that the energy rises gradually and consistently, so that the ritual makes sense. A student of mine once reported attending a large ritual where energy was repeatedly raised and dropped. Perhaps the flow of the ritual wasn't clearly thought through. She observed that there seemed to be conflicting intention among the facilitators. If you take a group on a spiritual roller coaster ride, you may all end up with migraines and whiplash.

For a ritual to be effective, you and the other participants must attune yourselves to its purpose and theme. To attune, you need a conscious connection to your body. Through the understanding and development of energetic skills, integrating your mind and body, you learn to embody the essence of the ritual theme.

Kirlian photography has shown that a plant first creates an astral form, then grows into that space. Think of applying this process to ritual construction. Energetic preparation for a ritual consciously prepares you for the ritual experience and creates the astral container that will hold the actual experience. If you don't energetically prepare yourself and any other participants for the ritual and consider the effect of personal energy on the ritual space, you may undermine all your hard work and site preparations. Learning to understand and use energy consciously will dramatically transform both your personal and group rituals.

All beings, plants, rocks, animals, and people are energy forms living in a sea of energy.[74] Everything affects everything else on both overt and subtle levels. Becoming sensitive to the level and quality of our own energy is a good place to start understanding energetics. Most of us are generally unaware of our energetic effect on our environment and the other beings around us.

You can become more aware of how you experience, affect, and work energy by regularly pausing in any activity to tune in to the energy around you. Feel how the energy you carry is affecting the environment and the creatures around you in that moment. With patience and discipline, you can develop awareness of how you hold and manipulate energy, greatly enhancing your skills as a magical practitioner and ritualist.

The following practice will help you become more sensitive to your personal energy within a physical space. Set aside twenty minutes to experience it.

Practice

In loose, comfortable clothes, lie down on your back and either close

---

[74] K, *Beginning True Magick*, 9.

your eyes or let them go softly unfocused. Take a deep breath. Fill your belly first, then your chest. Exhale slowly, letting your back sink into the floor. Take your attention to your toes. Curl your toes tightly as you inhale, and hold your breath to the count of four. Blow out through your mouth and relax your toes. Repeat.

Next, tighten your ankles as you inhale and hold your breath to the count of four. Blow out through your mouth, and relax your ankles. Repeat. Continue this exercise, tightening and relaxing your calves, thighs, buttocks, abdomen, chest, shoulders, arms, hands, neck, jaw, and brow.

Continue to breathe slowly and deeply. Survey your body to get a sense of your own energy level right now. Is it different than when you began? After you have a sense of your specific and overall energy, let your awareness expand beyond yourself into the physical space that you occupy. Once you have touched the edges of the room energetically, pull yourself in as you inhale, hold your breath, and condense your energetic body into your very center. Become very, very small. Crowd your consciousness onto the head of a pin. Release your breath and relax. Breathe yourself out to the walls again; expand to fill the room. Repeat. What do you sense in the quality of the energy of the room? Is it different than when you began? Check in with your own body again. Has your energy changed? Expand your awareness beyond yourself once more. Has the energy in the room changed? Has your personal energy merged with or been tempered by the external space?[75]

Personal Energetic Preparation

Before you participate in a ritual, it's vital to prepare intentionally. This greatly deepens your experience and sensitizes your mind to the subtleties of the ritual's theme. Begin your preparation as far in advance as possible. Preparation can be as simple as thinking about the occasion,

[75] Practice created by Falcon River.

letting impressions and feelings arise. The ritual's theme will begin to take shape within you, psychically and energetically, so that you begin to move into the reality that you're projecting.

Learning how to be in ritual space is the skill of bringing your self forth, bringing yourself fully into the present moment, into the energetics of the ritual's purpose. As children we are trained to disconnect from the present, as we do when watching TV or merely observing life. As a result, we are more practiced in *non*participation, in checking out rather than tuning in. Learning to become and remain fully present allows us to know with our senses what is actually going on energetically in a ritual. How can we attend to the needs of others if we can't sense what's going on in ourselves?

The following is a centering practice to benefit you in daily life. Centering before a ritual enhances your experience, brings you into the present, and helps to create conscious energetics.

Centering Practice #1

Stand with your feet shoulder-width apart, toes pointing forward, knees soft and slightly bent. Rock your pelvis slightly forward. Relax.

Feel that there is a helium balloon attached by a string to the top of your head. Let it pull your spine slightly upward. At the same time, send a taproot out the end of your tailbone and sink it into the ground slightly behind and between your feet. Feel the pull of the rising balloon lengthening your spine, even as your pelvis sinks slightly toward the floor, pulled by your taproot sinking deeper into the earth. Once your spine has come to a comfortable lengthening, rest your eyes on a point in the air about three feet in front of you and softly focus them there. Maintain your soft focus on this point for the rest of the exercise.

Let your arms hang limp at your sides. Now drop your inner vision into your nipples and contemplate the world around you from a "mammary" point of view. (Well, this *is* a Women's Mysteries tradition!) Turn your torso gently as you "look" to your right, then to your left. Sense the turning motion originating from a spot midway between your pubic arch and your belly button. This is called your "hara" or center. For women, it is the location of our womb space. Keep rhythmically turning your trunk from side to side, letting your arms swing limply, flapping against your sides from the centrifugal force of your motion. Do *not* turn your head with your torso as it turns. Keep your head facing forward as your torso twists.

As you continue to rotate your torso, become aware of your breathing. Breathe energy in through the balls of your feet. Bring it up through your legs to your heart. Exhale, sending some out each arm and the rest out through the top of your head. Inhale energy through the top of your head and down to your heart. Exhale, sending some out each arm and the rest down through your body and out through the balls of your feet. Repeat this breathing pattern for as long as you wish to indulge yourself in the pleasure of the motion. When you are finished, slow the motion down until you naturally come to a place of pause.[76] Know that you are an open channel for the energy and subsequent flow of the ritual. Trust in the Goddess.[77]

Centering Practice #2: Becoming a Tree in the Wind

Some women especially enjoy using this exercise to commune with trees. Take yourself to a forest or simply go outside and stand near your favorite tree. Stand with your feet hip-distance apart with your knees soft and your pelvis tucked beneath you. Allow your eyes to go soft (unfocused). Keeping your head forward, with your arms totally limp, begin to twist your torso to your right and left, placing your eyes in your nipples as in the prior practice, until your arms gently flog your sides from the centrifugal force of your twisting motion. As you begin the breathing and motion again, with each inhale pull energy up from the ground. Send down roots from your center. Extend your energetic body into the roots,

---

[76] Ibid.

[77] Starhawk's Tree of Life meditation from *The Spiral Dance* (HarperSanFrancisco, 1989), page 58, is another great source for this practice.

and then use them like a soda straw to reach down and suck up more energy with your next inhalation. With your exhale, run the energy out of your arms and out of the top of your head, lengthen your trunk, and expand your crown. Grow branches, buds, stems, and leaves, reaching for the sky. With the next inhalation, turn your leaves to the sun, cup them to catch the rain, and suck in the sky energy, pulling it down into your heart. Exhale, send a little back into the atmosphere through your branch-arms, and let the rest drain back into the earth through the balls of your feet, down through your energetic roots. Continue in this fashion: one breath from the earth and up to the sky, then a breath from the sky and down to the earth. Expand your root system to intertwine with and touch the spirit and body of the tree. Continue the breath and motion until your pleasure, and that of your tree companion, is complete.[78]

More Ways to Energetically Prepare for Ritual

THINK ABOUT LOGISTICAL ASPECTS OF THE RITUAL: What do you need to gather, bring, or prepare? Make a complete list of ritual items you need. Don't wait until the last possible minute to check to see if you have everything. The last-minute need to rush out for tin foil or matches will interfere with the energetic preparation.

PREPARE YOUR RITUAL TOOLS IN ADVANCE: Are there tools that need to be consecrated, cleansed, or prepared in some way prior to the ritual? For example, if you used your athame for a prior ritual to cut yourself free of an ex-lover, cleanse it thoroughly before using it again.

EAT LIGHTLY: Avoid large amounts of meat or heavy carbohydrates on the day of the ritual. The feeling of heaviness that comes with overeating can hinder altered states of consciousness.

---

[78] Practice created by Falcon River.

DRAW A DIAGRAM OF THE INTENDED RITUAL FLOW, MARKING THE TRANSITION POINTS AND ENACTMENTS ON THE PAGE: Think about the purpose of the ritual and how you have developed the theme. Use colored chalk or crayons to draw a diagram of the potential energy flow of the ritual. Draw how the energy might begin to rise, move, deepen, intensify, and release. Not all rituals look the same. Energy currents may change in color and pattern as the ritual progresses. Creating an image of the ritual flow in this way may help you work out the energetics of the ritual and understand how to align with it. When you work with a group of facilitators, showing a diagram of the ritual flow helps everyone involved understand where the energy needs to go at any given time. After the ritual, you can make a second drawing of what actually happened. This practice will help to sensitize your ability to feel the energy and determine if the energy flow was experienced as it was intended.

The flow of the ritual can also be expressed or demonstrated through movement, gesture, or dance.

CLEANSE YOUR PERSONAL ENVIRONMENT: Make a ritual out of cleaning your house, mowing your yard, organizing your cupboards, or cleaning out a closet or refrigerator. Many women use these activities as a moving meditation to quiet their internal chatter.

TAKE A WALK OR A HIKE: Use conscious breathing and movements to awaken, energize, and sensitize the mind and body together.

TAKE A PURIFYING BATH WITH OILS OR BATH SALTS ASSOCIATED WITH THE RITUAL'S PURPOSE.

ADORN YOURSELF WITH CLOTHING AND JEWELRY THAT YOU RESERVE FOR SACRED OCCASIONS ONLY.

ANOINT YOURSELF WITH A SPECIAL PERFUME OR SCENTED OIL THAT YOU ONLY USE FOR RITUALS: Be aware that you may have to abstain from using scents of any kind in group rituals to respect those with scent sensitivities.

CHANGE SOMETHING IN YOUR PHYSICAL ENVIRONMENT: One of my students does a little ritual in her office prior to each of the holidays. She changes the color scheme of her computer screen, so every time there is a seasonal quarter change, she changes the screen color to a seasonal color. Another student adds a seasonal chant to the bottom of her screen saver.

MAKE TIME TO THINK ABOUT THE OCCASION AND FEEL INTO IT: Find ways to personalize and immerse yourself in the ritual's theme, then move your understanding into the universal connection that the seasonal or personal ritual represents. For example, the ritual theme of Brigid (February 1) is one of spiritual dedication and renewal. The season of Brigid is a time of newness, of observing the growing sunlight, tender as a newborn infant, warm and sweet. A new solar cycle has begun to unfold, and the season is more about light than heat. The energetic preparation for a Brigid ritual calls for a reverent, contemplative, or meditative approach to the fire element, unlike the fiery exuberance and motion of a Summer Solstice ritual.

To begin preparing energetically for Brigid, I first think about the dominant energies present at this time of year in the sun and the Earth herself. I consider the newborn sunlight, so delicate and fragile, and the new shoots poking up beneath the earth's surface that have burst their seed casings. Reflecting on the feelings that are evoked, I dive into this imagery, in awe of the Goddess, who has shed Her skin and is reborn anew. The mystery of renewal is present; I feel humbled and grateful to be alive, able to experience the wonder of it all.

I consciously breathe with Her, like an infant tasting those first sweet breaths of life. I search with my consciousness to find a seed below the surface of the earth that is awakening to the call of life, and I merge with it. With the seed, I slowly crack my casing and begin to reach outside it. I send a tendril toward the waxing light and break the crust of the earth, individuating into the plant I am destined to become. Emerging from the seed of last year's harvest, I become who I have the capacity to be. It is to this spiritual becoming that I will dedicate myself at the Brigid ritual.

After doing this preparation, I can re-create the energetics of the seasonal theme at will and embody those energetics in the rite. I purposefully align my own energy with the season's energy, filling myself in mind, body, and spirit. This is the energy I will embody and carry to the ritual and work with there.

Energetic Preparation for Group Facilitators

Even a minimal amount of group energetic preparation makes a big difference in the overall experience for both facilitators and invited participants alike. Ritual facilitation is an act of spiritual service. After personal preparation, what group preparation do you need to best embody your "facilitator-selves," the ones who serve? Consider how you might come into resonance together.

If your group is facilitating for thirty to fifty participants or more, try to meet at least two to three hours before the scheduled ritual to set up the ritual space, review the ritual design, and go over any logistics that need attention. If you expect fewer participants, the review may take less time. Regardless of the number of participants, facilitators must make time to connect and come into resonance together. This is not the same as socializing. Coming into resonance brings the facilitators' collective consciousness into the ritual theme. This can be achieved by making time to be in circle together, holding hands, and breathing together in silence. You might include a chant or poetry that speaks to the ritual's theme and inspires the facilitators to connect with one another. Remind women that whatever capacity they choose in ritual is a valued act of spiritual service and that everyone who participates, from the greeters at the door and the women assisting in the parking lot to the woman aspecting the Goddess, is a ritual facilitator.

In a group ritual where teams of women are serving in different functions or ritual roles, it is very important for those women in each team to connect energetically prior to the ritual independently of the larger group. This seems to occur most naturally after all the facilitators have met together to review the ritual.

For example, the facilitators who are to invoke the elements and the Goddess meet briefly. They connect physically by holding hands in a circle, breathing together, and remembering that the elements they are calling into the circle are all interconnected like the uninterrupted line of the pentacle. If they haven't already done so in advance of the ritual, they briefly share aspects of their invocations with each other to ensure continuity between the ritual's theme and their invocations.

As important as energetic preparation is in advance of a ritual, so is allowing time afterwards to rest and integrate your experience. As part of your ritual preparation, consider what you might need right after the ritual and the next day.

Energetic Preparation for Participants

Ritual works best when everyone present is committed to the intention and the outcome. If you are planning a large, open-to-the-community seasonal ritual, you can expect the participants to have a wide range of ritual experience and skill. As a facilitator, you will want everyone attending to feel included. Newcomers to goddess rituals cannot experience a ritual in the same way as those who have participated in rituals before. For the benefit of the newcomers and any participant who wasn't part of the ritual planning, provide a brief but clear statement of purpose and a description in advance of the ritual through the invitation or publicity. This allows participants to prepare for the experience and come in the proper frame of mind. When you invite people to a party, you usually tell them what kind of party you are planning (surprise, slumber, birthday, etc.) so that they can have an idea of how to dress and what to bring. Giving women enough information in advance about what to expect at your ritual will help them align their energies with the ritual's purpose and intent (see examples of this in chapter 10).

If women are encouraged to be a part of the "circuitry" of the ritual rather than just passive onlookers being taken on a journey blindfolded, they can contribute to the group energy. In some traditions, newcomers are not expected or not allowed to participate in ritual work. They are asked to observe only. In the Dianic tradition, everyone who comes is expected to participate to the degree they feel comfortable, and passive observation is discouraged. The energetic consequences of not giving information to a group other than "come to a women's ritual" is the same as asking them to utterly trust you to take them on a trip without telling them the destination. Why should they trust you if you don't tell them where you are going and how you intend to take them there? Too often, women come to a ritual, step inside, and don't know where they are being taken. The result is, at best, hesitancy or reluctance to participate; at worst, chaos takes over and the ritual can break down entirely. Letting everyone know to some extent what is going to happen (what the ride is going to look or feel like) helps align them with the purpose of the ritual and will actively engage them in working toward the destination.

If your group sends out a newsletter, e-mail notice, or ritual flyer, recommend that newcomers to goddess and female-centered ritual at least do some suggested reading before attending their first community ritual. This discourages complete newcomers who just want to watch and check things out. If they do some reading, they may not know the final destination of the trip, but they will know what country they're traveling to.

When the group gathers for the ritual itself and you are ready to begin, welcome them and give them a brief description of the ritual flow and the sequence of the work. Giving the group some structure actually creates more freedom within the ritual. If women know what the parameters of the ritual are, they may actually feel safer to immerse themselves deeper into the experience.

Informing everyone about the ritual flow doesn't require you to reveal the mystery of the ritual. There are simple ways to describe what will happen, in what order, while retaining the mystery. Sometimes I use my hands to demonstrate the flow of energy as I describe the sequence of the ritual activities. You don't need to preview the ritual in detail. All you need are a few sentences that talk about the ritual theme and the energetic flow. During the ritual itself, you can continue to give simple guidance or instructions that move the ritual along. Even if you tell participants everything at the beginning, they won't remember most of it once they are in ritual space because they will be in an altered state of consciousness. And why should they remember it all? As participants, that's not their job. It's your job as a facilitator to know the details of the ritual plan and follow it through.

Decide in advance if your ritual will be conducted with participants and facilitators standing, sitting, or with options for both. Although there may be rituals best facilitated sitting down, in my experience standing is always best unless a woman is unable to stand for any length of time. Sitting encourages passivity and observation; standing helps sustain awareness and engagement. Movement also helps to raise and sustain energy. If you want a ritual with more energy, standing easily allows for dance and movement in place.

For a successful ritual, it is best for everyone to connect at the beginning. There are many gentle ways to join individuals into a focused and cohesive group. Even if a ritual group is already experienced at working together, connection is still needed to align all participants with the particular theme and purpose of each ritual. Bringing a group into resonance helps everyone become present and on the same page. Sometimes this energetic connection is called an attunement. The group forms a collective consciousness, a *feel*, a *tuning in* together as one body. This is an experience that usually develops organically in small, intimate groups who meet regularly. Larger groups comprised of strangers need the support of a conscious energetic attunement to achieve a similar collective consciousness that is so essential to the success of the ritual.

Cohesive Group Energetics

Try one or many of these suggestions:

* Ask the group to think about a question or reflect upon an image.
* Give a guided meditation on an aspect of the ritual's theme.
* Purify the space and participants with incense smoke, scented oil, or salt water (see "Admittance," p. 112).
* Teach the Centering Practice in this chapter to help women become balanced and fully present. Instruct them to send the energy released through their palms and around the circle in a deosil (sunwise) direction.
* Tell a story related to the ritual theme.
* Chant
* Drum.
* Share an appropriate thematic poem.
* Hold hands and breathe together.

Have Participants "Check In"

Having a brief check-in at the start of the ritual helps women feel included, present, and connected. Invite the women to hold hands. Ask them to go quickly around the circle, giving their names and a short personal sentence in accordance with the ritual's theme. This may take approximately 10–20 seconds per participant, but the time spent is surely justified when a group of strangers becomes a cohesive group of acquaintances. A check-in is especially effective for larger rituals where women will be largely anonymous once the casting of the circle begins. As each woman says her name, everyone hears that she is present and a little about her current state of being. The check-in helps give a larger group a sense of the intimacy that a smaller group has. To do the check-in, one facilitator has to initiate it and speak first to set the example, modeling a specific sentence structure that participants can fill in with their own names and thoughts.

Following are examples of some personal ritual and seasonal ritual check-ins:

> "I am Ruth, and I'm harvesting my book." (Fall Equinox)
>
> "I'm Jenny, and my fire is in my activism." (Summer Solstice)
>
> "I'm Julie, and I'm dreaming about opening a goddess store." (Yule)
>
> "I'm Sofia, daughter of Marnie, daughter of Sibyl, daughter of Ruby, and mother of Amy and Janet." (Reciting one's motherline for Spring Equinox)
>
> "I'm Sara, and to me, love is opening myself to pleasure beyond measure." (A handfasting or wedding ceremony)
>
> "I'm Dorothea, and for me, becoming a wise woman is learning to live wide open." (A croning ritual)

For variation, after each woman speaks, have the group repeat her name and statement in return. This is a way to use the check-in as a magical enactment to strengthen and amplify each woman's affirmation. Don't use this variation with very large groups as it doubles the time taken.

Yet another variation or addition to the check-in can be to invite women to express themselves with a movement that describes their feelings in that moment. The group can also reflect the woman's movement back to her so that she can see her own feelings. These last variations will take approximately 30-60 seconds per participant, so the size of the group needs to be considered.

Admittance

Formally admitting women into the ritual space is another effective way to settle down and focus participants and to connect women with the group energetics and ritual theme. A formal entry into the ritual space might include a personal welcome and anointing with a kiss, special scented oil, water, or incense smoke. Although in Dianic tradition it is customary to have women line up in order of age, with the eldest entering the circle first, this is not always practical with larger groups. Getting 150 women in age order could take quite some time! At the threshold of the ritual space, traditionally at the eastern gate of the circle, each woman is anointed or censed. She is blessed and welcomed by a ritual facilitator with the words, "I purify you from all anxieties and fears in the name of the Goddess," or "I/We welcome you into the circle of women." This type of formalized entry is best done with a smaller group. For larger rituals, women can pass through a candlelit "gateway" of burning incense or a line of drummers, pausing to allow the sound or smoke to cleanse and purify them.

Perfect Love and Perfect Trust

> *At the threshold* of the east gate of the ritual circle, a facilitator awaits. As each woman approaches her and prepares to enter, the facilitator issues the challenge,

> "How do you enter the circle?"
>
> The participant seeking entry replies, "I enter in perfect love and perfect trust."

...

The reply "I enter in perfect love and perfect trust" is often required when entering a Dianic ritual circle, and it is an important ideal in the Craft. Even when the words aren't said, the concept is implied. It is vital to our sense of emotional safety, so we can open to the ritual experience and allow the creative and divine to flow through us. It is not an exhortation to trust everyone in a gullible way, but to constantly strive within yourself, the group, your community, and the world, to *create* love and trust. It also issues a challenge to recognize the perfection in each person.

Since many women participating in goddess spirituality have little or no training or background in Wiccan traditions, these words may make some uncomfortable. In itself, "perfection" is a difficult concept—elusive, subjective, and burdensome, because our concept of perfection is often unattainable. So what does "perfect love and perfect trust" mean? How can this verbal commitment enhance safety and ease fears in a ritual circle?

For many, entering the circle in perfect love and perfect trust means they are willing to be honest and to communicate what is true for them, without judging or fear of being judged. Acting as each other's witnesses and listeners is an important part of group ritual. We often experience our own emotional healing through witnessing someone else's. The role of "loving witness" can be challenging for women, who are used to being judged not just by men, but by other women. In a place of love and trust, women can feel safe, be truly heard, and become vulnerable, because each woman has something personal at stake.

For some women, keeping perfect love and perfect trust means honoring a commitment to confidentiality. What is done and said in ritual remains in the ritual, to be kept private within the group unless it is agreed otherwise. Women may discuss their own experience freely but agree not to discuss their observations of others.

In a ritual circle, you may feel uncomfortable even while you're aware of being safe. The ritual may bring up unexpected emotions. You may feel challenged by the ritual's content, whether it's healing after sexual assault, losing a loved one to death, honoring one's sexuality, or focusing on the complex relationships of mothers and daughters. This very discomfort can be a catalyst for your own change and healing.

Whether she speaks the words or not, when a woman makes this commitment she wills into being a reality that the whole group can sense. "Perfect love and perfect trust" becomes an experience rooted in her body. When each of us commits to this ideal, this possibility, we bring our best selves forward to make it so.

What can be done if we come to the ritual carrying conflict with one another or knowing about a conflict? How can we enter in perfect love and trust in those terms? We can do this by making commitments in advance. Women in conflict may consider these commitments:

* I agree to communicate respectfully about any disagreement that arises during the ritual.

* If there's a dispute or problem, I'll assume that you didn't intentionally act to hurt me.

* If I experience something that bothers me during the ritual, I'll deal with it afterwards.

* If an agreement isn't possible, we'll ask ourselves where we could meet and hold the intention of perfect love and trust while holding conflicting personal feelings.

* I agree to not attend the ritual if we cannot come to a place of love and trust while holding conflicting personal feelings.

Learning perfect love and perfect trust may mean learning to work from the assumption that you are both on the same side. As women, we're not practiced at being allies in struggle. The emotional reflex we learn through living in the over-culture is that any conflict automatically means that we are adversaries to one other rather than allies having a problem that needs some work or awareness. For example, what if a circle sister put wine into the chalice, forgetting that one of the circle members is a recovering alcoholic? Without jumping to anger, the woman in recovery might remind her circle sister again, assuming that the circle sister simply forgot about the alcohol issue. The woman in recovery could also take responsibility for herself by bringing her own juice and chalice.

If women are considering working ritual together regularly, but are not trained together in the Craft, it may be important to talk about perfect love and perfect trust prior to entering the ritual space. This way, everyone is aligned with a definition they can agree on. Consider making a group agreement in advance as to how you will deal with difficulties that might arise in ritual. Having some simple agreements and basic understandings can help prevent hurt feelings and serious disagreements later on.

We may no longer consciously remember safety, intimacy, acceptance, and sisterhood, but we know on a cellular level what they are. We know the power of intention. If we commit to perfect love and perfect trust within the ritual circle, that commitment becomes an energy that creates and perpetuates its own reality.

With practice over time, we begin to remember these states of being; they once again become familiar and recognizable. We can then begin to transform into who we might be without patriarchal influences in our world and within ourselves. We begin to move differently in our lives, replacing our old, automatic behaviors and thought processes with a new goddess-empowered paradigm.

Practice

Continue your ritual making process with the personal ritual that you've already been working with. Create your personal energetic preparation to come into resonance with your ritual's purpose. If you have invited others, think of ways that you can bring your supporters and witnesses into resonance when you are ready to begin.

Practice

Choose three new examples from your personal list of rituals, or continue to work with passages you have already begun to experiment with. Do the following steps with each one. If you are doing this exercise as a group activity, choose new examples from each category of ritual listed in chapter 4.

1. Develop a one or two-line sentence of the ritual's purpose.
2. Identify the ritual theme.
3. Think of a few possible enactments for the ritual's core work.
4. Think of one energetic preparation to do prior to the ritual and one for the beginning of the actual ritual.

Example #1[79]

PURPOSE: To release the tyranny of our shame and embrace the magnificence of ourselves.

RITUAL THEME: Release of self-hatred (Release/Transformation/Affirmation).

ENACTMENT: Burn fashion magazines (Release). Make a picture collage of ourselves and our accomplishments (Transformation). Make a

[79] The three examples herein were taken from a workshop I presented at a women's conference in November 1998 in Seattle, Washington. I gave students a ritual-making topic and they did the rest.

declaration of thanks for who and what we are (Affirmation).

PRE-RITUAL ENERGETIC PREPARATION: Gather pieces for the collage prior to the ritual as a visual and moving meditation.

RITUAL ENERGETIC PREPARATION: Spend time in silence gazing into mirrors together.

Example #2

PURPOSE: We are coming together to honor the darkness as the creative container for the promise of light.

RITUAL THEME: Winter Solstice (Celebration).

ENACTMENT: Participants sit in front of a mirror in the dark and gaze at themselves by their own inner light. One by one, they light their own candle and make a one- word statement about their vision.

PRE-RITUAL ENERGETIC PREPARATION: Spend thirty minutes in the dark and immediately afterwards journal about the experience.

RITUAL ENERGETIC PREPARATION: Sit together in a circle in darkness. After ten minutes, go around the circle saying a sentence or two about darkness and creativity.

Example #3

PURPOSE: To create a space in our hearts, families, and communities for a child.

RITUAL THEME: A gathering of parents planning to adopt babies (Celebration).

ENACTMENT: Pass around a basket full of flower bulbs topped with a baby doll. Each person speaks to the symbolic child about hopes, wants, and what they have to offer as a loving parent.

PRE-RITUAL ENERGETIC PREPARATION: Think of what we want our future child to know.

RITUAL ENERGETIC PREPARATION: Enter the ritual space singing a lullaby, starting first with humming, and building to singing. The altar elemental tools are baby items: east, a rattle; west, a baby bottle; north, a hand-woven blanket; south, a toy.

Additional Practice

Design a ritual that uses no physical props, altar, or ritual tools. Practice embodying the energies you would have used through the physical symbols.

chapter 7

STRUCTURING A PERCEPTION

"Magic requires great amounts of practice and very little effort."[80]

"Ritual is structuring a perception."[81]

We have discussed developing the purpose, theme, and energetics of a ritual. Now it is time to consider what structure will most effectively support the ritual experience. If you think about ritual as the structuring of a perception, then the purpose of a ritual's structure is to support the perception by being an effective and appropriate container for the ritual activities.

Don't put the cart before the horse. You can't know what kind of container you will need before you have the purpose, theme, and energetics developed. If the ritual creation process starts with the structure and ends with the content, the ritual will be limited by the structure rather than the structure supporting the ritual. Form follows function; the architecture will vary, depending on the purpose and theme of the ritual. It's safe to assume that there should always be a beginning, middle, and ending.

For some women, the idea of imposing any type of structure on a ritual is "patriarchal." It is true that for centuries women have been oppressed by patriarchal religion and its dogma. For this reason, I believe, some women have a knee-jerk reaction to both structural and spiritual leadership, mistrusting it all as oppressive and confining.

Structure, in itself, is not inherently patriarchal nor oppressive. Structure is inherent in all of nature. Everything has organizational structure: crystals,

---

[80] From a conversation with Falcon River, Dianic Priestess of the Guardian Path.

[81] From a conversation with Rabbi Alexis Roberts.

leaves, DNA, snowflakes, and our own bodies are but a few examples. Some structures hinder the feeling of freedom, like bars on windows or tight clothing; some structures support it, like standing on top of a fire tower on a crisp autumn day or skimming across the water in a graceful sailboat. It is possible to create a structure that allows for spontaneity and creativity while providing safety within its clear boundaries. Like water in a kettle, it is the structure of the kettle that contains the water in one place long enough to absorb heat and boil. Where does water go without that kettle? It goes all over the place, meandering and unfocused. Water needs a container to give it a shape. Think of the ritual content as the water and its structure as the kettle containing the energy of the hot water, yet allowing it to move about within it.

Ritual Format

The process of developing a ritual format as it is described here is for group ritual, but it is easily adapted for solitary practice. The sequence of this ritual structure will be consistent for most Dianic rituals. The specific details and ways to combine the ritual structure with the theme will vary, depending on the ritual and the group or individual planning it. The size of the group may also influence the ritual format as well, allowing for greater or lesser degrees of specialization, depending on the number of facilitators available. Don't just follow the suggested form; think about and question the purpose behind it. Once you understand the purpose, then you can experiment with the form.

Building the structure of a formal ritual begins with the casting of a circle. Circle casting will be discussed in much greater detail later in this chapter, but it is worth noting here that it may not always be necessary to cast a circle. A cast circle contains and concentrates energy that is raised and focused for the release of a spell or a specific intention. If you only wish to invite the presence of the elemental powers to bless, honor, or witness the rite, as for a wedding or handfasting ceremony, a cast circle may not be needed and would restrict the free movement of guests in and out of the ceremony.

If you design a ritual and deem it unnecessary to include a cast circle, remember that you still need a definite beginning, middle, and ending. Just as any good story has a clear beginning, middle, and ending, participants in a ritual need to have definite closure to their experience. The following steps include the casting of a circle, but try experimenting in your rituals with and without a cast circle. Each step will be discussed in detail. You can evaluate the differences and determine which is more effective for different occasions. Remember: in any ritual or magical working, make everything you choose to do—or not do—a conscious decision.

The Steps (skip steps 5, 6, and 12 if you don't want to include a formal circle casting for your ritual. Also skip steps 7 and 8 if you don't wish to include invocations to the elemental powers or Goddess)

1. Gather what is needed and set up the physical space.
2. Prepare yourself: personal purification and energetic preparation.
3. Prepare the ritual space: purification and consecration.
4. Make a group connection: come into resonance.
5. Raise energy for circle casting.
6. Create the container: cast and seal the circle
7. Invoke the elemental powers.
8. Invoke the Goddess.
9. State the ritual's purpose at the center.
10. Do the core ritual work: the enactments.
11. Give thanks and libations.
12. Valedictions to the Goddess and the elemental powers.
13. Take down the circle.
14. Eat something and clean up.

Some ritual actions have been done over time with such success that they become part of a tradition. To keep faith with a tradition or to deviate from it is a decision to be made with mindfulness and respect. Understand the concept behind a ritual action before you improvise, alter, or add to it. The important point is to create the intention first and then make sure the ritual structure is appropriate to support it.

1. Gather What Is Needed and Set Up the Physical Space

In this activity, you attend to the practical details of the ritual. For example, if the ritual is in your home, you may wish to cover or remove objects like your television, computer, or some pieces of furniture. Remember to take the telephone off the hook, turn off cell phones or pagers, and secure pets that may be underfoot. Whether the ritual is in your home or at another site, make lists of everything needed in advance of the ritual, down to the aluminum foil that covers the altar and the matches, so you will have them ready when you set up. If you don't have all the physical details prepared ahead of time, it will significantly alter the flow of the ritual. If needed items are not there or have not been prepared, the energy of the ritual will plummet and focus will be lost as facilitators scramble to find missing articles or have to change the ritual abruptly. Preparation is part of the ritual, and the task of preparing the altar and the ritual space is a sacred responsibility. Rituals are beautifully enhanced when the work is done by women who feel called to provide service in this way. Physically clean the ritual space as you would if you were preparing your home for the arrival and visit of an honored guest; then set up the altar after cleaning the ritual space. Ritual energy begins to build from this point of preparation.

The Altar

Set up the altar to reflect the intention of the ritual, using physical symbols of the ritual's theme. This includes any cleansed and consecrated ritual tools that you plan to utilize.

Setting up the altar involves both hemispheres of the brain and serves to further create an energetic resonance. The logical left brain makes sure the matches actually make it to the altar, and the creative right brain sees the altar as "really needing this or that color." Allow your creativity to express itself as though you were creating a work of art—which, in fact, some altars are. Look for maximum visual impact, and avoid clutter: it is not necessary to put every stone in your collection on the altar when a single stone would do. Consider how easily tools can be reached and whether anything on the altar poses a safety hazard, such as candles that might be knocked over when the athame needs to be reached.

Are there to be other altars or working spaces in your ritual? If so, these need to be attended to with the same care as the main altar. Because sometimes these other altars or enactment areas may be set directly on the floor, particular attention must be paid to them to assure safety for yourself and others if they are to be illuminated with candles or contain liquids. This may include having a fire extinguisher nearby or towels to mop up spills.

2. Prepare Yourself: Personal Purification and Energetic Preparation

The purpose of self-purification is to transform from mundane consciousness into your magical self. In this shift of consciousness, the mind drops out of the everyday beta-wave state and into an alpha state. In the alpha state, we become more sensitive and can achieve a deep alignment with the energetics of the ritual. Changing your awareness from everyday consciousness to magical perception can be done in many ways; however, before any method can work, you must, on some level, be willing to be altered and open to a different set of eyes, ears, and physical sensations. This is clearly demonstrated in the act of self-purification, which brings you fully into the present time and prepares you for what you are about to do.

Wearing clean clothes or special ritual garb and adornments is one way to prepare yourself energetically for being in ritual. We commonly use the expression "dress for success," which is an energetic preparation for the workplace. Conscious dressing for ritual serves a similar purpose. It helps you to literally envelop yourself in the specific resonance you choose.

Another popular method of self-purification is to take a special bath prior to a ritual. Turn off the ringer on the phone or take it off the hook. Use music, candlelight, incense, or oils, and choose images to gaze at that will support your process of changing consciousness. Sink into yourself as you sink into the bath water and begin to awaken and align your entire being to the ritual's purpose. Complete your ritual bath with a self-blessing. Make eye contact with yourself in a mirror, and behold the Goddess within you. Study the details of your reflection and behold Her image in your own. Bless yourself and your body by anointing yourself with scented oil or salt water. Speak an affirmation that you need to hear.

The following is an example of a Dianic self-blessing that can be used for purification prior to ritual or at any other time. Once you understand the concept, make it your own by changing and personalizing any language you need to affirm for yourself. The "You" addressed in this self-blessing is the face of the Goddess reflected in the mirror (yes. I'm talking about you!), *and* the Goddess who is Creatrix of All. Make this a personal practice for the rest of your life.

> Blessed be my mind, that I may always think of You.
> Blessed be my eyes, that I may see Your ways.
> Blessed be my ears, that I may hear Your voice
> above all others.
> Blessed be my mouth, that I may always speak and sing
> of You.
> Blessed be my heart, that I may love myself and others,

as I love You.
Blessed be my breasts, formed in strength and beauty, to nurture myself and others as You have nurtured me.
Blessed be my womb and yoni, that I may know pleasure in creativity, as You have brought forth the universe.
Blessed be my hands, that I may do Your work.
Blessed be my legs and feet, that I may always walk and dance upon Your paths. I am Goddess.
Blessed be.[82]

Other purification methods for either solo or group ritual utilize the four elements. It is unnecessary to utilize all four. Choose the elements that most closely correspond to the nature of the specific ritual work.

Water: Wash your hands.

Anoint your third eye, or anoint a circle sister, with a blessing; anoint your womb as a symbol of connection with other women. Say, "I purify myself from all anxieties and fears in the Goddess's name."

Gaze into a hand mirror (another water symbol), saying "I am Goddess," then pass it to the next woman, saying "You are Goddess," until it goes all around the circle.[83] The woman who began the mirror ritual concludes with, "We are Goddess" as she holds up the mirror to the circle of women.

Air and Fire: Move incense over your body or over another with a blessing, such as "I welcome you into the circle of women."

Earth: Rub your hands and feet with salt from a bowl. If the gathering is for a rite of women's mysteries, anoint each woman's forehead with red ochre[84] or clay, accompanied with a blessing such as "I welcome you to

[82] Z Budapest, revised by the author and Jennie Mira.

[83] I learned this practice during my studies with Shekhinah Mountainwater in 1975–1976.

[84] A blood-red powder from earth containing a mixture of hydrated oxide of iron and clay.

this circle, daughter of Earth."

Shifting to magical perception prior to the consecration of the ritual space enables you to perceive the energy as it changes during the consecration. This shift to magical perception is developed from the art of paying attention and interpreting meaning. In small group ritual, purification may be done as part of a formal admittance into the ritual space, such as anointing and blessing women with water or incense as they enter.

After practicing the self-blessing or other forms of purification, notice how doing so changes the way you perceive energy in the ritual space. Refer back to chapter 6 for other ways to prepare energetically for ritual.

3. Prepare the Ritual Space: Purification and Consecration

Circle purification is an energetic cleansing that makes the ritual space neutral to psychic awareness.[85] You wouldn't think of starting a painting on a used canvas, or of writing a poem on a sheet of paper filled with someone else's script. It's the same with ritual. To purify the ritual space is to begin with a clean slate, so that the space has only the precise energy you put into it during the ritual. This work may be done either just prior to participants arriving for a group ritual, as a part of the group ritual, or at the start of a personal ritual. This ritual of purification and consecration sets an energetic base and begins to build a light container. It is a foundation for the magic of making the ritual circle.

The ritual circle is "a place which is psychically cleared, usually with physical cleaning, then banishing any incompatible thoughts, then requesting the power or presence of whatever set of deities, symbols, elemental beings, or images you wish, so that they protect the special atmosphere of the consecrated space."[86] In addition to cleansing the

---

[85] Green, *The Path Through the Labyrinth*, 43.
[86] Ibid., 42.

space of previous energies, purification aids in attuning yourself and others to the elemental powers and acknowledges the interconnectedness of the natural forces.

The ritual of purification marks the seven directional points and physical dimensions of the circle. These directions are the four cardinal quarter points (north, east, south, and west), with the addition of above, below, and center. In Dianic tradition, we correspond the special directions of above to the Maiden, below to the Crone, and center for the Mother, acknowledging the Goddess in Her oneness through Her triple form. You may wish to mark the four quarter-points with candles, stones, or other sacred objects, as discussed in chapter 5. If you don't intend to cast a circle, marking the dimensions of the circle is unnecessary, but clearing the ritual space of previous energy may still be important, depending on the physical location you choose. As a general rule, if the space has been used for mundane purposes or by someone unconnected with the Craft, it's best to cleanse the space.

To begin the purification process, mark the invisible limits of your working ritual space by walking the perimeter of the circle deosil, or clockwise. You will be walking around the circle four times total, each time carrying one of the elements in its *physical form*: incense for air (the rising smoke allows you to *see* air) or use a feather fan to move air, a lit candle for fire (a separate working candle other than the candle in its red holder denoting the fire element on the altar), a bowl containing water (a separate container than the altar chalice), and a bowl of rock salt for earth (or a bowl of earth). Potted plants or flowers can't be used to purify because their essence won't come into contact with the ritual space like rock salt or earth that can be tossed onto the floor or ground. Don't use an athame, wand, or staff to purify the ritual space: these are magical tools used to cast the circle or direct energy, and not actual forms of the physical elements.

The qualities of each of the physical elements energetically cleanse the ritual space in different ways according to their individual natures.

The smoke and scent of the incense rises and spreads. The candle's light illuminates and contrasts lights and shadows. Water can be sprinkled on the ground, as can salt or earth. As you walk the perimeter of the ritual circle, let your consciousness focus solely on the intention of cleansing. Drawing from personal experiences of the elements (read "elemental inventory" in chapter 8), awaken a memory of the elemental energy you wish to use for cleansing and embody the essence of that energy. To embody is to evoke, awaken, and activate a specific energy or feeling within yourself and to project it tangibly forward into the ritual space.

As you pick up each of the elements, bless it and reflect on the cleansing actions of air, fire, water, and earth. Feel a breeze wafting through the ritual space to clear it; let heat burn away undesirable energy, let rain splash over it, and let earth assimilate and transform what has been there before. Embody the elements as you hold the intention to purify the working area. I always silently repeat the phrase "Purified within, purified without" as my incantation for this ritual action. Its simplicity keeps me focused as I carry around the elements.

Begin purification of the circle in the north, as north is the traditional direction of all powers. The north represents physical manifestation or form, where we as human creatures most easily perceive and experience the elements. It is the point of origin for all physical form, where Spirit is birthed into manifestation. In old, pre-Gardnerian Craft, north is the place of all beginnings and endings.

Take your censer containing the burning incense representing air to the north quarter point of the circle and present it by raising the censer to that direction. After presenting air to the north, continue to walk the perimeter and repeat the presentation of the incense at the east, south, and west quarter points. You may wish to use your hand, a feather, or another symbol of air to move the incense before you. After stopping at the west quarter point, continue to walk to the north quarter, coming full circle to complete the perimeter purification. Then walk into the center of the ritual space and present the incense to the sky above, the earth below, and to the center, which is the Spirit point of the sphere. You might choose to enact this presentation by moving the symbol in a continuous spiral motion from the area in front of your third eye (above) to your womb (below) and back to your heart (center).

To purify with fire, carry a lighted taper or jar candle around the circle, projecting its light, illuminating all places in the space. You will begin in the north, as you did with the incense, stopping at all the quarter points and then walking to the center of the ritual space to present the fire to above, below, and center. You may wish to hold your hand behind the candle's flame so that your palm acts as a reflector, projecting the light before you.

To purify with water, it is traditional to dip into the bowl of water and sprinkle some drops on the ground in front of you at each of the seven points of the circle. Some women like to sprinkle the entire perimeter.

Salt is used to purify with a pinch dropped at each point or sprinkled around the entire perimeter as you walk. Remember that each of the elements is carried to the north first, rather than starting this process at the quarter point that corresponds with the element. It may take some getting used to, but it does make sense.

Take your time with purification. What makes a magical action "wrong" or "right" is not just what you are physically doing, but your frame of mind, your attitude toward beings on other levels, and your motives. Magic works through links forged on the inner levels.

For a group ritual, purification can be done with one, two, or four women, each carrying one of the four elemental symbols. It is visually beautiful to stagger the presentations by having each woman wait until the woman before her has reached the next quarter and moves on. That is to say, a woman will not begin to purify the circle with her element at the north point until the woman before her has moved from north to east and begins moving toward the south. When all women move around the circle deosil, it creates a visual and energetic spiral in the ritual space, creating pathways where the energy can flow and be magnified. From a practical standpoint, this staggered presentation prevents having the participants wait an extended time for the ritual to begin, as they would if each element made a complete circle before the next one began.

Consecration of the ritual space immediately follows the purification process. To consecrate means "to make holy," to "set apart," or, in this context, to energetically dedicate the ritual space to a magical working. Consecration of the ritual space energetically charges the newly cleansed ritual space with the intention that magic is welcome. Consecration follows the same presentation pattern as the elemental purification, and it can be done by a fifth woman or by one of the women who previously purified the space. There should be no interruption in the flow from the act of purification through consecration.

A bell with a long, extended tone is used to awaken the elemental spirits that reside behind the portal doors and inform them of an upcoming invitation. My favorite bells are the small Tibetan bells that are connected by a cord. One small tap together and the tone resonates for a long time, with overtones that help induce trance. Bar chimes or Tibetan bowls found in many stores can also be used due to their sustained tones. Using your voice as a bell can work by vocalizing tones at the quarter points, above, below, and center.

Elemental sounds can also be used to purify the ritual space because their vibratory levels approximate those of the elements. A bull-roarer or wind tube can be used for air; a tambourine, sistrum, or high-timbre rattle for fire; a rain stick or ocean drum for water; and a deep, resonant heart-beat drum for earth. Combining the elemental sounds with the physical symbols provides a visual, auditory, and kinesthetic experience.

4. Make a Group Connection: Come Into Resonance

The simplest way to help a group come into resonance is by simply holding hands and breathing together in silence. This simple act, done with conscious attention, helps bring everyone into the present time.

Chanting and/or drumming can also accomplish this. Deeper yet is to create a group connection that is also connected to, and balanced with, the earth and sky.

Review the Tree Centering Practice (in chapter 6) and apply it to group ritual. Connect with other women in the circle by first rooting yourself deeply and then interweaving your roots with those of your circle sisters. Then extend your trunk and interweave your canopy of branches and leaves above and spread from side to side to connect with your tree sisters. This practice brings individual women and the whole group fully present, into resonance, and centered for their work together. A group of individual women becomes a grove of trees with roots that sink all the way to the molten mantle of the earth's center and branches that reach the sun. As part of a human grove, it is possible to draw from the abundant and fluid energy of the earth and sky for yourself and your ritual without depleting your own energy.[87] This practice can be further developed so participants may assist in creating the cast ritual circle. (See "Creating the Grove: Energetic Support for Circle Casting" later in this chapter) This practice is also important for a ritual facilitator who is casting the circle (the ritual container). In order for her to effectively draw from an energy source (the earth, a tree, the energy raised by the other women in the circle for this purpose, etc.) and pull it through her to create the energetic form of the spherically shaped container, she must be centered.

If you incorporate this group tree-centering practice, you must remember to unweave the participants at the ritual's conclusion. First, facilitate the withdrawing of their canopies above with their branches at their sides, followed by their trunks, and last by withdrawing their entwined roots.

---

[87] This explanation was drawn from the grounding exercise found in *The Spiral Dance*.

5. Raise Energy for Circle Casting

In most Wiccan traditions and goddess-focused rituals, participants do not raise any energy prior to casting the ritual circle. I have found ritual much more effective when the elemental powers and the Goddess are welcomed into a space that is already charged and ready rather than a space that is empty. Therefore, I always raise some energy prior to casting the circle and invoking the elements. The Goddess and the elemental beings are your honored guests. Would you invite your honored guests into an empty room? Of course not. Imagine you've been invited to two different parties in two houses, side by side. The first house you come to is filled with people, but there is no furniture, no music, no pictures on the walls, no refreshments. People are just milling about, not really talking or connecting. You stop just long enough to look in and decide to check out the other party. You can hear the music from the porch of the second house. As you approach the door, you can smell delicious food and hear laughter and conversations. Inside, the home is beautifully decorated and you are joyfully welcomed as you enter. What party would *you* choose?

Each ritual will require different degrees and qualities of energy with which to cast the circle. The purpose of the ritual must be clearly understood in order to determine what quality of energy needs to be generated, and this quality must be communicated in some way to the participants so that they can produce it. Energy for circle casting can be raised in many ways: chanting, conscious breathing, unified sounding, movement, dance, guided meditation, drumming, and more. On a scale of one to ten, the group is going for an approximate "seven" in heightened vibration. Whichever method you choose, the purpose is the same: the power is not raised in order to peak it or release it, it is projected into the circle to be used by the facilitators during the ritual or to be used by the woman casting the circle.

The "MA" Chant for Energy Raising in Group Ritual

My favorite method for raising the energy needed to cast the circle is the "MA" chant. "MA" is the universal sound for mother. This chant is actually a continuous, unified sounding that begins in low tones and spirals deosil and upward in tone and motion.[88] This chant can be used in a variety of ways when directed with intention. It is most effective if you begin by humming. Keep the consonant sound, "mmmmmm," placed very forward in your closed mouth, humming the tone as though you were humming it out of your nose.[89] This sound is very much like the buzzing of many bees in a hive. Keep this hum going for a while without raising the pitch or opening your mouth. Feel your face and head vibrating. After a minute or two, drop your jaw into the vowel sound "ah." The larger the group, the longer it will take to unify the sound before dropping the jaw into "maaah." Don't rush it; try to feel when the moment is right.

I have found it best to have someone designated in advance to lead this process. Often, that someone is the woman who is either holding center in the group or someone taking responsibility to facilitate this for the ritual. Endeavor to keep the tone unified rather than going off into harmonies or odd descants. Remind women to stagger their breathing so the toning is continuous, rather than stopping together to take a breath and start again. The intention is to unify the group and build something together, rather than to assert individuality. Even women who think they're tone deaf can usually manage to approximate the group tone. Listen for the overtones that sound like bells ringing or spirits singing. Allow the energy of the sound to move deosil around the circle. Raise the pitches gradually as the vocal tapestry spirals tighter and tighter. Feel

---

[88] I learned the "MA" chant in my studies with Shekhinah Mountainwater. She originated it, and I have continued to use and teach it. Many other groups now use it, too. It has many applications, including raising power and overall energetic support.

[89] After working with the MA chant for many years, with advice from my friend and mentor Kay Gardner, I began to sound the consonant *mmmm* first before going into the *ah* of Ma. Doing so helps to create overtones.

the sound. If you are raising energy for the casting, don't let the energy peak, but build it up sufficiently to tangibly charge the participants and the space. In my experience, the "MA" chant, when properly done, builds up and fills the innermost center of the circle, creating a sphere of energy that will be drawn from to help build the walls of the cast circle. When there is sufficient energy raised to cast, drop the pitch that has been purposefully raised, to a low toned continuous hum. Now the circle casting may begin.

With the MA chant, or other methods for raising power, participants will experience energy moving within them and around them. However, without a properly cast circle this energy will eventually dissipate. It is for this reason that a cast circle is necessary: to contain the energy that has been raised. Not every ritual requires a cast circle.

6. Create the Container: Cast and Seal the Circle

The cast circle is a temporary spherical energy-form created to serve as a container for the energy that is generated and utilized by participants in a solo or group ritual. Simply put, containment boosts power. A cast circle is especially useful and necessary if a ritual incorporates spellwork where energy is raised to be focused, directed, and released toward an intention. The boundary of the cast circle also functions as a protective filter from undesirable influences outside the circle, and a shelter for those within.

Metaphorically, the cast circle is likened to the womb of the Goddess. Sometimes the ritual circle is referred to as a "sacred space" or "circle of art," meaning that it is set apart from the normal constraints of time and place, a space of potentiality that is created to be filled. I prefer using the words "ritual space" or "working space" to "sacred space," because the Goddess is everywhere, and thus all space is Her creation and, therefore, sacred. To perceive and experience "mundane" reality as sacred is a challenge and an aspiration for most spiritual seekers.

In the majority of Wiccan traditions, the circle is cast from within. It is understood, envisioned, and constructed as a semi-permeable membrane, allowing desired and compatible energies in and keeping undesirable energies out. References to the use of the ritual circle by witches, working with elemental spirits of earth, air, fire, and water, date back to 1608.[90] Different traditions cast their circles in different ways, and you may have already experienced some of them.

Conversely, the magical circle of the medieval ceremonial magician was cast from the *outside*, to protect the magician from the beings he or she summoned into the circle. The spirits or deities were commanded *into* the circle to do the magician's will. The attitude, language, and posturing of the magician reflects a very different intention from how most contemporary witches approach their power relationship with the universe. Commanding or ordering spirits is a form of patriarchal magic, which seeks to gain or assume power over entities, spirits, or deities. Witches and goddess worshippers, on the other hand, know themselves to be part of Her universal creation, which includes all beings, seen and unseen, and therefore they wish to invoke elements of Her creation to join them in the circle, rather than keeping themselves separated from them.

Dianic Casting For Group Ritual in the Early Years

I was originally taught to cast the circle at the same time invocations

[90] This example was drawn by Francesco Guazzo, an Italian Ambrosian monk who came to be regarded as an authority on Witchcraft. He wrote *Compendium Malecarum*. From the introduction of *The Witches' Craft* by Raven Grimassi (Llewellyn Publications, 2002). Invoking the elemental powers is different than invoking elemental beings associated with the elements. Traditionally, these elemental beings are gnomes (earth), salamanders (fire), sylphs (air), and undines (water). Although these beings can be invoked for a magical working, in most instances women need to choose to invoke elements and elemental energy rather than elemental beings. These beings live in their own realms with their own rules and demand attention in the same way that a human being might. You cannot just invoke them and leave them to their own devices during the ritual. They will find it rude, and unexpected consequences may result.

were addressed to the elemental powers.[91] I believe that this form of circle casting evolved in Zsuzsanna Budapest's early Dianic circles, which were often quite large and comprised mostly of women without any formal Craft training. Participants largely did not know how to energetically support the construction of the ritual container and many had no real experience of what to expect. Large, open seasonal and lunar rituals for mostly untrained women presented a different set of energetic problems and considerations in contrast to traditional Craft denominations where rituals were usually practiced in closed covens of thirteen or fewer, and where members were trained by coven elders with experience who did most of the ritual work.

The early Dianic form of circle casting involved raising energy, then casting the circle in conjunction with invoking one quarter of the circle at a time, until the circle was closed. When I originally learned to cast this way, it was the same facilitator who both cast and paused at each cardinal direction to invoke. When the casting responsibility was shared by four women, each spoke her invocation and cast her section of the circle, walking as she cast, and then delivered the sword or athame to her waiting circle sister, who greeted her with a welcoming kiss. In my first coven, Moon Birch Grove, and later in my larger community, Circle of Aradia, we used this form of casting for many years.

This form of casting gave participants, often a group of fifty to two hundred women, something to see and do instead of waiting in boredom for the large circle to be cast around them. Rather than let the energy dissipate, by casting the circle in tandem with invocations and lots of energetic support through sounding, women tended to stay engaged and in a heightened state of anticipation.

I mention this early method of Dianic circle casting to honor our herstory, although I no longer practice or teach this form of casting. I

---

[91] McFarland Dianics (from the Texas-based tradition created by Morgan McFarland) invoke the powers at the four directions entirely before casting the circle. This form invites the guests in and builds the container around them once they arrive.

found this method to not be magically sound. It simply is not as effective as casting the circle entirely first before inviting the elemental powers and the Goddess to enter. The following description is a useful guide to understanding the concept of circle casting as we currently teach it, in groves of Temple of Diana, Inc.

The Cast Circle

The cast circle functions as a boundary in much the same way that our personal boundaries function. As women living in a patriarchal culture, with violence against us a daily occurrence, we put up personal boundaries every time we walk down the street, choose what to wear or not to wear, or whether to meet or avoid a gaze. Although we put up boundaries constantly, most of us would be at a loss to explain how we do it. Imagine that you are coming out of a restaurant and walking across the parking lot to your car. It's after dark, and your car is on the far side of a crowded lot. How do you protect yourself energetically? Do you puff yourself up or make yourself invisible? Do you communicate a don't-mess-with-me attitude with your body? Remember other times when you were aware of putting up a boundary and how you felt. Was it not made by a conscious decision that you created by willing it to be so? When we consciously put up a boundary, we feel more protected, more solid around that which is most vulnerable within us.

Similar to the creation of your personal boundary, it is your will and energetic skill that build and maintain the energetic boundary of the ritual circle; therefore, it is important to have a sense of how to build, project, and maintain the energy necessary to put up and sustain the cast circle.

Casting a circle is the creation and projection of an energy field in the shape of a three-dimensional sphere.[92] The equator line is located where the sphere touches the ground upon which you stand or sit. The

---

[92] Farrar, *The Witches Bible*, Vol. 2, 83.

top half of the sphere is above the ground; the bottom half is below the ground. The top of the sphere is as far above you as it is below your feet. This projection is an energetic field that is consciously constructed in the physical location of the ritual space.

The casting of the circle follows deosil, the direction of the sun cycle, the direction of manifestation. This practice originates with ancient Celtic religious practice where following the motion of "right hand-wise" was considered in harmony with the movement of the sun.[93] We teach casting the circle beginning at the northeast point of the circle and moving respectively to the east, south, west, north, and back to the northeast again to close and seal the circle. After the circle is entirely cast and sealed, invocations are offered in the east (air), south (fire), west (water), and north (earth) quarter points. Lastly, the Goddess (at the center point of the sphere) is invoked into the circle.

Envision a peeled orange divided into four equal sections and pierced through the center by a soda straw. As the circle is cast, the orange is reassembled, segment by segment. Each orange section corresponds to one of the four quarters to be invoked. The outer wall of the circle is built by putting the peel back on the orange, section by section, pulling a semicircular arc of energy around you from one quarter to the next until you are fully enclosed. Some women can see the sphere and it is also possible to feel the boundary by placing a hand against the "wall" of the circle and sensing the heat and gentle resistance against your hand if you push gently on it.

The following practices may help you to better understand what is involved in casting a ritual circle. Practice these exercises often prior to ritual, as they will support you in feeling comfortable with the concept of the sphere and help to sensitize you to projecting and maintaining energy. These practices will prepare you for using the athame (or sword) to cast.

---

93 Spence, *The Magic Arts in Celtic Britain*, 35.

Practice #1

Put your hands in front of you and begin to rub them together very briskly. After about 20–30 seconds, they will feel hot and charged with energy. Construct a small sphere of energy within the curve of your cupped hands. Open your hands to support the sphere in front of you. Really look at it or sense it. Note its weight, or lack of it. Note its color, or lack of it. Can you see into it? Can you see through it? Get a clear sense or feel of the three-dimensional spherical form. When you have examined it thoroughly, cup it again with your hands, bring your cupped hands up to your mouth, and breathe it back into yourself.

Practice #2

Do this practice with a partner. Sit across from your partner and decide who will begin first. Partner A creates an energy band by briskly rubbing her hands together and then slowly expanding her hands until they are as far apart as the length of a loaf of bread. With eyes closed, she focuses on maintaining the energy band between her hands as Partner B, with deliberate intention, cuts through the energy band using the side of her hand or a finger like a swift knife. After Partner B has passed through five or six times, Partner A then brings her hands back together slowly, and the partners switch. Wait to share and compare experiences until both of you have finished the practice.

The purpose of this practice is to become sensitive to subtleties, changes, and disruptions of energy. Women usually experience disruptions in the energy band as temperature shifts, tingling, or feeling that the energy has "dropped out." You may also feel no change at all. There is no right or wrong experience. Just be curious.

Practice #3

This practice builds on the previous two and is best experienced in an enclosed room about ten feet by twelve feet. Stand in the center of the room and determine where the cardinal directions are. Face the northeast point and put your hands together in front of you. Begin to rub them together very briskly until they feel hot and charged. Construct a small sphere of energy within the curve of your cupped hands. Open your hands to support the sphere in front of you. Bring the energy ball up to your face. What does it look like? Smell it. Does it have a scent? Does it have sound? Bring it up to your lips and suck some of the juice. Then put it in your mouth and roll it around on your tongue. Swallow it.

Feel the energy permeating your being, flowing out of your center, down your legs, and out your arms, beyond your fingertips. Take a deep breath and fill the room with a long "ahhhh" or a tone from deep within you. Feel your sound permeate the room and touch the four walls.

Point your fingers toward the wall at the northeast point and send the energy out of your fingertips to the wall. Begin to turn deosil, touching all four walls of the room, marking the walls with your energy until you have come full circle back to the northeast point. Remember to scribe an arc across the ceiling that extends above your head and another arc that extends below your feet. When you are finished, you should be standing in a sphere of energy that is slowly spinning in a clockwise direction.

Spend some time inside the sphere. You may choose to sit in stillness and silence. You may choose to walk or dance within its boundaries. What does it feel like inside there? Warm? Cold? Tingly? Breezy? Still? Are there colors? Sounds? Voices? Are you alone? If not, who is there and why? When you have spent as much time as you wish within the sphere, go to the center and take a deep breath. Your eyes may be closed or open with soft focus. Begin to breathe in the energy of the room, starting at the northeast point and turning counterclockwise. Breathe the energy back into your fingertips and into your center.

Give thanks to the elemental teachers for what you learned, releasing your thanks with your breath back to the universe.

Energy Projection with an Athame or Sword

Only the tools of fire, the athame or sword, can cut, cauterize, and seal the circle away from mundane time and space. Toy wooden swords and plastic athames are not tools of fire, and ought not be used by the serious practitioner. Experiment before you make a decision for or against using an athame for any of the circle-casting methods. Using an athame is well worth the effort once practiced.

Practice:

Stand in a relaxed manner with your feet on the floor, and hold your athame in your strongest hand or with both hands if you are using a sword. With open, soft, or closed eyes, breathe into your belly until you are relaxed. Without lifting your tool, draw energy into your body. Draw up from the earth through the balls of your feet and down from the sky through the top of your head. Run the energy traveling through your body down your arm, into your tool, and out the end. Be aware of how the path of energy moves through your body, out your hand, and through the tool. If you are using a heavy sword, it may be necessary for you to use two hands. In this case, you must learn to run energy down both arms, through your hands, and into the tool.

Now, repeat this exercise with open, closed, or soft eyes, and extend your arm, pointing the tip of the tool toward a point in the room. Use your intention, your focused will, to run the energy you have gathered through your body, out your hand, and through the tool to the focus point. Inhale and bring the energy in; exhale and run it out through the tool. Repeat. Practice this until you can feel the energy moving out the tip of the tool. I always hold my athame so that my index finger is extended over the top center of the blade toward the tip of the blade. It is easier for me to send energy from the end of my index finger into a tool.

Casting the Circle: Solitary Ritual

If you are casting a circle for solitary work, do the Centering Practice #1 in chapter 6 which, when done properly, will even out your personal energy field. Once centered, scribe the boundary of your ritual area with your athame, beginning in the northeast and moving deosil to complete the circle, projecting energy to create a surrounding sphere. After you have cast the circle and sealed it, begin your invocations at the east quarter and proceed deosil to the other quarter points of the circle, offering invocations to the other elements (invocation is discussed in detail in chapter 8). Then invoke the Goddess at the center.

Casting the Circle: Group Ritual

> *"… there are these moments of intimacy where the universe is felt through our veins, and to experience that, even occasionally, might be worth everything. To do what we might be destined to do, to co-create and do that in healing, pleasurable ways, is to align with something beyond, but not excluding, ourselves."*[94]

In creating ritual space, purification sets the energetic tone and begins to build a light container; the "MA" chant generates the energy that will be used by the caster to cut the ritual circle (the temporary Temple space), away from time and place. The membrane of the cast circle is built by projecting energy through her athame or sword from *inside* the circle.

Unlike purification of the space, which begins in the north, the casting of the circle, as we teach it, begins in the northeast. The northeast is the point of manifestation (where earth and air meet, life begins) and it is with the casting of the circle that the group ritual formally begins.

In the narrative example that follows, I describe casting and sealing the

---

[94] Excerpt from, Reflections on the Theology of Simone Weil by LaChelle Schilling, February 19, 2018. https://feminismandreligion.com/2018/02/19/reflections-on-the-theology-of-simone-weil-by-lachelle-schilling/

circle from the *outside* of the circle of participants. Depending on where the ritual is taking place, indoors or outside, and security issues, she may either seal herself *inside* the ritual circle or she may seal it from the outside and remain outside of the cast circle for the ritual's duration. She is the one who will cut participants in or out of the circle in event of an emergency and someone needing to leave. This woman also serves the ritual as a "gatekeeper" (see Chapter 13).[95]

> *The circle of* women have raised sufficient energy by chanting, drumming, moving, or sounding with the "MA" chant to raise the vibration within their bodies and the ritual space. The ritual facilitator designated to determine when sufficient energy is raised to begin the circle casting drops the pitch that has been raised into a low continuous hum, signaling the group to transition. The facilitator casting the circle now begins her work.
>
> In the northeast point of the circle, the casting woman points her athame to the ground outside of the circle of women. She pulls a thread of energy from the power raised in the center of the circle, above and below, and runs the current through her own body and down the length of her athame. As she fixes her gaze on the point where she will mark the start of the casting process, she raises her athame, projects energy through it, and starts the process of cutting the circle of women away from ordinary time and space as she walks deosil to create the circle. The leading edge of the blade cuts the boundary of the circle as the following edge cauterizes and seals

---

[95] To expand the facilitation experience with others, you will need one woman to cast, four women to invoke the elemental powers, and one woman to call the Goddess.

it. The casting woman walks slowly, cutting and sealing until she has ended back where she began. Pointing the tip of her athame to the ground, sealing the sphere, she speaks the words, "The circle is cast, we are between the worlds, and the Goddess blesses her women! Blessed be!" Once the circle is cast, the women are enclosed in an energetic container that sets them apart from everyday perception and envelops them in the magical, timeless realm of ritual space. The Temple of the cast circle has been created.

Creating the Grove: Energetic Support for Circle Casting

The following method of circle casting is best for a group that has practiced together over time. Facilitators and participants may contribute energetic support besides continuing the humming during the casting and invoking, by assisting in the creation of the walls of the circle as it is cast. This results in a more stable and strong container to work in.

First, the group must be centered as a tree (review Centering Practice #2 in chapter 6). Envision the World Tree, who is the Goddess in Her aspect as the Tree of Life, at the very center of the circle. See/feel Her trunk and roots extending deep underneath the surface below you. See/feel Her crown extending high above you, Her branches spreading a canopy of leaves, encircling the circle of women.

As the facilitator moves around the circle, casting with her athame or sword, she will pass behind each woman in the circle. At the moment the woman with the athame passes behind her, each woman draws energy from above and shoots it down to the lower root axis of the World Tree, sinking her own tree roots into the ground in a semi-circular arc, attaching them at the base of the World Tree. She sends her roots to seek those of her other sisters, who are reaching with their own roots, and together they entwine to weave a root web of support for the bottom of the sphere. Almost simultaneously, the woman draws energy from below and shoots it up to the crown axis of the World Tree, reaching with her own crown branches emerging from the top of her head in a semicircular arc and interweaving them with the canopy the World Tree. She lets her crown branches entwine with her sisters who are also reaching with their own branches, and together they weave a canopy top of the sphere. This energetic support by the participants creates an energetic weft and warp weaving, making it very easy for the woman casting to cut the sphere away from mundane time and space.

Once the circle is cast, the participants do not have to remain in place nor maintain what has been built. Maintaining the cast circle for the ritual's duration is the job of the ritual facilitators serving in a guardian capacity. Instructions on deconstructing of the grove is included in Step 12.

7. Invoke the Elemental Powers

After the circle is cast, all present turn to the east to open themselves to the spirit of air. (Those residing in the southern hemisphere will of course adjust directions/elements accordingly.) The woman who invokes stands just outside the circle of women, in "living chalice" posture with her feet apart, at approximately shoulder width, to form the base of the chalice, and her arms raised, her hands slightly cupped to form the bowl of the chalice. This posture also represents the World Tree, which connects the heavens with the underworld in the phrase "As above, so below." The upraised arms are the crown of the tree, the trunk is formed from the navel up, and the pelvis, legs, and feet represent the tree's base and roots.

> The facilitator who invokes stands just outside the circle of women facing the east cardinal point. With her arms upraised, she opens herself to be filled with the precise imagery, feelings, sounds, and the specific qualities

> desired of air. Embodying the ritual's intention, she takes a deep breath and sends her invocation to the spirit of air, making her request that the guardian of the element open the portal door between the world of spirit and the world of manifestation, the container of the cast circle. She immediately follows her invocation with an invoking pentacle, scribed in the membrane of the cast circle, to provide an entry portal for the invited elemental teachers.

Invocations continue with the spirit of fire at the south point of the circle, the spirit of water in the west, and the spirit of earth in the north, with circle participants turning in place to face the directions as the elements are invited to the circle. After the invocations are complete, the facilitator invoking the Goddess steps to the center of the circle, and with open arms raised, invites Her to bless the ritual's intention.

When you invoke you are creating a portal between the worlds. The properly cast ritual circle is a place between the worlds, a parallel universe in which to work and access other realms. When you cast a circle, you are selecting from all possibilities those specific qualities from which to manifest your goals or the intention of the ritual. Creating this alternative space requires the invocation of earth, water, fire, and air in order to bring these forces into this temporary plane of existence. These elemental forces are the ones that we as humans can recognize, use, and know. Therefore, the pentacle, which symbolizes the elements combined with spirit, works as a metaphor for the universe we are creating, manipulating, and selecting from.

Many Wiccan traditions mark the four directions by scribing a pentacle in the air immediately following an elemental invocation. The scribing of a pentacle provides the elemental powers that are invoked with a "door" into the space of the circle through which they may enter and exit.

The pentacle is an ancient symbol for the door or portal that contains all the elements. The aesthetic of its practiced use awakens the forces within us, affirms the interconnectedness of life, and triggers layers of psychological meaning.

In the Dianic tradition, when invoking the elements during ritual, an earth pentacle is drawn at each quarter immediately following each elemental quarter invocation. When you draw these earth pentacles, you do so with the understanding that you are creating a doorway only on your side of the veil (the physical or earth plane) into the ritual circle, a place cut away from time and space. You still must qualify which aspects of each elemental power you are requesting.

To draw an earth pentacle, use your hand, or preferably your athame, and begin at the spirit point at the top of the star and scribe down to the bottom left point of earth. The drawing of the pentacle continues in a fluid motion up and diagonally to the right point of air, then straight left across to water, and down diagonally to the right to fire, and back up to the left to spirit at the top. Then, in a continuous motion, draw a circle from the spirit point, moving clockwise to connect all five points of the star until the circle is completed. Continue the gesture by pointing your hand or atheme directly from this top point of the star to the ground. This concludes the invitation to the elemental spirit in the other realm to enter into this plane of existence: spirit realm to earth plane.

Some Dianic witches use the Gardnerian practice of scribing a different elemental pentacle at each of the four directions. There are four elemental pentacles, each drawn differently by starting the scribing from their representative point of the pentacle until the star is formed. If you choose to do this, you will still need to qualify in your spoken invocation those qualities of the element you are choosing to invite into the circle. The following is a portion of an invocation to air showing how the scribing of the pentacle is done in conjunction with an invocation.

She who invokes sends her invocation on her breath to the spirit of air, asking for blessings on the ritual's purpose.
"We invoke thee, power of the east, spirit of air,
You who lift us to higher awareness,
You who clear our minds of confusion.
Bless us with focus on our spiritual paths.
Grant us clarity in our continuing journey
toward knowledge.
We call you from our hearts to be with us now."

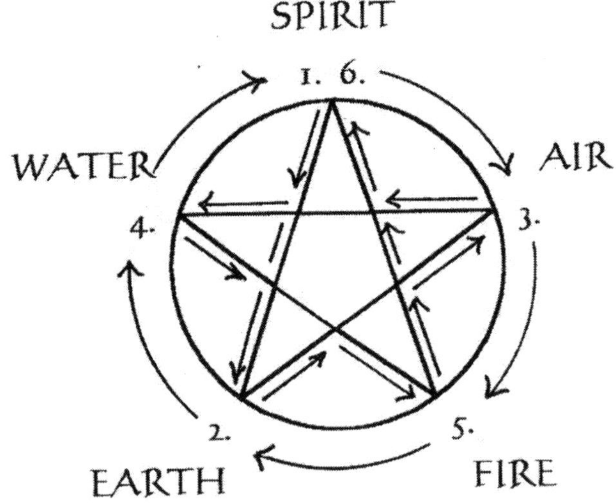

Invoking Earth Pentacle

With her athame in her hand, she inscribes an invoking pentacle into the air in front of her, opening the portal door in the physical realm of the ritual circle. In a continuous motion from completing the deosil encircling of the star, she guides the tip of the blade from the point of spirit, down the middle of the pentacle, and ends with the athame pointing to the ground. The pathway from the other realm to the ritual circle is made.

She concludes immediately with "Blessed be!"

...

Many women's circles and individual ritualists do not scribe pentacles in conjunction with the invocation and valediction. This may be due to their tradition's practice, lack of training, or personal preference. As mentioned before, it is important that you understand and make a conscious decision whether to do a given ritual action or not and why the choice is made. In order to become fluid with the precision and power of the use of pentacles in invocations, practice scribing invoking and revoking pentacles hundreds of times.

Here are some things to remember: It is very important that the energy that has been raised for the circle casting be maintained. This is easily accomplished by maintaining a gentle humming sound at a low but consistent tone to energetically support the woman who is speaking the invocation. In fact, throughout the ritual, use the sound vibration of the group hum to support the energy anytime it begins to lag. The humming is not just a background noise: it is the practice of maintaining energy through sound. It is the buzzing sound of the sacred hive, and it is the job of the facilitators as "melissaes"[96] to maintain the hum. There are many times in ritual where silence is important, but when you are working with energy to keep things charged or to raise power, conscious sounding is very effective. If women feel tired, humming helps to raise the energy level in their bodies and helps to sustain them through the ritual.

---

[96] Melissae, which translates as 'the bees' were priestesses in ancient Greece, and served in the temples of several goddesses. The Goddess as the Great Mother was sometimes titled Melissa, literally, 'the Queen Bee.'

A word about invocation: In many Wiccan and contemporary goddess traditions, the attitude, language, and style of approaching the invisible forces is that of an ally, not of a master. The elemental powers are invited, never commanded, to attend the rite; as Riane Eisler notes, "control and influence are not the same." The cast circle is a space that is shared with the forces that are called in order to honor and align with them, and to ask them to bear witness, for protection, or for blessings and aid. We are a part of them, and they are a part of us. The forces invoked are respected allies. The invitation to the elemental powers may be offered by spoken words, song, movement, gesture, percussion, or other sounds developed from understanding the energetics of the element.

The language of the invocation, whether spoken, sung, danced, or played, should reflect the purpose of the ritual in the choice of metaphors, images, and requests for aid. The question to ask when preparing an invocation is "What attributes or aspects of the element can support the ritual's purpose?" Since every ritual is unique, generic invocations to the directions cannot possibly address the specifics of your ritual. Standardized invocations are used in some traditions throughout the year with the understanding that the continuing repetition of the words gives them power over time. Standard invocations might be used as a baseline format for seasonal rituals and might contain consistent references for the ritual theme, but even here, it is preferable that invocations should be tailor-made for the specific work chosen. Refer to chapter 8 for more on invocation.

8. Invoke the Goddess

After the invocations to the elemental powers, the Goddess or goddesses are invoked at the center of the circle. She is called forth from within the women in the circle. She births the women, and the women birth Her into the womb of the cast circle. The Goddess is embodied by the woman who invokes Her.

An in-depth discussion about invoking the Goddess can be found in chapter 8, "The Art of Invocation."

9. State the Ritual's Purpose at the Center

The purpose of the ritual is usually incorporated into the Goddess invocation that is spoken at center, including which attributes She brings that align with your purpose. After the invocation, the ritual's purpose can be spoken again, but oriented to the participants this time, not to the Goddess. Now, the core ritual work can be shared with more detail and may include some of the logistics to expect. Stating the purpose aloud is essential in order to focus and join the group together for your work. Even if everyone already knows why they have gathered, it is still important to verbally state the purpose within the context of the ritual itself. The minds of the women will receive the purpose on a deeper level.

10. Do the Core Ritual Work: The Enactments

After the invocation to the Goddess and the ritual's purpose is stated, it is time to participate in the core work of the ritual, as discussed in chapter 4. Remember that a ritual is a creative, living thing. It is an experience in the process of becoming. Allow for spontaneity, inspiration, improvisation, and occasional chaos.

When you are facilitating a group ritual, the facilitation skills you need vary depending on the type of ritual you are creating. To use theatrical terms, if you are the sole facilitator for a group, you may have to act as stage manager, director, and performer simultaneously. Over time, and through repeated practice in ritual facilitation, you will gradually be able to take on increasing degrees of responsibility for the outcome of the ritual. Though it is not always possible, it is wise to practice these skills before the ritual, rather than experiencing them for the first time during the ritual, so that any unexpected problems can be addressed.

As a facilitator, you must never lose sight of the fact that a ritual is an experience co-created by both participants and facilitators. When women choose to speak, have the courage to be vulnerable to their words. When women choose to move, have the courage to truly witness and participate in their expression. In choosing women to assist in facilitating a ritual, consider their skills and abilities before assigning their tasks. In addition, the enactments must be consistent with the ritual purpose and theme. Years ago, I attended a large group ritual where a woman who obviously had no understanding of energetics was put in charge of leading group dancing. While a huge Lammas bonfire burned wildly in the night to drums and a flute, she insisted on leading a group of 200 people in a dance that had the pace and motion of a funeral procession. Not only was her dance choice terribly inconsistent with the theme of celebrating the First Harvest, but she seemed unwilling to join in with the festive energy of the participants. Her lack of flexibility and courage to move with the spontaneous energetics of the ritual aborted a wonderful opportunity for free-form dancing or a group dance that was more appropriate to the ritual's purpose. (For more information about ritual facilitation, please refer to chapter 10.)

The Cone of Power

The women have just spoken aloud their desires and lit their candles for their wishes. I am about to facilitate the building and release of energy toward the manifestation of those wishes. The higher the energy is raised, the deeper women must be centered and rooted. Together, we spiral the energy deosil and build it up into the spiral shape of a cone. Energy spins round and round the circle of women and spirals upward and tighter,

> upward, tighter, to a pinnacle of intensity. The air is charged with life force and electricity. I can feel it in my body and within the ritual space. We sharpen the point of the cone into a laser beam, and with a great shout we release our focused energy and will toward our goal.

• • •

Raising a cone of power is essential to the practice of spellcraft if a spell is to be part of the core ritual enactments. Raising the cone may take the form of ecstatic dancing, chanting, and drumming, sounds and movement that pulse and vibrate the body. It is best to have a designated ritual facilitator or ritual priestess who has experience or is adept at being able to sense when the energy has peaked to call the release. The release is like a group orgasm. Like the flight of an arrow on release of the bowstring, a rush of energy enveloping your entire being lifts off from your body, leaving you relaxed and fulfilled.

Learning the art of magical release takes lots of committed practice. With enough practice, patience, and a willingness to make mistakes and evaluate herself honestly, the ritual facilitator can develop a sense of when the energy has built to its peak and release it just moments prior to when she anticipates the energy will begin to drop. Remember that what goes up, must come down. Eventually women will begin to tire, but don't let the energy drop before the group releases the energy that has been raised. To get women who are dancing wildly to release their energy simultaneously is often challenging. Within a group ritual where there is ecstatic dancing and drumming, high energy can sustain itself for a long time, building itself higher and higher with the potential for "mini-peaks" before the final pinnacle is reached. This energy build-up is analogous to an orgasm, which builds, plateaus, builds again, and peaks. It is important to let the energy beat and pulse naturally, even if it feels chaotic and you have a fear of not being in control of the group.

If you are fortunate enough to have good ritual drummers[97], a designated ritual facilitator should observe the pace of the group and signal the drummers to adjust their pace accordingly. She can signal when it is nearly time for the release so that in a matter of seconds, the drummers can crescendo and halt their drumming with one final beat, thereby indicating the end of the dancing and the release. If you don't have the support of drummers, you can begin to hum or chant "MA," gathering more and more women into the beehive sound, gradually raising the tones higher and higher. Once women catch on that something different is happening, it is easy to grab hands, connect, and, using your voices, raise the roof and let the sound and energy go. If there is no one able or willing to call the release, the peak can be sensed by the entire group as one body (with lots of practice), and the energy can be then released by the intuitive group mind.

In the Dianic tradition, we affirm our magical will immediately after we release the energy toward the spells. We chant aloud together, "By all the power of three times three, as we will it, so shall it be! As we will it, so shall it be! As we will it, so shall it be!" With each repetition of the last phrase, the chant gets louder and louder. It is very powerful to hear a chorus of women shouting out this phrase in focus, strength, and mutual support.

Be sure to completely release the energy accumulated in your body toward the spell. Allow time for the release to be complete. Don't rush it. Feel it through, see it through, and move it through until the energy has been completely released and dispersed. Give it your all when the facilitating priestess says "Now!" If you are the facilitator, encourage a full release of energy to the spell. If a full release is not achieved individually, remind women to continue releasing the accumulated energy toward the group effort.

---

[97] Ritual drumming requires an understanding of how percussion can support the ritual flow, energy raising and release. Ritual drumming is about service to the ritual, and not about jamming for fun or as a performance.

Many women "ground" any perceived "excess" energy after releasing energy toward a goal without analyzing what this really does. I propose that this practice actually reinforces women holding back a complete release. Holding back in our lives is a way that we self-sabotage. Holding back a complete release in our spellwork sabotages the spell. Grounding is taught as an antidote for women who describe feelings of agitation, inability to sleep, and general crankiness after doing a ritual. If women experience this feeling after a ritual, further release toward the goal is needed instead of grounding to get rid of the energy. Rather than draining the excess energy back into the earth, complete the release by focusing it on the spell goal for which it was intended. Use your breath to exhale and allow any remaining energy to fully release toward the goal. Let's not reinforce women holding back life force in our rituals.

If a woman can be compared to a chalice, and the water contained within it is the energy that she has raised to be released, what is left if the water in that chalice is tossed into the air? An empty chalice ready to be filled again. Make more magic.

When the core ritual work has been completed and the energy released, ask women to take hands and reconnect. Breathe. The transition between releasing a cone of power and its communion afterwards allows the spin of the cast circle to slow to a place of pause, which will be necessary before opening up the circle widdershins. Some women enjoy taking a few moments after the release to express gratitude to the Earth, the Goddess, and for the beauty and pleasure of the moment. After the cone has been released completely, allow a minute or two for the group to relax, look around at each other, and appreciate community. Just as in sexual release, most women relax into a sense of communion with their deep selves and, hopefully, their sisters. Allow a few moments for this communion between the women and the Goddess before moving on. Sometimes women will break into giggles and laughter. Encourage women to connect with their hands and simply breathe together. Dare to pause in the moment and simply be.

If you have not raised and released a cone of power, taking a short pause when the ritual work is complete serves this purpose also. Begin a low hum to help the women realign with each other without raising power.

With the core enactments complete, the ritual comes to a close with libation(s).

11. Give Thanks: Libation

A libation is akin to a ritual "toast" that is solely about gratitude. Traditionally, the chalice is used to give a libation to the Goddess with thanks for her presence in the rite. Lift the chalice, express your gratitude, dip your fingers into the chalice, and gently sprinkle or spill a few drops on the earth before you sip. After the Goddess has been given a libation, give thanks to anyone or anything else you wish. If you are facilitating a large ritual, it is best for one woman to give the libation on behalf of the circle.

If you are having a small group ritual, pass the chalice around the circle so that others have the opportunity to give appreciation. Libations can provide many moving and sweet moments. Remember, libation is a time for giving thanks, *not* for making more requests.

If a circle has not been cast, make concluding remarks after thanks have been given so that the ritual is formally ended in the minds of the participants.

12. Valedictions to the Goddess and Elemental Powers; Take Down the Circle

> With libations given, participants once again reconnect with their hands in circle, humming and swaying gently. She who invoked the Goddess steps into the center of the circle. She breathes deeply and raises her arms,

> opening her heart and soul in gratitude to the Goddess for Her presence. Bidding Her a loving farewell, she and the women in the circle respond in with, "Blessed be!" Valedictions follow, moving widdershins, beginning with the spirit of earth at the north point of the circle, the spirit of water in the west, the spirit of fire in the south, and the spirit of air in the east. Circle participants with raised arms, turn in place to face the directions as the elements are thanked for their presence.

Now is the time to thank your honored guests, the Goddess and the elements, and escort them to their respective doors. This is the formal closing of the ritual before the sphere is taken down. Begin with the Goddess at the center point. (For more information about the valediction of the Goddess, please refer to chapter 8, "The Art of Invocation."). Valedictions (thanks and farewell) to the elemental powers are made next, moving widdershins, starting with the valediction to earth and moving from north, to west, to south, to east.

If you are doing a solitary ritual within a cast circle and your core ritual work is complete, taking the circle down follows the same process as for a group ritual. Give your thanks to the Goddess at the center, begin your valedictions to the elemental powers, and then take down your circle.

Scribing Pentacles: Valediction

When the core ritual work is completed, libations are first given to the Goddess at the center. This is followed by libations to the powers called at the quarters, beginning in the north and moving counterclockwise around the circle to west, south, and concluding in the east. Be a good host who escorts her special guests to the door, waves them through, and closes it gently, but firmly, behind them. Follow each quarter valediction immediately with a revoking pentacle. This is an earth pentacle reversed, scribed into the air beginning at the earth point at the bottom left of the pentacle, moving diagonally up and to the right to the spirit point at the top. Continue this line from the spirit point diagonally right down to the fire point, then diagonally left up to the water point, straight across to the right to air, and back down to the left to earth. From the earth point, the circle surrounding the star is completed widdershins. Then lift the athame straight up through the middle of the pentacle, back to spirit. Reversing the pentacle is closing the door between the earth plane of the circle and the realm of the elemental powers. The facilitator (or facilitators) who invoked usually does the valedictions.

The following valediction of earth demonstrates the scribing of the reversed pentacle in conjunction with a valediction.

> *She who bids* farewell gives thanks, and all bid a loving farewell to the powers of earth.
> "Power of the north, spirit of earth,
> You strengthened and nurtured us on our spiritual path,
> Drawing us ever closer to you.
> We thank you for your sustaining beauty that nourishes our spirits as we journey toward knowledge.
> We bless you, as you have blessed us, and we thank you from our hearts for being with us. Hail and farewell!"
>
> Immediately with her athame, she scribes a revoking earth pentacle in the air before her, closing the door of the physical realm behind the honored elemental guest. She concludes immediately with "Blessed be!" The

> women in circle respond in unison, "Blessed be!" All turn to the west for the next valediction to begin...

...

Take time with your valedictions. If you want the elemental powers to take you seriously, you must, in turn, take them seriously. You are not just reciting pretty poetry into the air. Although valedictions are often shorter in length than invocations, remain connected and speak from your heart. Maintain the same kind of intensity and focus as you did when putting up the circle. As you say a respectful farewell to the powers that were called, allow the energy in your body to wind down. Restore the space energetically to what it was before the ritual began. Returning to regular consciousness is critical, otherwise a part of your psychic energy continues to flow out in search of an energetic form that no longer exists. This can be exhausting and depleting to your physical health.

Taking Down the Circle

> The valedictions are complete, and participants in the circle connect their hands together again to lend their energy in taking down the circle, with a gentle hum. The casting facilitator with the athame or sword has been waiting in the northeast, prepared to open the circle once valedictions have been made. The casting woman pierces the boundary of the sphere with her athame, and extends her blade while walking the circle's perimeter widdershins, until she has come full circle back to the northeast, opening what was sealed. She lowers her athame and declares, "The circle is open, but never broken, and the Goddess blesses her women!" The taking down or opening of the circle is complete.

***

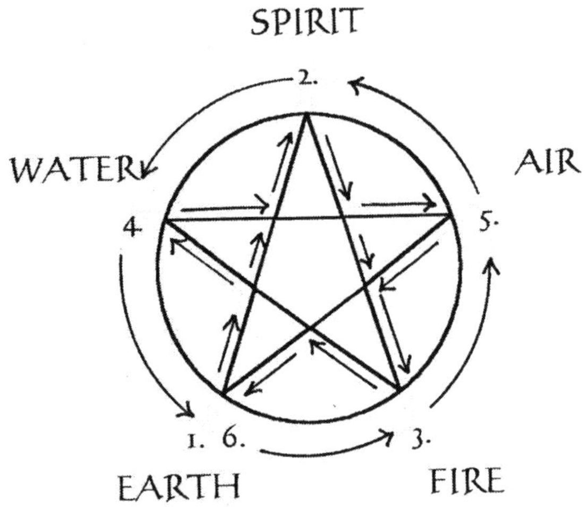

Revoking Earth Pentacle

Deconstruction of the Grove

If you have constructed the circle in the grove or World Tree form previously described, take it down using the following method. As the facilitator with the athame moves widdershins around the circle, taking it down, she will either pass in front of or behind each woman, depending on whether the women are turning to face each quarter or remaining facing the center during the valedictions. At the moment the casting facilitator passes by, each woman will retract her top branches from the crown axis of the World Tree and from the webbing at the top of the circle with her circle sisters. Almost simultaneously, she will retract her branches from side to side from around the circle's perimeter and from the other tree sister's branches on the sides of the circle. Lastly, she will retract her roots from below her, detaching from the lower root axis of the World Tree and from the root webbing with her sisters at that point. Gather this energy of the retracted tree at your heart. Exhale and relax.

Women remain in place until the casting facilitator has completed taking the circle down and announces the circle open.

Take some moments to reflect on your experience and to become fully present before socializing.

13. Eat Something and Clean Up

Ritual makes for hungry women! Consider having a potluck feast afterward. In the Dianic tradition, before eating or drinking anything ourselves, we nourish our sisters. Offer food to a sister, saying "May you never hunger," and offer drink, saying "May you never thirst." Depending on the ritual theme, there may be particular festive foods that are shared. I strongly suggest eating healthy, nutritious food before hitting the desserts. Choosing to have everyone bring vegetarian food allows all women to partake in the feast.

Practice

Choose a ritual that you have developed through your work with this book. Review the activities and ritual flow both visually and energetically. Notice how the physical sensations in your body change while you imagine the scenes as the ritual moves along. This sensation is the shifting of energetics within the ritual as they are anticipated in advance.

Driving a mountain road feels much easier after having driven it once. In a smaller way, going over the ritual journey visually and kinesthetically beforehand has enabled me to find the possible potholes in the ritual road, anticipate curves, and make necessary changes. I must have the feel of the ritual's pace to anticipate what might be needed. A sister priestess once shared that she looks at the ritual flow to see if it makes organic sense. If she has to struggle to remember the next activity, the activity may be inappropriate or out of place, like hitting a wall or blind curve. Explore the ways that you best internalize, perceive, or understand a ritual's flow.

Practice

With each ritual you are working with, address these questions:

* What kind of container energetically and structurally will best support your ritual?
* How will your ritual formally begin and conclude?

chapter 8

THE ART OF INVOCATION

Lady of Moving Form, Seen and Unseen,
Enter, we ask of Thee, in colors three.
You who birth the living seed, universe, and melody,
Charge the center of the spark,
We who call You from the heart.
Lady of Moving Form, Seen and Unseen,
Enter, we ask of Thee, in colors three.
Keeper of the living Tree,
Queen of Love and Mystery,
Charge the center of the spark,
We who call You from the heart.[98]

Invocation is the magical act of inviting a deity or spirits into a specific time and place to witness, to grant a request (as in a petition), for protection, or to praise, thank, or honor Her or them. An invocation is spoken in the same way that one utters a prayer: it is a communication from the heart that is spoken with the need to be heard and responded to. Invocations and prayers differ in that prayer calls for the favor or blessing from a deity in a specific circumstance; invocation calls for the presence of the deity in some form and in a specific time and place.[99] The language of invocation and prayer may be similar if the intention is

---

[98] "Lady of Three" from the CD *The Year Is a Dancing Woman*, Vol. I, from the author (Dancing Tree Music, 2003).

[99] From the article "The Essence of Air" by Raymond T. Anderson, *Circle Network News*, Vol. 20, No. 4.

communion with a deity or when asking for guidance or aid. Invocation is often a prelude to some form of spellcraft or ritual enactment.

Always invite the Goddess and the elemental spirits with respect and love, never by commanding or demanding in tone, attitude, or words. Although there are magical and ritual traditions that order the gods and spirits around, it is offensive, disrespectful, and arrogant to even consider approaching deity in this manner. This latter approach to invocation is a patriarchal attempt at domination over nature and is akin to the act of summoning or conjuring a spirit or deity, commonly used by ceremonial magicians. It has no place in Dianic feminist rituals.

Not every ritual must include invocation. The need for invocation is determined by the ritual makers, based on the purpose and content of the ritual. As with the casting of the circle, invocation is an option, not an "always." Invocation is usually done somewhere near the beginning of a ritual. Sometimes the invocation of the elements or the Goddess includes a statement of the ritual purpose; however, only stating the purpose of the ritual is no substitute for an invocation. You can't just state the purpose and expect the elemental powers or the Goddess to show up automatically.

Building An Elemental Inventory

"The world is full of magic things, patiently waiting for our senses to grow sharper"[100]

Earth, water, fire, and air are the main ingredients of the great cosmic soup. It is through the gift of Spirit that the Goddess stirs the Great Cauldron, animating the elemental forces and blending them together into energetic forms. Energy, like an invisible yet tangible thread, swirls around and within, affecting and being affected by every living thing. Energy is the life force that animates us, moves us, heals us, and transforms

[100] William Butler Yeats

us. Energy manifests as color, light, and vibration: the frequencies of matter. We, and all other life forms, are created from the same material as the stars. What differentiates us from a butterfly, a rock, or a moving stream is how our "stuff" is distributed, in greater or lesser percentages.

When we invoke the four elements, we address the spirits of earth, water, fire, and air. We are addressing the elemental energy, which is the archetypal force or spirit within the physical form. The magical and ritual application of these energies is based on the purpose of the working or ritual and the quality of the elemental power best suited to the purpose.

In any ritual where the elemental powers are invoked, it is vital to identify the specific elemental aspect(s) that are aligned with the ritual's theme and purpose. Within each element there are a wide range of aspects. For example, in working with the element of air, do you wish to invoke hurricane-force winds or gentle spring breezes? Consider the range of aspects that may be called on from the various elemental powers and what gifts or blessings might be requested for the specific occasion. Because every element expresses itself in a range of dimensions there can be no generic invocations. Water can range in extremes from tear to tidal wave, and everything in between. What aspect(s) of the elemental power is needed for your ritual, invocation, or magical working?

Within your personal memories you have many paths that can lead you to a deepening relationship with each of the elements. The following practices will help you discover those pathways and make your memories more conscious and available for use in both magic and ritual. These practices will help you build what I call, an *elemental inventory.* An elemental inventory is much like a "sensory reference library"—an inner inventory of personal experiences with each of the elements to help you access your authentic connections to these diverse forces.

Air Practice 1

Find a quiet place in the time and space of your life. Step outside to feel the air if you can. Breathe deeply and soar out of the present. Fly back in time on the wind of your memories. What do you see? What do you hear? Where are you? What does it feel like? Are you lying on a beach in Maui, feeling the air caress your body gently? Are you in the desert during a windstorm being knocked over by the strong force of the winds? Are you taking shelter from the rain under a storm-tossed tree? Are you skydiving? Are you hang-gliding over an expanse of meadow? Are you breathing in the sweet scent of new-mown hay? Blowing a dandelion flower gone to seed into the wind with a hundred wishes? Become a bee, and visit as many fragrant flowers of your memory as you can. Take in all the sweetness, then buzz back to the present.

Air Practice 2

Choose one personal memory from an experience with air. Take yourself back to that place now, and fill yourself with that memory. Recall that experience of air with *all* of your senses. What do you notice physically happening to you as you fully recall this experience of air?

What internal energetic shift, if any, did you notice as you filled yourself with the memory of air? Repeat this practice with a different memory of air that has a different quality. Compare and contrast these experiences, and file them away in your elemental inventory under "air".

Air Practice 3

You have gone into your memories to realize the connections to the air element that you already have. Now go outside and make a memory on purpose. Add it to your elemental inventory. Repeat this practice as often as you are able.

Fire Practice 1

Light a candle and illuminate the pathway to your memories of fire. Can you remember your favorite birthday cake? What did you wish for in this first act of candle magic? Did you get close enough to feel the warmth on your face? Walk forward into your memories to your favorite campfire.

What does the fire sound like? Who are you with? Are you alone? Where are you—in a forest, on a cliff, beside the ocean? Is it night or day? Are you cooking? Are you trying to view your future in the coals? What did you see in your first experience of scrying into fire? Walk yourself forward again, visiting other favorite memories of fire, pausing where it pleases you, until you return fully into the present moment. Complete this exercise by pinching out the candle flame between moistened fingers or with a candle snuffer. Use this candle again when you need to invoke the essence of fire for your own personal work.

Fire Practice 2

Choose one personal memory from an experience with fire. Take yourself back to that place now, and fill yourself with that memory. Recall that experience of fire with *all* of your senses. What do you notice physically happening to you as you fully recall this experience of fire?

What internal energetic shift, if any, did you notice as you filled yourself with the memory of fire? Repeat this practice with a different memory of fire that has a different quality. Compare and contrast these experiences, and file them away in your elemental inventory under "fire".

Fire Practice 3

You have gone into your memories to realize the connections to the fire element that you already have. Now go outside and make a memory on purpose. Add it to your elemental inventory. Repeat this practice as often as you are able.

Water Practice 1

Draw yourself a bath. Slip into the tub and glide back through your memories of water. Do you remember taking a shower under a rainspout? Did you live in a neighborhood where people turned on the hydrant on a hot day? When was the first time you skated on ice or immersed yourself in a hot spring? Did you ever go skinny-dipping on a moonlit night or stand on a glacier? Have you ever steamed yourself in a sauna and run out naked into the snow? Go as many places and visit as many forms of water as you can: rain, rivers, oceans, bathtubs, hot springs, clouds, steam, ice, glaciers, wells, lakes, geysers, running streams, frost, floods, snow, tidal waves, dams, or rip tides. How do the differing qualities affect you? Swim back to the surface of your consciousness and let your memories float there, then scoop them up in the nets of your present mind and store them in your elemental inventory.

Water Practice 2

Choose one personal memory from an experience with water. Take yourself back to that place now, and fill yourself with that memory. Recall that experience of water with *all* of your senses. What do you notice physically happening to you as you fully recall this experience of water?

What internal energetic shift, if any, did you notice as you filled yourself with the memory of water? Repeat this practice with a different memory of water that has a different quality. Compare and contrast these experiences, and file them away in your elemental inventory under "water".

Water Practice 3

You have gone into your memories to realize the connections to the water element that you already have. Now go outside and make a memory on purpose. Add it to your elemental inventory. Repeat this practice as often as you are able.

Earth Practice 1

Make a physical connection with earth. Stand barefoot on the grass or ground or hold some soil in your hand. Take a walk into the cavern of your deep mind. Notice how cool it is as you enter. The walls are moist and a breeze, like a soft breath, caresses your face, coming from deep within the earth. You can easily see to walk, as the light emanates from within. Find a resting place, perhaps a sandy beach beside the meandering stream that has carved this cavern. Lie down and let yourself be held by the earth's embrace. And as you are held, let your memories emerge from the rock like the continuous flow of moisture seeping through the cracks in the stones, dripping down into the meandering stream of your consciousness.

Do you remember your first batch of gourmet mud pies? Picking tomatoes in your grandmother's garden? Rolling down a steep, grassy hill? When was the last time you stepped barefoot into really fine mud and squished it between your toes? Relive moments you have spent with mountains, deserts, sand, caves, rocks, quicksand, corn fields, earthquakes, and landslides. When you are ready to leave the cavern, pluck your gemstone memories from the stream and store them in your elemental inventory pouch.[101]

Earth Practice 2

Choose one personal memory from an experience with earth. Take yourself back to that place now, and fill yourself with that memory. Recall that experience of earth with *all* of your senses. What do you notice physically happening to you as you fully recall this experience of earth?

What internal energetic shift, if any, did you notice as you filled yourself with the memory of earth? Repeat this practice with a different memory of earth that has a different quality. Compare and contrast these experiences, and file them away in your elemental inventory under "earth".

Earth Practice 3

You have gone into your memories to realize the connections to the earth element that you already have. Now go outside and make a memory on purpose. Add it to your elemental inventory. Repeat this practice as often as you are able.

---

[101] Ibid.

Repeat these practices with the various elements until you have relived a wide range of aspects from your personal memories. With "witch consciousness," intentionally seek out and cultivate new experiences, adding them to your elemental inventory for sensory reference in future workings.

Elemental Invocations

All the experiences in your elemental inventory can be brought forward to the present and used in invocation. Now you have the embodied knowledge you need to invoke a very specific quality of elemental energy from each direction to empower your ritual.

> "I call you, powers of the west, spirit of water,
> You whose waves flow smooth and strong,
> Changing shape and dissolving form,
> Sliding off rocks, holding on to nothing,
> Let me ride the waves with you and trust the flow of life.
> Teach me to let go and swim in your mystery,
> Knowing that all things must flow and change
> And slip through our fingertips.
> Be with me now. Blessed be."

One way to identify the elemental energy of the ritual is to categorize your ritual occasion. Look at the emotions surrounding the occasion. How do they correspond to each element? What aspects of air, fire, water, and earth can change or offset a force that is present in the situation? How can the elemental forces be used to bring the situation into balance? If you need to, refer back to chapter 5 for a discussion of the elements and their correspondences, or let your natural intelligence guide your way.

Elemental Invocation Practice

MEDITATE

Create a comfortable, relaxing space. Breathe yourself into a place of quiet in your inner landscape. Walk into a circle in that landscape and turn to the east. Hold in your outstretched hands a symbol of your ritual and offer it to the spirit of air. Who comes forward to accept this offering? A person? A being? A creature? Is there a breath at the base of your neck? Is there a breeze that ruffles your hair? Is there wind that sways the tree branches? Ask the spirit of air to support you in your ritual endeavor, and thank it for answering your call.

Turn now to the south and repeat your offering to the spirit of fire. Continue turning toward each of the remaining directions of west and north, repeating your offering as before, until you have communicated with all four elements and have received their guidance.

WRITE/DRAW/SCULPT/MOVE

When you are finished, turn around full circle counterclockwise, taking a deep breath at each direction and noticing any changes in the landscape. As your awareness returns, write down words, draw or sculpt some of the imagery, or move yourself with the sensations accessed by the meditation.

Basic Guide for Elemental Invocations

The following guide can be used as a tool to understand the components of elemental invocation. Once understood, the suggested format and structure may become more stylistically flexible. If you are working solitary, use "I" language, and if you will be speaking for a group, use inclusive "we" language. Feel free to use the less formal "you" rather than "thee" as you feel called to address the elemental powers.

"I call thee, spirit of the _____ (east/south/west/north),
Power of _____ (air/ fire/water/earth.).
You who are _____ ." (Describe the attributes you wish to invoke from that element in the language of lyrical praise.)

Follow this by asking for what you need (specific blessings, guidance, or attributes) from the element. Invite that elemental energy to help you with the request:

"Bless me with _____ ," or "Guide me to _____ ,"
or "Teach me to _____ ,"
or "Show me _____ ."

Conclude your invocation with:

"I call you from my heart to be with me now.
Blessed be!"

The following are some elemental invocations that are variations on the format shown above:

"I invoke you, spirit of the west, power of water.
Calm and deep, serene in the mysteries of
the unknown,
Bless me with the ability to trust myself in
unknown waters,
That I might swim with confidence and without fear.
I call you from my heart to be with me now. Blessed be."

"We call to you, spirit of earth,
Who brings in the spring and covers the ground with scent and color, You who give food to all that need.
Show us the harvest of our creations.
Let us not pass by the rose on the vine without inhaling her scent.
Fill our bodies with the sensual celebration of living.
We call you from our hearts to be with us now.
Blessed be."

"I invoke thee, power of the east, spirit of air,
Whirlwind of freedom, source of my singing breath,
Breathe love into my heart.
Whisper awareness with your fragrant scents.
Help me to clear away all fear that clouds my mind's opening to love's sweetness.
I call you from my heart to be with me now."

"We call to thee, powers of the south, and welcome you, spirit of fire,
You who dance our bodies in passion and bid us
rise to action!
Bless us to know the strength of our loving
And to know the power of our united will.
Teach us how to forge ourselves into tools of change.
Aid us to heal our earth, our sisters, and ourselves from oppression, within and without.
We call you from our loving hearts to be with us now."

Seasonal Elemental Invocations

Go outside. If you can't actually go outdoors, find a way to bring the outdoors in. Open a window. What does it smell like? Is it warm or cool? Is it sunny? Overcast? Raining? Snowing? Freezing? Are the days or nights lengthening or shortening? Can you see any animals? Hear them? Sense them? What are they doing? What do they look like? What is the general mood of people around you? How are they dressed? What about the trees and flowers? What is growing in your garden or not? Why?

At this season, in your part of the world, how is air most likely to manifest? As a warm spring breeze or freezing blast? How does fire manifest? As a long, hot day or does it seem as if the sun barely rises above the horizon? What about water? Are you experiencing monsoons or is the ground parched? Does water flow at this time of year or can you walk on it? What is the ground like at this season? Are you smelling the fresh-turned path of a plow or choking on dust with each breath?

In thinking about the season of the year, consider the seasonal qualities of each element and its energy. How might you request this power to assist you with your ritual. Honor the connections that come to you intuitively, follow the trail of your thoughts, and notice where it leads you. Write about where you go and what comes to you, either in fragments or full lines. Try using the suggested format for elemental invocations. Fill in or round out the written fragments until you have invocations that you feel best embody the concept and essential elemental energy of the season.

Fall Equinox Invocation to the North

Grandmother Earth, Crone keeper of the north, we call you.
You are rich sweet soil, dirt grit ground,
Round orange squashes bursting from the fields.
You are a blanket of wheat woven gold,
The rhythm of the mountain humming in our skins
As we walk, walk, walk upon you.

Now is the season to sing our shadow selves awake,
Teach us, Mother of brittle brown leaves.
Mother of bones and wings,
Bring your boldness, being, and body to our circle tonight.
With your Crone fingers, braid us into the strong rope of community, That we may sustain and heal ourselves and the world.
Be with us now, grandmothers. Blessed be.[102]

Fall Equinox Invocation to the West

We invoke thee, spirit of water,
Place of beginnings and endings,
Watery womb of creation and dissolution,
Great cauldron of rebirth,
We stand at the equinox and face your great sea.
Dark and deep, we gaze into your waters
And descend into the season of reflection.
Bless us with courage to return to you;
To see ourselves as we truly are,
A mirror reflection of our Great Goddess.
We call you by our wombs, and by our sacred bloods,
To be with us now. Blessed be.

Spring Equinox Invocation to the North

We invoke and call you, powers of earth,
By pulsing soil and budding branch,
By our bodies aching to open to your touch.
We have gathered to celebrate the great reawakening of your body from winter's sleep,

---

[102] Jennifer M. Murphy.

And welcome the return of the laughing Maiden
To Her dance of life.
Bless us to awaken to spring, to stretch our bodies as your blossoms already reach for the sun, that we, too, might dance
To your powerful rhythms.
Inspire us with understanding, that we might know our bodies' strengths
And pleasures as we awaken the Maiden Goddess in ourselves.
We call you from our hearts to be with us now.
Blessed be.

Spring Equinox Invocation to the South

Sizzling sister goddesses of the south!
Sultry serpent spirits, rise up.
Your burning, blood-red thread winds through us,
Up our spines like snakes. We call you! Rise up.
Stir the cauldron of creativity in our bellies.
Spark the laughter that lives under our skins.
Rise up.
The Wheel has turned, and it is time again
To loose the secret song of remembering upon us.
Let it simmer in our bodies, salty and hot.
Let it awaken in our souls and our sexuality.
Rise up, sacred fire queen, and bless us
With your heat, your light, your love, in our circle tonight.
Be with us now! Blessed be.[103]

---

[103] Jennifer M. Murphy.

Winter Solstice Invocation to the North

Element of earth,
You who are the winter cave of hibernation,
The hag who is the white peaks of snow-capped mountains.
We can feel your rumblings:
Animals in slumber,
Gestating seeds, ripe with the promise of life, at rest.
We call you as we enter this season of transition from longest night. Beginning the stretch to awakening,
We call you from our hearts to be with us now. Blessed be.[104]

May Eve Invocation to the West

We invoke and call thee, powers of the west,
Pulsing moon-tide currents flowing with the mystery of her sacred rhythm.
Primordial waters reflecting her pearlescent moonlight,
Life-giving sea-foam waves of passion,
Come, anoint us with your presence and join us as we come together
To honor the powers of our moon-time waters
And the sacredness of our life-giving bodies.
Be witness as we celebrate the mystery of your ancient rhythm.[105]

Summer Solstice Invocation for the East

Guardian of the east, Mother Wind of Summer,
we call you to inspire our circle!
Sweet summer air, will our noses with sage and new-mown grass;
fill our ears with hissing sprinklers and hummingbirds, bees

---

[104] Ramona Reeves.
[105] Ellen Pele.

buzzing.
You give us the power to know our truth and to speak it loudly and with conviction.
You send the Santa Anas, hot off the desert,
scattering palm fronds in the streets and making us restless,
making us dance with the crackling energy of desire.
Embers of desire lie in our bellies, waiting coals of possibility.
Mother Wind, feed them with your vital breath,
set them ablaze that our path may be brilliantly lit!
Be with us now! Blessed be![106]

Be-Speaking Elemental Invocations

Feminist theologian Mary Daly (of blessed memory) created the word "be-speaking," and she defines it as "bringing about a psychic and/or material change by means of words; speaking into be-ing."[107] To be-speak an invocation, you must be fully present with what you are saying.

Do you remember your elemental inventory? Now is the time to access that information. Prepare yourself energetically, and trust that the poetry of the season is alive inside you. Embody the frequency, the resonance, and the vibration of the elemental power you are inviting. Let your words emerge from your center. Let the tone of your voice change in range, pitch, quality of sound, and meter of delivery as each element is invoked. Like tuning into the band-wave frequency on a radio, dial up each directional "station" to hear the elemental music clearly. Make an authentic connection to the quality of elemental energy you seek. For example, air sounds in the environment tend to be very soft, breathy, and relatively high-pitched. Air words are clear, thought-provoking, clever, and should give the feeling of expansive, open spaces or be soaring in

[106] Jennifer M. Murphy.
[107] Daly and Caputi, *Webster's First New Intergalactic Wickedary of the English Language*, 65.

their delivery.

Fire sounds in the environment are those that are relatively high-pitched, clear, bright, shrill, carry well over distance, and seem to cut through other sounds. Fire sounds grab our attention by irritating our nerves. Fire words are simple but passionate, higher pitched, with a faster-paced delivery; words that rise, outburst, or simmer (as seasonally appropriate), with sibilance accentuated.

Water sounds in the environment are soft but definite, midrange in pitch, and give us the feeling of caressing or stroking. These are sounds that cause our muscles to relax. Water words flow in a stream of consciousness. They are dreamy and poetic, with connective phrasing and rhythmic undulation in their delivery.

Earth sounds in the environment are definite or heavy, and low-pitched, often sub-sonic. These are sounds that seem to rattle our bones. Earth words are solid, like large stones; simple but carrying weight. Delivery of an earth invocation would be slower paced and with a deeper pitch.

When you are speaking an invocation in a group ritual, remember that you are the conduit between the elemental energies and the will of the women in the ritual circle. You will need to project your voice, speaking out so that everyone present can hear and feel the invocation. This is particularly critical if you are outside, where sound can easily be lost. Personal ritual invocations need not be spoken with such projection, but it is still best to speak them aloud, and make the contact needed. Speaking aloud gives the elemental forces within you an opportunity to come fully forward. It is a form of self-witnessing. How and what you hear within ritual space may be different than how and what you hear in a state of ordinary consciousness. Try invocation both ways, aloud and silent, to hear, see, and feel the differences for yourself.

As you become more sensitive to ritual energy, you will feel the energy in the room shift or drop, depending on what is happening at the time. In some Wiccan traditions, invocations are passed out and read from a printed page. This can have a profound and unpleasant effect on the energy of the ritual, and the invocations can sound and feel flat. Whether you are preoccupied with memorizing exact words or speaking them from a page, there are energetic consequences. If you rely on the left, linear side of your brain completely for delivering your invocation, there won't be much change in the energy of the ritual space. However, when you be-speak your invocation and you truly embody the essence of the Goddess and the elements, the energy builds rather than drops.

Practice

Write an elemental invocation and be-speak it aloud. Speak your invocation again, applying the additional information above. Notice the differences.

Invoking the Goddesses: The Power of Naming

I invoke thee, Tiamat, great serpentine creatrix
From the beginning of all beginnings.
You who swam the primordial waters of the worlds
Before the formation of the lands.
You, who play in the ebb and flow of creation,
The void that potentials all things.
Uncontrolled One, Flowing One, with scales and tail,
Of sea-green hair and eel eyes of fire,
You who are within me, arise.
Teach me to flow in your watery ways,
To let go of the land that crumbles in my hand
Even as I fear to let it go.
Be with me as I dare to risk, change,
And open to my creativity.
Help me to open my hand.
Soothe my fears in your boundless ocean,

And let me ride your waves to my unfolding path.
Be with me now and always.

Once you are familiar and comfortable with invoking the elements, you are ready to practice invoking the Goddess(es).

When you invoke the Goddess, or a specific goddess, whom are you addressing? For me, invocation is an external and internal experience of communing with Her. Both experiences meet at a central point within me. The Goddess exists within and without simultaneously. In calling Her forward, I am awakening Her within myself and asking that She come into my conscious awareness. At the same time, I am calling Her from Her own realm where She exists independently of me. For example, when I have a need to strengthen my autonomy, energize my political activism, and awaken the part of myself that is strong and independent in defending the rights of women, I invoke the goddess Diana or Artemis. It is a multilayered process. I am a part of Her; She is a part of me. Once I invoke Her, I open myself to embody Her. This is different than becoming Her. For me to experience Her presence, She must already live within me, so that I can recognize Her energetic presence when She arrives.

Think of the name of a goddess as the container of Her energy and attributes carried upon the breath of the spoken word. The vibration contained in the sounding of words, and the life force in our breath, travel between the seen and unseen realms, creating a pathway for the Goddess to enter the ritual circle. The name of a goddess must be carefully chosen. The attributes of the deity invited must resonate with the desired qualities to be utilized in the ritual. If you are seeking physical manifestation, address an earth goddess. For mental powers, choose an air goddess. For creativity, call for a water goddess. Passionate emotions and life-force energy are usually associated with the realm of re goddesses. If you are going to address a specific goddess, get to know Her before calling on Her. A relationship with a goddess is a two-way street. Before you ask something of Her, be prepared to give something to Her.

Addressing a specific, desired quality may sometimes be more successful than choosing a specific goddess, who may contain other aspects unrelated to the ritual's purpose. If it is written in a book that you must call on a specific goddess for an issue, and you really have no clue as to who or what She is about, I do not recommend that you address Her by name. It is far more important to know what you need than who you need it from. If you are very clear about what it is you need, then you can address your invocation to "She who gives this" or "She who blesses with that." Then She who fits the need can come. Clear intention, accompanied by resonance, when embodied by the woman invoking, will draw the desired helper even if she is not called by a specific name.

Many goddess names, when translated from their original languages, are actually "job descriptions," describing a goddess's major attributes or associations. If you are worried about calling the Roman goddess Ceres (whose name translates as "create") because She is virtually unknown to you, perhaps you could address Her in her primary function as "She who brings forth the grain," or "She who creates abundance from the seed." You are then calling upon any creatrix goddess of the land who can help you.

Addressing the Goddesses by Their attributes and function, rather than by name, is an ancient and universal tradition. I most often address Her in Her totality, by the title of Great Goddess. Because the basic forms of most Wiccan traditions are drawn from European or Mediterranean origin, influence, or inspiration, refraining from specific names and focusing instead on the desired aspects of that Goddess may help to make everyone attending feel included regardless of their training or cultural background. By invoking Her in less specific ways, you can honor all cultures without speaking from ignorance regarding one.

To study the various goddesses throughout the world's cultures, learning about their natures and aspects, doesn't mean that you must work with all of them. The goddesses you work with the most come to know you as you know them. Except for rare cases, it is the goddesses with whom you cultivate a relationship that you will invoke most often.

You may also wish to invoke a quality you desire using a more abstract form of invocation. An abstract invocation can be as simple as "Peace, come to me. Peace, come to me." In speaking this simple phrase, concentrate on the precise energetics that you desire. Fill yourself with the essential quality of peace you are seeking. Speak out of that embodied place of peace. Its coded message will be easily read by the psyche.

Invocation and Issues of Cultural Appropriation

I have attended rituals over the years where goddess names are invoked for what feels like a good ten minutes. It has never been clear to me why this happens or what purpose this serves. Is it spontaneous emoting or someone showing off how many goddess names she's memorized? Is she simply reciting a roster out of a book that says to call twenty goddess names in alphabetical order as each direction is invoked? How many goddess names are enough?

Please do not invoke a block of international goddesses just because it says to do so in a book. What do you know about who you are invoking? Why are you calling them? Names are like magical telephone numbers. Would you dial up a stranger or casual acquaintance and ask her to help you? Would you dial up five? Are you certain that all the goddesses you've called will get along with each other in the same room? Any magical work done when inviting the wrong goddess—in other words, a goddess who would not be appropriate for the ritual's purpose—will likely fail. If you invite the wrong goddess, and the intention of your ritual is not clear, the results can be frightening or worse. Before invoking strangers, cultivate and invest in quality relationships with a few goddesses.

Many names of the Goddesses have been lost. The burning of ancient libraries, patriarchal repression of our Goddess heritage, and the fact that early peoples did not write Her name have contributed to this loss. Emotionally it feels so good, so healing, to speak Her names, especially after centuries of fear and the gynocide of the Burning Times. As an alternative to invoking a roster of goddess names during invocation, a group could make a place of honor within a ritual to speak, but not invoke, as many names of the Goddess as women can recall. This would honor and praise the Goddess of Many Names in all Her diversity.

By invoking goddesses from many cultures, we also must look at the bigger picture and be aware of other connected issues. Invoking multicultural goddesses within a ritual touches on issues of cultural appropriation and needs to be considered by anyone who is involved in planning public rituals. Many women of European descent don't think twice about invoking goddesses outside their own culture. They don't stop to consider issues around cultural appropriation. This lack of perspective comes from a position of privilege, however unconscious it may be. Some women seem to have the attitude that they have an inherent right to invoke any goddess from any tradition, lift Her entirely out of Her cultural, ethnic, or religious context, and ask Her to serve their purposes. This issue is especially relevant when the goddess in question is from a living tradition, such as the Yoruba goddesses of the living traditions of Africa and Brazil, goddesses of India, and the legendary female figures of First Nation North American religious traditions (who are not considered actual goddesses by Indigenous North Americans).

Women can learn to be respectful guests around goddesses of cultures other than their own. Just as it is critical for all people to cultivate an awareness of multiculturalism, it is equally important to understand the diversity of female deities of other cultures. There is, however, a line between being a respectful guest who acknowledges other goddess forms and attempting to take over your hostess's home and asking her to serve you. The most disrespectful behavior is claiming to be a priestess of a goddess from a living tradition without the appropriate training from that tradition. A lifetime of white privilege makes this issue sadly difficult for many white women of European descent to consider or understand. Perhaps a way to begin changing the perspective of privilege is to work first with goddesses within your own culture and ethnic heritage before working with those from other cultures. This work alone could take a lifetime and, in fact, it is only in very recent times that goddesses from more than one culture have been invoked in Wiccan ritual. It is only within the past three decades that women of European descent began to discover that they had a goddess heritage.[108]

Women can develop deep, personal relationships with specific goddesses, sometimes embracing a goddess from within their own culture, ethnicity, or race, while some are drawn to a goddess outside of their ethnic or racial roots. As priestess at your own altar, your relationship with various goddess forms is subjectively real and can be honored. Those experiences may include goddesses from other cultures who come to you in dreams, meditations, and metaphor. If you choose to devote yourself to a goddess outside of your own racial heritage or ethnicity, and that goddess is part of a *living* tradition, be willing to travel to study with a priestess of that tradition. This is necessary in order to work properly with that goddess form respectfully and responsibly. If the tradition is no longer active, you are still responsible for studying Her and learning all you can so that She can be related to appropriately.

Creating Goddess Invocations

When choosing a goddess to invoke for a personal ritual that includes a petition, it is best to choose a goddess whom you know something about, both intellectually and intuitively. Sometimes, however, you may not know which goddess would best assist you in your query. The following practice is an entirely intuitive process for writing a goddess invocation asking for guidance or aid. Leave yourself open and willing to receive whoever may come to you. Open yourself and explore what Her presence and essence communicates without words.

[108] Thanks to the pioneering works of women's spirituality foremothers (of blessed memory), Marija Gimbutas, Merlin Stone, Monico Sjoo, Patricia Monaghan, and others.

Goddess Invocation Practice

PONDER

Create a comfortable, quiet space. Breathe yourself into deep calmness. Conjure up one of the significant life events from your list that needs and deserves a ritual. Walk yourself into it. What does it feel like to be there? What do you see? What do you hear? Take out a pencil and pad, and begin to take notes.

WRITE/DRAW/SCULPT/MOVE

Write, draw, sculpt, or move your body as you think about and feel into the occasion or issue. Express your emotions, physical sensations, and perceptions of the issue. Defy your inner critic and dare to express yourself freely. After all, no one is there to see you.

MEDITATE

Move your consciousness out of the event and into a place outdoors where you feel powerful—your favorite place to just hang out and *be*. Maybe this place is an actual location. Maybe it's a part of your inner landscape. Take a look around you. Look to the east. What do you see, hear, and feel? Look to the south, the west, and the north, and explore in the same way. Continue turning clockwise until you have come full circle. Take time at each direction to notice details.

Standing at the center of your own inner circle, raise your arms and ask that a goddess who would be the most helpful and appropriate to assist you with your ritual make Herself known to you. As She arrives, turn to greet Her. Thank Her for coming. Ask Her how you should address Her, by name or title. Accept what She says without question. If She says nothing, don't worry. Honor what She does not say as much as what She does say. Thank Her for coming to you. Watch Her go back to where She came from. Now, face the north again, then turn counterclockwise to the west, then south, then east, noticing carefully any changes in the landscape. Take out your pencil and pad again, and take a few notes.

As with any guided meditation, the images, deities, and symbols revealed, or the lack of them, are all information that you can use for deepening self-knowledge. Take what you receive without trying purposely to change or impose anything upon what your deep mind gives you, even if you don't know yet what it means or you find it unsettling.

There is elemental information embedded in the language and imagery you experienced in the goddess meditation. Pay attention to the elemental essence of the goddess who came forward in your meditation. Notice the direction from which She arose. These noticings[109] can be keys to the overall elemental energetics of the ritual theme, as well as inspiration for the ritual enactments that can follow the invocation. What dominant elemental energy is present within the imagery of this meditation? What ritual enactments might you be inspired to follow up with, based on this imagery?

WRITE

Pour the essence of your experience with the goddess onto the paper before you. Let your words flow with the poetic or lyrical language of your senses. Poetry has the power to evoke our emotions by engaging both our feelings and our bodies, giving us unique access to even deeper knowing. Attend to the details of Her appearance and Her essence. You may find it helpful to begin with the words, "You who are the..."

Basic Guide for Goddess Invocations

The following is a guide for writing the petition or invocation to the goddess you have just connected with. It follows a sequence that identifies the deity desired, the aspects and qualities needed for aid or support, and the specific aid requested for the ritual occasion. Use this guide as a tool for including the important components of the invocation. Once you understand the components, the suggested format and structure may

[109] I like to use the word *noticings*, which I learned from Falcon River, to honor all the ways that individuals can perceive an experience through visual, auditory, and kinesthetic stimulus.

become more stylistically flexible.

When writing invocations for personal use, use "I" statements and details that are personally intimate. When writing group invocations, use "we" statements and imagery that is more universal, inclusive of others, and expressive of the group ritual's purpose.

> "I invoke thee, ______," or " We call you ______."

Fill in Her name or title. If She didn't give you a specific name, refer to your notes concerning Her appearance or energetic essence. A respectful way of addressing Her might be "Lady of the raven hair," or you might simply say, "You who came to me."

> "You who are the ______."

It is here that you praise Her. Describe Her attributes that you are asking Her to assist you with, or what you know of the one who appeared to you in the meditation. Include phrases or fragments from what you wrote down during your stream-of-consciousness writing. You called Her to you in response to a need, so what did She bring or show you? State those qualities and, in appreciative language, describe them.

> Conclude this part with "You who are within and without."

This statement affirms that She is a part of you as well as part of the greater whole.

> "Bless me/us with ______," or "Guide me/us to ______."
> or "Teach me/us to ____," or "Show me/us ______."

Drawing from the need identified in the first part of this exercise, craft phrases that best fit your situation and the way you can receive Her guidance. Ask her for specific blessings, guidance, assistance, or qualities you need, that She is able to provide. Write from your heart, and inform her of your true needs. Keep your invocation concise. What is the bottom line of your need? Make your requests with loving reverence and respect.

Conclude your invocation with:

> "I/we call you from my/our heart(s) to be with me now.
> Blessed be!"

How long should an invocation be? It should be long enough to convey the invitation and align with the essence of the power being called. The best invocations I have heard range from five to fifteen lines, depending on what needs to be said and how it is said. A minute in length is usually long enough. Avoid going on too long. In group ritual, an invocation that is too lengthy can cause the energy in the circle to drop. Be careful not to repeat what you may have already said unless you are structuring your invitation to include a chorus line or call-and-response pattern, in which everyone in the group participates. Repetition with no clear purpose is boring.

Here are some examples of personal and group-oriented goddess invocations, written by either myself or former students, using variations of the basic format.

> Sweet Sea Foam Golden One, Aphrodite,
> Rising from inside our very hearts,
> You who shower us with rose petals and salty tears,
> You who continually flow with feelings, fluidity dancing in balance Between joy and loss, gentleness and hot-blooded passion,
> Togetherness and solitude,
> You who teach us to love ourselves deeply and well,
> And to love each other

With all the life and presence we can bring forth, we call You.
Bless our circle with Your beauty, wash us clean of patriarchal lies
That we may see You and feel You in each other, in the trees, the rocks,
And most of all in ourselves.
We open ourselves like flowers to You, Goddess.
Be with us now![110]

I invoke thee, You who came to me from the south.
You who are regal, tall, lean, and burn down to the essence.
You who are fuel and flame,
A calming presence in the center of the firestorm.
Your guidance in helping me decide the next step on my spiritual path.
Please lead me to the appropriate decision.
Help me to clarify what I must do.
I call You from my heart to be with me now. Blessed be.[111]

I welcome You, Goddess of the west,
Mari, Lady of shimmering waves,
You who bring joy. Quencher of soul's thirst.
You who rain upon my parched dreams.
You who are within and without.
Flow over me so that I may open to love's possibilities.
I call You into my heart now.[112]

We invoke thee, Great Goddess,
You who create, animate, and bind all elemental forces

---

[110] Aphrodite Invocation by Jennifer M. Murphy.
[111] Invocation by anonymous student during a ritual-intensive weekend course that I taught.
[112] Ibid.

Into Your awesome web of relationship.
We gather at Summer Solstice to honor and celebrate Your fire essence in all its forms.
We call You to our circle, into us, from within us,
To bless us with the passion and ability to transform ourselves through Your gift of Spirit.
To heal ourselves. To heal one another.
To heal our home, our earth.
We call You by the flame that purifies,
And by the fire of our will that burns eternally.
Blessed be the Goddess of Life who kindles the flame!

Be-Speaking Goddess Invocations

Remember that to be-speak an invocation, you must be fully present with what you are saying. Let the words arise out of the lips of the Goddess who resides within you, and speak to Her who also resides without. *Hear* your own words, your own voice; *listen* to what you are saying. Experience your voice, spoken or sung, as a pathway for Her to enter. Listen for the echo of your own voice speaking, singing back to you. Know that you can do more than you think you can.

The goal of invocation is to speak with such an openness of mind and heart that you come into resonance with Her. This can be difficult to do if you are holding a piece of paper and reading your invocation. If you read your invocation, your eyes and mind are on the printed page and not with Her. Remember that the purpose of invocation is to connect with Her. Preparation is most important because it gives you the energetic experience that your words will emerge from. Therefore, writing an invocation prior to the ritual helps to clarify the purpose of your invocation. Use the writing practice as part of your energetic preparation, but during the actual ritual, as you are able, trust yourself to have a conversation with Her. Do you write down exactly what you are going to say before you phone a friend to ask a favor or have a heart-to-heart chat? You might make notes of points to cover if you intend to have a long conversation, but most of the time, you just dial the number and talk when the connection goes through. Initially you may want to memorize your invocation and valediction, but with experience, you will move beyond this. Once you are experienced with invocation, you will rarely, if ever, need to prepare a script in advance.

A coven or ritual circle can be a wonderful place to jump into the waters of improvised invocation. Be-speaking does not necessarily have to involve words. Invocation can be communicated entirely with movement, in silence, or with music, drums, percussion, or breath. Whether in solitary space or a supportive environment, women can learn to trust that they can communicate directly with the Goddess, unaided by a script or cheat sheet. As long as you convey the essence of what you are asking for, a simple, concise invocation can be magnificent.

Practice for Spoken Invocation

Hold your written invocation in one hand, and stand in "chalice" posture with your other arm raised, hand upturned and open. Return to the special place where you were in the earlier meditation. Stand once again at the center of your own inner landscape and speak your invocation aloud to Her. Speak slowly enough that you can feel the words reverberating in your body. Feel the spaces between the words as well as the words themselves.[113] As She arrives, turn to greet Her. Welcome Her into your being. Spend as much time as is mutually pleasurable in sacred communion. At the appropriate time, bid Her a loving and respectful farewell.

Afterwards, take a few moments to note any response you may have experienced. Did you experience any changes in the energy of your

---

[113] Adapted from a class exercise created by author and poet Deena Metzger, with whom I studied writing weekly in 1988–1989.

environment after speaking your invocation? Did you notice any changes or shifts in energy within yourself?

Alternative Practice for Invocation

As with the above practice, return to the circle of your own inner landscape. Unencumbered by words, reach for the Goddess in whatever way you find most fulfilling. Move to Her, drum to Her, sound to Her, breathe to Her. Create a pathway, and then wait for Her to come. Embrace Her when She arrives, and spend some time in sacred play together. At the appropriate time, bid Her a loving and respectful farewell.

Afterwards, take a few moments to note any response you may have experienced. Did you experience any changes in the energy of the room after expressing your invocation? Did you notice any changes or shifts in energy within yourself?

Invocation Without Words

As the essence of the elements and the Goddess becomes embodied within you, experiment with other ways to invoke the Goddess and the elemental powers. For women who more naturally express themselves kinesthetically, movement, dance, and symbolic gesture can be as effective as words. Percussion and other instruments have elemental qualities. To name a few, breathy whistles, certain bells, some vibra-tones, or flutes can be used for air; sistrums, some rattles, or tambourines are good for fire; rain sticks or ocean drums can be used for water; and deep-toned hand drums can convey the element of earth. These can be played in groups or layered on top of one another to create an elemental musical composition.

You may wish to create invocations that combine words, sounds, and movement. At one Spring Equinox ritual, I improvised a center invocation with two priestesses who express the Goddess best through dance. Spontaneously, we opened to the flow and invoked the Goddess in song and movement in a powerful collaborative invocation.

Valediction

Words such as "revocation," "dismissal," "releasing," "disbursing," and "banishing" have all been used to describe thanking and saying farewell to invited spirits and deities prior to opening the circle at a ritual's conclusion. None of these word choices have ever felt entirely appropriate to me, since they all assume a one-down power position of the elemental powers or deities to human beings, rather than that of allies or co-creators. Therefore, I have begun simply using the word "valediction" when describing the ritual act of sincerely thanking and formally withdrawing the invitation extended through the invocation to the powers that have been invited. "Valediction," originally from the Latin *vale*, "goodbye," and *dicere,* "to say," means the action of saying farewell and a formal farewell address or statement. Valediction as a magical act, when accompanied by the energetic component of scribing a pentacle, is intended to lovingly escort the invited guests of spirit back to the portal door they entered through and back to their realm, respectfully closing the door behind them as they depart.

Unlike invocations, this is *not* the time to ask for more blessings and support, and can be shorter in length. In creating valedictions for the Goddess and the four directions, refer back to the words spoken in the invocations to thank and bid farewell to any goddesses or specific powers that have been invoked. Allow the events of the ritual to inspire your words so that the two prayers have similar sound or feel that links them together. There is nothing more unnerving than hearing the goddess Kali, or someone's ancestral spirits from the Burning Times, invoked at the beginning of a ritual and not hearing them named, thanked, and bid farewell to at the closure. It can also be disconcerting for the invocation and valediction to contrast wildly. If you plan to invoke in rhyme, be prepared to bid farewell in rhyme also. Overall similarity of style among all the invocations and valedictions is also important. In an open public ritual, if one woman wants to do rhyming invocations and valedictions, and the rest of the facilitators do not, the rhyme will stick out awkwardly. It is best to have some similarity of style between all the invocations and valedictions, rather than end up with one rapper and a Shakespearean sonnet in the same ritual. Respect the powers you invite and take them seriously, and they will respect you and take you seriously.[114]

The Goddess is always thanked and given a formal farewell before thanking and bidding the elements farewell. Use "I" if you are having a solo ritual, and "we" when speaking on behalf of a group.

Basic Guide for Goddess Valedictions

Address the Goddess by Her name or title.

> "You who are the _____."
> "I/we thank You for _____."

Briefly reference the attributes you invoked from Her or experienced during the ritual. Give thanks to Her for the blessings, guidance, or presence that were asked for in the invocation using lyrical praise language, concluding with:

> "I/We thank You from my/our heart(s) for being with me/us."
> "Hail and farewell! Blessed be!"

Or,

> "I/We thank You from my/our heart(s) for being with me/us, and I/we bless You as You have blessed me/us. Hail and farewell! Blessed be!"

---

[114] Paraphrased from author Marion Green.

Basic Guide for Elemental Valedictions

> "Spirit of the ______ (east/south/west/north), Power of ______(earth/water/ fire/air). You who are________ ."

Briefly reference the attributes you invoked and/or observed during the ritual. Give thanks for the blessings that were asked for in the invocation using lyrical praise language, and concluding with:

> "I/We thank You from my/our heart(s) for being with me/us. Hail and farewell! Blessed be!"

Or,

> "I/We bless You, as You have blessed me/us, and bid You farewell. Blessed be!"

I have often heard valedictions that end with "Go if you must, stay if you will. Hail and farewell." In fact, because this was said so commonly in Wiccan and Pagan groups in the 1980s, I used to say it myself. Eventually I realized this is a mixed message! Magic is serious business. When you invite a guest over for dinner, do you really want to give them the choice to stay as long as they please, or is it your intention to spend a specific amount of quality time with them? In this book, we have focused on the importance of having a clear intention for your ritual, a precise understanding of the specific elemental energy you wish to invoke, and a clear intention for each ritual enactment. Having clear beginnings and clear endings is just as essential. This clarity of intention must follow through to the end of the ritual to ensure the success of the ritual magic, as well as the safety and wellbeing of all the participants. Escort your invited elemental guests back to the door, and kiss them goodbye and goodnight. I have heard too many stories of flash floods, fires, and tornadoes following rituals where the elemental spirits were not respectfully, lovingly, firmly, and clearly bid farewell. Changing the words "go if you must, stay if you will" to "go as you must, blessing our will" is a simple suggestion for women used to the now-familiar liturgy who are seeking a new and clearer intention.

Here are some examples of seasonal invocations with their corresponding valedictions.

Fall Equinox Invocation to the East

> We invoke thee, elemental spirits of the air.
> By the winds of autumn that chill the air and show us that winter is at hand, we call the power of the raven.
> Come to us, whose cries herald the coming of the Crone's season. Pierce the chilled air with your sounds and waken us to the great transition.
> Carry us upon your wings, and upon the winds, to the silence and peace that is the center of the cyclone.
> Bless us with the gift of balance that is this season's message.
> We call you from our hearts to be with us now.
> Blessed be!

Fall Equinox Valediction to the East

> Spirits of the east, power of the raven,
> We thank you from the heart for being here.
> During the balance of the light and dark of this season, we thank you for your gifts of silence and clarity so that we might grow in wisdom.
> Go as you must, blessing our will. Hail and farewell.

Spring Equinox Invocation to the North

We invoke and call thee, powers of earth,
Ancient mother whose dark, cavernous womb pulses and throbs,
Giving birth to new life, Mountain-peaked breasts nourishing fertile fields and wild flower meadows,
You who plant the seed, then birth us and sustain us,
You who give us the strength to grow strong and bloom with the joy of living,
Come be witness to our awakening. Blessed be![115]

Spring Equinox Valediction to the North

Powers of Earth, Ancient Mother,
Womb and breasts, seeds, birth, and sustenance,
Thank you for giving us life and the strength to grow and bloom into being.
Thank you for being witness to our awakening.
From our hearts we bid you hail and farewell! Blessed be!

Practice

* Choose a personal ritual for yourself. Write invocations to the four directions and a Goddess invocation for the center. Write their corresponding valediction. Practice creating invocations and valedictions hundreds of times.

* Choose a seasonal ritual theme. Meditate on the significance of the occasion in order to understand which energies might need to be invoked. Improvise your spoken invocations to all four directions

115 Spring Equinox invocation and valediction by Ellen Pele.

and to the Goddess. Improvise your valedictions. Practice hundreds of times.

* Using the same ritual theme as the exercise above, invoke the four directions and spirit with movement, dance, or sound. Practice hundreds of times.

chapter 9

THE YEAR IS A DANCING WOMAN

The year is a dancing woman who is born at the coming of spring.
The year is a dancing woman; of her birth and death we sing.[116]

Women are once again ritually celebrating the seasons and cycles of nature, as did their ancestors from all corners of the globe. The return to a consciousness where nature is revered and celebrated evolved naturally from the ecology and feminist movements of the late 1960s and '70s. The growing interest in Dianic and other goddess traditions, feminist ritual, and the Pagan roots of Western religion are providing more ways to celebrate nature's eternal, cyclical themes of birth, death, and rebirth.

These revivals of pre-Christian and Wiccan religious traditions over the past few decades have been the primary inspiration and source material for many of the ritual customs and the overall flavor of the Pagan holy days being practiced by witches and other modern Pagans today. These seasonal ritual themes focus primarily on the fertility cycle of the Goddess and Her male consort. Most Neopagan and Wiccan traditions celebrate the sexual and fertility cycle of nature exclusively in heterosexual terms, with particular emphasis on the life and death cycle of the God within the Goddess's eternal, rotating journey throughout the seasons. Where the Goddess is eternal and immortal, the God is seasonal. He is born from Her, mates with Her, dies at the appointed season, and is reborn again through Her.

In the Dianic tradition, where the Goddess is the sole focus of religious practice, the cycles of women's lives merge and overlap with the Goddess'

[116] Mountainwater, *Ariadne's Thread*, 193.

seasonal, mythic cycle. As previously discussed, the Goddess always contains the God within Her, as He is a variation of Her; one of Her sacred creations like the trees, the rocks, and all other creatures. While acknowledging that His seasonal journey is different, Dianics do not celebrate the God's mythic journey through the wheel of the year as part of Her and our Mysteries. Dianic tradition creates rituals that celebrate the changing and eternal Goddess as She transforms throughout the year and women's likewise cyclical nature.[117]

In earlier times, the seasonal rituals were concerned with the cultivation of the land and the interdependence of animals and people with the elements. A way to understand the mysteries of the holy days, or Sabbats, is to understand how Nature herself encompasses the interdependent aspects of reality that include the agricultural, pastoral, wildlife, botanical, solar, lunar, planetary, and mythic. The ancient celebrations of the seasonal changes enabled the ancestors to consciously put themselves into Mother Nature's cycles of time, to know when to plant, sow, and reap—how to survive and thrive. It was Nature herself who instructed the ancestors about what to do at the holy days, and local customs developed for each village. The land itself dictated the traditions that evolved and passed down in each locality.

Never have there been so many written sources, so widely available, that discuss the folklore and traditional customs that our ancestors practiced. There are many books that incorporate old customs into new rituals from a Pagan or Wiccan perspective, as well as books specifically on folklore and old seasonal customs. I highly recommend learning about the old ways and their meanings in earlier times. Learning about old customs and traditions is a wonderful way to deepen your understanding of the significance of the seasonal rituals and to have continuity with the past. Some old customs can be incorporated into contemporary seasonal rituals or inspire creativity.

---

[117] Other women's holidays based on the research of Jane Harrison are included in Z Budapest's *The Holy Book of Women's Mysteries*.

The holiday customs of the villages noted in this chapter are by no means universal. Rituals and celebrations are specific to a time and a place. Similarly, if you choose to include elements from earlier times in your rituals, it may be necessary to ascribe new meanings for women living in our time so that the ritual is relevant for the participants; as Marion Green writes,

> We all need to realign ourselves with the actual seasons and not blindly follow a calendar which was designed for the convenience of keeping the church's faithful in step with each other. We need to examine the symbols, the gifts, the associations with each festival as we come to celebrate it, so that it actually means something to us, as individuals or as members of a community.[118]

Our lives cycle around the wheel of the year, growing and changing as we move through the earth's seasons. Pre-Christian peoples in northern Europe calculated the passage of time in moon phases, and because of this, the ancient Celtic calendar had a moon-number of nine great festivals that marked the changing of the seasons and guided farmers to their various tasks. These festivals were the Winter and Summer Solstices, Fall and Spring Equinoxes, and the cross-quarter days of Imbolc or Brigid, Beltane or May Eve, Lammas or First Harvest, and Samhain or Hallowmas, which fall at the mid-points between the solstices and equinoxes. The ninth festival was Twelfth Night (called Epiphany in the Christian calendar), which celebrated the end of Midwinter. The date of Twelfth Night is now reckoned as January 6, but in some villages it was held well into the middle of January; in ancient Celtic tradition, on the festival of Twelfth Night a young man or woman, at about the age of twelve to fourteen years, gained their adult name and clan status.[119]

---

[118] Green, *Natural Magic*, 100.
[119] Green, *A Witch Alone*, 46–50.

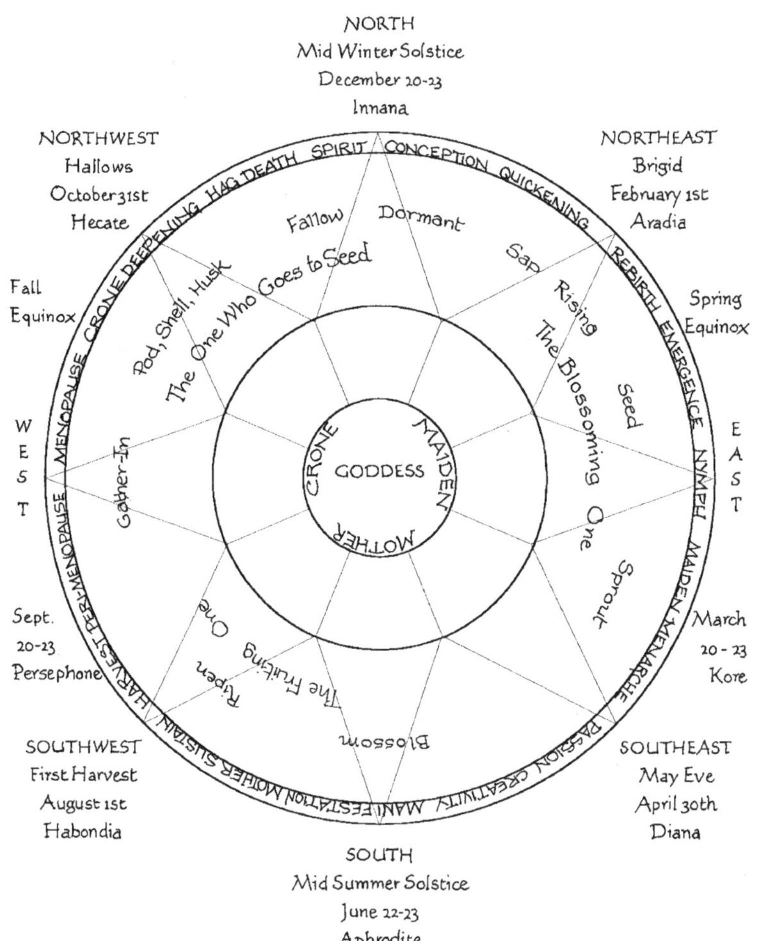

NORTH
Mid Winter Solstice
December 20-23
Innana
NORTHEAST
Brigid
February 1st
Aradia
Spring
Equinox
EAST
March
20 - 23
Kore
SOUTHEAST
May Eve
April 30th
Diana
SOUTH
Mid Summer Solstice
June 22-23
Aphrodite
SOUTHWEST
First Harvest
August 1st
Habondia
Sept.
20-23
Persephone
WEST
Fall
Equinox
NORTHWEST
Hallows
October 31st
Hecate
SPIRIT
CONCEPTION
QUICKENING
REBIRTH
EMERGENCE
NYMPH
MAIDEN
MENARCHE
PASSION
CREATIVITY
MANIFESTATION
MOTHER
SUSTAIN
HARVEST
PERIMENOPAUSE
MENOPAUSE
CRONE
DEEPENING
HAG
DEATH
Dormant
Sap
Rising
Seed
Sprout
The Blossoming One
Blossom
The Fruiting One
Ripen
Gather-In
Pod, Shell, Husk
The One Who Goes to Seed
Fallow
GODDESS
MAIDEN
MOTHER
CRONE

The Women's Wheel of the Year

In more recent times, the earth's cyclic flow was divided into eight parts and marked by eight festivals. These eight divisions of the year are marked at the solstices and equinoxes, as well as the four cross-quarter days noted above, which came to be known as the greater festivals or greater Sabbats. These agricultural festivals gathered the community members together and gave structure to their lives, indicating when to proceed with the activities of breeding livestock, planting, sowing, reaping and harvesting the land, and storing food for the winter. People honored the changing of the seasons with seriousness and reverence, for without the cooperation of nature, their lives would be lost.

> The wheel of the year is not just a matter of changing from one season to the next. Beneath the manifestation of seasonal change, there is also change within the subtle energies of the earth. These energy patterns affect us all (consciously or unconsciously), so by understanding the flow and direction of that energy, we can move with it, and in harmony with it, as true inhabitants of our planet Earth: belonging, part of, and flowing on all levels of our being.[120]

In the Dianic and other goddess traditions,

> [the Goddess's] shapeshifting follows the cycle of the year, each season having a distinct character, yet each owing without a clear boundary into the other. In the springtime the Goddess manifests as the Virgin, the Blossoming One. As she shapeshifts into the summer, she becomes the Mother, the Fruiting One. In the Fall and Winter, she becomes the Crone, the One Who goes to Seed[121] and

---

[120] Kindred, *The Earth's Cycle of Celebration*.
[121] Wilshire, *Virgin, Mother, Crone*, 22.

> falls back into the earth's dark womb, from which She is transformed once again into the Blossoming One.

This is the mythic cycle of the Goddess, the eternal cycle of birth, death, and rebirth. Each seasonal transition initiates a unique aspect of the Goddess and its correspondence to the passages of women's lives. In making this correlation between women's lives and the natural cycles of the earth, sun, moon, and stars, we deepen in our understanding of life itself.

If you pay close attention and observe how the body of the earth is transforming throughout the year, she will speak to you, as she did to our ancestors. She will guide you toward what kind of ritual making to do. It is important to note that although the Wiccan holidays are largely based on the seasons of northern Europe, seasonal cycles are universal and occur with variations everywhere. My intention in citing the Celtic seasonal customs is to illustrate only one of the many rich seasonal traditions that also exist elsewhere throughout Europe and beyond.

All natural cycles begin and end in darkness. This is why pre-Gardnerian, traditional Craft rituals begin in the north for purification and casting. The metaphor of the Goddess birthing all things from the darkness of Her cosmic womb is present within the life cycle of all living things. According to Celtic tradition, the new year begins in darkness, just as the sun's cycle begins at the darkest point of the night, and each new day begins at sundown on the previous night.[122] In Celtic tradition, therefore, the cross-quarter holidays would be celebrated on the night before the holiday itself. Thus Hallowmas would be celebrated on October 31, Brigid on February 1[123], May Eve on April 30, and Lammas on July 31. We begin our ritual-making journey around the wheel of the year from the beginning of the dark season, the holiday of Hallowmas.

---

122 Alba, *The Cauldron of Change*, 46.

123 The holiday of Imbolc is celebrated on January 31st. Dianics have celebrated Brigid on February 1st, and have chosen this date for initiations.

Note that although I have given many details of enactments from Dianic seasonal rituals, I purposefully have not published specific seasonal rituals from the Dianic tradition in their entirety. Although details of our tradition are generally not oath-bound, and with open community rituals largely the norm (with the exception of initiation at Brigid), publishing all of the details from our long-standing seasonal rituals in a book violates my code of ethics. To do so would also not be in keeping with the intention of this book: to utilize the knowledge you have learned and the skills you have practiced through this book to create, experience, and facilitate your own meaningful seasonal rituals.

Hallowmas • October 31 *Deepening*[124]

Also known as Samhain (pronounced "sow-in," meaning "summer's end"), All Soul's Night, All Hallows Eve, Hallows, and Halloween.

Hecate

She walks the roads every moonless night.
Watching the stars to Her heart's delight.
With a blazing torch and whispered song,
The path of destiny She travels on.

She moves through darkness like a knife.
Her dreams are seeds of future's life.
To taste the sweetness with the pain,
Is to know how much the flower needs the rain.

The place She waits is where three roads meet.
The past, the present, and future greet.

[124] All of this section's descriptive Sabbat headings are taken from "The Chakras and the Wheel of the Year," seasonal themes developed by Mooncat and Shekhinah Mountainwater in *Ariadne's Thread*.

To meet Her there where the horned owl flies,
Is to ride the pale stars down from the skies.

She'll take you up, then She'll take you down.
She'll take you under and turn you 'round.
And when She's done, at the dawn light's rise,
You'll meet every gaze with brighter eyes.

Oh Old One of the midnight rhyme,
Bless Your daughters in our time,
As we take to roads in the moonless night,
To seek the wisdom of Your ancient sight.[125]

Night is noticeably lengthening as the dark half of the year marks the first day of winter. With the last of the harvest gathered and stored away, the livestock were brought in from the summer pastures close to home. Those animals not likely to survive the winter were slaughtered and their meat preserved for winter stores. In earlier times, this was a time of sacrifice, of divination for the new year and communion with the dead. To the ancestors, this season was a time of endings and rest, and the night of October 31 was a moment in time that belonged to neither past nor future, to neither this world nor the otherworld.

In Ireland the customs of November Eve varied greatly from village to village. The beloved dead were remembered and honored by candles that were formally lit, one for each departed relative. If the deceased had died in the family home, a candle was lit in the room where the person died. It was a night where communication with the dead was possible and a time where one could ask favors from the ancestors. It was also time to escort the souls of those who had passed through the veil between life and death.

---

125 Song by the author from the CD *The Year Is a Dancing Woman*, Vol. 2.

Halloween was also called "the night of mischief or con." Bands of young people would go door to door begging for bread or money. Since the people knocking at the door might be faeries or ghosts in disguise, the holiday was taken very seriously, and it was of utmost importance to give them something. Pranks were played on persons generally held to be mean or unpleasant. Divination customs included the lighting of bonfires and scrying into the hot coals or ashes to foretell the future for personal reasons, such as marriage and the success of next season's crops. Especially important was the foretelling of weather for the coming year, often done by observing the winds at midnight, which would indicate the prevailing wind during the coming season and warn of storms.

The practice of "trick or treat," where children disguised as ghosts and goblins walk from door to door asking for candy, is still celebrated in the majority of neighborhoods in the United States. Séances, scary stories, and spooky games to foretell the future are still played at today's Halloween parties by young and old alike. The image of the Old Crone riding Her broom across the moon is displayed in store windows and in homes. I find it fascinating that most people are unaware that these images and customs survive from ancient Pagan religions. How interesting that most Americans continue to celebrate the ancient Pagan holiday that acknowledges death in the cycle of life.

Mexico's Dia de los Muertos or Day of the Dead is celebrated in many parts of the United States and "is the result of a fusion between a medieval Spanish-European tradition honoring souls of the dead and pre-Columbian indigenous rites of the dead."[126] In the mid-tenth century, Pope Gregory IV established All Soul's Day and the Feast of All Saints on November first and second, respectively. Dia de los Muertos is a time set aside in many families to honor their ancestors by bringing offerings of yellow marigolds, photographs, copal incense, fanciful toys, food, and alcoholic libations to special altars and to the gravesides of

[126] Article on Dia de los Muertos from Museum of Cultural History, Los Angeles, California, 1982.

relatives for family reunions. The atmosphere of this festival is lighthearted and loving.

Within the mythic cycle of the Goddess, in Her aspect as Crone, the Goddess deepens into Herself and enters the dreamtime, the place between the worlds where past, present, and future exist simultaneously to rest until renewal. The time between Hallomas and Winter Solstice can be understood as the liminal space between the end of the old year and the beginning of the new. The challenge of the season initiated by this night is to enter a place of stillness and simply be where you are: not moving forward or backward but being utterly present, suspended in the space between past and future. It is here that we listen to the voices in the crackling fire, rain, and wind. We let ourselves sink into the arms of the grandmothers. We enter the dark season of the year to dream and remember before we begin to make our return after Winter Solstice, and the new solar cycle is conceived.

> Our delights, our ripening, is a long story to be told over and over in various ways. We begin to make our return. We turn and return to everything that has come to us and see it in relation to the whole. We embody the cycle of return. We make the giveaway of all we have tasted, touched, loved. We become our meaning. We retain the distillation, then concentrate as our circle comes in closer to the center. We can see full circle while looking ahead. We dance the spiral dance, weaving our energies with that of the universe. We invite the presence of memory and prophecy.[127]

In the Dianic tradition, Hallowmas is probably the most ritually packed night of the year. It is an opportunity to leave behind all that has caused you harm in the year closing behind you and carry forward all that is in

---

[127] Hart and Lanning, *Dreaming*, 130.

accordance with the highest good. This holiday incorporates many of the thematic categories discussed in chapter 4, so you might choose to select only a few aspects to work with, rather than all of them in one evening.

Hallowmas Meditation

Relax and deepen into yourself. Breathe deeply into your belly. Inhale. Exhale. Continue to breathe deeply; float on the wind of your breath to the crossroads of your deep mind. Three paths lead away from the place where you are standing. It is night, and you are alone in the light of a waning moon. As you gaze down one of the roads, become aware of someone walking toward you. The figure draws closer. It is your old-year self walking toward you.

Touch her face and gaze into her eyes. Look into her soul and know that your own soul is gazing back at you. What beauty do you find there? What is absolutely exquisite about this being? What needs to evolve? What needs to be accepted? Step forward into communion with your old self. [pause]

Now, turn to the next road. Another figure is coming slowly toward you. She is the goddess Hecate, the wise Crone and guardian of the crossroads. She lives deep within you as your wise self and comes forward when you must make choices at times of transition. She stands before you and hands you a gift of guidance to help you open to new possibilities in the year ahead. Receive Her gift, even though you may not yet understand its meaning. Gaze into Her wise eyes that can see your past, present, and future. Breathe in your willingness to open to the unknown, which contains the seed of possibility. Breathe with Her again as you step forward into communion with Her. [pause]

Turn to face the third road. Its path leads off into the darkness. All life, all consciousness, all birth and rebirth emerges from darkness. You have the opportunity to begin anew if you can only learn to trust the darkness and embrace its wisdom and unseen possibilities. In the darkness of the night, take your first step down that road into the unknown and back into your conscious mind.

...

Seasonal Questions and Ideas

REVIEW YOUR SPIRITUAL GOALS AND PERSONAL VALUES:

* What do I leave behind in the year that has passed, and what do I take with me?
* Whom do I need to forgive? From whom do I need to ask forgiveness?
* What actions can I take in order to open and listen to the Wise One within?
* What is my resistance to listening for Her voice?
* How can I best honor the crones in my life?
* What do I already see or feel that shows what I am moving toward in the year ahead?

REVIEW THE YEAR THAT HAS PASSED WITH INTROSPECTION AND RETROSPECTION: Use the Hallowmas meditation to gain perspective on your past, present, and future.

INVOKE AND/OR HONOR YOUR BELOVED DEAD AND SPIRIT GUIDES: Create an ancestral altar to honor your beloved dead. Ring a spirit bell, call their names, and speak from your heart to them. Do not demand that they come to you, but invite them to be present if they wish to. At the end of the ritual, remember to formally bid them farewell if you have invited them into the ritual space.

REMEMBER THE BURNING TIMES: In Dianic tradition, Hallowmas is the night where we especially remember and honor the women and children who were tortured to death as witches, healers, herbalists, midwives, and heretics during the Inquisition. Learn about the life and death of a woman murdered during this period. In your Hallows ritual, share about her life, read a story, or perform a mystery play to memorialize her.

RITUALIZE THE RELEASE OF PATRIARCHAL MANIFESTATIONS AND COLLUSIONS IN YOUR LIFE.

GIVE AWAY OR DONATE YOUR OLD CLOTHES.

HONOR THE CRONES AND HAGS ("HAG" FROM THE GREEK WORD FOR "HOLY") IN YOUR LIFE AND IN THE SEASONAL CYCLE OF THE GODDESS YEAR.

WELCOME IN THE CLOSE OF THE YEAR BY LIGHTING CANDLES. HONOR THE FATES, WHO ARE ESPECIALLY PRESENT ON HALLOWMAS. DO A DIVINATION FOR THE NEW YEAR.

PREPARE YOURSELF TO TRANSITION INTO THE SEASON OF SPIRIT: Ritualize your descent into the cauldron of change, and prepare yourself to be in a place of stillness.

CREATE A FEAST FOR THE DEAD: Choose foods that are red in color to honor your beloved dead.

Winter Solstice • December 21

Conception/Communion

Also called Midwinter or Yule (meaning "Wheel").

Invocation

> We call you by the winter winds that chill our bones
> and awaken our minds.
> We call you by the warmth of the hearth fire that gathers and comforts.
> We call you by still waters, whose mirror leads us to inner journeys.
> We call you by the quiet earth that waits and dreams.
> We call you by the visions we make and the love we share.
> Great Goddess, who contains all things, bless our rite
> as we celebrate the rebirth of spirit. Blessed be!

Winter Solstice comes at the dead of winter and marks the longest night. Being a solar holiday, the exact date fluctuates each calendar year between December twentieth and twenty-third. The ancestors saw this season as a time of faith and the rebirth of spirit. In ancient celebrations of Midwinter, on hilltops and in homes, fires were lit with ceremony. People huddled around the blazing Yule log and lit ritual fires outside to encourage the sun to return. In many old Pagan traditions, later adopted by the Christian calendar, it was at this time of the year that the Star

Child, sacred son of the Mother, was born. He represented hope during the hard months of winter.[128] The Winter Solstice was a time of magic and faith. By projecting and energizing hope for the sun's eventual return and the earth's renewal, the people made a "spiritual cradle" or psychic space for the newly conceived light to eventually fill. In Norway, people still wish each other *God Jul*, meaning "Good Wheel," a winter holiday blessing for a "good turn" around the wheel of the year once again.

In Dianic cosmology, the Goddess is *not* the fertile mother giving birth at this time of year to a physical being. Few creatures give birth in the middle of winter where fewer offspring can survive. On the contrary, the Goddess is the Hag of Winter, who goes to seed and becomes bone; therefore, the age of women honored in this season ranges from eighty-four years to the time of her death. The Goddess births, sustains, and devours the life She creates in order to re-create again and again. At Winter Solstice, it is the Goddess as hag who begins to release Herself from the physical world and conceive Herself anew as the Infant Light so the new solar cycle can begin. She contains the seed of Her own rebirth. Unlike a physical child who can be seen, She conceives the spirit of the infant sun, a spirit child, the daughter of light, who can be sensed but not yet seen, an invisible point in the vast darkness. This time brings the promise of light, not the actual delivery. Winter Solstice can be described as the dark moon cycle of the sun. The light is there but no one can see the light, nor fathom it until later. The actual physical presence of the light returning isn't experienced until the wheel of the year turns closer to the holiday of Brigid (February 1), the festival of the waxing light.

The holiday of Winter Solstice celebrates the presence of spirit and the power of faith and hope that our visions of the future will come into manifestation. All we can do in the middle of winter is pray and hope that the light will return. Winter Solstice is not about having the light. It is about carrying hope and trust while moving toward a vision that

---

[128] Green, *A Witch Alone*, 49.

we will work to make a reality. It is a time of patience, like that of an expectant mother who can sense the spirit of the child within but must wait until the actual quickening to know that physical life is truly within her. We must wait in the darkness of Midwinter, and this is not easy for most of us who are not comfortable with the dark, silence, resting, and dreaming.

In the darkest part of the year when the days are shortest, Nature asks us to slow down and enjoy a cup of warm tea, to be with loved ones, to listen rather than to speak. Under the ground, the earth silently sleeps. Seeds rest in suspended animation, and the animals hibernate. In contrast, we humans rush frantically to the malls, stressing ourselves with activity when we really yearn to rest, dream, and gather strength in our bodies for the coming season of renewal. For many people living in the United States, taking time to rest and dream is seen as a sign of laziness. However, nature teaches us that resting, drawing inward for a time, is present in all living things. Rest is necessary for growth that comes later in its season.

The sun will return: our modern knowledge of astronomy tells us that this is a fact we can depend on. Unlike our ancestors, to whom the cycles of light and dark, the heat and rain, meant life or death, food or starvation, we need only go to the supermarket and buy everything we need. Urban dwellers usually forget about the farmers who provide our food and our continued dependency on the cycles of nature. We don't have to actually make magic in the darkness to encourage the sunlight to return, but what we have lost, perhaps, is the awe and wonder of the darkness. Because of the pervasive use of electricity, especially in urban areas, we often have to create the experience of darkness in order to perceive the light. With such ingrained cultural and religious emphasis on the light, always the light, we forget to value the dark. Just as "death belongs to life, half of day is night,"[129] half of the year moves toward darkness and then rests in it.

Midwinter invites us to dream in the dark, to become still and listen to

---

[129] From the song "Out of the Darkness" by Frankie Armstrong.

the wise self within, the old, wise hag present in every woman. Winter is Her season, and She lives on the edge of spirit, able to access both this world and the next. She is the old one who is already in your future, looking back into this moment at the choices you made, the values you chose to follow, the paths you took. Dreaming is Her power, and She patiently waits in the dark with wisdom and guidance. It is often this wise self whom we try to avoid in our constant rushing toward the light, whom we choose not to see with our inner eyes.

The dark season challenges us to surrender to our dreaming, to trust that the strength of the earth will support our weight as we sleep. It is out of the darkness that flowers eventually emerge, babies are born, and inspiration for poetry and ideas is nurtured toward the page and through our voices. In the deep, dark places in ourselves, we find the inner truth about ourselves. In this winter season of so many people prematurely rushing toward the light, remember to slow down and do winter's inner work. Celebrate the dark, where the inner life is honored and nurtured. Sometime during this season, take some time for yourself to go inward, to find out what your dreams are.

Seasonal Questions and Ideas

REVIEW YOUR SPIRITUAL GOALS AND PERSONAL VALUES:

* What am I visioning and hoping for?
* What dreams do I carry inside?
* How do I keep my faith alive?
* How do I nurture a state of awe and wonder of the universe?
* What can I do to encourage the rebirth of spirit in my life, my family, and my world?
* What can I do as an individual and in my community to create a space for the Goddess?

SPEND TIME CONSCIOUSLY IN THE DARK: Take some time to relax into yourself. Find ways to honor the darkness, the dreamtime, the time of visioning and imagining. Practice using your inner senses in the dark.

LIGHT A CANDLE IN THE DARK TO HONOR A DREAM OR LONG-TERM VISION YOU HAVE FOR THE COMING YEAR: Remember that the candle flame represents your inner spirit light, representing hope and faith. Pass the flame on to others.

MAKE OR GIVE CANDLES AS GIFTS OF SPIRIT, FAITH, AND HOPE.

LIGHT EIGHT CANDLES IN A CIRCLE, ONE FOR EACH OF THE HOLIDAYS: Extinguish each one at a time, starting with Brigid, acknowledging each holiday that has passed, until all is in darkness. Pause in the darkness. Light a candle at the center, to begin again.[130]

CREATE AN ALTAR TO HONOR YOUR ANCESTRAL MOTHERS.

STAY UP ALL NIGHT IN THE DARKNESS AND WAIT FOR THE SUNRISE.

SLOW DOWN AND TAKE MORE TIME TO REMEMBER YOUR DREAMS EACH MORNING.

SHARE A FIRE AND WARM FOOD AND DRINK WITH YOUR LOVED ONES.

LEAVE FOOD AND WATER OUT FOR BIRDS AND OTHER ANIMALS.

SAVE SEEDS FROM THE HARVEST FOR NEXT YEAR'S GARDEN OR FLOWER BED.

---

[130] From a Mother Night ritual by Ristandi.

LISTEN TO OR TELL STORIES OF TIMES PAST.

Brigid • February 1

Stirrings/Quickening

Also known as Imbolc (pronounced IMM'bolk, meaning "in the belly"), Festival of the Waxing Light, Bride/ Bridgid's Day, Oilmelc (meaning "ewe's milk"), Groundhog Day (in the United States), Badger's Day (in the United Kingdom), and Candlemas (February second).

Brigid

Hear my words, I'm calling from your heart,
And calling from your mind.
I am the spark that kindles the flame,
And nurtures all in kind.
For a jewel of light has been at every root,
And lies within the soil's clay,
And it cradles the babe of our visions and dreams,
And sends all creation into flight.
Take my hand, I'll pull to free your stance,
I pull only at first.
And when you push on to make out a path,
The waiting seedpods burst.
There's a fountain that flows from deep within the rock, And
satisfies the thirst in all,
And it cools the brow when the hammer falls,
And smoothes the way for the birth.
So speak my name, I'll come to any door,
And come at any hour,
And when you raise your voice and your heart,
Your innocence is power.

And the healing of love can sweeten bitter tastes,
And wash the poison from the wound,
And it fills every sail to ride upon the sea,
And guides every vessel homeward bound.[131]

The earth begins to waken from winter's sleep as the pale sunlight grows stronger with each passing day. The first signs of renewal appear as the crocuses bloom and early lambs are born in the snow. The hope and faith sustained through the winter cold and darkness has turned to a certainty. Seeds that have been resting in the earth crack their casings and send out a root, initiating the discovery of individuation.

In ancient Ireland, this cross-quarter day marked the first day of spring, and the first stirrings in the womb of Earth Mother were celebrated as farmers started their preparations for spring sowing. This holiday marked the beginning of the lambing season, and was the first dairy produced after the long winter. Like all of the cross-quarter day fire festivals, divination was done to predict the prevailing wind and weather conditions in the season to come. To see a badger or hedgehog (or groundhog in the United States) emerging from its burrow to forage was a sign of good weather. If she stayed out, it was a sign that mild weather was coming. If she saw her shadow and returned to her burrow, the winter would be longer. We still carry on this tradition as each February 1 people gather in Pennsylvania to see Puxatawney Phil, the famous groundhog, emerge from his burrow.

The time between Yule and the Spring Equinox was called the Cleansing Tide. It was a time of thinking and planning, of assessing what had been achieved and what unfinished work could readily be cast away. It was a time when all things were washed clean or swept away. In ancient Rome, February was cleansing time, "the month of ritual purification."[132] During the season, a new tide of life started to flow through the whole world of nature, and people had to get rid of the past and look to the

131 Song by Cyntia Smith, recorded with the author, on the CD, *The Heart Is the Only Nation.*
132 Farrar, *Eight Sabbats for Witches*, 65.

future. Spring cleaning was originally a nature ritual.[133]

In Irish folk tradition to this day, St. Brigid's Day[134] is still celebrated on the first of February. In addition to being a goddess of poetry, inspiration, divination, smithcraft, and healing, she is also a patroness of cattle, dairy work, and is closely bound up with food production.[135] Traditionally, a young girl dressed in white and wearing a crown of rushes was escorted from house to house by a group of other young girls. She would give a blessing for an egg, a penny, bread, sugar, or cakes.[136] During this time, seed saved from the previous year's crops were mingled with the new. Water from wells dedicated to Brigid or Bride was sprinkled on the house and its occupants, farm buildings, livestock, and fields to invoke the blessings of the goddess, so powerful and beloved She was transformed in later years into a saint by the Catholic Church.[137] Many old customs associated with the Celtic goddess Brigid continue to this day, such as picking rushes and weaving them into sun wheels, also called Brigid's crosses.

In the mythic cycle of the Goddess, She shapeshifts from the hag that entered into spirit at Yule, conceives Herself anew, and mysteriously emerges at Brigid in the form of a young girl dressed in white. It is the greatest of Women's Mysteries, demonstrating the eternal and ever-changing nature of the Goddess who never dies,[138] analogous to the transition from the waning dark moon to the waxing new crescent moon in the sky each lunar month. For Dianics, the transition time between Brigid and Spring Equinox symbolizes rebirth and the time of infancy and early childhood. There is no way to predict the precise date at which She transforms herself from the hag to infant again. Part of this Mystery is to feel the change to know it has happened.

---

133 Ibid., 66.

134 In the fifth century, St. Brighid of Kildare took over many of the goddess's qualities and aspects. Matthews, *The Celtic Spirit*, 102.

135 Danaher, 13.

136 Ibid., 25.

137 Ibid., 37.

138 *A Witch Alone*, 51.

In the Dianic tradition, February first is called Brigid after the Celtic goddess and is the time when formal initiation into the Dianic tradition takes place. Of all the rituals in Dianic tradition, the initiation ceremony is the only one held secret. Initiation, from the Latin *inire,* means "to go into"; *initium*, "a beginning." We are initiated into mystery, into the awakened self.[139] Our ritual of initiation is known only to those women who have received it, and only initiates may facilitate this ceremony of welcoming in new Dianic witches. If a woman is already initiated, then she rededicates herself at Brigid. Throughout the season of the earth's awakening, like the tiny seeds within the earth, breaking their casings and stretching their tiny tendrils out and up toward the earth's surface, it is a time of personal individuation, of formally declaring who you are. Out of the dark earth, close to the heartbeat of the Mother, a woman defines her spiritual path to herself, and names and claims it.

Seasonal Questions and Ideas

REVIEW YOUR SPIRITUAL GOALS AND PERSONAL VALUES:
Ask yourself the following seasonal questions:

* What am I spiritually dedicated to?

* What are my spiritual goals for the coming year?

* What is stirring inside me that seeks to grow? How will I nurture this growth?

* How will I deepen my connection to the Goddess who is both within and without?

DECLARE YOUR SPIRITUAL JOURNEY ALOUD: Declare your spiritual focus for the year. Make a dedication to the Goddess regarding your personal and spiritual growth. Light a white candle as you make your dedication.

---

[139] Hart, *Dreaming*, 32.

DEDICATE YOURSELF TO LEARNING ABOUT A SPECIFIC GODDESS FOR THE YEAR.

WEAR WHITE TO SIGNIFY THE NEW CYCLE OF THE WAXING LIGHT.

THINK OF WAYS TO GIVE BIRTH TO YOURSELF AND OTHERS SPIRITUALLY.

TAKE A RITUAL BATH: using a loofa, scrub off the winter layers from your skin.

CLEAN AND PURIFY YOUR HOME AND WORKSPACE FOR THE YEAR.

Spring Equinox • March 21

Emergence

Also called Ostara or Eostre.

Laughing Maiden is a-borning,
Laughing Maiden is a-rising,
Laughing Maiden is a-flying,
Spring is come, spring is come.[140]

The arrival of the Spring Equinox marks the balancing or equal length of day and night and the onset of warmer weather. The exact date fluctuates each calendar year with the solar cycle and falls between March twentieth to twenty-third. The equinoxes are times of equilibrium, of balance, of suspended activity and, by their nature, they are times when the veil between the seen and unseen is thin. Times of change such as these are also frequently times of psychological and psychic turbulence.[141]

[140] Chant by the author from the CD *The Year Is a Dancing Woman, Volume 1*.
[141] Marian Green.

Although in spring we are poised at equilibrium, our energy and psyches are in a state of anticipation, ready to move forward into the season of rapid growth. In the Northern Hemisphere, this time began the Sowing Tide, the time of preparing the earth for planting.

This holiday is sometimes known as Ostara, named after the Scandinavian goddess of spring, or by Her Anglo-Saxon name, Eostre or Ostre, from the root word *estrus*, when animals come into the fertile time of their reproductive cycle,[142] and the German word *Ostern*, which denotes an eastern orientation and the dawn. The Christian holiday of Easter took its name from this word and associated itself with Eostre's theme of resurrection from death, celebrated in a sunrise ceremony[143] on the Sunday after the first full moon after the vernal equinox. The Irish Catholic holiday of Saint Patrick's Day occurs near the middle of spring, and, like Easter, it utilizes many pre-Christian themes and symbols. Decorated eggs—often dyed red, the color of life—are found all over Europe and symbolize the rebirth of nature. The chocolate rabbit is the Goddess's sacred hare in disguise.[144] It was also customary to wear a new set of clothes in celebration of the earth's birthday.

Spring is a time of earthly regeneration, the time of birth and rebirth. The seasonal energy is one of emergence, expansion, and the drive to implement the visions begun in winter's dreaming. The air is charged with a newness, fresh and exciting, bidding life to shake off the inner world of winter and to step fully outside into a renewed world.

In the Goddess's mythic cycle, the Maiden goddess of spring is reborn from the earth, emerging out of winter's confines into the bursting flowers and budding greenery of new life.

> The world is again recreated in all its teeming diversity, and we stand in awe of Her miraculous will and the power that is

---

142 Kindred, *The Earth's Cycle of Celebration*.

143 Grimassi, *Encyclopedia of Wicca & Witchcraft*, 281.

144 Green, *A Witch Alone*, 52.

> woman. And a promise made to a dying world in the fall is fulfilled in the spring. For know ye the mystery that without life there is no death and without death no renewal, and the Great Goddess rules it all.[145]

In the cycle of Women's Mysteries celebrated in the Dianic tradition, we celebrate our young girls and welcome the Maiden of Spring lovingly back into the world. We rejoice in the renewal of the earth, honoring the eternal connection of mothers and daughters, of women borne of women. We retell the pre-Hellenic myth of Demeter and Kore/Persephone (the Greeks called her Kore, meaning "maiden"), in which the daughter of the Earth Mother chooses to leave her mother to follow her own calling in the world as Persephone, the Queen of the Dead, yet returns annually to reconnect with her mother and renew their eternal bond of love. We bless the young girls, in our community and in the world, pledging to help them be strong and safe. We honor the spirit of the young Maiden within each other and ourselves. This holiday initiates the seasonal cycle of the Maiden goddess and the time of childhood just prior to the coming of age into womanhood with the onset of menstruation. We dance to awaken ourselves and the earth, and symbolically or actually plant seeds to nurture the goals we set at Brigid.

Seasonal Questions and Ideas

ASK YOURSELF THE FOLLOWING SEASONAL QUESTIONS:

* What wisdom am I bringing with me from the dark of winter?
* Who am I becoming?
* What am I awakening within myself ?

COVER YOURSELF WITH A DARK CLOTH: then emerge into colorful, open spaces.

---

145 Alba, *Cauldron of Change*, 183.

CELEBRATE AND ENERGIZE YOUR BECOMING.

BUY OR MAKE SOME NEW COLORFUL CLOTHES.

CELEBRATE AND HONOR THE MAIDEN GODDESS WITHIN AND WITHOUT.

DO A SPRING CLEANING OF YOUR HOME, ALTAR, AND MIND.

GATHER WITH FRIENDS AND PLAY FUN PHYSICAL GAMES: DANCE AND SING!

PAINT AND DECORATE EGGS: perhaps with symbols of your wishes for the coming season. Learn the ancient art of pysanky egg decorating.

SHAPE SWEET COOKIE DOUGH INTO SNAKES AND RABBITS.

BEGIN YOUR SPRING GARDEN: Dig your hands into the earth and loosen the clods in preparation for planting. Plant the eggs you decorated in the soil to "grow" your intentions.

FILL YOUR HOME WITH SEASONAL FLOWERS OR BRANCHES. HONOR THE CONNECTION BETWEEN MOTHERS AND DAUGHTERS: Use the season to heal or honor the bond with your own mother or daughter.

SIMULATE A BIRTH CANAL TO WELCOME THE MAIDEN GODDESS BACK TO THE MOTHER.

"HATCH" YOURSELF: Create a form of pressure or resistance to simulate breaking through a seed's shell casing under the weight of the earth. Enact becoming an active participant in your own becoming.

BAKE A BIRTHDAY CAKE: Honor the Maiden Goddess's return.

TELL OR READ STORIES ABOUT COURAGEOUS YOUNG GIRLS.

DANCE A CIRCLE DANCE TO HONOR THE CYCLE OF REBIRTH AND RETURN.

CREATE WAYS TO REMEMBER AND HONOR THE YOUNG GIRL WITHIN YOURSELF AND OTHERS.

NOTICE THE FLOWERS THAT BEGIN TO COME OUT: Meditate on the courage and strength in such vulnerability.

SPEND TIME WITH A YOUNG GIRL OR A GROUP OF GIRLS: Find ways to support, protect, or empower them.

May Eve • April 30/May 1

Menstruation/Flowering

Also known as Beltane, Bealtaine (pronounced *b'yol-tinnuh*), Walpurgisnacht, and Maiden Fire[146]

The May Queen Is Waiting

I'll prepare the furrowed earth for your sweet body.
The stars are rising in the moonlit sky.
The May Queen is waiting.
Her voice reaches as you sleep, can you awaken
To live the wonders of your dreams?
The May Queen is waiting.
Restless in the night, the full moon light,

[146] A new name for this holiday by Dianic HP Cerridwyn RoseLabrys.

Carving magic patterns in the land,
She waits for you to return again.
Do not keep Her waiting.
You startle, wake, and stare, heart is beating.
The new earth quickens as you rise.
The May Queen is waiting.
Feel the pulsing ground call you to journey,
To know the depths of your desire.
The May Queen is waiting.
Moving through the night, the bright moon's flight.
In green and silver on the plain,
She waits for you to return again.
Do not keep Her waiting.
Her temper stings if you refuse to taste Her honey.
Surrender as enchantment brings
The first light of dawning.
Move with Her in sacred dance,
through fear to feeling,
Bringing ecstasy to those who dare.
Living earth is breathing.
Loving through the night in the bright moonlight,
As seedlings open with the rain,
She'll long for you to return again.
Do not keep Her waiting.
Do not keep Her waiting.
Do not keep Her waiting.[147]

In Ireland, as in most parts of northern Europe, May Eve signaled the first day of summer, and the principal customs and ceremonies of May

---

[147] By the author, from the CD, *Songs of the Otherworld.*

were those welcoming summer. Summer brought the Growing Tide, when things begin to come to fruition, ripen, and fulfill the promises of spring. May Eve was marked by the lighting of bon fires and various rites to ensure fertility among the herds and to bring a good harvest.[148] The old name for this feast at the beginning of May was Beltane, which means "bright fire."[149] Although the holiday has various spellings, it consists of two components: bel and tan. "Bel is known to be an ancient sun god name ... Tan is Celtic for fire, so here there is a double principle of God, or good."[150] In old Ireland, the cattle were taken to the summer pastures, where they would remain until Samhain. All of the spring work, including tilling the soil to produce the crops, should have been finished by May Day. The most common custom was that of venturing out after dusk on May Eve to pick fresh flowers that would be brought home before dawn on the following day. The hawthorn, or May bush, would be set out in front of the home in the same spirit in which we set out our flags on a national holiday. Sometimes the May bush would be decorated with eggshells, ribbons, colored paper, and flowers.[151] Beltane was a time of revelry and bawdiness, stimulating the sexual energy of life-making. The maypole, outlawed in Ireland in 1792, is probably one of the most overtly sexual ritual customs associated with this season.

May Eve's dark counterpart across the wheel of the year is Hallowmas, and traditionally both holidays were the hinge holidays of the year, where inhabitants of the worlds of ancestral spirits, otherworld beings, and humans might cross paths. The faerie faith was strong in many Celtic lands, and protective measures were taken on the chance that mortals and immortals might encounter each other from sunset on May Eve to sunrise on May Day. Faerie abductions were feared, and it was thought that infants were especially in danger of being switched for "changelings,"

---

[148] Davidson, *Myths and Symbols in Pagan Europe*, 39.

[149] Knightly, *The Customs and Ceremonies of Britain*, 159.

[150] Green, *A Calendar of Festivals*, 49.

[151] Danaher, 88.

the children of the faerie folk. Offerings of food or drink were left for the faeries so that they might be kind to their mortal neighbors.

In the mythic cycle of the Goddess, the Maiden becomes initiated into womanhood through her first menstruation, her first bloods. With the onset of menarche, passion awakens, and girls begin the transition to becoming young women, entering into the Mysteries of womanhood. The young goddess becomes the Virgin, She Who Is Whole Unto Herself, possessing herself and possessed by no one. This does not, however, imply that she is a virgin in the strictly physical sense; in fact, she may choose to have many lovers, either male or female, according to her desire, but none can claim her exclusively as their own.

The Dianic tradition is unique in that our seasonal celebrations openly honor young women's first menarche, women's uterine blood, and the creative forces within the earth and ourselves. Women's uterine blood as the source of physical fertility is also symbolic of our ability to create, whether through childbearing or by the many other forms our creativity might express itself. Our woman-blood is life. We celebrate and bless young women who have begun to menstruate during the previous year. In this season, we especially honor young women from ages twelve to twenty-one years. We bless our female bodies and honor the power of our emerging sexual and sensual selves. This is also an especially appropriate time to do healing work around childhood sexual abuse, body hatred, and misogyny.

Seasonal Questions and Ideas

ASK YOURSELF THESE SEASONAL QUESTIONS:

* How do I honor my own sacred blood?
* How do I honor the blood of other women?
* What holds me back from opening to my desires, from participating in and celebrating life?

LOOK AT THE INTERNAL RESTRICTIONS YOU HAVE PLACED ON YOUR BODY, HEART, AND MIND THAT KEEP YOU FROM FULLY PARTAKING IN THE SACRED AND SIMPLE JOYS OF LIVING. MAKE CHANGES.

FIND WAYS TO CELEBRATE HAVING A FEMALE BODY: Do self-blessings for yourself and with other women.

DRESS AND ADORN YOURSELF IN A WAY THAT CELEBRATES YOUR BEAUTY: Dance in front of a mirror.

EXPLORE THE NOTION THAT LIFE IS YOUR LOVER: Find safe and healthy ways to fully explore and honor your sensual/sexual self. Open to the senses of touch, taste, scent, and hearing.

MAY IS A WONDERFUL MONTH TO CELEBRATE THE FIRST BLOOD OF YOUNG WOMEN IN YOUR COMMUNITY: Create a ritual to welcome them into the circle of women. Affirm their strengths and values. Encourage them to resist the negative voices of patriarchy that come through fashion magazines, television, and film.

CREATE A FIRST BLOODS RITUAL FOR YOURSELF AS YOU WOULD HAVE WISHED IT TO BE.

CREATE A SEXUAL HEALING RITUAL FOR YOURSELF AND/OR OTHER WOMEN.

MAKE LOVE WITH YOUR LOVER, YOURSELF, YOUR GARDEN, YOUR LIFE.

CELEBRATE BIOPHILIA[152]: loving life.

---

[152] A term created by feminist theologian Mary Daly, after noting that there was no term in the English language for loving life, only for loving death (necrophilia). She defines biophilia as the original lust for life that is at the core of all elemental emotion; pure lust,

Summer Solstice • June 21

Union

Also called Midsummer's Eve/Day or Litha.

Summer, Summer

Summer, summer, milk of the heifers
We have brought the summer in.
Yellow summer, brilliant daisies,
We have brought the summer in.
Barley is rising, lilies are blooming,
We have brought the summer in,
Fields are golden, corn is reaching,
We have brought the summer in.
Boughs are laden, birds are singing,
We have brought the summer in.
Meadow streams and roe deer grazing,
We have brought the summer in.
Fires in the hearth, our homes protecting,
We have brought the summer in.
Over the farmlands, smoke is drifting,
We have brought the summer in.
Torches blazing, circle dancing,
We have brought the summer in.
Wine is flowing, voices soaring,
We have brought the summer in.
Midsummer bonfires, lovers jumping,
We have brought the summer in.

---

which is the nemesis of patriarchy, the necrophilic state. Daly, *Webster's First New Intergalactic Wickedary of the English Language*, 67.

Health and long life, good fortune bringing,
We have brought the summer in.
Summer, summer, milk of the heifers
We have brought the summer in.
Yellow summer, brilliant daisies,
We have brought the summer in.[153]

Summer Solstice marks the peak of the solar cycle at Midsummer. In the midst of the longest day of the year, we simultaneously begin our return to the dark half of the year. The exact date of the Summer Solstice fluctuates each calendar year between June twentieth and twenty-third. At Winter Solstice, the underlying energy is about visioning; the seasonal energy at Summer Solstice is active: it's about doing and expanding, living the dream envisioned in the dreamtime of winter. At the peak point of summer bloom, prayers for blessings on the crops are asked of the Goddess. The earth is fertile, and the womb of the Earth Mother is now ripe with life as She begins to pour forth Her creations in the form of growing fields, trees, flowers, and animals.

Two fire traditions were practiced widely on Summer Solstice, sometimes called "Bonfire Night." One old Irish custom dictated that a community fire was to be lit exactly at sunset and had to be watched and tended until long after midnight. The communal fire was built and lit by the inhabitants of a whole town or several towns and celebrated with music, dancing, fire jumping, singing, and other ceremonies. The family fire was a smaller fire lit by members of each household for the benefit of their particular household or farm. The family fire was a quiet affair in which protective ceremonies were the main concern. In some villages, the inhabitants took embers or ashes from the family fire, or from the community fire, and threw a portion into each field or on

---

[153] Song by Cyntia Smith and the author from their CD, *The Heart Is the Only Nation*. Chorus translated from the Gaelic by Jim Duran.

the four corners of each field in order to protect them from damaging weather, such as drought or hail storms. The cattle of the farm were herded together and driven through the smoke of an outdoor bonfire. In Ireland, this was also a traditional time for medicinal herb gathering.[154]

In the mythic cycle of the Goddess, the Maiden Goddess experiences the joy of union with Her creative, sexual, sensual self and becomes pregnant with Her creations. Thus, this holiday begins the Goddess's transition from the Maiden to the fertility cycle of the Mother Goddess as maker/creatrix. The age range of women honored in the season from Summer Solstice to First Harvest is from approximately twenty-one to thirty-one years of age.

In the Dianic tradition, Summer Solstice is a holiday honoring the many ways that women are fertile and creative in their lives; the ways that, as women, we metaphorically and literally use our bloods. All women, regardless of whether they physically give birth and parent children, become "Mother" when they nurture, sustain, and protect life—the human species or other species—through their life's work and activism. In Dianic tradition, we also honor the fire element in our personal and collective lives and use it symbolically and energetically to strengthen, sharpen, and forge our will to the fall of patriarchy in the world and within ourselves. Energizing our individual and collective creativity, we use the metaphor of the sun's power to magnify and illuminate our awareness and actions toward a more egalitarian and loving world for everyone. Using our voices and the power of dance and drum, we celebrate union within ourselves and with others, honoring fertility and creative expression of all kinds. By standing over a small cauldron fire, we use the power of fire to cleanse ourselves of negative body images, particularly those around sexuality. By leaping over a fire as was done in ages past, we energize the fruition of our projects and passions.

---

[154] Danaher, 134–149.

Seasonal Questions and Ideas

ASK YOURSELF THESE SEASONAL QUESTIONS:

* Where is the fiery, life-force energy in my life? How is it manifesting?
* How will I (or how do I) feed my creative fire? What is its fuel?
* How do I use my blood?
* How am I a "mother"? How do I nurture, sustain, and protect my creations?

JUMP A LITERAL OR SYMBOLIC BONFIRE: Use the seasonal ritual theme to feed, ignite, and magnify your personal and collective will. Dance and move your body to feel the heat of your life force.

HONOR MOTHER GODDESSES THROUGHOUT THE WORLD AS CREATORS OF LIFE AND LOVE. MAKE, BUILD, OR CREATE SOMETHING WITH YOUR HANDS, VOICE, WRITING, OR MOVEMENT IN HONOR OF THE MOTHER/MAKER WITHIN AND WITHOUT.

HONOR THE MANY DIFFERENT WAYS THAT THE CONCEPT OF "MOTHER" CAN BE EXPRESSED THROUGH THE MAKING OF CHILDREN AS WELL AS THE MAKING OF ART, MUSIC, CAREERS, ETC.: Celebrate she who creates, sustains, and protects.

This holiday is also an appropriate time to honor a woman or women within your community who choose not to bear children or who cannot have them, yet who channel their creativity into other works.

EXPLORE PASSION, CREATIVITY, AND GROWTH AS RELATED TO THE FIRE ELEMENT: Use the fire element to strengthen, sharpen, and forge your will to the fall of patriarchy. Empower yourself to act! Dare to live your life according to your values! Commit or recommit yourself to ending patriarchy within and without.

CELEBRATE FERTILITY IN ALL ITS FORMS.

MAKE LOVE A LOT: Dedicate the energy to a specific creative focus.

LIGHT CANDLES OR BONFIRES FOR WHAT YOU DESIRE IN THE SEASON OF GROWTH AND ABUNDANCE.

First Harvest • August 1

Ripening

Also called Lammas (Loaf Mass), Lughnasa, Feast of the First Fruits, Habondia, or the Threshold of Plenty.

Tree Lessons

There was a lass, and a bonny lass
Did enter a sacred grove,
She's turned her east, she's turned her west,
To see the trees all grow.
The hazel, the oak, the ash, and the willow,
How lovely you do grow,
If I could learn your seasons well,
The greater wisdom I will know.
She made a wand from the hazelnut branch,
To lead her to a owing stream.
She bent and drank from the waters there,
And knew true poetry.
It's then she stood beside the wise oak,
And held an acorn in her hand.
She met the mighty Guardian of the Door,
Protector of times past.
She came unto the ash tree of old,

That grows between the sky and earth.
She felt the spin of all the worlds,
Like the quickening of birth.
At last she came to the bending willow tree,
Who harbors magic and mystery.
She danced to the song of the wind in the leaves,
And knew sweet ecstasy.[155]

Sunlight is noticeably beginning to decline as the wheel of the year turns toward the dark half of the year. The beginning of August marks celebration of the First Harvest. The fertile Earth Mother is abundant with life, as evidenced by the golden fields of grain and the ripening fruits of autumn. Like the cornucopia, She pours forth Her blessings of abundance. The traditional Celtic name of this holiday, Lughnasa, stems from a word meaning "the commemoration of Lugh." Lugh, the Celtic fire and light god, appears in Irish legend as a leader of the Tuatha De Danann ("the peoples of the goddess Dana").[156] Like so many of the pre-Christian gods, he undergoes death and rebirth seasonally within the eternal cycle of the Goddess. This holiday is also well known as Lammas, from the Saxon word *Hlaft-mass*, meaning "Feast of the Bread."[157]

In Ireland, farmers hoped to have the first crops ready for gathering at this date, which traditionally began the harvest. It was against custom to cut any corn or dig any potatoes before this day.[158] A ritual meal was prepared and eaten from the fruits and grains gathered on the first day of the harvest. This feast was usually eaten at a festive gathering that involved an excursion to some traditional site, usually a hill or mountaintop, or beside a lake or river. Garlands made from stalks of corn, which we call

---

155 Song by the author, Cyntia Smith, and Shekhinah Mountainwater, from the CD, *The Heart Is the Only Nation*.

156 Farrar, *Eight Sabbats for Witches*, 102–105.

157 Grimassi, *Encyclopedia of Wicca and Witchcraft*, 227.

158 Danaher, 166.

wheat in America, were worn in honor of the corn goddess. It was a social and flirtatious time for young people, accompanied by music, dancing, and fire leaping. It was also a traditional time for weddings. In earlier times, trial marriages that lasted a year and a day began at this time. They could be dissolved the following Lammas by simply having the couple stand back to back and walk away from each other, one toward the north and the other toward the south. Other couples, who had decided to deepen their commitment, would join hands for life.[159]

In the mythic cycle of the Goddess and in Dianic tradition, we honor the abundant Mother Goddess whose love pours forth as food and beauty for Her daughters and their children. While the focus is on abundance, it is also a time to make appropriate sacrifices to the Goddess in Her aspect as reaper. First Harvest causes us to look at what must be weeded, thinned, cut away, or prioritized, so that the full harvest to come is insured. Since most women no longer grow their own food, their personal harvest is that project or life goal that they set into motion, nurtured along, worked hard for, and now have manifested. The age range of women honored in this season from First Harvest to Fall Equinox is approximately from thirty-two to forty-nine years of age.

Seasonal Questions and Ideas

ASK YOURSELF THESE SEASONAL QUESTIONS:

* What can be or needs to be sacrificed for my harvest?
* How do I share my abundance with others?
* How do I manifest my power?
* How do I support myself and others in attaining or manifesting life goals?

SACRIFICE TO THE GODDESS AS REAPER THOSE THINGS,

---

159 Alba, *Cauldron of Change*, 209.

BEHAVIORS, OR ATTITUDES THAT WILL HINDER THE COMPLETION OF YOUR OWN PERSONAL HARVEST: Weed out, pinch back, or thin out anything not essential that might impede its fruition. Look at the priorities in your life and review them to see if they are consistent with what you say you want or need. Initiate any necessary changes.

CELEBRATE THE ABUNDANCE OF THE EARTH BY MAKING AND SHARING A FEAST OF FRESH SEASONAL FRUITS, GRAINS, AND VEGETABLES.

BAKE BREAD AND TASTE THE GIFT OF LIFE: Shape it into a goddess figure, and share the bounty of Her body at a seasonal ritual or feast.

GIVE THANKS FOR THE GIFTS AROUND YOU AND FOR GOOD FORTUNE IN YOUR LIFE.

FIND WAYS TO TASTE WHAT YOU HAVE ACCOMPLISHED IN THE GROWING SEASON.

HONOR YOUR LEADERSHIP SKILLS OR THE WAYS IN WHICH YOU HAVE SUPPORTED OTHERS WITH WISDOM.

TAKE A FESTIVE PICNIC MEAL TO THE MOUNTAINS, OCEAN, RIVER, OR ANY NATURAL PLACE OF BEAUTY.

SEND INTENTIONAL ENERGY THROUGH DANCE AND SONG TO INSURE A HARVEST OR THE COMPLETION OF PROJECTS, ETC., WHICH YOU HAVE BEEN NURTURING ALONG.

COMMIT OR RECOMMIT YOURSELF TO ANIMAL AND/OR ENVIRONMENTAL ACTIVISM: Protect Earth and her creatures from further pollution, extermination, or abuse. Attend to recycling. Teach and encourage others to do the same.

FIND WAYS TO GIVE BACK TO THE GODDESS FOR HER GIFTS.

SHARE WITH OR PROVIDE FOOD TO THOSE WHO HAVE LESS THAN YOU.

CELEBRATE YOUR LIFE ACHIEVEMENTS: Even if you are a younger woman, honor those milestones that have brought you to your best self.

Autumn Equinox • September 21

Descent

Also called Harvest Home, Mabon, or the Festival of Thanksgiving.

Celebrate her ripening spirit
Celebrate her blossoming truth
Celebrate the fruits of our labors
Mother Goddess, we celebrate you![160]

Once again, light and dark are balanced in equal length of day and night. The exact date of the autumnal equinox fluctuates each calendar year between September twentieth and twenty-third. Whereas Spring Equinox symbolically manifests the equinox's equilibrium as that of an athlete poised for action, the Autumn Equinox's theme is that of rest after labor. It is a time of rebalancing after intensive work. In earlier times, the autumnal equinox marked the middle of the harvest season and began the intensive preparation for winter. This season was known as the Harvesting or Reaping Tide, "a time of inward turning as well as

---

160 Chant by Lori Richards, from the CD, *The Year Is a Dancing Woman, Volutme 2*.

celebration. It was a time of great cooperation within the community, of celebration and hard work to ensure that as much as possible of every foodstuff was carefully gathered in and preserved against the barren months of winter."[161]

In Ireland, there is Michaelmas (around September 29), which traditionally was the time of the goose harvest and a time to begin picking apples for making cider.[162] The Harvest Home was a feast given by the farmer for the workers, both paid and voluntary. The last sheaf of wheat was prominently displayed, generally hung in the house and replacing the previous year's last sheaf. This last sheaf itself was called the "cailleach"[163] or "hag," and the way the last sheaf was cut was held by many to affect the destiny of its cutter.[164] The last bit of corn in the farmer's fields was the visible symbol of the end of harvest, and all over Ireland, the cutting of it was attended with some ceremony. Harvest knots—small ornamental twists or knots of plaited straw—were made and worn as a sign that the harvest was complete.

In the mythic cycle of the Goddess, the Mother Goddess is completing the physical activity of creation. Analogous to the peri-menopausal years, she ceases to bleed and birth and begins her physical transition to Crone with her descent toward the inner world of spirit. In Dianic tradition, the Fall Equinox is celebrated as the witches' Thanksgiving. It is a time to taste the personal harvest of our hands. We give blessings and gratitude to the earth for the abundance with which she nurtures her children and prepare ourselves psychologically and energetically for the Crone's season of winter ahead. At this time, in community, we honor women who are in their peri-menopausal transition time and those women who have crossed the threshold to young cronehood. These young Crones are

---

[161] Green, *Natural Magic*, 102.

[162] Danaher, *The Year in Ireland*, 190.

[163] The Cailleach (KAHL'lee-ak) is the Old Woman or Grandmother who rules wintertide. Matthews, *The Celtic Spirit*, 96. The custom of calling the last sheaf the "calilleach" is a tribute to her powers and hopes for her blessings.

[164] Danaher, *The Year in Ireland*, 190.

women whose bloods have entirely stopped and have gone through (or at least half way through) their second Saturn return, somewhere between fifty-seven to sixty years old.

In ritual, we enact the descent of the goddess Persephone into the earth. She who has gone through Her journey as Kore, the Maiden Goddess, daughter of Demeter, now becomes Queen of the Underworld. We cover ourselves with a black cloth as we welcome the darkness and the wisdom contained within.

> We celebrate the time of lengthening darkness when the night equals the day by putting to rest all the activities of the summer. We gather the last from the garden, returning to the earth what we have received. We put our summer tools away. We pack away our light clothing. We choose a few good books with which to spend the coming season. We gather with friends that we have not seen all summer. We share a harvest meal in the peace of the gathering twilight. Our talk is of the fullness and strength stored for leaner times, of what we have earned, of what we take with us into the winter.[165]

Seasonal Questions and Ideas

ASK YOURSELF THESE SEASONAL QUESTIONS:

* What is my personal harvest?
* What have I brought into manifestation this year?
* What can I do to honor the generosity of the earth that sustains me?
* How might I thank my loved ones and acquaintances who have supported my creativity this year?

---

[165] Harding and Laning, *Dreaming*, 115.

* How can I best acknowledge and celebrate myself for hard work completed this year?

AT SUNSET, SAY FAREWELL TO THE POWERS OF THE SUN: Give thanks and praise for the heat and light that helped the crops to grow and nurtured your body.

THINK OF ALL YOU HAVE NURTURED SINCE SPRING: Name what you have brought to fruition by the work of your own hands and through the blessings of the Goddess. Appreciate what you have. Celebrate the fruits of your labors by dancing, naming, eating, etc., your personal harvest. Indulge yourself in the pleasure of plenty.

CREATE A SACRED MEAL OF SEASONAL FOODS: Share the abundance. Eat slowly. Savor being alive.

FIND WAYS TO GIVE BACK IN RETURN FOR ALL YOU HAVE RECEIVED: Feed the hungry. Pick up garbage along city highways, parks, or beaches. Plant trees.

ACKNOWLEDGE THE EARTH MOTHER FOR HER ABUNDANCE: Renew your commitment to help Her heal. Look for activist opportunities and join with others in protecting Her from pollution and other forms of environmental attack.

BEGIN PREPARING TO TURN INWARD FOR WINTER: Make time to notice the internal and external seasonal changes. Notice the gathering flocks of birds, changing of the leaves, the shortening daylight. Put your garden to bed, fill your bird feeders, put away your summer clothing. Go to bed on purpose to dream.

LIGHT CANDLES DEDICATED TO THE WISE WOMEN IN YOUR PERSONAL LIFE, THAT THEY MAY BE VALUED AND HONORED IN OUR COMMUNITIES AND IN THE WORLD AT LARGE: Let the crones in your life know that you love and value them. Bake them their favorite cookies.

HAVE A CRONING CEREMONY: This is a wonderful time for a woman newly crossing the threshold into her life as a young crone to have her croning ceremony. Refer to the ritual-making guidelines in chapter 3 to create a personal ritual for yourself or for another who is of age.

Each year at our Autumn Equinox ritual, we ask that the new crones come forward so that the younger women may present them with a special pouch on a cord that contains a hazelnut, symbolizing contained wisdom. The crones are each asked to speak briefly and share some of their life wisdom with the community. Their words are written down by scribes, who record and preserve the words of the wise women into a collection for the community.

RITUALLY CREATE A TRANSITION INTO THE SEASON OF REST BY GOING INTO A "SEEDAL" (AS IN "SEED IN THE WOMB" + "FETAL") POSITION: Do this by curling up with your legs tucked into your body. Cover yourself or have another cover you with a dark veil to symbolize the seed going under the earth for the winter. Consciously change your own energy from activity to rest by slowing down your breathing. Feel the earth's pull beneath you, and know yourself as a part of her as you ritually slow down, going inward and under to seek the wisdom found in the darkness.

Practice

Using the ritual-making process provided in this book, design and facilitate or participate in a seasonal ritual for the closest upcoming holiday. Record your ritual design and experience in your ongoing ritual-making journal.

chapter 10

FACILITATION AS SPIRITUAL SERVICE

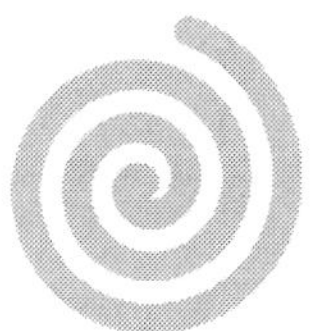

Group ritual has become both a meaningful spiritual practice and a valuable social activity for growing numbers of women. Ritual groups or covens often evolve into a circle of friends who share personal problems and joys.

Ideally, small and inexperienced groups will get together on a regular basis to plan and do rituals, and then take the time to evaluate them and discuss issues related to ritual making. A ritual group is a place where women can take risks—and make really big mistakes. These mistakes—which can include everything from a confusing choice of enactments to a poor ritual structure to invoking a goddess who decides to wreak havoc in your circle—often become the best teachers. Learn from what worked and what didn't. Smaller settings provide a more intimate personal place to gain ritual experience, where feedback can be given and received within a supportive circle of mentors and learners. You are not going to learn anything if you aren't willing to take risks and stretch your abilities. Keep growing through gaining ritual experiences and constructively evaluating them.

The vast majority of women are learning about ritual as they go, and small group rituals provide a great opportunity to acquire not only ritual skills, but facilitation skills.

Facilitating in an Ongoing Ritual Circle

Many women drawn to Dianic tradition, women's rituals, and goddess traditions live in small communities; many consider themselves fairly isolated. Women gathering in these communities are likely to share similar levels of experience, inspire one another, and learn ritual skills through trial and error. There may not be any other groups practicing goddess and female-centered ritual in their area; there may not be an elder nearby to teach or train them in ritual and magical skills. The experience of these women will be different from those practicing in larger cities that may have access to more resources and training. It takes a lot of courage and determination to self-educate, to dive into areas where you don't have guidance, to gain experience wherever you can get it, and to fall on your face as a group when a ritual goes awry.

Unfortunately, there are many women who have done a lot of reading about goddess traditions and believe that just because they've read about ritual, they are instant ritualists or priestesses. Reading about rafting the Grand Canyon and actually having the skill, courage, and experience it takes to do it are very different. Although scholarship is very important and can help to inform your ritual concepts and ideas, in order to become an effective ritualist you must be able to integrate intellectual concepts and information with hands-on, energetic skills and an open heart. It takes time, experience, and practice. This integration of skill and knowledge can create a ritual experience that is moving and transformational.

Unless a woman establishes a ritual group with herself as the focus point or leader, most women's ritual circles work with a consensus model of decision-making. Groups sometimes form to practice ritual skills and everyone usually starts out with the same level of experience, or lack of it. If you are part of a circle, or choose to form one, rotating responsibility allows for all women to learn and be supported as they are learning.

No ritual role or job is less or more rewarding than another when you learn to embody the Goddess in your service to women. Every woman in a group has something to offer. Identifying the abilities, skills, and talents within a group can be fun, as well as eye opening.

In my experience, women often have no desire to serve in a ritual facilitator capacity. A circle sister should be encouraged and supported to take risks, but if she feels unprepared or unwilling to fulfill a facilitator role, respect her right to decline. Facilitation should be voluntary. Always offer each other the opportunity to *stretch*, rather than *stress*, your abilities. If a circle sister is nervous or self-conscious, others in the group with more confidence can support her by honoring the skills she already has and making space for her to grow in her confidence. Constructive feedback should be encouraged when she takes on new responsibilities. In my first coven, Moon Birch Grove, circle sister Sylvia did not have any interest in facilitating ritual; what she loved to do was cook! To the group's delight, she made seasonally inspired meals for each Sabbat. This was Sylvia's gift, offered in service to the group. Given that space of honoring, Sylvia later developed into a fine storyteller of goddess myths. If your circle is a supportive environment for practicing skills and learning by trial and error, everyone will grow in their abilities and confidence in their own time and in their own way.

If you are interested in learning how to facilitate others in ritual, it is important to learn how to truly participate in one yourself. What are your responsibilities as participants in a ritual? What can we learn from being a participant that can help us become better ritual facilitators? When asked about their responsibilities as ritual participants, some of my students listed these points:

* Stay focused, centered, and present.

* Lend energy when energy is required.

* Follow instructions given by the facilitators.

* Respect any guidelines or safety requirements.

* Avoid side talk.

* Take care of yourself. Check in with yourself periodically during the ritual.

* Take responsibility for your own experience.

When a woman facilitates ritual, she gains valuable experience that could eventually move her toward becoming a ritualist or an ordained vocational Priestess, should she desire it.[166]

I use the term ritual "facilitator" rather than ritual "priestess" when working with women who are learning ritual facilitation skills. Although a ritual priestess is a facilitator, a facilitator is not always a ritual priestess. The word "facilitator" more accurately describes the role of the woman taking responsibility for the ritual or an aspect of it. A facilitator is a woman who makes the way easier; as an act of service, she assists in creating the experience of the participants. Like a guide on a journey, the facilitator's responsibility is to hold the vision, the purpose; to keep the compass, to know what the ultimate destination of the ritual journey is, and help everyone get there and back safely. If you were leading a group on a hike, you'd have to watch the trail and set a pace that matched the energy of the participants or be prepared to motivate them to match yours. It would be your responsibility if someone got lost or wandered too near the edge of a cliff. Like the leader of the hiking group, as you gain experience in facilitation, even though you may not have hiked on a particular trail, you know the forest, have the feel of the pace needed, and can improvise as the weather changes or other factors arise. Always have a magical first-aid kit on hand for bruised egos or raw emotions.

When a woman first begins to gain experience as a ritual facilitator, she may find herself memorizing lines, words, or movements. Gradually, though, a change, a shift, happens: a glimmer, a revelation, or deepening as to what ritual facilitation is really about. This shift of awareness moves from simply following the ritual structure or form to being part of, and guiding the flow of, the ritual's purpose. Sensing and guiding the ritual's intention as a flow of energy that has a shape and direction is a skill

[166] I capitalize the word "Priestess" in this chapter to designate a vocational or ordained Priestess, or a woman who is considered a Priestess by her community due to her ongoing spiritual service, and refer to the lowercase form to denote a woman who occasionally volunteers her service in a priestess capacity or occasionally with others in a small group such as a study group.

gained from a deep understanding and practice of energetics. It means not only holding the ritual intention and shape, but also being fully present in the moment-to-moment experience yourself. This is part of the transitional experience from being a ritual facilitator to potentially becoming a ritual Priestess.

You begin to identify when a ritual is flowing well because it feels like a light switch being turned on—a feeling of rightness, a physical experience of a perfect fit. A good metaphor would be learning to play a guitar. At first, your fingers struggle to remember chords and move in proper time. You are ever conscious in trying to remember where your hands need to be. Your fingers need to develop the strength to hold the strings against the frets. As you master the skill and the strength, you are no longer conscious of having to place your fingers on the right frets. Your brain and muscles remember automatically, and instead of thinking and struggling, the music just comes through you. For more on The Priestess, see chapter 13.

Facilitating Public Ritual

As a group or coven continues to grow, sometimes members will extend an invitation to friends or interested women, and sometimes to the public at large. If you belong to a small ritual group and you consider opening your rituals to others, it is wise to acquire a lot of experience in small-group practice before opening rituals to the general public. Gently widen your experience by opening up a little at a time. When the group feels ready, plan your next ritual to serve six more women on a handpicked, invitation-only basis, and see how that works out. If the group feels confident that they can responsibly handle a group of twenty, then next time perhaps expand to twenty-five or thirty. Evaluate how it went.

Opening gradually to women you know will help maintain the deep, intimate quality of your work, which might be lost if an invitation is extended publicly to unknown women in numbers larger than your group is equipped to handle. Keep sight of what originally brought your group together. Stay with what strengthens you individually and collectively. Take time to experiment, learn, and evaluate, rather than rushing into public ritual facilitation right away. Before offering public rituals of your own, it is more responsible to learn and stretch one's limits within a class setting (or your ritual circle or coven) or to assist a mentor experienced at facilitating larger rituals.

When taken out of a small, intimate group into the larger public sphere, there is a danger of rituals becoming performance-oriented and losing the essential, personal experience that makes them so meaningful. The challenge of offering open, public rituals is to construct a complete experience that is moving and transforming for each woman within a specific time frame while providing effective facilitation. If your group is considering offering large rituals, the pros and cons should be carefully discussed. Since it is nearly impossible to anticipate the cons if your group has never offered large open rituals, please consider the guidance in this chapter.

Larger community or open public ritual gatherings are not the best venue to experiment with utterly untried ritual skills. In offering public ritual, it is the responsibility of the facilitators to provide the participants with a meaningful spiritual experience. Public or open community rituals are *not* about the facilitators meeting their own personal spiritual needs. Facilitating others is about doing what best serves the participants; it is *not* about what role a woman would personally like to take on, or because a woman wants to have the experience, using the community ritual as a laboratory for her own gain. Alas, it is usually time and experience that will help someone come to this understanding.

Within the ritual facilitator's circle in my community, women gain an understanding that whoever gets to do what in any given public ritual is based on what is best for the ritual. Women are encouraged to gain experience in ritual situations apart from larger community rituals. They slowly and gradually accept more difficult ritual tasks or roles as their skills develop, and as they are observed by the more experienced facilitators. It is sometimes difficult and uncomfortable to have an open and honest discussion with a woman who wants to take on a ritual role for which she is not yet ready. Yet we rely on each other as a committed group of women to have the courage and communication skills needed to raise these issues when necessary. If you or others in your community do not have these communication skills, seek out resources to learn them and practice them together. Each woman should be given the opportunity to participate with the skills she currently has, explore ways her skills might best fit the ritual, and be supported in continuing to develop and practice more challenging skills.

Lessons regarding skill, or the lack of it, can be driven home the hard way—by abandoning someone to fall on her face. I, however, have not been willing to stand by and allow this to happen; it risks the well-being of the community and, perhaps, the facilitator herself. Even though it is difficult to play the heavy at ritual-planning meetings, avoiding the issue of lack of skill is, ultimately, cruel and dishonest. Constructive evaluation is sometimes the most loving support you can give a sister.

Once there was a woman in my community who was not especially articulate in her speaking ability. She wanted to become a ritualist so badly that she consistently volunteered for ritual roles that required especially keen verbal skills and the ability to think on her feet. Instead of allowing her to experience her lack of skill through a vey public failure, she was supported to serve in areas where she had natural talent, doing things that she enjoyed, like creating the visual imagery for the ritual space and the altar. We asked her to facilitate in ways that did not require extensive verbal skills. Her heart was in the right place and her passionate commitment to ritual service kept her open to learning. She learned to invite, and become comfortable, with constructive criticism and feedback even while struggling with her self-esteem and hurt feelings. About a year later, while facilitating a ritual where there were long periods of silence, she had a revelation. She explained to me after the ritual, wherein she had been given what she initially felt was a minor role, that her concern in facilitation had been about what she could do to feel visible and be seen. Her revelation was that there are no minor roles in a ritual. She realized that every role is important if it is approached that way. I was proud to ordain this woman as a temple Priestess several years later.

Some years ago, a situation arose during a planning meeting for a community Hallows ritual in which the goddess Hecate was to be aspected. This specialized ritual work is demanding, even for an experienced facilitator. I had a particular woman in mind to do this work who was an adept ritualist and a crone, having previously demonstrated the ability to do prolonged and focused ritual priestess work. During the planning meeting, though, two young women were anxious to aspect Hecate. Although these women were experienced ritual facilitators, I felt strongly that Hecate needed to be aspected by someone who was both physically a crone and had demonstrated the depth required of a ritualist to take on such a role. Although these younger women's feelings were initially hurt, they later shared that they understood my decision after observing the ability of this crone to sustain Hecate's presence for several hours.

As previously mentioned, public ritual is a worship service, not a therapy session. It is not the place to take on emotionally volatile issues unless you are prepared to deal with the reactions that may arise. Although you may wish to do more advanced ritual work, attempting this with inexperienced women often backfires with unhappy results. An open ritual, large or small, based on the mythic descent of Innana to the Underworld, or focusing in detail on issues of child abuse, or other violence, should not be attempted without great consideration and professional therapeutic support on hand. Work with themes that will be nurturing, empowering, and even a little challenging without going beyond what can be handled responsibly. Women's rituals can be emotional enough without deliberately opening wounds in a public setting where you have no idea who is attending or what their background may be. Be responsible to your guests! If you feel you have the experience and intend to do ritual around potentially difficult or intense issues, I strongly recommend women with counseling or crisis intervention backgrounds be designated to intervene should someone need assistance.

One of the drawbacks to offering open public rituals is that they can sometimes be attended by an emotionally needy or mentally ill woman who enjoys drawing attention to herself in public places. This woman may use the ritual space to act out. Especially for this reason, having women designated to work with difficult or emotionally sensitive people is advisable. Facilitators who are skilled in emotional support and crisis intervention can take the woman aside and work with her while the ritual continues relatively unaffected.

Preparing Newcomers

When inviting a guest to any ritual, whether it is a small coven rite or a larger open community ritual, women must take on a degree of responsibility for the welfare of newcomers. In my Los Angeles community of the 1980s – 1990s, it was not unusual to have 150 participants at open seasonal rituals. We suggested in the public ritual notices that no one invite guests until after they themselves have personally experienced, and become educated about, our rituals and our tradition. So, if you are a woman making an invitation to a newcomer, be respectful to your guest and the circle by sharing with her, through conversation, books, or videos, information about real witches and the goddess movement. Preparing your guest in advance enables her to participate at a deeper level. If you are an experienced facilitator, remember when you were a beginner, and consider what you would have wanted to know before and during your first ritual. Extend this kindness and consciousness to every new woman each time you step forward in Her service to invite newcomers.

After welcoming women to a public ritual, you might ask for a show of hands, asking "How many women are here for the first time?" Acknowledge that most of the women attending do not know each other and may be coming from very different backgrounds or experiences. Just acknowledging that fact will help the group feel safer and more connected. It may be important to say, "We are a group of lesbian, bisexual, and heterosexual women" or "We are a group of women from many races, cultures, and diverse backgrounds." Whether this statement is absolutely true or not, it still acknowledges the variety of experiences and backgrounds that women come from and the fact that women bring their differences and their similarities into the ritual space.

Give participants enough information to empower them to fully partake in the ritual. Provide women with the basics of ritual etiquette, guidelines, and the ritual structure. Set the parameters that create physical and emotional safety; for example, "Once the circle is cast, no one will be walking in or out of the ritual space" or "We can raise our voices as loud as we want," etc. If they are not informed, participants may be respectful, but they may not open up because they don't know that it is permissible to do so or may not feel safe to do so. Information is especially important for large community rituals where newcomers are invited to attend. Since there is no way to really know the experience level of everyone present, make comments that are inclusive and affirming. Explain that by following the ritual etiquette guidelines, everyone's experience of the ritual will be optimally magnificent and powerful.

Give women an opportunity to leave if they realize that the ritual may be a different kind of gathering than they thought it might be or if the ritual is going to run longer than they scheduled time for. You may wish to publicize the time frame in any advance publicity. It is helpful to announce the time frame at the onset of the ritual, saying, for example, "The ritual is expected to last approximately two hours. If you think you will not be able to stay for the entire ritual, please consider leaving now, and return again when you can participate fully." In this way, no blame has been laid, and the invitation to return at a later time has been extended.

Here is an example of some pre-ritual guidelines created in the 1990s. These guidelines are still announced at the beginning of open community rituals of Circle of Aradia, a grove of Temple of Diana in Los Angeles. These announcements are specific to large community rituals with an abundance of facilitators and participants. Feel free to adapt these announcements for your own use at larger or open community rituals. When you may have women attending who have little or no previous experience of what is expected of them during a ritual, announcements such as these are an act of support for newcomers and gentle reminders to regulars so that everyone can have the best ritual experience possible. Ritual guidelines are best spoken by a woman with a bright personality or funny sense of humor.

Ritual Guidelines

WELCOMING ANNOUNCEMENT: "Welcome to everyone, and happy (Spring/May/Solstice/Hallowmas, etc.). I am (give your name). I especially want to welcome women who are here for the first time. (You might ask for a show of hands so that you can see how many newcomers there are.) Here are some guidelines designed to create an optimal experience for everyone:

FACILITATORS: Women who are facilitating this ritual tonight, please raise your hands. If you are new to our rituals and have questions, many of these women are available to speak with you after the ritual is over.

SMOKING BAN: There is no smoking in the building (if you are meeting outdoors, state your preference with this) due to extreme fire danger. If you need to smoke, please do so outside the building, after the ritual is completed.

DOOR: The outside door is now locked for your safety (add this if you are indoors). If you cannot stay until the end of the ritual, approximately __ hours, you may wish to leave now, and return another time when you can more fully participate.

GUARDIANS: At the four directions of the circle, and elsewhere, there are women providing service in a guardian capacity. Women serving as guardians tonight, please raise your hands. These women serve the ritual in a variety of capacities from providing security for us to helping maintain the energy of the cast circle.

CIRCLE: Once the ritual has begun and the circle has been cast, please do not break the circle. If you have an emergency and must leave, please see the ritual facilitator at the east gate of the circle (indicate where that is) so she can cut you out of the circle properly and let you out. (Ask this woman to raise her hand.) It is extremely important to maintain the boundary of the cast circle and the energy we are containing inside of it. *Please don't ask to be let out unless it is really urgent.* Upon returning, go immediately to the east gate, where you will be let in properly. This applies to both indoor and outdoor rituals.

Does everyone here understand this?
(Pause for response.)

CHAIRS: There are a limited number of chairs available for women who are physically challenged and cannot stand for a length of time. Please make these chairs available for those women. Thank you for your understanding.

DRUMS: Please stay clear of the drums when dancing or moving during the ritual and the feast. These instruments belong to the musicians and are their sacred tools and may not be available to be played by anyone else.

ALTAR: Since women often bring personal and sacred objects to ritual, please do not touch or handle anything on the altar that is not yours or that is not purposefully provided by the facilitators for your use.

If applicable: Please light only your own candle using the designated working candle only. Do not light your candle off of any woman's personal candle or any of the altar candles.

FOCUS: Our community rituals are participatory. This ritual is for you and everyone else here, so please work to stay focused so that our magical work together stays as powerful as it is intended to be and refrain from mundane conversation during the ritual. We will have time to socialize during the feast afterwards.

FOOD: When the circle is opened for the feast, please give the women who have facilitated a five-minute lead-time to the food. This also goes for our honorary Crone, Mother, and Maiden for the evening.[167]

CLEANUP: Everyone who helps to facilitate our rituals is a volunteer. Before we can start the ritual, we need ten additional volunteers who can stay until the end of the feast to help with cleanup. (Wait for at least ten women to raise their hands.)

WHEN CHILDREN ARE PRESENT: Moms, please be involved with your child or children during the ritual and afterwards. Everyone else needs to be aware of possible little people underfoot.

CLOSING: Thank you so much for your patience and for listening.

> Have a beautiful and powerful ritual! Happy (Spring/May/Hallows/Summer/Fall, etc.)."

It is best to refrain from giving participants in-depth instructions for the core ritual work until you are further into the body of the ritual. They

---

[167] From the earliest days of the Dianic tradition, the eldest woman at the ritual became our honorary Crone for the evening. A woman was also selected as honorary Mother, based on being pregnant with child or pregnant with possibilities. The youngest became the ritual's honorary Maiden. It was the Maiden's job to make sure that the chalice was always full and to attend to the needs of the Crone.

will forget during the transition from the announcements to the cast circle. If your ritual is open to the general public, remember that you will have to address your instructions to the least-experienced women. It is okay to teach a little as you go. Newcomers or women who have different ritual practices or traditions especially appreciate this.

Suggestions for Facilitators

Design the Ritual Carefully

Try to anticipate women's needs for safety and information, especially if you are offering a public ritual. Before thinking about the ritual enactment possibilities, consider the following questions. They will help you decide how much explaining and instruction the participants may need before and during the ritual. Remember, no matter what size group you are working with, as a facilitator you must choose enactments for the ritual intention that are accessible to all participants regardless of their skill or experience.

QUESTIONS

1. Are the women attending familiar with each other?
2. Do the participants work in ritual together on a regular or semi-regular basis?
3. Have they ever attended a goddess-oriented or woman-focused ritual before?
4. Do they share a cosmology or spiritual practice?
5. What level or levels of ritual experience are likely to be present?

Weave Threads of Personal Contact with Each Woman into the Ritual Fabric

Engage women with the check-in process mentioned in chapter 6, or with ritual enactments that foster individual connection. You must make a judgment call as to which ritual enactments will serve the greater ritual experience while still creating a feeling of intimacy, visibility, and personal contact, touching each woman attending. Let each woman know that her presence at the ritual matters. Make a connection with and between all who are present.

Consider Time and Space

Be realistic. Develop a general time frame for each section of the ritual so that you can determine how much individually focused work can be allowed. Alter any ritual plans that require intricate logistics unless you have a lot of extra help facilitating. Be aware that rituals, which are manageable in small groups, may require extensive and complicated stage management when they are enlarged to include more women. A ten-minute activity or enactment in a group of thirteen women can take an hour in a group of fifty.

Sharing

Women love to talk and have a lot to say, but after the fiftieth woman tells her entire life story to the question "What is your dream?" you may regret having asked this question. When given the opportunity for focused attention from others, some participants will speak longer, regardless of the reality that fifty other women are waiting for their turn. Instead, have a facilitator model the form of the response, such as, "I'm Ruth and my dream is to finish writing my ritual-making book." Offer a structure for the length of a particular sharing to a sentence or two. If this breaks down at some point, be prepared to interrupt and gently reaffirm the instructions.

If there are many people doing individual work that needs the entire group's focus, the energy level is likely to drop while others wait to speak or share, regardless of the good intention to energetically support everyone. At some of my community's seasonal rituals, where the number of participants may be up to 150 women or more, the ritual space is set up for personal work to be done in groups so that several activities are going on simultaneously. For example, at our May Eve celebration, several altars are set up around the hall so that women can spend time ritualizing the release of internalized cultural attitudes about the female body and then reclaim and honor their bodies as reflections of the Goddess. While this individual work is going on, there is ongoing chanting and/or drumming to support their work. Women are able to work at their choice of altars in a loosely guided order. This avoids long lines while women move from one experience to the next.

Keep It Flowing

A facilitator must be prepared to keep the ritual flow moving to its destination by gently guiding along the activities. When things take too long because participants have been left unaided, the group's energy can drop. For example, if participants are instructed to light their candles individually, speaking out their spells when they feel ready, this will usually lengthen a ritual because women tend to hesitate before stepping forward. Too much pausing between each participant affects the energy. One option is to have groups of women step forward, quarter by quarter around the circle, to light their candles together. Alternatively, a team of facilitators could carry lit candles to every woman in the circle so that the ritual can flow smoothly without waiting for every woman to walk up to the altar to light her candle.

Less is often more. One or two simple yet profound enactments are infinitely more powerful than a three-hour multi-enactment mini-series. The energy level needed to sustain a three- or four-hour group ritual is considerable. Construct a ritual wherein the energy is raised, focused, directed, and released in one continuous flow, not raised and dropped repeatedly. Try to send women home empowered, exhilarated, and well spent, not exhausted and drained.

Transitions

Be especially mindful of the transitions from one section of the ritual to another. The challenge is to gracefully move the energy in the direction it is intended to go. This may require just a few sentences, like picking up a stitch, and that is it. Be wary of too much talking with little activity in between.

Note: Because transitions can be challenging work, they are best left in the hands of more experienced facilitators.

Maintain Clear and Cohesive Spiritual References

If your ritual is being done within a particular spiritual tradition or shared cosmology, keep explanations clear, cohesive, and consistent so that the entire group can be a part of it. If you choose to take a departure from the familiar, prepare the participants in advance or be prepared to include a considerable amount of teaching time during the ritual, otherwise women will feel excluded. I once attended an opening ritual at a large goddess festival where the facilitating group chose to share completely new references for invoking the quarters. The facilitators didn't take the time to explain their new cosmology. I observed that everyone but the facilitators felt completely disconnected from this ritual. Initiating a new system such as this without any explanation was an especially inappropriate choice for a festival that had invited women from all over Europe and the United States.

Cultivate Awareness, Respect, and Appreciation for Diversity

It is important for any woman who is interested in ritual facilitation to become educated in issues of diversity and cultural awareness. If you are speaking to a group of women from diverse ethnic, racial, sexual, or class backgrounds, be aware that you cannot speak for all women. If you are a white woman and you intend to facilitate ritual seriously, consider the importance of diversity work. Look for ways to include all women's experience by naming the real issues in society and incorporating these issues in your ritual work.

Perhaps because of the lack of guidance that elders traditionally provided in times past, there has been a tendency for some women's circles to become melting pots of many disparate spiritual traditions. With an attitude of "anything goes," some eclectic groups combine so many diverse spiritual and cultural traditions that the content of their spiritual practice becomes diluted beyond a point of recognizable origin. Watering down traditional knowledge can lead to unintentional superficiality and a misunderstanding and misuse of original intent. At worst, it can lead to magical disaster. For example, lighting a purple candle in the Hindu chakra system represents enlightenment, power, and spirituality. In traditional Craft, a purple candle represents uncontrolled female rage. Another example is using patchouli oil in a love spell, where it is a repellent in traditional Craft.

For many years, sisters of color have been consciousness-raising about white women's appropriation of their spiritual and cultural traditions and have been frustrated by white women's refusal to consider the issues that have been raised. For many white women of European descent, especially those born in the melting pot of the United States, borrowing from other cultures may feel natural. However, the assumption that other cultures are simply there for the taking or that people of a culture want to share their spiritual heritage with others outside their culture bears examination. White privilege creates blindness. It is true that women of other cultures will sometimes share their spiritual practices with white women, but this is not always the case. It should not be assumed that because a spiritual practice is shared with a white woman that she then owns it and can practice it on her own or teach it to others.

Included in this blindness of white privilege is the unconscious assumption that white women's experience is the model of all women's experience. Aggressively taking on the work of unlearning racism is crucial for any white woman, and it is especially critical for those facilitating group ritual or those women on the priestess path. This work is painful to undertake, as each woman must examine the extent to which she has internalized the values and perceptions of the dominant culture. As she begins to unlearn her internalized racism, she becomes sensitized to the realities of women of color. This growing awareness will influence how she will serve women as a ritual facilitator or priestess.

Publicizing Rituals

If you advertise through posted flyers, a newsletter, e-mail, or on the Internet, be as specific as you can about your ritual. State the purpose of the ritual and the general theme. If women need to have read something specific, or be familiar with any particular mythic stories, seasonal symbolism, or ritual practices in order to fully participate, provide resources where they may easily obtain the needed information.

If your open ritual (open to the public) is exclusively for women, and by this you mean female-sexed participants, check your state or country's anti-discrimination laws. A growing number of states and country's have anti-discrimination laws making it illegal for females to exclusively gather for whatever reason. In many states, males who self-identify as women are now legally allowed access to what were previously private female spaces. If you want to be able to have your open rituals exclusively for women you may need to apply for religious protections that separates church and state, and attain "church" status. Unless a women's circle has religious protection, a circle may not be able to insure that all participants are biological women.

Consider whether or not you need women to RSVP before the ritual, the last date to respond, and whether you will admit women who did not RSVP. For security reasons, you might not wish to give out the ritual location unless a woman has made direct contact with you.

Here is an example of the type of information sent out for a Circle of Aradia seasonal ritual that was included in the community's newsletter for decades. Consider the following guidelines and items mentioned, and feel free to alter them as needed for your own circumstances.

Winter Solstice Ritual and Feast

* Saturday, December 21, 7pm, (location)
* The hall will be open at 6:30 pm; please arrive early so we can begin on time.
* Doors will be closed by 7:15 pm.

On the longest night of the year, we renew our spirits, celebrate our visions and ideas that give birth to form, and honor the Goddess, who carries us through the winter season. Our community will ritually welcome the new babies born this year. We will meet indoors at (location address). Mothers with newborns must call the CoA hotline no later than December 10. Everyone who plans to attend must RSVP to the voicemail before Thursday, December 17 at (phone number). Leave a message including your name, telephone number, and how many women you plan to bring. Also, let us know if you are a newcomer or if you are bringing your daughter(s). If you are a newcomer, or if you are bringing your daughter(s), please read carefully the information below. *Please do not call CoA the weekend of the ritual, as we are extremely busy preparing and probably will not be able to process your call.*

These participatory rituals are created exclusively for biological females and serious seekers only. Each woman contributes to the rite's successful focus and intent so that the entire community benefits from our cooperative efforts to work magic! Once the circle is cast, we cannot admit latecomers, so please arrive on time so you will not be locked out.

Healing Meditation at Community Seasonal Rituals

As a community, we want to respond to those in need of healing (physical, emotional, or spiritual) with loving intention and action. If someone you know desires to be named in our community healing meditation to be done at this ritual, please phone Circle of Aradia (phone number here) no later than two days before the ritual with the name of the individual needing healing. Messages left less than forty-eight hours in advance may not be processed in time to be included in the ritual.

WHAT TO BRING: Decorations for our communal altar (optional) and healthy vegetarian food/drink to share (absolutely no alcohol, please). Wear comfortable, festive clothing and supportive shoes (the door at the location is terrible for bare feet). In honor of our Earth Mother, Circle of Aradia will not provide paper goods (with the exception of napkins) for the feast. Please bring your own plate, cup, and personal utensil. A donation of $__ is requested to cover the hall rental and other related expenses, but no woman will be turned away for lack of funds. As in years past, CoA will also be collecting nonperishable food and supplies for our ongoing food drive for the homeless and for the CoA food bank. Preferred items are rice, pasta, dried beans, and hygiene supplies. There will be an area at the side of the building for your donations.

FOR NEWCOMERS: Newcomers are warmly welcomed! We want your experience to be optimal, so we have created these guidelines in your interest. Women new to goddess spirituality must be advised that the ritual is a participatory religious service and is not structured to be a first introduction to the goddess or to feminist Witchcraft; therefore, if this is new to you, please read one of these suggested books before attending the ritual: *The Spiral Dance* by Starhawk, *Ariadne's Thread* by Shekhinah Mountainwater, or *Women's Rites, Women's Mysteries* by Ruth Barrett. If you are planning on bringing newcomers to the ritual, please be responsible to them and CoA by preparing your guests in advance for what generally to expect, since our rituals are participatory and for serious seekers only.

REGARDING CHILDREN AT THIS RITUAL: We recognize that most of Circle of Aradia's seasonal rituals are not designed to meet children's needs. Many of our rituals often include our response to the realities of women's lives in patriarchy. Emotional intensity and adult issues may be included. For these reasons, the public seasonal rituals may not be appropriate for children of any age. This ritual may not be appropriate for girls under eight years of age, other than babes in arms. If you are a newcomer considering bringing your daughter, we ask that you first attend a ritual by yourself in order to have an idea of what to expect. Then you can decide if the experience is appropriate for your daughter. These guidelines are suggested to ensure your daughter's well-being. When leaving an RSVP, please make sure to indicate if you are bringing a child with you.

LOST AND FOUND: Items left at community rituals are collected and kept for one six-week cycle. If you are missing personal items from the past, please call CoA and leave a message.

DIRECTIONS TO THE RITUAL: (Include instructions from several directions and a map of the immediate area, if possible.)

Alcohol and Drugs

In order for ritual to deeply affect the psyche and remain in the memory, it is best to avoid the use of alcohol, marijuana, or any psychotropic drugs (natural or synthetic). Most of us do not have a cultural or spiritual context for the responsible use of these substances, as some people in other parts of the world do. Dianic ritual is intended to empower and strengthen women. It is intended to help us heal from abuse we may have experienced at the hands of a drunken or drug-using parent or spouse; it is intended to help us heal from our own addictions and patterns of self-abuse that result in drug and alcohol addiction. In order to insure a safe and truly transformational ritual experience for all involved, communicate in advance your policy on the use of alcohol or drugs at your rituals.

Children at Rituals

Not all rituals are appropriate for children's participation. Careful thought should be given to which ritual themes are appropriate for children to participate in. As a mother myself, I have been personally against the inclusion of children in rituals where intense adult issues are included or are the focus. For example, a twelve-year-old girl will not benefit (and may in fact be harmed) by being present while an adult woman does intense emotional release work around being sexually assaulted as a girl. Ritual themes and enactments that deal with issues outside of a child's experience or her ability to comprehend can be frightening and emotionally damaging. Design age-appropriate rituals for and with children using processes from this book if you wish to have them present. Generally, children respond to ritual as they do to play, and ritual can be another creative way to teach spiritual values and ethical behavior. For seasonal community gatherings, either create a ritual that is inclusive and appropriate for all ages or consider creating a second ritual specifically for all of the community's children if there is a need.

In my Dianic community, we have an age limit of up to three years for boys at adult rituals. Since our rituals are completely female-focused and based in Women's Mysteries, we are committed to maintaining a separate ritual space for women and girls. Sons of Dianic witches are supported and encouraged to learn about the Goddess and to participate in seasonal celebrations with their families, in other groups for both women and men, or Men's Mystery circles.

Ritual Support Descriptions

If you have the good fortune to work with a large group of facilitators, the following ritual support should be considered, especially when offering larger open rituals. In presenting these job descriptions, I realize that most readers of this book have no intention of offering large open rituals or have the numbers of women to facilitate. If you have only a few women to work with, each woman may need to take on several responsibilities in addition to facilitating the ritual itself. If you plan on facilitating a ritual on your own, these descriptions may help you to plan with greater awareness or to have some back up strategies if needed.

Keep in mind that each ritual support description requires a specific set of skills, including personal and social skills, the ability to organize, and magical ability.

Road Woman

The road woman is the contact person for the ritual facilitators and responsible for the details and overview of the ritual (she has the ritual "map"). She handles physical logistics and emergencies before, during, and after the ritual. It is best if she does not take on another ritual role so that her full attention can be on logistics. However, most often the road woman is the same woman who serves as high priestess or the primary ritual facilitator. This role can be compared to a stage manager for a theatre production. The road woman stays in close communication with the primary ritual facilitator at all times, unless they are one and the same.

Clean-Up Coordinator

This facilitator makes sure that the rented space is returned in as good, or better, shape than before the ritual began. She understands the cleanup requirements of the hall or site owners, and supervises, delegates, and works alongside other cleanup volunteers and stays until the very end of the evening. This job is often overlooked, but its value is essential if the group wishes to return to that site again. Otherwise, like me on too many occasions, you will have to spend hours afterward scraping the candle wax off the floor of the rented hall.

Sacred Space Coordinator

This is a wonderful service role for a facilitator who loves to create the visuals for each ritual theme. She is the contemporary version of a temple priestess. She is responsible for the set up of the central altar and knowing what ritual tools are needed for the ritual. This coordinator also makes sure that there is a fire extinguisher and a well-equipped first-aid kit on hand (this can also be a responsibility of a community guardian facilitator if you have someone serving in this capacity).

Special Needs/Mother and Child Attendants

It is always greatly appreciated if there is at least one facilitator designated to assist mothers with small children and women who are blind, deaf, or have other special needs. This facilitator is available to provide chairs for those who cannot stand in circle for any length of time.

Ritual Drummers

These facilitators offer spiritual service in the form of percussion and other instrumental sounds. They have knowledge of how to use drumming for ritual energetic support and have worked out in advance with the other facilitators how they can best serve the ritual design. They work closely with the primary ritual facilitator(s), particularly for raising and releasing the cone of power should the ritual include this.

Graces

These are facilitators who pick up the RSVPs for the ritual and return phone calls as needed. They also welcome participants at the door after they have checked in and direct them to where to put their personal and ritual items for the evening. A newcomer's first experience of a group is through a grace, so this job is important in setting the tone of the ritual and helping all women feel welcome.

Door Attendant

This facilitator collects donations at the door as participants arrive, asks them to sign the guest book, and gives out information as needed.

Feast Coordinator/ Food Receiver(s)

If your ritual includes the sharing of food and drink, this facilitator is responsible for organizing the feast, setting up the tables, paper goods, etc., and receiving the food when participants arrive with their pot-luck items.

Guardians

Guardians serve in several capacities. Community guardians are facilitators who serve the ritual through handling physical logistics and security in or around the ritual facility. If parking for the ritual is challenging, a guardian assists women with parking. These women make sure that outsiders will not disturb the ritual. They also may help to place chairs for women who are unable to stand for the duration of the ritual. A woman serving in a guardian capacity is responsible for making sure the facility is secured once the ritual is ready to begin by locking the doors. It is recommended that at least some women serving as guardians have current certification in CPR, and basic first aid. They also monitor the ritual circle for disruptive or mentally disturbed participants and notify designated crisis-intervention facilitators.

Ritual guardians are facilitators that serve the ritual by energetically maintaining and supporting the container of the cast circle and giving specific energetic support to the other ritual facilitators. Ritual guardians work in partnership with the ritual priestess(es) to ensure the success of the ritual experience. More on this partnership is discussed in chapter 13.

East Gatekeeper

This facilitator serves in a ritual guardian capacity. She is posted at the east gate of the cast circle. With her athame, she "cuts" women out of the cast circle and back into the circle if someone must leave during the ritual. This woman must have the energetic skills necessary to do this work if required.

Ritual Flow Woman

This facilitator lets the participants know the specific nature of the ritual's work and how the group will work the energy of the rite. She may also be the central facilitator responsible for facilitating the ritual's energetic flow, generally the work of the high priestess (or the woman holding center for the ritual).

Psych Support

These facilitators are available for crisis support as needed. If possible, they should be trained therapists or social workers. They should also be able to provide magical containment when working with a woman in distress, so that the woman in crisis does not affect the ritual.

Invocation Coordinator

This facilitator makes sure that the content and style of the invocations to be delivered are consistent with the seasonal theme. This is best done in advance of the ritual. She confirms which ritual tool (athame or sword) will be used for casting the circle and makes sure that it is brought and ready for use, or if the invoker(s) and casting facilitator will use their personal athames.

Purification Coordinator

If purification of the ritual space is shared with several facilitators, this coordinator makes sure that all purifiers understand how they are going to work the space together. She also makes sure in advance that the physical elemental symbols are on the altar and ready for the ritual.

Altar Facilitator

This facilitator assists participants at the altar by answering questions or helping place their candles or other altar items on the altar.

Fire Attendants

If you are planning to have a ritual that includes fire of any sort, including an altar full of lighted candles, at least one or more fire attendants are necessary. These facilitators must be able to resist going into trance during the ritual and must stay close to the fire with eyes alert. A multi-rated fire extinguisher is useful for any kind of fire, and these facilitators should know how to use it.

When Problems Arise

Because participatory ritual is a living, moment-to-moment experience, sometimes even the most thorough ritual planning can be unraveled or certainly affected by unforeseen physical, logistical, and emotional issues that spontaneously arise. Determining what is actually a real problem and what to do about it can sometimes be challenging. Some unforeseen occurrences in ritual space are not real problems, but others might be.

I have a phrase that goes, "Sometimes it's just the match." This refers to the fairly common occurrence of lighting a candle with intent, as in a spell, and struggling with matches that won't strike up. Some women ascribe a deeper spiritual meaning to this frustrating experience, while others simply offer another matchbook in the hopes that this new set is dryer or fresher. A simple solution is to provide a specific candle (the "working" candle) on the altar for others to light their candles or matches from.

Once, at an outdoor Summer Solstice ritual, I was giving a seasonal invocation that was to be followed by the lighting of a smokeless fire (a blend of Epsom salts and flammable rubbing alcohol) in an iron cauldron. After ceremoniously declaring, "Let the fire festival begin!" I touched a lit fireplace match to the Epson salts and alcohol contained in the cauldron and waited for it to ignite. Nothing happened. Baffled and embarrassed at the lack of fire, I had to quickly improvise, with some humor, and move the ritual ahead anyway. I discovered later that the alcohol I had purchased was the non-flammable kind.

What do you do if you are facilitating a spellcasting and the participants can't seem to generate enough energy to send off the spell? Ask for help to correct the problem: "Let's raise some more energy here. How about a few jumping jacks?" or "Let's get more energy moving!" You might also begin an energizing chant and add clapping, drumming, or dancing. If the purpose is to get the work done, make sure your efforts are not being wasted by trying to send out a spell with no fuel to get it to its destination.

I want to share a couple of the rarer moments I've experienced in facilitating public rituals, not to discourage you from offering them but to give you a reality check on what can occur and how those situations were responded to. Some situations justify halting the ritual by physical or verbal means, for instance, if a woman verbally attacks another woman in circle or says something racist, homophobic, or hateful. Years ago, at one of my community's public rituals, women were lighting their candles and speaking aloud their desires for all to affirm with a resounding "Blessed be!" A newcomer lit her candle and asked that "all the foreigners leave the country and go back to where they belong." The room of seventy-five women went dead silent. No one affirmed her wish. After a pause, the next woman stepped up to the altar, and the candle lighting continued. As a principal facilitator at that ritual, I decided to speak with the woman at length after the ritual, since the other participants had responded as one body by not affirming her spell. If faced with the same situation today, I would stop the ritual and address her words immediately, taking the opportunity for a teachable moment for everyone present. If the woman's response were hostile, I would likely invite her to leave the ritual, cut her out of the cast circle, and then resume the work after first facilitating the group coming into resonance again. In that ritual, we facilitators did not uphold our responsibility to the participants to provide and maintain safe space for all. Over the years since then I have worked to further educate myself about racism and have learned to deal more responsibly with similar incidents.

Rarely, a situation may arise that no one is ever prepared for, yet action must still be taken. At the start of a community Fall Equinox ritual back in the 1980s, Teri, a woman in the community, came to the room where the facilitators were preparing with news that her daughter, Kim, had just been abducted, sexually assaulted, and was in the hospital.[168] Since all of the facilitators knew Kim and Teri, we were all distraught. Women waiting for the ritual to begin could feel in the air that something terrible had happened but did not know what it was. We all knew that we could not, and would not, put this news completely out of our heads and hearts until afterwards, and so we decided to incorporate the sharing of this news into the ritual. I announced to the gathering that something terrible had happened in order to validate women's heightened awareness that something was wrong, and I told them that the news would be shared in the ritual later on. We proceeded to ritualize the culmination of the harvest season in a dance of celebration before preparing for entering the dark half of the year.

Teri was then invited to the center of the circle of ninety or more women, and told everyone in tears of grief and anger what had happened to her daughter. The room exploded with sobs, wailing, and shrieking outrage. I watched the energy in the room hit the roof and spin around the room. As intense and chaotic as it was, I also stood in awe at the compassion and righteous rage of the women responding to another sister's pain. The wound was raw and open. Uncensored, women called out many things, including asking for the death of the rapist. Fortunately, I trusted

---

[168] Names have been changed.

that what goes up must come down and knew that rather than trying to control what was happening, I needed to wait it out. Then an amazing thing happened. One of our ritual priestesses, who had been aspecting the Goddess as Crone, and rocking in a rocking chair at the center of the circle, suddenly stood up. The circle hushed. Summoning all of Her strength, She said that the perpetrator was Hers and that justice would be served. Women then began to call for justice and that the perpetrator be caught within the moon cycle. With the intent on justice, the energy was gathered and sent out as a group spell.

Directly after the ritual concluded, some newcomers fled the hall, feeling so uncomfortable with the raw emotions that they never returned. Others responded that it was one of the most empowering and moving experiences they had ever had. In the days and months that followed, there continued to be feedback about what had occurred at the ritual. We learned that Kim, upon hearing the outrage, support, and love expressed on her behalf, was determined to identify the perpetrator, should he be caught. The police soon captured him, and Kim's testimony was instrumental in his prosecution. She credited the caring of the community at that ritual for her courage to testify and for the initiation of her healing process.

Practices

When you feel confident enough, facilitate a simple ritual. Evaluate your experience of facilitating according to some of the criteria in this chapter.

If you already facilitate ritual regularly, volunteer to facilitate in a capacity you have not considered before (this is assuming that you have practiced and demonstrated the skills to do it).

If you are already experienced in facilitating the ritual content, consider volunteering to facilitate a more "mundane" aspect of the ritual. Evaluate what you learn. Stretch your abilities until you are flexible.

chapter 11

VISIONING NEW RITUALS

This chapter will offer a few vignettes and suggestions for women's life-cycle rituals. They are either from actual rituals or are a composite of rituals created by my students, others, or myself, following the ritual-making process described in this book. These simple, lyrically written ritual vignettes are intended to stimulate your mind and spirit and give you some direction in thinking more expansively in your ritual design. The stated purpose of this book is to empower you to create your own rituals, not to follow prescribed recipes. These scenarios offer you a place to start.

Menstruation/First Bloods Ritual

This scenario represents one of many "first bloods" rituals to welcome a girl into young womanhood. If you are helping to design a first bloods ritual, spend some time with the girl and explore what she would find meaningful. Do not assume to know what she would like to experience or what guests she would like to have participate. In working with many women whose first menstruation experience was traumatic or insignificant, when I ask them to imagine in retrospect the menstruation ritual they would have liked to receive, they imagine it from their adult perspective and not as the emerging young woman they were at the time. These perspectives are very different. Support the girl's needs and work with her to create a beautiful, empowering, and unforgettable menstruation ritual to carry her into womanhood.

> Sacred blood of the Mother runs through my veins,
> And with each lunation, scarlet She rains.

Mother to daughter passes this gift.
Blessed be the Mother, within us She lives.[169]

The women of Jacqueline's family and her closest friends are informed that Jacqueline recently had her first menstrual period, and they are invited to celebrate this passage. They arrive at the family home dressed in red and bearing gifts, anticipating the ceremony with great excitement, knowing that the great transition from girl to young woman has begun. An altar is set up in the center of the room with flowers, red candles, and photographs of Jacqueline's ancestors. When everyone is ready to begin, the women take hands in a circle. Celia, Jacqueline's mother, takes her daughter's hand, and they enter the circle of women. Jacqueline gazes at the photographs of her maternal grandmother, her mother, and herself—the continuum of her woman-line. Celia takes a bowl of scented water and blesses the body of her daughter with pride and joy, teaching her how to bless herself each day and to honor her blossoming sexuality. She looks into her daughter's eyes and says the following Maiden Blessing:

I bless your mind that you may know the wisdom of the Goddess.
I bless your eyes that you will see your true beauty, within and without.
I bless your ears to hear Her wise voice above all others.
I bless your mouth to praise life.
I bless your heart to love and be loved.

[169] Chant by the author from the CD, *The Year Is a Dancing Woman, Volume 1.*

I bless your breasts to nurture yourself and those you love.
I bless your womb and yoni that you may know creativity and pleasure as a divine gift to share in sacred ways.
I bless your hands to make the world a holy place.
I bless your feet that you may walk paths of wisdom and understanding.

Celia now addresses her daughter as "young woman," declaring that although she will continue to watch over and guide Jacqueline into adulthood, now their mother/daughter relationship is expanding to include sisterhood. Celia's mother, Jacqueline's grandmother Audry, presents Jacqueline with a red-stoned ring. This is to remind her granddaughter of her sacred blood as a source of creative power in her life and to value the power and responsibility of sexuality and creativity.[170] Celia and Audry light red candles in Jacqueline's honor and give her a final blessing of love and acceptance. The other women in the circle pledge to support Jacqueline's journey into womanhood as she is formally welcomed into the circle of women.

...

Birthday

Here is a witchy alternative to the traditional cake and candle ritual. At your party, instead of lighting the birthday candles and then making a wish, bring out the cake and hand out birthday candles to all the guests. Offer a variety of colors to choose from so that the color of the candle

---

[170] I have incorporated some details from the menstruation ritual from *The Holy Book of Women's Mysteries* by Z Budapest (Wingbow Press, 1989), 77.

selected by each person can have significance. One by one, each of the guests puts her candle on the cake and speaks a blessing or wish for the honored one, and then lights the candle for her wish. This is a wonderful and loving experience for the honoree to hear from her friends and family. It also creates a warm feeling of intimacy among everyone because something real and heartfelt is happening.

After the candles have been lit (and yes, the wishes must be brief in order for the cake not to go up in flames), the honoree also lights a candle for herself for the year. Then sing the "Happy Birthday" song if you wish. The honoree takes a bite of cake first, with the consciousness of taking the wishes literally and symbolically into herself and into her new year of life. This activity restores the proper sequence of a spell.[171] To allow the candles to burn down all the way, the blessing candles can be placed in a bowl filled with earth, salt, or sand instead of on the cake. In order to energize the spell, the candles will have to burn all the way down, so the bowl of salt or sand is magically the best option.

Wedding or Commitment Ceremony

One of the roles of a priestess (or ritual facilitator) is to help design a ceremony that is an accurate reflection of the couple's spiritual values and relationship. For me, this usually involves meeting with the couple and inviting them to participate in the creation of their ceremony. Although I always come to this meeting prepared with plenty of tried and true ideas from past ceremonies I have facilitated, it is important to include and/or incorporate the wishes of the couple since the ceremony is about them.

I have always reminded the invited guests that they are present to witness the covenant made between the couple and to energetically support them. In ceremonies that I facilitate, there is special attention paid to affirming the interdependent relationship between the couple and their extended family and community.

[171] My Moon Birch Grove coven sister, Pat Devin first introduced this new birthday custom to me in the early 1980s.

The priestess welcomes the families and guests to the happy day. She explains that the altar before them was created by the lovers and speaks of the meaning of commitment. Invited guests are asked to turn to look at one another to acknowledge the importance of their presence in the couple's lives and to understand that they are the community container in which the couple's relationship takes place. The couple enters into the circle of loving support together and is welcomed by the priestess. All rise, and the universal elements of air, fire, water, and earth, and the Goddess, are invited to bless the couple with gifts for a long and happy life together. Both sets of parents, if present, light a candle, symbolizing the joining of their families, and a chalice is passed to family and friends to fill the cup with special blessings and words from their hearts. Before the lovers drink in these blessings, they offer the chalice to each other, saying, "May you never thirst."

To symbolize how their loving relationship nurtures their families and community, the couple breaks a loaf of bread in two and together they personally feed each guest, saying, "May you never hunger." Lover's vows of commitment and blessings are spoken and sealed with a ring or token of the heart. The priestess also asks the guests to make a commitment to the couple to offer them encouragement and growth as individuals and as a new family. After the couple receives a final blessing from the priestess, they are pronounced "partners in this lifetime, lovers in trust." To seal the ceremony, the lovers join hands and prepare to jump over a broom, symbolic threshold of fertility and prosperity. With joyous encouragement from their loved ones, they jump from the west to the east, marking the new beginning they are making in their lives.

...

Celebrating Sacred Sexuality

Charge of the Star Goddess, written by Doreen Valiente, is a beloved piece of liturgy embraced by numerous modern Witchcraft traditions. In the *Charge*, the voice of the Goddess says, "All acts of love and pleasure are my rituals." Communing with the Goddess through the physical act of lovemaking is an ancient ritual that has retained its importance into contemporary times in both Tantric yoga and modern Witchcraft. In a world that strives to separate our hearts from our bodies, lovemaking as a sacred ritual reconnects and heals, bringing our most intimate relationships to ever-deepening levels of connection and ecstasy.

The lovers have prepared separately for their union by bathing and meditating. The room has been prepared in advance with candles, flowers, and devotional offerings that they have carefully chosen. As they meet at the appointed time, they greet each other through their eyes, meeting in perfect resonance, unafraid to see the Goddess in each other. The lovers take turns anointing each other's bodies with scented oil, kissing each part of their beloved's body, and speaking words of blessing. They lie close to one another without physically touching, and, breathing together, stretch their energy fields to each enclose the other in a loving and protective sphere. Pleasure arises from the bases of their spines as serpent fire is ignited between them. Slowly and reverently, they begin to touch, each sensation a devotional offering to the Goddess, as their individual bodies become a single heart beating as one. There is no goal to achieve or race toward; the pleasure of each successive present moment is experienced fully. They move in a sensual dance as the worship of their beloved guides them. Sensation is not localized, but runs throughout them in exquisite streams of electricity until the time when the energy is released. Love is being made in the world.

...

Ritual to Conceive a Child

I've known many women who became pregnant without making a conscious decision to do so. I've known others who had great difficulty getting pregnant, whether by sex with their male partner or through aided insemination. This vignette was inspired by a ritual performed by women of the Trobrinand Islands in Papua, New Guinea, that I read about many years ago in Bronislaw Malinowski's book *Magic, Science, and Religion*. Malinowski writes that when a woman wishes to conceive, she bathes in the ocean at high tide where the *baloma* (spirits of deceased persons) that have transformed into *waiwaia* (non-incarnated spirit children) dwell and await reincarnation. In the late 1980s, imagery from this ritual inspired me to write a song called "Parthenogenesis":

Legs parted to the sea.
Legs parted to the sea.
What is she doing in the sea foam?

What is she doing?
She is giving birth to herself.
Dance of joy to the stars,
Loved by the silvery ocean,
She is born in waves of pleasure and emotion.
Stepping into icy waves of motion,
She balances entwined around the kelp,
Translucent cells are pulling in her stillness,
The very will of life creates itself.[172]

Tracie stands at the shore of the Pacific Ocean as the day breaks. Listening to the rolling waves and seagulls' song, she allows her own body's rhythms to entrain[173] with the ocean's ceaseless pulse. She prays to the Mother of Life as Primal Womb to open her own womb. Tracie makes an offering of grain to the waters and anoints her body with the salt water. Wading into the lapping waves, she stands, legs apart, opening to the birth waters of the Great Mother, that they may mix with her own juices. In communion with the Mother of Creation, Tracie prays for the gift of a child.

...

Ritual for Entering the Circle of Mothers/Baby Shower

In the cycle of Women's Mysteries, this life-cycle event offers a tremendous opportunity for the mother-to-be, with clear intention, to have a meaningful experience that also empowers her psychically and

---

[172] From the author's CD, *Parthenogenesis.*

[173] Entrainment is the quality of two similarly timed beats to link up and become synchronized in each other's presence (Grahn, *Blood, Bread, and Roses,* 13).

physically. This ritual can also be easily adapted for lesbian couples who choose to birth children and for single mothers.[174] The ritual planning begins by asking the mother-to-be some questions. What are her needs? What does she hope to experience in giving birth and in parenting? What kind of verbal and hands-on support does she wish from her friends and family within the ritual itself?

> *In order of* age, the invited women are admitted into the circle to be anointed by Holly, a close friend of Lisa, the mother-to-be. Holly touches each woman's brow with ocean water, representing the creative womb water of the Goddess, from which the spirit of all life emerges into form. Women join hands in one circle, and Holly invites the elemental powers to bless Lisa and the child she contains in her womb. As planned, the circle separates into two smaller circles, side by side. One circle consists of women who do not parent children, have not given birth to a child, or have chosen not to become a parent. The other circle is comprised of women who parent children and who have physically given birth. Lisa walks to the center of the first circle, wearing a skirt that hangs low on her hips to proudly display her pregnant belly. One by one, she embraces and receives embraces from the women in that circle and says farewell to the life she has known prior to birthing a child and accepting the responsibilities of parenthood. Her friends acknowledge that she will be stepping through a doorway and will be forever changed. They all affirm that they will stay supportive

[174] A version for lesbian couples is included in my chapter "Lesbian Rituals and Dianic Tradition" in *Lesbian Rites: Symbolic Acts and the Power of Community* (Ramona Faith Oswald, editor).

and connected to her.

Holly escorts Lisa out of the first circle to the edge of the circle of mothers, symbolizing the transition she has now begun. Lisa is welcomed into the circle of mothers, first by her own mother or by a close, motherly friend. Her bare belly is blessed with red ochre, symbolic of the life-giving blood of the womb.

The circles rejoin into one as Lisa is honored and blessed by the entire circle. Holly takes a ball of red string and ties a bracelet around her own left wrist. She passes the ball to the woman on her left, who ties the string around her left wrist. The ball of yarn is passed around the circle in this way until all the women are bound together by the strand of blood-red string. The group pauses to look around the circle and acknowledge that they are united through the blood of their wombs. A scissors is passed, and each woman cuts the string that binds her to the woman on her left, leaving a bracelet on her wrist that she will continue to wear until the birth of the child. The women focus their energy and prayers for a safe and healthy birth. Holly instructs them to cut their string off and bury it with gratitude after the child arrives.[175] Lisa is presented with gifts with which to create a birthing altar to use as a focus before and during labor. The ritual gifts reflect Lisa as the embodiment of the Goddess, who brings forth and sustains life in strength and love. The Goddess and the elements are thanked, and the

---

[175] From a Blessing Way ritual conducted by midwife and Priestess Lonnie Rose, of blessed memory.

circle is opened. After the sharing of food, additional gifts for the care of the infant, like those usually associated with the traditional baby shower, are opened.

...

Wiccaning/Baby Welcoming and Family Blessing

A ritual to welcome and bless a newborn is a wonderful occasion to celebrate within a community. It sets a loving, energetic web of support between the baby's parents and extended family and friends. To give as an example, I've chosen a two-part ritual. In the first part, Women's Mysteries are honored. In the second part, the ritual opens to include other extended family and friends of either sex. In this scenario, the new parents are lesbian. This kind of ritual is easily modified if the baby's parents are heterosexual.

Jo and Karen invited their families for a special celebration to welcome their new baby daughter, Genevieve, born just two weeks earlier, into their family. Shortly before the larger celebration that will include the male members of the baby's extended families, Karen (the birth mother), her partner Jo, their mothers, Karen's grandmother, and a few close female friends gather for a private ritual. Karen's best friend Julie facilitates the ritual that begins with the calling of the elements, asking that the baby be blessed with love, strength, creativity, health, and the power to communicate well. Karen and Jo are welcomed into parenthood by the passing of their baby from the arms of Karen's grandmother to Jo's mother to Jo, and from Karen's mother to Karen. The ritual continues with three blessings witnessed by the circle.

The first blessing is from Karen and Jo to their new baby. Expressing some milk from her breasts, Karen anoints their daughter's brow, speaking words from her heart, saying, "I anoint you, beloved daughter Genevieve, and bless you with life, health, prosperity, and love." Jo follows, blessing Genevieve with strength, protection, and creativity.

Jo and Karen's mothers give baby Genevieve her second blessing for close family ties, with promises to teach her how to cook and make rustic furniture someday. They bestow upon their daughters special necklaces that honor them as mothers. The third blessing is given by Karen's grandmother, who blesses Karen and Jo and her new granddaughter with words spoken from her heart that Genevieve grow up in a world of gentleness and free of prejudice. A Goddess Mother, chosen by Karen and Jo, who will be the spiritual guardian of the child her whole life, speaks her commitment to stand by Genevieve and mentor her into adulthood.

When this part of the ritual has been completed, Julie welcomes the male family members who have been waiting in another room into the circle. Julie begins by acknowledging the hard work Karen did in carrying the baby, the labor and birthing, and the huge change in Karen and Jo's lives. She speaks of the couple's strength and commitment as new parents, and to Karen's ability to feed and sustain her baby from her body, as the

Mother of Life sustains us all. Jo offers a chalice filled with fruit juice to her beloved Karen and promises to love and sustain her and their child, understanding that she must, for a time, turn her attention completely to nurturing their new daughter. Karen offers the chalice to her partner, Jo, and promises to love and sustain Jo through the times to come. Together, they promise before their family and friends to nurture their relationship as they nurture their newborn.

The community circles around the parents and infant. A round of blessings is given by family and friends: words of welcome and good wishes for the infant and loving support for the new mothers. As the circle sings a chant that praises life, Karen and Jo, carrying Genevieve in their arms, walk three times clockwise around the circle to seal the blessings of their loved ones.

...

Honoring the Choice Not to Have Children

In patriarchal societies, a woman's worth is measured by her fertility and birth-giving, especially within a marriage, whether she has made an actual choice to have a child or not. Lesbians and heterosexual women who make the choice to not have children often have to defend themselves to family, friends, and the culture at large. Women who are childless by choice are judged as "selfish," "unfulfilled," "incomplete as a woman," "un-feminine," "unnatural," "child-haters," and a "disappointment" to their families. These women often say that they feel invisible in conversations with other women where the unspoken cultural expectation from birth to physical maturity is to have children.

The Goddess in Her aspect as Mother, Creatrix, Maker, or She Who Manifests can include *all* women, regardless of whether they have physically borne children or not, or whether their womb has been removed by a hysterectomy. The womb of a woman (or her "womb space", if she has had a hysterectomy) still serves as the metaphorical, if not literal, symbol of a woman's creative potential and power.

When a woman chooses a path of service that nurtures, supports, sustains, or protects life, whether that is the human species or another species on the planet, she is manifesting the Goddess's attributes as Mother. This is a woman who may be a doula or midwife for women who birth children, a childcare provider, a teacher, counselor, or a political, environmental, or animal activist. A childless woman may sustain her community through service to women and the human family as a healer, a physician, or a woman who runs a community center where women can find a safe place to be.

A childless woman can celebrate herself and identify with the Goddess as Creatrix when she births her ideas into form as art, music, writing, dance, and her career. A woman who chooses another primary way to manifest her creative power in the world needs to be honored and respected for her choice, not condemned.

This ritual scenario comes from a closed women's circle that gathers monthly to support one another's personal growth through ritual making. The group is comprised of lesbians, bisexual and heterosexual women, most of whom are childless by choice. One woman has miscarried several times and is still hoping to get pregnant someday. She decided to participate in her group's ritual because of the possibility that she may never be able to conceive, and she wishes the strength to move forward into that possibility.

> *Each woman has* brought a symbol of her creativity with her. They begin the ritual with each woman speaking

aloud the internalized, harmful voices of her culture, religion, parents, and her own self about childbearing. As the words are spoken they are written down, and the paper that contains them is burned to release each woman from others' expectations. The ritual space is then purified with herbs to clear the energy and make a transition space for women to honor the choices they have made.

A circle sister, Cyndy, speaks about the womb as the literal and symbolic source of potential and fertility that each woman knows. Her words honor their womb blood as the source of creative power, to be channeled how each woman chooses. She encourages the women to reclaim their wombs as their cauldrons of creation. In turn, each woman blesses her womb, anointing her belly with scented oil. She says aloud what she creates and how she sustains and protects her creations: how she is a Creatrix. As she speaks about her creativity and how she nurtures and protects life, she adds her symbol to the group altar. Each woman follows Cyndy's example and declares how she uses her woman-blood to create beauty and meaning in her life, then adds her own symbol of her creativity to the altar. The ritual concludes with words that honor their choices and all the many ways women use their creative energies.

...

Croning Ritual

The word *crone* is a reclaimed word that describes a woman whose womb bloods have stopped (the average age of menopause is 52) for a minimum of a year and who has reached, in astrological terms, her second Saturn return. This is the second return of the planet Saturn to the point where it was at the woman's birth. The first Saturn return occurs between the ages of 28–30 and is a maturing cycle. Astrologer Gretchen Lawlor says, "The second Saturn return occurs somewhere between 58–60 and is as potent in the structuring of the next 30 years as the first Saturn return around age 29 set the tone for the 30s, 40s, and 50s. The second Saturn return completes an era, and with its intense biographical review and pivotal decisions launches one into a 'third destiny.' Themes of the third destiny include the work of mentoring, of seeding the future, of leaving a legacy, and strengthening the light body for transition out of the physical."[176]

The combination of these two passages signifies the passage of a woman into elder status, as a young wise woman or "Earth Crone."[177] It is a convergence of physical, psychological, and psychic changes that brings a woman to this threshold as Earth Crone. Crossing this threshold is an occasion for ritual. Her later transition from Earth Crone to Stone Crone or "hag" is another passage to honor through another ritual.

The words "hag" and "crone" are both words that, in recent years, have begun to be proudly reclaimed and restored to their original ancient and honored meanings. Hags and crones are the "magic makers and transition-easers, the healers and distributors of age-old sacraments."[178] *Hag* comes from the Greek *hagios*, meaning "holy," especially as applied to the principle of female wisdom, Hagia Sophia.[179] *Hagios* is also a cognate

---

[176] From a personal conversation.

[177] A term created by chantress, artist, and ritualist Carolyn Hillyer to denote a young crone. She refers to an older crone as a Stone Crone, and the old woman who is passing through the veil of death and rebirth as Bone. Carolyn's CD, *Old Silverhead*, is a brilliant recording dedicated to women's life cycles. www.seventhwavemusic.co.uk

[178] Wilshire, *Virgin, Mother, Crone*, 21.

[179] Walker, *The Women's Encyclopedia of Myths and Secrets*, 388.

of the Egyptian *heg*, a pre-dynastic matriarchal ruler who knew the words of power, or *hekau*. In Greece, this hag Goddess aspect became Hecate, the crone or hag as Queen of the Dead. These terms are being used again to denote respect for elder women in Dianic community.

A younger woman who has entered menopause can surely create or receive a ritual to mark the ending of her bloods, whether this occurs through her natural body processes or through surgical intervention such as a hysterectomy. The ending of the bloods alone, however, is not enough to achieve cronehood. It is possible for some women as young as thirty-nine years old to go into menopause.[180] A woman this young might have stopped bleeding, but she would not have lived long enough to accumulate the life experience or wisdom that is internalized by her late-fifties. It is this life wisdom that makes a woman a crone.

Women entering their fifties, and sometimes even much younger, experience great fear and anxiety about aging. In patriarchy, once a woman is perceived as past her reproductive or sexual prime, she becomes valueless and invisible. A croning ritual can be an important rite of passage that helps women transition into this next phase of their lives, which is otherwise experienced in isolation. The ritual of croning acknowledges a woman's value as a woman of wisdom and as a person to be cherished and respected. Each woman's needs are different, and in the creation of her ritual, it may be important for a woman to first acknowledge the negative attitudes about aging that she has internalized from the dominant culture. Once these negative attitudes are spoken aloud, she may not feel the need to address them within her ritual, or at least may not need to address them in any great detail.

Croning Background

Sharon is turning fifty-eight years old and recognizes the importance of creating a positive context in which to experience her cronehood.

---

[180] Northrop, 532.

She is a single professional woman who was married many years ago and whose baby son died three days after birth. She feels the oppression felt by many women who do not mother children and feels deeply hurt by the invisibility of childlessness and growing older. She experiences anxiety around financial security, her health, and whether she will be alone in her later years. Sharon has done a lot of ritual work in the past year to release past shame around her nonconformity and wants to give gratitude for being an older woman and a person of joy. She wants to have her ritual in the presence of about a dozen women of all ages whom she knows will support a positive perception of herself growing older.

> *The participants gather* as the ritual space is purified with sage from the hills surrounding Sharon's home. A single circle forms, and women deepen their awareness and connection to one another as the four elements of air, fire, water, and earth are invoked, followed by a sung invocation to the Goddess as Grandmother, our primal ancestress. The purpose of this ritual is spoken as friends are welcomed and given instructions on the ritual's content by the facilitating priestess. Inspired by an enactment called "The Decades," adapted from a croning ritual from the Feminist Spiritual Community of Portland, Maine,[181] the younger women in the circle share a brief story about their lives in the decade of their twenties, naming something significant about that time. The other women (thirty years and older) share in a few words an image or phrase that characterized the twenties decade in their own lives. Sharon speaks last, naming significant events of that decade in her life.
>
> When this has been completed, women in their thirties and

[181] *Celebrating Ourselves: A Crone Ritual Book*, edited by Edna M. Ward.

upward take a step forward to form another inner circle, leaving the women in their twenties in the circle behind them. The same sharing process is repeated by women who are living in or have lived through their thirties. Then women who are forty and up take another step forward. The same process repeats itself with the forties and fifties, up to age fifty-six.

The crones, women who are ages fifty-eight and older, step forward again. A wooden staff decorated with symbols meaningful to Sharon is placed on the ground as a symbolic threshold. Sharon is invited to step over the staff and is welcomed into the circle of ancient women's wisdom. She is draped in an embroidered mantle signifying her new status and handed the wooded staff, which she now holds proudly. The crones speak loving words of comfort and empowerment to the new wise woman, sharing that the best is yet to come. Sharon declares aloud her desires and visions, filling this new phase of life with her intentions for health, love, financial security, and the ability to do meaningful work.

To return to a single circle, the crones rejoin the women in their fifties, who rejoin the forties, etc. until the one circle is reformed again. The older women congratulate each other for making it through so far, and the younger women welcome them back. The ritual concludes with Sharon's libations of gratitude for the gift of life. The circle is opened and the feast, which Sharon lovingly insisted on preparing herself, begins.

...

Coming Out as a Lesbian

Blessed be the fire of our desire.
Blessed be our courage.
Blessed be our love.[182]

Rituals specifically addressing lesbian lives were first made available by Dianic tradition. Union ceremonies for lesbians, described as "trysts," were first published by Z Budapest in 1980.[183] Declaring a lesbian identity can bring fear and distancing from others. By ritualizing this important transition, lesbians create a cauldron of support that brings the newly "out" lesbians into communion with others. For lesbians to honor their unique rites of passage within the dominant culture reflects a deep commitment to end patriarchal oppression both personally and globally. In naming and claiming lesbian rites, we restore meaning, value, and a sense of the sacred to our lives, the lives of our lovers, and loved ones.

The women gather at the lakeside to give themselves and one another a ritual they had previously never conceived of being able to experience: that of celebrating women loving women in the open, of lesbian community, and of honoring their path as Amazons in the world. At the water's edge, the elements are invoked, and women then look toward a collection of driftwood that forms a natural arched passageway to the other side of the riverbank. Some women stand on the other side of the passage as a single drum beats to their breath. As each woman approaches the passage, she briefly tells the

---

182 Chant by Sue McGowan and Delyse from the author's CD *The Year Is a Dancing Woman*.
183 Budapest, *Feminist Book of Lights and Shadows*, 120–122.

others of her awakening and process of coming out to her lesbian identity. At the threshold of the passage she is asked, by a woman on the other side, "Who are you?" and she responds, declaring, "I am Ruth, and I am a lesbian!" One by one, each woman tells her story and crosses the threshold amid the cheers of her sisters until all the women are on the other side of the passage. A chant begins: "Blessed be the fire of our desire. Blessed be our courage. Blessed be our love," as women move into freeform dancing, expressing their joy. A cauldron is lit to ceremonially honor lesbian sacred sexuality, as women continue to dance and feed each other sweet mangos.

...

Ritual for Divorce or Separation

When a relationship ends, willingly or unwillingly, the ties that bind often endure long after. There are emotional and energetic ties, especially if the relationship involved a sexual partnership. The following example of a ritual for ending a relationship is taken from my own divorce ritual with my daughter's father, William. I feel very thankful that he chose to participate in the ritual with me, knowing our relationship was over, the divorce papers had been filed, and the child custody arrangements worked out. If he had chosen not to participate with me, a variation of the same enactment could have been modified for me to do the ritual alone. This was a very difficult ritual for both of us to do. Feelings of hurt, anger, blame, regret, and relief combined in a complex emotional soup. I believe that participating in this ritual made it possible for us to remain on civil terms over the years as we parented our daughter from separate households.

He knocked on the door of the home that we shared together during our marriage. I let him in and invited him to sit down in the middle of the living room floor. We sat cross-legged, facing each other. I placed a white taper in a holder in front of each of us. We sat in silence for a couple of minutes, containing within us the heated words that already had been spoken aloud many times.

I took up a match and spoke blessing words that I could honestly say, wishing him a good life. I then lit the candle in front of him. He did the same, wishing me well, and lit the candle in front of me. Each of us then reached out and grasped the candleholder directly in front of us and slowly pulled it back across the carpet and away from the other person. We sat in the palpable silence of the enactment for a few moments. I then tied a string from my wrist to his, representing the connection we had. I took a scissors and severed it. He got up and left without another word passing between us.

...

Ritual for a Survivor of Sexual Assault

This release/transformation ritual was created by a group of eighteen women in a ritual-making workshop I taught decades ago at a Lesbian Witchcamp near Vancouver, Canada. The women created and participated in eight personal rituals that covered a variety of themes over a five-day period. The level of experience within the group varied from women who were complete newcomers to Dianic ritual to witches with many years of experience.

The ritual was created for a survivor of a sexual assault. Healing rituals can also be created for survivors of incest and childhood abuse. As I have already mentioned, a ritual with content of this nature should be undertaken with utmost care and responsibility. I recommend the attendance or facilitation of an experienced therapist who has expertise in ritual construction and energetics. This is the kind of ritual that women create out of a need to heal and return to fuller participation in life, and it illustrates ritual's potential to empower women in their lives. Because of my prior experience with this kind of intense ritual, I facilitated the more difficult parts, allowing Susan (the survivor) and the group to feel more relaxed.

Background

Susan is new to women's ritual and has never before experienced being witnessed and supported by women in a ritual circle. She wants to heal from some continuing emotional and psychic effects of being sexually assaulted three years earlier. She thinks that she has worked through the worst of it and feels the need to help other survivors of sexual violence. She wants to deal with the experience on an emotional level with group support, sharing her anger and sadness at what she has lost. She also wants to share her feelings of relief in moving through it.

Ritual Purpose

Susan says, "I want to honor my feelings of anger and sadness from rape and share my relief in moving through it." Susan wants a group of supportive women to participate in various parts of the ritual and to witness her as she does some deep personal work.

Theme

In order to make her internal connections with the ritual, Susan meditates on the ritual purpose while opening herself to Going Wide

Practice: filling her ritual space with the ambiance of the five sensual correspondences of sight, sound, smell, taste, and touch. Susan shares with her ritual group that she saw the colors of purple, black, and green. She describes seeing the ocean at sunset and hearing the song of dolphins. In her meditation, she heard chanting, drumming, and saw a fire. She smelled lemongrass, and there was a circle of women holding hands. She tells the group that she wants to drink something sweet during the ritual.

The rest of the ritual is created by the group with Susan's full participation and final approval. The group discusses personal preparation for this ritual in which there will be energetic support, witnessing, and an energetic container for Susan to work in. We also discuss what we will do if our own emotions are brought to the surface, especially those of other rape survivors. Two women volunteer to be available for others who might be in crisis. We discuss and agree that it will be especially important for the group to stay centered and emotionally present for the duration of the ritual. Women agree that showing feelings doesn't automatically mean that someone is in crisis or in need of intervention. We also agree that if it appears that someone is in actual crisis, she will be asked up to three times if she needs anything. Prior to gathering, everyone takes a couple of hours for their own preparation, and we observe silence for forty-five minutes prior to the beginning of the ritual.

The Ritual

LOCATION: The ritual takes place by the shore of a lake. There is complete privacy. A short distance from the lakeshore is a fire circle. It is evening, and the sun is going down.

THE ALTAR: We gather early to help build the altar. Susan is meditating elsewhere and preparing for the ritual with a support person. She has given some altar items to others so that they will be on the altar when she arrives: her chalice, healing crystals, fresh lavender, and a dolphin image. A candle that was lit from Brigid's flame at Kildare, Ireland (which contains in its wick the flame of Brigid, a Celtic goddess of healing), a bowl of water, and other healing objects are brought by others.

The ritual space is purified with incense and water. Most of the group lines up at the entrance of the ritual space with Susan at the end of the line. There are some women drumming a steady, meditative rhythm. One by one, the support women approach the threshold of the ritual space. As facilitating Priestess, I challenge them, "How do you enter the circle?" They each answer the question with "I enter in perfect love and perfect trust." By saying this, each woman makes a personal commitment to creating a space of love and safety for Susan and each other.

The group forms a circle and begins to chant the sound "MA," creating with our voices a sound vibration that will raise personal and group energy for the circle casting, which extends out to include the beach and the lakeside. I invoke the elemental powers and the goddess Brigid, asking for healing and blessings for this work.

We escort Susan down to the water's edge. I give her a few rocks, telling her to begin throwing them into the water, asking her gently to breathe and to keep breathing as she lets out a sound with each throw of a rock. Susan appears a little reluctant or emotionally stuck, so I assist her in getting into a physical posture designed to bring feelings to the surface by making her physically uncomfortable. As she bends over with me, I instruct her to stand on one bent leg, lifting the other leg high behind her,[184] using just one finger on each hand to lightly touch on the sand below her. Her only support is the one bent leg. With our heads bowed low, we begin to make sounds as the posture becomes more tiring and difficult to hold. After a while, I suggest that she switch legs, which she does. Women by the water near us are making sounds with us, encouraging Susan's anger to emerge.

Susan turns again to the river and begins to throw rocks, this time with vocal sounds emerging authentically from her pain. Rock after rock is passed to her, and she appears entranced with her process of throwing and vocalizing her anger and grief. When she has finished, she spontaneously undresses and jumps into the cold lake with a cry of joy. After swimming for a couple of minutes, she returns to the shore, where she is dried off by the waiting women.

We escort Susan back to the ritual area where women bless her with sacred waters from Brigid's well. This is done to consecrate Susan's body as her own temple. The group begins to chant words praising the Goddess who brings healing and change, "She changes everything She touches, and everything She touches changes."[185] After blessing Susan's body, women individually speak blessings of healing and empowerment while she sips hot mint tea.

---

[184] This is a posture that I learned from Richian therapy in the early 1980s.
[185] Kore Chant by Starhawk.

> Spontaneously, the women enclose Susan in a group hug, a final envelopment of love and support. The group begins singing another chant about healing and the ocean as they rock Susan gently in their arms. The circle is opened, releasing the energy that has sealed the ritual container with grateful thanks to the elemental forces and the Goddess of Healing.

***

In the days following the ritual, women processed their experiences. Susan felt that the ritual helped her move into a new perspective on her life that she had not previously been able to access. She felt relieved of the burden she was carrying and felt that she could now go on with her life. Others shared that by supporting Susan, they had healed a part of themselves that had stayed victimized by their own experience of assault. Women acknowledged that although some of the ritual experience was emotionally intense and painful, the careful psychological and energetic preparation in advance of the ritual empowered them to remain present and to spiritually serve Susan. I felt that the group did a beautiful job of creating and facilitating this ritual experience, and it was one of the most emotionally moving ritual experiences I have had. The women worked and focused together beautifully and selflessly. They recognized the importance of the ritual they had created and how powerful their organized focused intention was. They were able to experience their ability to make a difference in the life of another woman and how their own lives were touched in turn.

It is rituals like this one and others that are drawing women to the Dianic tradition, women's spirituality groups, and to ritual making. Dianic ritual is about women's lives, experiences, joys, and sorrows, whether done alone or within a group of women. To learn how to create ritual is to learn how to heal ourselves and others, to joyfully participate in life's blessings, and to feel spiritually connected. When done with care and consciousness, ritual is a powerful tool for personal and social transformation.

chapter 12

EVERY RITUAL IS A TEACHER

Your willingness and ability to evaluate a ritual experience is critical if you hope to improve your skills in ritual design, facilitation, and participation. Because Dianic ritual is a moment-to-moment, living and breathing experience, what you originally envisioned and what you eventually end up with may seldom match exactly. This does not mean that you will never have a "perfect" ritual. It means that your idea of the perfect ritual will evolve as you grow in your ritual-making skills and your practices of visioning, planning, and facilitating. Some rituals will flow very well; at other times they may feel as though you are wrestling a greased pig. Always remind yourself, with a lot of compassion and a great deal of humor, that every ritual is a teacher.

Ritual is, by nature, a subjective experience for each participant. You might think you have just facilitated the ritual from hell when a woman comes up to you in tears and thanks you for a life-changing experience. That woman managed to have a life-transforming experience regardless of the problems experienced by you and the other facilitators, and for her, the ritual was the catalyst for that success. Perhaps you've attended a ritual and felt deeply moved, whereas the friend who came with you was thoroughly bored. You've probably wondered if you were both at the same ritual at the same time.

Given its subjective nature, on what basis do you, or can you, evaluate a ritual? The questions offered in this chapter will help to guide you in evaluating your rituals so that ideas and ways to improve them can be more easily understood. These same questions can also be extremely useful to consider in the planning stages of a ritual. The ritual experience, made conscious, will teach you.

First, keep records of rituals that you create or attend. This will make it easier for you to refer back to them from year to year. Some rituals become traditions over time if the same enactments are repeated yearly and taken to an even deeper level by the facilitators and participants. Rituals will also change and evolve in response to changing needs within a group or community. Keep notes that record suggested changes and improvements for the next time. What you think you will absolutely remember will appear fuzzy a year later.

After the ritual, let your impressions and experiences sit for a day or two before you begin to compare your experiences with others, especially if you are evaluating a ritual that you helped create. If you designed and facilitated a group ritual, devote a separate time or meeting with the other facilitators to share your experiences of how the ritual went. For many years in my local community, there would always be three meetings for each of the public seasonal rituals. The intent of the initial meeting, called the ritual design meeting, was to arrive at a clear purpose and create a working outline in developing the ritual theme, or to review the previous year's ritual and decide how much of it would be repeated. Quite often this meeting would draw fewer women. The ritual planning meeting followed a week or two later, and all the women who wished to facilitate in some form would attend to flesh out the outline and designate ritual responsibilities. The post-ritual evaluation meeting was held a week or two after the community ritual to discuss what worked, what didn't work, and to record any recommended changes for the following year in the community ritual book. Although these meetings took time and commitment from everyone, the learning process was invaluable. Two effective formulas for giving and receiving constructive evaluations are included at the end of this chapter; they work equally well in post-ritual evaluation meetings and in everyday life.

If there are no regular meetings planned to evaluate your rituals, make sure that there are other communication methods in place so that a more informal evaluation is managed. Letters, notes, e-mails, and phone calls to a central person in order to share reflections and ideas for improvement can be put in a file and stored with the ritual outline for another time.

In evaluating a ritual, it is crucial to consider all of the forces that were operating during the ritual. This can include the energy that you or others came into the ritual with, the ritual environment itself, the level of experience of the facilitators and participants, any "outside" factors such as large-scale current events or personal issues, and the effect that the combined forces had energetically. A ritual can be evaluated by looking at all of the points of the creation process mentioned in this book, including the development of the ritual purpose, the theme, the altar setup (if included), the energetic preparations prior to the ritual, the working of energy during the ritual, the ritual's structure, and the ritual's facilitation.

The evaluation questions below can help you improve your skills as both a facilitator and a participant. Tailor the questions to your situation; not all questions will apply to every ritual, and others can be easily adjusted to apply to your own ritual experience. Some rituals may be solitary and therefore self-facilitated, or they may be held in a closed coven (a ritual group not open to including others) where the ritual is both created and facilitated by its members. Other rituals may be ones where one woman entirely creates and facilitates the ritual for another woman or group. Still others may be created by a group for a single woman. Many of these questions are written for a group of facilitators who create and facilitate rituals that are offered to the public.

Remember, the most important aspects to explore when evaluating or deconstructing your ritual experience is to look for *why* and *how* something either worked well or didn't. When deconstructing a ritual, use the phrase, "This worked well *because* . . ." or "That didn't work *because* . . ."

Let us begin.

Evaluation Questions

Evaluate the Ritual Location

The location for a ritual makes a difference. Whether your location is indoors or out, the space must be able to serve your needs. Working outdoors has its own set of challenges and joys. You must be able to adapt to wind, water, heat, or cold. Security can be a major issue; always post a guard. Women who are called to the path of service as a community guardian might provide security for all of your rituals, indoors and out. Sound generally carries poorly outdoors as compared to a contained room. You must be able to project your voice and energy so that everyone attending can understand what is being said. Sometimes it is harder to feel the energetic connection across a very large circle outside, especially if women are accustomed to working indoors.

Even with all of the extra challenges, the benefits of doing ritual together on the living body of the Mother, under sun, moon, or stars, outweighs any negatives. Communion with Her is more intense in every way possible. Once women become accustomed to being outside, the rituals work very well.

* Was the physical location appropriate for the ritual?

* Was there enough privacy and adequate security?

* How did the environment affect your experience positively or negatively?

* Was the space large enough to comfortably accommodate the expected numbers?

* Was it seasonally appropriate? For example, if it was winter or summer, were women comfortable with the temperature, elemental exposure, and accessibility?

* What about parking?

* If a feast was included at the ritual, was there a place for the food to be stored and served?

* How close were the toilets? Were they accessible for everyone?

* Was the ritual space accessible for women with disabilities?

* If the ritual was held in an indoor space, were you sharing the building with other events that disrupted your ritual? Were you able to lock the doors before the circle was cast?

* Were the acoustics of the room supportive of speaking or singing?

* If there were windows that looked out to the public, were you able to cover them?

* Were you free to make as much noise as you wished without someone calling the police?

Evaluate the Practical Details

* Were things prepared and ready for use? It is simply best to have more of what you think you might need (candles, matches, incense, etc.)?

* If magical tools were used, were the tools consecrated and charged?

Evaluate the Altar Setup

Review the use of colors, tools, symbols, and images for the elements and the Goddess.

* How did you feel about the altar? Did it reflect the intention of the ritual?

* Was it easy to work with? Were the things you needed to work with within reach? Was it attractive and inviting?

* If candles were lit, were they placed safely away from flammable items and dancing women?

Evaluate the Personal Ritual Preparation

* Did you and others go into the ritual sufficiently prepared emotionally, energetically, physically, and psychically? If not, why not?

* How did preparation, or the lack of it, affect your experience of the ritual? How will you improve in your preparations next time?

Evaluate How Participants Were Welcomed Into the Ritual Space

* If you came to the ritual as a participant, did you feel welcomed and accommodated?

* Did the facilitators clearly explain the ritual purpose and enactments?

* Considering what "safe space" means to you personally, did the space feel emotionally and physically safe?

* Did the facilitators act to ensure a focused ritual experience?

Review the Use and Style of Invocations and Valedictions

* Did the language of the invocations and valedictions reflect the purpose of the ritual?

* Was the imagery seasonally and thematically appropriate?

* Were the blessings or aid requested from the elemental spirits appropriate? For example, don't ask the earth element to bless you with blossoming spring flowers in the dead of winter. This does not correspond with the seasonal cycle of the Northern Hemisphere.

Did the Ritual Enactments Chosen Correspond Well to the Ritual Theme?

* Did you resonate with the symbols chosen for the enactments?

* Were the enactments clearly explained in accessible language?

* Did the enactments take enough time? Too much time?

* Was the energy of the ritual appropriately maintained during the enactments?

At the beginning of the ritual or as the ritual is proceeding, give brief and lyrically voiced explanations of the proceedings, symbols, and ritual actions. In this way, participants will clearly understand what is going on. Giving them what they need to hear and see empowers them to participate at their own level of experience, since their very presence indicates that they are there to participate.

Evaluate the Ritual Design

* Were all the perceptual modes (visual, auditory, and kinesthetic) considered and incorporated into the ritual design?

* Was there so much sitting that women who needed to move got bored and fidgety?

* Was there so much dancing that women who need to focus on visual imagery felt left out?

* Was there too much to look at all at once?

* Too much talking?

* Too much silence?

* In retrospect, would you design this ritual differently?

Review the Transitions

* Were the transitions between the enactments smooth, abrupt, or awkward?
* If you could repeat the ritual again, would you design it differently? If so, how?
* In hindsight, what might have been some other possibilities?

Transitions are a ritualist's specialty. They are often the most critical and challenging parts of any ritual and can make or break a ritual's flow. The skill lies in the way that a facilitator simultaneously contains and guides the energy of the ritual unobtrusively, holding the complete picture and moving the ritual into the next section. She may need to take the spiraling energy of a free-form dance and focus it into a collective point of stillness and unity. As you practice facilitating and grow in your ability to embody the ritual, you will learn to sensitively guide energy from one phase to the next.

Energy Flow and Ritual Energetics

* Did the ritual flow well from beginning to end, as it was structured to do?
* Was the choice of energetic preparation effective?
* Were you able to embody the theme of the ritual?
* If energy was raised, how was the energy used? Did it work?
* Was the type of energy raised appropriate to the ritual theme and purpose?
* Was it released completely?

Group Focus

Sometimes participants become nervous or bored and may start chatting with others while ritual work is being enacted. This is detrimental to the ritual focus, distracting or disturbing for the women who are trying to work, and disrespectful to everyone else. Facilitators must find a way to intervene without embarrassing the talkers and causing more disruption in the ritual flow. Without intervention by a facilitator, other participants may feel that they are not being taken care of.

* How cohesive was the group's focus?
* Was there a sense of all or most of the women in the circle being present energetically?
* Were the women able to work with the ritual intention as one mind?
* If you came into the ritual in a conflicting mental or emotional state, were you able to center and become fully present during the ritual?
* What parts of the ritual felt more or less focused, and what may have been the contributing factors? Look at this question for both internal and external distractions.

Evaluate the Length of the Experience

* Were you being realistic about the time needed to complete the ritual, or were you even thinking about it at all?
* Was there enough time to do everything that had been planned?
* Was it too long or too short?

Even a simple ritual can take much longer than you might realize. In a large group with diverse levels of experience, it is hard to keep the momentum going and the energy flowing. If you are working a ritual as a solitary, time is completely flexible. You are not accountable to others and the issue of time need not be a concern at all. Your experience begins when you begin and ends when you end it.

* If you designed the ritual for or with others, was the amount of ritual work planned appropriate for the skill level and energetic capacity of the participants?

Evaluate Your Experience as a Facilitator

* Did you enjoy giving service to the group or an individual? Why? Why not?

* Were you comfortable in a facilitating role?

* Were there enough facilitators for the ritual you designed?

* Were you truly able to step aside and allow yourself to be used as a tool in the Goddess' service?

* Is this something that you would wish to continue doing?

* What skills do you believe you need to develop in order to become a more effective facilitator?

* How will you nourish yourself and remain centered as you step forward to serve?

* As a facilitator, did you do your personal ritual work prior to the ritual?

Occasionally I've heard a facilitator say that she "didn't get anything out of the ritual" she helped to facilitate. If you come out of a ritual you facilitated feeling resentful that you didn't get anything out of it, or complain that all you did was give, then perhaps you have crossed over the line from service to self-sacrifice. When I facilitate a ritual, especially in a large open seasonal ritual, I do not expect to get my personal needs met when I am in a service role. I make sure to do my own related ritual work sometime prior to, or soon after, the group ritual.

Evaluate the Ritual Guardian Facilitators

* Would the ritual benefit from designating one or more women to ensure safety, keep time (if appropriate), maintain the container of the cast circle, or provide specific energetic support to facilitators and participants?

* If a circle was cast, how successful was the container?

* If specific energetic support was asked for and given, was it what you wanted or needed?

Evaluate the Effect of the Ritual

* Do you have a sense that the ritual initiated genuine change in the participants and facilitators alike?

* What gives you this feedback? Verbal communication or observation? Your personal intuition?

* Gather information from various sources before you make your final evaluation.

Evaluate the Success of the Ritual's Purpose

* Did the ritual accomplish what it set out to do?

* Did the ritual feel finished or complete?

* Was the ritual theme more challenging than the facilitators and participants anticipated?

Most rituals are designed to be a complete experience. Other rituals are done in installments or phases. I've heard some women express in exasperation, "I thought I'd already dealt with that issue years ago!" Some issues, such as healing from sexual abuse, dysfunctional family history, mourning, and other traumas may need to be revisited as layers of the issue are removed and brought to awareness. While it is true that a woman may have already dealt with an issue at one point in time, the unconscious mind continues to process it and may reveal more pieces or aspects of an event that need to be examined and healed. Fortunately, other rituals can be created to further process and support the healing evolution of the issue. It is imperative that you carefully consider your responsibility in facilitating yourself or others in areas where you may lack the skill or knowledge to deal with potentially volatile issues. Other rituals can be done regularly as "maintenance," such as rituals for the continual health of one's family. These rituals may require less evaluation once a satisfactory pattern is established that fulfills the ritual's purpose.

Evaluate the Ritual-Creation Process from Initial Planning to Final Cleanup

* What did you learn about yourself and about working with others?
* In the process of creating the ritual with a group, how was power shared?
* Did everyone feel that the ritual was created for them—that they had "ownership" of the ritual?
* What were the factors that contributed to the feeling of ownership or the absence of that feeling?

The goal of ritual planning should be the success of the ritual. In my community, when a ritual is initially designed, facilitators gather together and brainstorm, throwing ideas for enactments to support the ritual's theme into the cauldron. After enough energetic ideas have been tossed in, we pull out the ones we feel will best serve our purposes and set them into a ritual structure. Each woman learns to contribute her best ideas without having a personal attachment to the group's final decisions. It is not essential that everyone offer ideas in the planning of a ritual. However, what is most important is that everyone is able to participate if they wish to. If a suggested enactment is utilized in the ritual and doesn't work out well, we simply discard it or adapt it for future use. One of my roles as high priestess and ritualist is to assist in guiding ritual design. The more ritual experience a group has, the less work I have to do.

Evaluate Your Most Memorable Moments of the Ritual

Reviewing what worked in the ritual and, more importantly, why you think it worked, is equally as important as noting what didn't work. People tend to focus on problems and ignore or take for granted their successes. Make sure to acknowledge both the individuals and the group as a whole for work well done.

Practice

Evaluate your experience of ritual with the questions in this chapter. Evaluate a ritual you attend as a participant and a ritual you create and facilitate. Record your answers in your ritual-making journal.

Giving and Receiving Constructive Feedback/Evaluation

The ability to give and receive constructive feedback and do self-evaluation is essential to your growth as a ritualist. Criticism, however, focuses on what is wrong and is often presented in immobilizing or hurtful ways. Sometimes criticism is disguised as feedback. This is destructive to relationships, groups, and movements.

> Feedback/evaluation is often seen and used as a more balanced process meant to help you see what you are doing

> well, what was not successful, and what you may want to think about doing differently. Feedback/evaluation is interactive—it means giving as well as receiving information. Feedback/evaluation can help you see your strengths as well as what needs further development or change.[186]

The following formulas for giving constructive feedback/evaluation and for doing self-evaluation are simple and useful. Their language structure promotes mutual responsibility and support.[187]

Practice these forms of constructive feedback until they become natural in their delivery. The immediate, positive results will encourage you to practice. If you are working with an ongoing group, everyone will benefit by learning and practicing together. When a group comes together as allies to review a ritual and examine it for its beauty and its places for improvement, the growth, bonding, and positive benefits for individuals and the group alike are enormous.

In the formula for feedback/evaluation, the woman giving the feedback must include what she would want to have experienced in addition to what she believes did not work. A healing way to respond to constructive feedback/evaluation by women in the group is to respond with a spoken or written self-evaluation. This helps others to know that you understand what they said and what alternatives you have considered for future actions that might benefit everyone. Reviewing your part in a ritual without waiting for feedback from others will support your personal growth and improve your work as a ritual maker.

---

[186] From "Transforming: Conflict, Communication, & Leadership to Build Community," a workshop facilitated by Rae Atira-Soncea (of blessed memory) and Marian Farrior for the Spiral Door Women's Mystery School of Magick and Ritual Arts, 2004.

[187] The formulas for constructive critique come from Radical Therapy "criticism/self-criticism."

Constructive Feedback/Evaluation Sample Format

When you do/did/said (observation[188] or specific words), I feel/felt (emotion), and what I want you to do in the future or what I would have liked you to have done is (action/want), because of (the purpose it will advance).

EXAMPLE

When you (observation: cracked a joke in the middle of the silent part of the ritual), I felt (emotion: irritation). What I want you to do in the future is (action/want: to allow the intentional silence to remain uninterrupted), so that (the purpose it will advance: the group can go even deeper into the ritual theme, which the silence is meant to facilitate).

Constructive Self-Evaluation Sample Format

When I do/did/said (observation of my actions or specific words), I caused (effect of my action), and from now on I will do/say (action for doing or saying it better or differently) because of (purpose it will advance).

EXAMPLE

When I (observation of my actions: cracked a joke during the silence), I (effect of my action: could see that it caused you and others to feel angry and perplexed), and from now on I will (action for doing it better or differently: deal more responsibly with my own

---

[188] Observations refer to specific actions, as in "She said or did ____." This is not a judgment, such as "She is selfish." To observe without judgment is difficult. Judgment, diagnosing, and interpreting events obscures what is actually happening. Try not to mix what you observe and how you respond to and interpret it.

> discomfort with being in silence because (purpose it will advance: then I, as well as others, can receive the maximum benefit from that part of the ritual experience, and others will know that our rituals allow for very deep personal experience).

Practice

Practice constructive evaluation hundreds of times using the formulas. Learn and grow. Get back on the horse and ride again. Evaluate your experience every time. Make this mirror your ally.

If you are doing ritual regularly with a group, ask for constructive feedback of all kinds. Ask your circle sisters to practice and use the formulas for constructive evaluation. Be kind and honest with your feedback; learn and grow together.

Every ritual is a teacher.

chapter 13

THE PRIESTESS

The role of the priestess awaits re-definition in the twenty-first century. Its keynote must be service, not power.[189]

With the resurgence of women's interest in Dianic tradition, goddess traditions and women's ritual, the role of the priestess is being revived in contemporary times. With growing interest in ritual making and more women gaining experience in facilitating ritual, we must ask ourselves many questions. Where are the role models for contemporary women who are interested in learning about ritual facilitation or the ritual Priestess path? If you imagine yourself as a Priestess, or a ritual Priestess, what are your expectations for yourself? What are your expectations based on? Do you have any models for spiritual leadership other than religious leadership models from patriarchal religions?

There is a tendency to romanticize the ancient priestess, placing modern-day sensibilities or feminist values on what we imagine to be a glowing, utopian picture of the past. However, there were thousands of temple priestesses in Asia Minor, most taken from the lower social orders, who were relegated to simple or menial labor.[190] Daughters of poor families were picking up the temple garbage, and that was all they could hope to attain.

High Priestesses were given station by inheritance, "often born into royal families, thus priestesses by birth. They were also queens of the land as in Crete, Egypt, and Anatolia. Their ritual enactment of planting

---

[189] Ozaniec, *Daughter of the Goddess*, 300.

[190] Goodrich, *Priestesses*, 1.

and harvest ceremonies ensured fertility and prosperity for all. They lived in both small or huge cloistered communities. All were educated for religious duties, and separated by performance and aptitude."[191]

Ancient ritual priestesses were trained to embody the Goddess and thereby provide direct contact with Her to the community they served. There was a religious and cultural understanding that individuals who were too weak personally, physically, or intellectually to reach Her by their own efforts could connect directly with Her via their connection through the priestess.[192]

As contemporary women on the Priestess path (those women seeking ordination), our primary function is to create or to become a channel, a chalice, for an experience of the Goddess. In this way, we continue to function as the priestesses did in ancient times. Whether it is through ritual, writing, art, scholarship, dance, music, or organizational skills, the twenty-first-century Priestess becomes the container who helps create sacred space wherein women can connect with the Goddess. Her service may be to help others integrate life passages by providing facilitation services and energetic support at joyous events like births and cronings. She must also be prepared to escort the dying as they cross over and attend to those in mourning.

The noun "Priestess" is the title of a woman who has studied and trained, who has gained experience as a spiritual leader, and who has grown adept in the propagation of her spiritual tradition or specialized area of ministry. She serves a community in a vocational capacity, and can teach what she knows. She has trained rigorously, developed specific skill sets, and carved the many facets of her skills into a diamond of her own self. It is the journey of becoming a Priestess that has shaped her. This woman has dedicated herself to her work and has perhaps been accepted as a Priestess by the congregation, circle, or community she serves.

If her central focus is ritual, she must excel in ritual making, facilitation,

---

191 Ibid.,I, II.

192 Ibid.

and the energetic skills required to execute those duties. If she is a temple Priestess, she must have the skills and vision to create altars, ritual tools, and an environment where women can experience a temple of the Goddess. If she is a healer Priestess, she must know how to keep herself whole and centered as she serves her community, animals, or plants who are ailing. Her most important tool is learning how to bring herself fully present in the moment. She is accountable and responsible for her service over the long haul. She experiences herself as an instrument of service to the Goddess and Her women. She works consciously to be a living presence of the Goddess in her words and deeds.

The Priestess is responsive to her commitments, even when she doesn't always feel like it. This does not mean, however, that she sacrifices herself to her detriment or becomes a doormat for others' needs. Self-care is essential in order to have the internal resources to offer service. To facilitate others, a woman must be able to come to them as a full vessel. It is difficult to flow when the well has run dry, when one's strength and energy are depleted due to lack of personal maintenance. A woman responsive to her commitments also knows her limitations and makes appropriate referrals when necessary.

On the other hand, one cannot control unexpected life events. There have been many times when I've been asked to serve when what I really needed was a few weeks of rest. At these times—the sudden death of a community member's partner, parent, or companion animal—I've just done what was needed and summoned the strength to be there to show up and serve. The Goddess has never failed to give me strength and guide my service.

Too often the complexity of the process a woman undergoes in becoming a Priestess is minimized or misunderstood. A woman who is learning to become a Priestess will undergo a process of self-transformation that is difficult to describe and can pose many challenges while offering much enlightenment.

Hearing the Call of Service: The Priestess Path

"To be a leader, you must first learn to serve."[193]

The path to becoming a Priestess begins with a calling; Her voice speaking to your spirit, awakening you to the knowledge that your life has a specific purpose. You may experience the feeling of "coming home" that so many women describe upon awakening to the Goddess and Her ways. Becoming a Priestess is a deep and dedicated process of learning how to use and serve with this awareness. One may have the feeling that the Goddess is calling you and you must answer, but, ultimately, you alone must choose whether to serve or not.

While there are women who find meaning in providing spiritual service, if her service is not her vocation, she can set it aside when interest wanes or too many conflicts arise. There are contemporary practitioners who publically claim the title of Priestess without the training or deeper understanding of the responsibilities involved with spiritual service. This confuses and undermines the role of the vocational Priestess and her work.

Why is service integral to priestess work? What does it mean to serve others spiritually? In many ways, spiritual service is about empowering a community to identify and support its own needs. For me, serving women is serving the Goddess: I don't see any difference. When I am ministering to women, my challenge is to open my heart, mind, and hands, letting Her work through me. In many ways, being a good leader is also like being a good mother: listening, setting boundaries, helping others see how their behavior affects others, and being negotiable with some bottom lines.

Loving the Goddess, and even having a personal relationship with a particular aspect of Her, is basic to Dianic Witchcraft and its practitioners.

---

[193] Priestess Jennie Mira.

Feeling that a particular goddess speaks to you is a part of the practice of Witchcraft that can develop over time. Some women call themselves Priestesses out of a desire to express love, commitment, or devotion to a particular goddess. Loving the Goddess, in itself, does not make one a Priestess, just as being a devout Jew or Christian does not automatically make one a rabbi, priest, or minister. The term "Priestess" is not just about one's self-defined identity.

The word "witch" can describe a woman who is completely self-defined, practicing alone or with others without performing acts of service to a community. It is not possible, however, for a Priestess to be completely self-defined. She is identified by her legacy of spiritual service in her community.

What is a community, especially a spiritual community? The *Oxford Universal Dictionary's* definition of *community* is "a body of people having common organization or interests or living in the same place under the same laws; common character; agreement; identity." Many women consider themselves involved in many communities. Thus, "community" may include the larger global sisterhood of women, the geographic area where one resides, special interest groups, and spiritual circles. All of these circles require various levels of participation and intimacy.

My initial reaction when a woman says that she wants to be a Priestess is to alternately howl and laugh inside! "Why would she want to do that? Is she crazy?" It is, at times, so incredibly hard! My usual response is to do my best to talk her out of the idea.

What is your motivation for leadership? The title of Priestess sounds mystical, powerful, and conjures up fantasy images of flowing robes, crescent tiaras, charged magical tools at your fingertips, and rooms full of chanting, awe-eyed devotees lingering on your every muse-inspired word. You dispense wisdom directly from the Goddess Herself, channeled in perfection to the unquestioning multitudes that wait and depend on your guidance.

If that's your vision, get another hobby.

If you are a ritual Priestess, the reality is this: you will be the last one left in the rented hall, scraping candle-wax droppings off the floor with a razor blade.[194] Even though you try to delegate volunteers to help with the cleanup, when women slip through the cracks at the end of the night, it is *your* butt on the line because you rented the place. *You* will be blamed for everything and anything that goes wrong—not just in the ritual, but possibly in the lives of all the people who attend the event. You will become the archetypal "mother to the masses," with everyone's feelings and unfinished business with their parents, their bosses, and their last lover who dumped them all projected onto you. You will be sick of politics and held to a standard of personal conduct that no one can, or should, maintain. You will want to quit many times over, all the while knowing that the only path that exists is forward.

Why would you consider the Priestess path? Do you want attention from your community? Do you think you will feel better about yourself? Do you want to feel extra special or important? If you say "yes" to any of these questions, seek a different path. If your need to do this work is ego driven, your expectations are based on a fantasy that will not sustain you when the hard reality sets in.

In considering the responsibility of becoming a Priestess, you should consider the following questions: What does the title of "Priestess" mean to you? Do you feel that there ought to be criteria and standards for Priestesses that women can expect from someone who calls herself by that title? If you could set these standards, what would they be and why? What standards do you set for your own Priestess work? How do you know that you have met your own standards? What expectations do you have of a woman who calls herself a Priestess? Why do you think you are good Priestess material? Do you have a loving and compassionate heart? Is it your passion to serve the Goddess through serving women and Mother Earth as a vocation? Do you have proven creativity and skills? Do you wish

---

194 As part of the ordination ceremony for ritual Priestesses, I give an ice scraper for picking up candle-wax droppings.

to offer them in service to others? Are you deepening your skills in order to help others? What experience do you have in taking on leadership responsibilities? Do you feel that you are, or would be, a good group facilitator? Do you have the ability to communicate well and connect compassionately with others? Have you acquired skills and practice in conflict resolution and group process? Are you afraid to be accountable for your actions, say you are wrong, or to apologize when it is due? Have you made a commitment to the ongoing process and journey of knowing yourself, accepting both your challenges and strengths?

Working to evolve beyond our patriarchal conditioning and to build a world based on feminist values is a very challenging task, yet this personal commitment is essential for Priestess work. What personal work have you done to examine any internalized racism you may have? What personal work have you done around examining issues of class, sexism, and homophobia? A woman on the Priestess path must understand that this examination, called "self-facing" in my community, can be extremely painful. How a woman communicates and uses and shares her energy is dependent on her vigilant awareness of herself and the unconscious tendencies and unexamined habits she has learned from her culture.

If you have the desire to empower and assist others in making their lives more meaningful, you might be on the right path. You will need great courage, will, and discipline to develop yourself as a tool of spiritual service. Once you become a Priestess, you have made a commitment for life.

In discussing what it is to be a Priestess, I realize that every woman who takes on the mantle of Priestess does not share my standards and expectations. I ask a lot from women who train and step up to serve, just as I continue to ask a lot from myself. I want only the best for women, therefore I want Priestesses to be prepared to stand alone, if necessary, and to be able to work in partnership alongside their sisters in community. To serve in a community as a Priestess, a woman will ideally undergo specialized training and personal development. The process takes years and involves patience, personal sacrifice, and dedication. It takes years of hard work to gain knowledge and experience, integrate it, practice it, and then understand how to serve with it. A woman on the Priestess path learns to understand that time is her friend. It gives her the accumulation of experiences that will enrich and transform her into someone who can serve her community effectively. The years of training, thinking, experiences, challenges, and visioning contribute to the quality of her work in the world. If her training is deep, she will not be the same person who began the journey. Like the goddess Inanna, she will descend through the seven gates to the Underworld, hang dying on the hook of her fears and doubts, and rise again to the heavens. She will doubt and question *everything*. She will likely continue to question everything for the rest of her life.

Service is not servitude, as in placing yourself or others either above or below. To work effectively, there must be a relationship of mutual honor between the Priestess and the women she facilitates and serves. Service becomes self-destructive or martyrdom when it becomes a harmful burden, a yoke, and is disconnected from its previous or original motivation. It is important for a Priestess to set and keep a standard of self-care in which she models healthy living practices and healthy relationships. She must be able to receive support from her sisters. She must confront her own internalized misogyny, be self-respectful, and present the consistent expectation that her community treat her with respect and love as well. It is imperative that she develop the skills of discernment and learn to gently diffuse a challenging situation.

As women raised in a patriarchal society, we are all too skilled at participating in our own abuse. By the time a woman has reached the point where she feels resentful, she has long ago crossed the line between service and self-victimization. When this happens— and it will—she should pause and ask a trusted elder or another Priestess for feedback and help in order to regain her energy and perspective.

Models of Leadership

Many women have justifiable concerns about leadership, spiritual or otherwise. We have few models for leadership beyond the up/down, high/low, leader/follower examples of the dominator model of hierarchy in patriarchal culture. The patriarchal model for leadership is based in oppositional dualism: "leader" and "follower." Merely the use of the word "leader" implies that there are passive "followers," and due to patriarchal hierarchy, which is based on power over others, many women have knee-jerk resistance to anyone who establishes themselves or who is perceived by others as a leader. Many women want nothing to do with "leadership" and close their minds to the possibility of it being based on egalitarian practices and mutual respect and appreciation for skills or knowledge gained and shared by all members of the community.

Sometimes hostility or disrespect is directed toward a woman experienced in a particular area or specialty who takes on a leadership role. Because many women are still learning to understand self-empowerment, some of them may expend energy trying to "take down" women whom they consider to have more power, in order to supposedly "equalize the playing field." Feminist writer Mary Daly describes this reaction as "horizontal" violence, where women and other oppressed people release their frustration by oppressing one another rather than focusing attention "vertically" on the power structures of the dominant culture.[195]

As mentioned above, a woman on the Priestess path must be vigilant in examining the unconscious tendencies and unexamined habits she has learned from her culture. I believe that another one of these unexamined tendencies crucial to recognize is that American culture is in all-out war against mastery. I use the word "mastery" as it is used in the martial arts. Mastering the physical, psychological, and energetic skills required to achieve, for instance, a black belt in Aikido is a path that requires discipline, openness to learning, and the patience and persistence to

---

[195] Daly, *Outercourse*, 233.

work through plateaus. The black belt is not a goal, it is a journey. The journey is the destination. A master or *sensei* of the martial arts black belt is still a student. Mastery is a path, not a title or a credential. It is the process of recognizing and achieving potential. So it is with the Priestess path. The more I know, the more I know there is to learn, and I must endeavor to have an open beginner's mind.

Many Americans—women and feminists included—haven't looked very closely at how colonized their minds are by patriarchy's powerful child: corporate culture. The corporate domination of our culture teaches only the bottom line and demands instant results—fast temporary relief, just add water or take this pill. We live in an instant-gratification culture, where anyone can read a couple of self-help books and be an instant "expert" on any topic, including Wicca. Everything is available for purchase, preferably cheaply. We're supposed to get there fast and easy, and it's often easy to hide our resentment at the fact that there is no quick way to mastery behind the defense of a "level playing field."

Imagine if one of those same women who worried about level playing fields wanted to become a plumber and had the opportunity to apprentice with a master plumber. It would probably never occur to her to challenge her teacher if she made a recommendation about pipe sizes or diagnosis for a malfunctioning kitchen sink. She would never cry "Patriarchy!" or think to say "Who are you to tell me what I should be doing?" I believe that becoming a Priestess is similar to becoming a master plumber or carpenter, a concert pianist, or a martial artist. It is a vocation of spiritual service based in acquired skills, experience, dedication, responsibility, and continuing openness to more learning.

In her development of cultural transformation theory, Riane Eisler distinguishes between two kinds of hierarchies. One kind of hierarchy is based on threat or fear of pain. She calls this type of hierarchy a *domination hierarchy*, inherent in a dominator model of social organization. The other type of hierarchy, an *actualization hierarchy*, is described as more flexible and far less authoritarian. This second type of hierarchy is based on greater complexity of function and higher levels of function or performance.[196] In applying this theory to social systems, hierarchies of actualization equate the use of power with the power to create and to elicit from oneself and others their highest potential.[197]

It is Eisler's description of an actualization hierarchy that best describes the leadership role of the Dianic Priestess and High Priestess. As a High Priestess, I am responsible for the perpetuation of my tradition even as I am empowered to evolve it. The traditional coven structure of most Wiccan traditions does not require nor aspire to a democracy. The High Priestess is a teacher of the Mysteries who ideally supports and empowers her students/coveners to learn and grow until they know enough to form their own group. This is how the Craft was, and still is, perpetuated.

The branch of Dianic tradition revived by Z Budapest evolved out of a feminist movement determined to eradicate all patriarchal, power-over manifestations, including the notion of hierarchy. Unfortunately, the concept of an actualization hierarchy, based on acquiring greater levels of skill, experience, and responsibility, has not been widely explored, understood, or supported to a great degree. Instead, to many feminists, all forms of hierarchy are viewed as inherently oppressive, and often there is insistence that every woman's voice should be accepted as carrying the same weight as those with more experience. Consensus decision-making has been widely adopted in many Dianic and goddess spirituality circles as the only valid form of group process from which to resolve or decide anything. This is a wonderful ideal to aspire to, and one that can work especially well when a ritual group is comprised of women with similar or equivalent knowledge or skill. However, a circle comprised of peers is very different from a traditional coven model, where teachers are guiding their circle through a prescribed progression of learning and experiences.

The majority of women coming to the Goddess through the feminist

196 Eisler, *Sacred Pleasure*, 79.
197 Ibid, 404.

movement have never had the benefits of apprenticing to elders in a coven structure, so the benefits of this learning model are outside the scope of their experience. It is understandable, especially as so many women have had to teach themselves in solitary or small group practices, but the reality is that mastering the subtle energies of magic, let alone the dynamics of a group and group ritual, ultimately requires critique and feedback. Many women cannot imagine a hierarchical structure that might actually guide, support, and empower them in their learning process. In the coven blessed to have experienced teachers, all voices cannot carry the same weight because they cannot draw from the same level of experience to inform their choices or decisions. It bewilders me when women new to the Craft actually believe that their opinion about how a magical working should be carried out ought to be valued over the experience of their teacher. When less experienced women who don't know what they don't know argue with a more experienced woman or teacher, frustrations on both sides often ensue. Would you consent to brain surgery by an eager first-year medical student who has only read about how to do it? I certainly hope not, but you probably would feel safe coming to consensus about where to go out to dinner. Actualization hierarchy is about recognizing individuals who perform more complex functions, not about who is a better or more valued human being. The values of Dianic tradition acknowledge each woman's contribution of creativity and knowledge while honoring and respecting our elders, teachers, and Priestesses. Shall we not also begin to honor their dedication to mastery?

How can we develop more egalitarian models for leadership? How do leaders emerge? For some, "leadership can be a function of charisma, seniority, knowledge, experience, consensus, or default (or more likely some mixture of these elements) . . . [For others,] the role of leader is fluid and can be borne by the right person for the given situation."[198]

---

[198] Fisher, "The Priestess Path," 16.

Women's groups, in general, often have very unrealistic expectations for their leaders. When a woman who is, or is perceived to be, in a leadership role makes a mistake or behaves outside of her community's expectations, the fallout is often severe. When our female leaders behave like humans, we are disappointed. We are too often quick to think the worst of our own leaders, assuming that the leadership in our groups and communities must be patriarchal. While it is vital to hold our leaders accountable for their actions or hurtful, unethical behavior (just as we must be responsible for our own behavior and actions toward others), we are quick to judge harshly, based on assumptions, and too often without evidence that some oppressive act has actually been committed.

Riane Eisler writes that

> definitions of leadership in the context of the society that we are trying to leave behind, and definitions of leadership for the society we are trying to create, are very different. But we still have to function within society as it is, so we have to have standards that are realistic for our leaders and for ourselves.[199]

Eisler continues,

> Social movements reflect and even sometimes magnify the problems that they are trying to change, and this results in what psychologists call "displaced aggression." You don't dare attack the person who will really hurt you, so what do you do? You attack your own sisters, your own leaders, instead.[200]

It is important to understand that we are living in a crucial transition

---

[199] From an article by Riane Eisler in *Woman of Power* magazine, issue 24, page 26.
[200] Ibid.

time in the world at large where the patriarchal model for power, what Eisler calls the "dominator model," is being contrasted with a growing global movement toward a "partnership model." Women and men in many parts of the world are developing new models and theories for power that are based on equitable, relational ways of living.

Developing a greater understanding of how the dominator model manifests itself, both personally and globally, is a vital first step in developing new ways of being. These egalitarian ways of being must be practiced and lived on a daily basis by every person consciously involved in the process of this transformation of modern culture. Since spiritual, political, economic, and social awareness is interconnected, this living experiment offers a great opportunity for participation. Through this experiment, and by sharing our processes and ideas, we will teach each other and ourselves what we need to learn about new models of power.

Answering the Call

So why would anyone become a Priestess? If it is what you are here on Earth to do, any negative experiences or fears cannot deter you from your passion to create and serve in this way. With the right attitude, challenges will only make you stronger, providing you with invaluable life experience, personal growth, and the knowledge that you are contributing in a uniquely powerful way to the lives of others. As you work compassionately alongside your sisters to heal from your own internalized oppression, you will be adding strength to the evolution of human consciousness that the Goddess represents. You will be a part of the morphogenetic field that is growing to restore the Goddess and Her teachings to Her daughters.

Priestess Specialties

In the Dianic tradition, we do not have degrees such as first, second, or third degree, as some other Wiccan traditions do. Instead, we have recognized developmental stages of learning and skill that can evolve into expertise or answering one's calling to become a Priestess. These stages are called *initiate* (a woman who has studied the minimum of a year and a day and chooses to self-initiate or be formally initiated as a witch), *Priestess* (a woman who has developed her ministry), and *High Priestess* (a Priestess with many specialties who can perpetuate her tradition and create and maintain community). Most often, the High Priestess is also a ritualist who can facilitate the rites of our tradition and holds the center energetic in the rituals (explained later in this chapter).

In the Dianic tradition, a Priestess develops, and then names, her own path of service in her own words. For example, I have ordained, among others, women who named their Priestess path of service as "Priestess of the Wild Moon," "Priestess of the Veil" (a death midwife), "Priestess of Her Voice," "Priestess of the Signs and Symbols of Astrology," "Priestess of Her Mysteries," "Priestess of Visual Arts," "Priestess of Mothering," "Priestess of the Singing Spirit," "Priestess of the Guardian Path," "Ritual Priestess," "Priestess of Her Wisdom," and "Temple Priestess." Some of these ministries are highly individualized and personal, such as "Priestess of Her Voice." In the herstory of the Dianic tradition, very personalized ministries such as these were not expected to be taught to others, even though these women were expected to provide spiritual service through their specialty's naming. It is my hope that, as our tradition evolves, all Priestess specialties be encouraged and able to be taught and mentored so that options for service may be visible to others called to the same work.

Thus far, ministries such as Ritual Priestess, Guardian Priestess, Drum Priestess, Temple Priestess, and Priestess of the Veil have developed specific skill sets that are bodies of work associated with that ministry which can be taught to others drawn to the same calling. For the purpose of this book, however, I want to discuss the Priestess specialty with which I have the most experience.

The Ritual Priestess

In addition to being an ordained High Priestess who teaches classes in the practice of the Dianic tradition, I am also a ritual Priestess by calling and vocation. Learning to become a ritual Priestess is not for the faint of heart. If you fear chaos, the unexpected, or the unforeseen, choose another vocation. A ritual Priestess regularly finds herself in challenging situations that are not at all what she originally planned.

There are many books on goddess spirituality and the Craft who use the word "priestess" to refer to any woman who facilitates in ritual. They make no distinction between the verb and noun forms of the word. For me, the verb, "priestess" as in "to priestess a ritual," describes the actions of a woman who takes responsibility for various parts of a ritual in a ritual circle setting, while the nown "Priestess" describes the vocational Priestess.

The ritual Priestess is a facilitator whose spiritual service is to act as a creator and guide for the ritual experience. She must have knowledge and skills in all aspects of ritual making, including ritual design, the ability to create invocations, knowledge of how to utilize sacred tools and symbols, and expertise in energetics. She must have the ability to monitor, sense, shape, and direct the energy created by the group toward a focused purpose. She must also be equipped with skills in counseling, communication, and organizing.

A ritual Priestess must have a working knowledge of what is needed for each seasonal Sabbat and lunar phase, with respect to both the physical needs of the ritual (someone has got to remember the matches) and an intuitive sense of the energetic needs. She must be capable of creating and facilitating rituals that link the cycles of the Goddess with Earth's seasonal cycles and the cycles of women's lives.

A ritual Priestess is responsible for, and must be capable of, providing a welcoming and emotionally safe space for women. Her behavior and attitude deeply affect the experience of everyone present. If women become emotionally open during the ritual, as they may be, they are, in a very real sense, temporarily entrusting their psyches to her care. Ritual Priestessing is not just about what you know, what you have read, or what skills you can demonstrate in a ritual circle, but just as importantly how you are *with* the women whom you serve or facilitate. A ritual Priestess must understand that her service does not end when the ritual is over. Service includes the preparation before the ritual begins, the ritual itself, and the period of days, weeks, or months afterward when women are experiencing the transformational effects of the magic they have created. The ritual Priestess may continue to provide guidance, support, and containment for their experience throughout this process. She must be willing to see through to the end what she helped initiate. This is her sacred responsibility.

I believe that the most important skill the ritual Priestess must learn is how to bring herself, fully centered, into the present time. This is critical because she must simultaneously embody the energy of the ritual space, be at one with the flow of the ritual, and direct it as it unfolds. She must develop impeccable, clear personal boundaries, so that she can sense and experience the differences between her own energy and the energy of an individual or group she is facilitating. This is fundamental in order to serve effectively, both inside and outside the ritual space. Within a cast circle, she holds the center point, allowing the Goddess to work through her, listening to Her voice *while* directing the intended work and flow of the rite. This means expanding her energetic field to hold and fill the larger container that comprises the ritual space. She must expect to improvise as the energy shifts among the participants and become flexible with the ritual structure while maintaining its essential intention.

When I am really working the energy in a ritual, I am completely centered and open. I must get out of my own way in order to be receptive and flexible. I must have the skill to rapidly move from one state of consciousness to another as necessary to track where the ritual is going and what is supposed to happen next, remember that I have a candle to light, and all the other lists of things that I have decided to include in the ritual. Meanwhile, I am feeling into the energy, sensing what is happening with the participants and anticipating what needs to happen next. On top of all this, I am supporting and maintaining the integrity of the cast circle. This fluid awareness can be developed by learning to identify the pathways of your own mind and by the disciplined practice of moving rapidly through expanding and contracting states of consciousness.

The Ritual Priestess directs, not controls, the ritual flow. Like a maestro conducting an orchestra, she has the baton and directs the orchestra's pace and dynamics while being at one with the music. If she doesn't feel the music, the musicians will not respond as well as they might if they felt her connection to their playing. There is a dynamic between the conductor and each member of the orchestra, and when that energetic is happening, you have an inspired musical experience. So it is with the ritual Priestess and the ritual participants.

Advance ritual preparation is essential in order to embody the ritual's intention, become fully present, and serve the participants. This advance preparation differs with individual ritual Priestesses. For some, preparation starts a week ahead; others take even more time to prepare. Preparation may include consciously slowing down, quiet contemplation, making something to adorn oneself with, "feeling into" the ritual theme, taking a pre-ritual bath, doing a self-blessing, or singing and chanting. Others may sit at their altars and ask themselves questions: What am I feeling? What energies do I need to help me serve in this rite? Discovering how to best prepare to serve is a wonderful opportunity for self-intimacy and personal empowerment.

When I serve in my capacity as High Priestess in ritual, my primary function is to hold the center energetic (more on this below) of the ritual. Unless another woman is designated to do so, it is my responsibility to bring the presence of the Goddess as the Great Mother into the container of the cast circle. Although I may serve as the primary ritual facilitator, my responsibility is not to be the focus of the ritual or a presence at the center of the ritual, as if starring in a play or show. My facilitating role is to appear and disappear as the ritual needs me to become visible or invisible. My primary responsibility is to embody the energetic flow of the ritual, to energetically contain the larger container of the ritual, to monitor the energy, and to guide the flow forward in accordance with the ritual's intention. My visible presence is only important as a part of helping the group's energy to be cohesive and to support the women in doing their work.

Holding the center energetic is an advanced and invaluable skill for women who facilitate rituals and who are interested in ritual Priestessing. "Holding center" means that the ritual facilitator physically and energetically embodies the ritual theme to the extent that the ritual's thematic energy emanates from her entire being, evoking that energetic intention from the other women participating, and together they fill the ritual space with it. If the facilitator is doing her job, others can actually feel this process happening, even though they may not consciously be aware of its source.

A ritual Priestess must learn to embody the intention of the ritual, not only the structure. The ritual's structure must be able to adapt to the situation or group of women, while the intention remains the same. The ritual structure exists only to support the intention. If the form does not allow for the possibility of spontaneous creativity and improvisation, the ritual will strangle from an inability to breathe. It will be boring, stagnant, or uninspired. I listen to the voice of the Goddess singing through the ritual. I keep my eyes open for Her arrival, and welcome Her when She comes. Once, at a Spring Equinox ritual, a little girl was holding onto her mother's hand and dancing in place, clearly wanting to move freely. As a chant to the Maiden Goddess rose and the energy soared, I drew her forward into the center of the circle to dance the Maiden Goddess with my support.

Given breathing room, a ritual lives to address what is meaningful in that moment for that group and for that occasion. Words and gestures emerge as they are inspired from the heart and the Goddess, not from a script. Be flexible. Dare to spread your wings and risk falling. If the only route you know to a given destination is on the highway, and there is an accident slowing traffic to a snail's pace, you will be late or miss your purpose for the drive. If you are flexible and know alternate routes, you can get off the freeway, take other streets, and get to your appointment more or less on time, accomplishing the task at hand. The willingness and ability to improvise in the moment with humor and grace are necessary skills for any serious ritualist.

Shekhinah Mountainwater used the word "seasoned" to describe a Priestess who has had years of experience in service. I also describe some Priestesses as seasoned who demonstrate expertise in their specialty as adepts. Because a seasoned Priestess aligns herself to the theme of the ritual, she simply speaks or acts out of her connection to the Goddess in service to the ritual's purpose. After years of experience in learning, practicing, preparing, and honing her skills, when she enters ritual space, she simply opens herself to the Goddess and trusts her training. As one of my students put it, "Read the energy and do what's appropriate." As simple as this sounds, it is the result of experience gained over time, the ability to put creativity and intuition into service, the willingness to make mistakes, and the ability to self-critique each ritual.

A ritual Priestess's repertory contains all the skills and experiences she has internalized over the years, enabling her to jump into the unknown and think on her feet. Every ritual has its challenges; some are greater than others. For example, what would you do if a dear relative of the bride died suddenly just a day prior to the wedding ceremony? As the facilitating clergy, how would you acknowledge that experience in the ceremony? If you don't, it will be there anyway, looming like an elephant in the living room. After preparing a wonderfully deep ritual, you might discover that you are working with a group of women who don't relate to anything you are saying and are looking at you like you have four heads. How might you be flexible in these various situations?

You have to be prepared to adjust to the environment, as well as the level of understanding and experience of the women participating. Sometimes you have to change, adapt, or throw out the whole thing and create something else that will meet the needs of that group of women. What happens when you have been asked to facilitate an outdoor group ritual for two hundred women and the microphone you are given is dead? What do you do when you arrive to facilitate an outdoor ritual at a festival, having planned to lead a free-form group dance, and realize that the ritual site is pockmarked with gopher holes? Bear in mind that women come to rituals because they are interested and have a need for a meaningful spiritual experience. Ritual Priestessing requires physical stamina, mental and emotional flexibility, and a huge sense of humor. When I was introduced to "guardian" facilitators a new world of possibilities opened to me, making my energetic multi-tasking so much easier!

Partnering with another woman (or more) who choose to provide service to the ritual in a guardian facilitator capacity became another named Priestess path at the turn of the 21st century.

The Guardian Priestess[201]

I want to introduce this discussion of the Guardian Priestess by explaining why I am devoting a large section to this priestess specialty. There are many other Priestess specialties related to ritual making, such as the Temple Priestess, whose work includes the artful and inspired creation of sacred space, altars, and related crafts. Another ritual-related Priestess specialty is ritual drumming, where a woman combines her understanding of energetics with her proficient skills as a drummer to assist a ritual in innumerable ways. Given that this book is about ritual design, energetics, facilitation, and the exploration of spiritual service,

[201] The first edition of this book included a chapter on "The Guardian Priestess". I removed it from the second edition before submitting the manuscript for publication. It was time to update this material for its return in this third edition.

the inclusion of the guardian role in Dianic ritual is significant. The skills necessary for guardian work have always existed in Dianic Craft, but they did not coalesce into an articulated body of work until the late 1990s. Ever since my first experiences of working with women doing this specialized body of work, I recognized it as a distinct calling, connected to, but different from the work of a ritual priestess. It is my hope that by giving some of the her-story of this path, and how we are continuing to evolve and teach the necessary skills, more women will find a supported place for themselves to offer this type of service in Dianic circles. It is also my hope that ritual priestesses will understand how this path of service can support and complement their work.

While sitting at my kitchen table in the Spring of 1998, visiting with one of the founders of the Re-formed Congregation of the Goddess, a Goddess spirituality organization based in Wisconsin, our conversation turned to a group of women in her local community who were creating a new path of service they called, "guardian." At spiritual gatherings these women volunteered to direct traffic at the ritual site, welcomed participants and helped them carry their belongings into the ritual space. They took note of any possible difficulties, not only potential troubles from outside the ritual space (such as intruders), but also any problems that might arise from within the ritual space once the circle was cast. They attended to the energy of the women arriving, looking out for those with special needs including alerting the facilitators to any personal or situational issues before the ritual got underway. Once the ritual began, these women provided energetic support to the cast circle and the other facilitators throughout the rite. My ears perked up. Although I had always worked with women who provided various forms of energetic support, because after all, this is what we *do* together, I had never considered the possibility of energetic support being a specialty of spiritual service like other paths of service a woman might consider on the Dianic priestess path.

Working as a ritual priestess for over two decades at that time, I thought I had a fairly clear understanding of my responsibilities. During ritual

I did everything. Modeling "She Who Is Whole Unto Herself" to excess, for twenty years, I embodied "She Who Must Do Everything Herself At All Costs." From creating, shaping, monitoring and maintaining the cast circle to facilitating the ritual's content, I boosted and directed the group's energy to a focused purpose. I kept a far eye on the entrance to the parking lot so that we would not have any unexpected, hostile guests while I embodied the Goddess for the ritual's duration. I constantly adjusted my actions and consciousness to work with the shifting energies and changes in circumstance both inside and outside of the cast circle. This energetic juggling act was exhausting, even for a seasoned ritual priestess. Nonetheless, these were the energetic skills I had always taught and insisted that every woman interested in ritual priestessing must understand and eventually master. It had never occurred to me that the cast circle, and the woman, or women, facilitating the ritual from within it, could effectively be supported, physically and energetically, by other women whose specific calling was to provide physical and energetic support.

Recognizing that I, myself, had been serving in a guardian Priestess *and* a ritual Priestess capacity for years, I was immediately struck with the importance of what these women in Wisconsin were doing. I was thrilled to join in their efforts toward naming and defining a new path of service within the Dianic tradition, a path of service that had clearly been there all along, hidden in the Mysteries. I began to work with a few women in my local Los Angeles community who resonated with this new path of service as guardian ritual facilitators. Although these women had little formal or unified training for providing this new articulation of energetic support, they lovingly applied their intuitive knowledge and abilities to supporting our community ritual gatherings.

In May of 1999, I attended a women's spirituality conference in the Midwest where I had my first taste of working with more experienced guardian ritual facilitators and specifically, with a woman named Falcon, whom I was to discover had extensive magical skills, and who I would come to know as an adept guardian facilitator. As a visiting Priestess from California, I was asked to cast the circle on Saturday night for the main ritual of the gathering, at which the founder of the feminist Dianic tradition, Z Budapest, was to be given special honors. Falcon, and the other guardian facilitators assisted me in preparing and purifying the ritual space. When this was complete they then took up positions in each cardinal direction, where they remained for the duration of what was to be a very long evening. After women entered our carefully prepared ritual space, I began to cast the circle and immediately felt a stream of energy coming toward me from all four directions. I am accustomed to facilitating rituals for large groups, usually 150 to 200 women, and there is always a lot of energy to draw from. However, this time, a stream of energy actually seemed to be intentionally directed toward me. As I was focused, in that moment, on casting the circle, I gave no thought to the source of this extra energy. I later discovered that the source of this energy came from the very same women that had been spoken about at my kitchen table.

When the main enactments of the ritual had been completed, I was asked to witness and support Z Budapest as she was being honored. After Z received the honors of the community, she turned to me and whispered that she had never been formally ordained. So right then and there, I spontaneously returned to her what she had given to me more than 20 years earlier (at that time): a full-fledged, Dianic ordination in front of 150 adoring daughters of the Goddess!

As Z and I turned to greet the Goddess in the final act of the ordination rite, I immediately understood the benefits of working with skilled guardian facilitators. As I was lifting Z's face to the Goddess, I felt as if I was physically being lifted up. I had never before received such a tangible experience of energetic support, and this time it was quite clear that the support was coming from and through the women standing at the four directions, Falcon in particular. A well of energy was mine to draw upon far beyond my own regular reservoir. After the rite, I flew through my hour-long performance of Goddess music and hit my dorm-room bed, collapsing into a deep and restful sleep. The feelings of exhilaration continued into the next morning with none of the usual morning-after ritual exhaustion, I had come to expect after years of leading large, public rituals.

The woman I described as an adept guardian, Falcon, became my life companion, and was the first woman to receive Dianic ordination as a Priestess of the Guardian Path. Our initial meeting at this conference came when she attended a workshop that I was teaching on energetics, and I attended her workshop teaching inter-species communication. As our personal relationship grew, we soon began to combine our magical and ritual skills with our teaching experience to midwife this new and ancient path of spiritual service within the Dianic tradition. The foundation of the guardian path is in the practice of energetic support, whether in partnership with other women or other sentient beings, such as trees, animals, plants, the spirits of the land, and the elemental powers of nature.

Energetic partnership, as it is more commonly understood in other Craft traditions, generally occurs between a Priestess and her consort or Priest. As previously stated in this book, those Wiccan traditions celebrate a cosmology based on a male/female duality. We however, are Dianic, and our cosmology is not based on dualism, but on a Goddess-centered paradigm of wholeness. Therefore, in recognizing and including guardians as facilitators and priestesses, we do not seek to mimic a partnership model based on a heterosexist division of labor. We have instead, named and expanded on the kind of energetic support that Dianics have always had in our communities and ritual circles. Women working in partnership and giving energetic support to other women is intrinsic to the basic concept of feminism. As the saying goes, empowered women empower women. It is called sisterhood.

In a ritual context, all support roles are facilitator roles, and women who serve in ritual in *any* capacity, are ritual facilitators. This includes the woman who greets you at the door, to the women invoking the elemental powers, to the women assisting participants in the parking lot. However, through the process of bringing the guardian path forward, we have been able to identify and articulate specific skill sets involved with this area of ritual service. Not all women have the capacity or inclination to serve in this way, but for those who do, the work is deeply rewarding.

For us, the re-emergence of the guardian path is part of the continuing return and rebirth of ancient Amazon consciousness, first re-kindled by the early feminist movement. In her book, *The Double Goddess: Women Sharing Power,*[202] author Vicki Noble notes that, until very recently, Western history has dealt with Amazons strictly as fiction and myth. She relates that hundreds of recent archeological finds in southern and eastern Russia are verifying the fifth century B.C.E. accounts of the Greek historian, Herodotus.[203] Herodotus (as well as other ancient historical sources) described Amazon tribes as having two queens: a "warrior" queen and a "priestess" queen. According to Herodotus, the "priestess queen" governed over internal domestic affairs; the "warrior queen" governed the external affairs of the tribe by maintaining the boundaries of the tribal territory and defending the land and the people.[204] Archeological excavations of Amazon burials at the border between Russia and Kazakhstan conducted since the 1950s have found the remains of warrior women and priestesses buried with their horses in full armor with shields, swords and daggers at their side. Other excavations at the same site have found women buried with divination mirrors, portable altars, incense burners, and jewelry.[205] In her research, Vicki Noble writes that this form of female rule can be documented from ancient times into the early period of the Common

---

202 *The Double Goddess: Women Sharing Power*, Vicki Noble, Bear & Company, 2003.

203 *The History*, Herodotus. Translated by David Greene, University of Chicago Press, 1987. Cited in "Double Queen of the Amazons", Vicki Noble, *The Beltane Papers*, Issue Eighteen, 1999, p. 6.

204 *The Double Goddess: Women Sharing Power*, Vicki Noble, Bear & Company, 2003, p. 183.

205 "Double Queen of the Amazons," p. 6.

Era; from Africa and the Mediterranean all the way to western China and Tibet.[206]

Images of the double queen appear as two seated female figures on thrones, often sharing a torso, sometimes also joined at the head, and date from the Neolithic and Bronze Ages in every Near Eastern civilization.[207] These intriguing images have been interpreted by scholars and archeologists as representing two women, two Goddesses, twin sisters of various alternating forms (one light, one dark), mother and daughter, two female rulers, priestess queens, queen-mother and queen-sister, and symbols of matrilineal descent.[208] Vicki Noble suggests that, "The double Goddess represents a characteristic female approach to government — the equal sharing of power between two women in a classic division of labor that can be seen through all the ages until patriarchy was firmly established..." She goes on to theorize that, "the Double Goddess embodies the planets, the moon, and the earth in one composite figure. The female centrality of Earth and Moon remained in later classical periods as the widespread Mystery Religions of Isis, Demeter-Persephone, and Artemis of Ephesus."[209]

The emerging information and speculation about this dual form of ancient female rule has inspired me, Falcon, other Dianics, and Goddess women, to examine a possible ritual corollary in the collaborative relationship between the ritual facilitators working at the center of the circle, and those ritual facilitators serving in a guardian capacity to provide support from the circle's edge. At the center of the circle, the facilitators attend to the internal content and structure of the ritual, while the facilitators working in a guardian capacity attend to the physical and energetic maintenance and safety of the ritual space from the edge or beyond.

---

[206] Ibid.

[207] Ibid.

[208] *The Double Goddess: Women Sharing Power*, pp. 6, 21, 37, 68, 73, 79.

[209] "Double Queen of the Amazons," p. 7.

We propose that the physical structure of a large group ritual, the container of the cast circle itself, can also be interpreted as a metaphor for the double queen. In this model, the cast circle is comprised of three concentric spheres. We see the ritual facilitators and the participants inside the circle as symbolic of the Earth, embodying the Goddess and birthing Her into the container of the cast circle. The facilitators serving in a guardian capacity encircle them as the moon circles around the earth. Those facilitators who choose to work further beyond the edge of the cast circle, perhaps patrolling the perimeter of the ritual site, represent the planets beyond the moon, moving constantly about the earth. In yet another analogy, the facilitators serving in a guardian capacity embody the Goddess in Her moon aspect, as Diana or Artemis, Amazon, fierce protector and nurturer of women, children, and all Her creatures; while the facilitators and the participants in the center embody Gaia, the Earth. It is our belief that this concept of double queen rule, Gaia, the Earth, and Artemis, Her protector and nurturer, has lain hidden within the Mysteries and cosmology of the Dianic tradition: one of those truths hidden in plain sight for decades.

Large group rituals with 40 or more participants can allow for these specialized jobs to be utilized on an expanded scale, depending on the number of facilitators available with the appropriate skills. Ritual groups or covens of five to thirteen women can explore this concept on a much smaller scale, with one or more women giving energetic support from the edge. It is important to remember that ritual jobs are not about fixed roles or "type-casting", but should be based on a woman's ability to do what the job calls for. Empower your circle sisters by encouraging everyone in the group to gain ritual skills by working in many capacities. Ways for women to work together in partnership for ritual are being remembered and reclaimed. We support the exploration of this partnership model that suggests amazing, empowering possibilities for present-day women's ritual.

Energetic Support

What is energetic support? The answer to this question would require another book! Many times over the years, women have offered me "energetic support" for healing or for a magical working. Their offer could mean many different things: thinking positive thoughts about or for me; visualizing me healthy; lighting a candle for my prosperity; even hands-on help with physical projects. Without a mutually agreed upon definition of what kind of energetic support I needed in a given situation, their offerings frequently were not what I wanted or needed at all.

During a ritual, unless I know exactly what women mean when they offer energetic support, and whether I can be certain that they have the skills to deliver it, I can't relinquish any of my responsibilities. As the High Priestess, I must be absolutely certain that the facilitator offering her service has the ability to do what she says she is offering. The wellbeing of the participants and the other facilitators depend on a facilitator's practiced skills, consistently demonstrated and verifiable. This ensures everyone's safety, enabling everyone to fully open and give themselves to the ritual's purpose.

So, what do I mean by energetic support? A woman who is skilled in the art of providing energetic support is able to draw energy from the four directions, from above and below and all around her. She is able to gather, hold, shape, and focus that energy, and then direct it like a laser beam to support a particular person or magical intention. For example, in our rituals, women serving in a guardian capacity may work in partnership with women who are facilitating the core enactments of the ritual and who do the invocations and valedictions of the elemental power. Because guardian facilitators are trained to provide energetic support to these women, each of our invoking facilitators now has a well of energy to draw upon that far exceeds her own reserve. As a result, her invocations are more powerful and are more strongly felt by all the participants.

I have been surprised to experience resistance from some ritual facilitators to receiving energetic support. Accustomed, as I was, to having to do it all themselves, they assume an offer of energetic support is a criticism of their abilities rather than an opportunity to experience support from others in a ritual context. Yet these women agree that women supporting other women, i.e. sisterhood, is the foundation of feminism. As I stated earlier, in rejecting the patriarchal power model of dominance and subordination, we seem to have confused becoming "whole unto ourselves" with becoming "She Who Must Stand Alone At All Costs." Could it be that, as feminists, we have swung from one end of the pendulum to the other? In bringing forward the concept of an energetic partnership of women sharing power in the ritual, we offer a different possibility for cultural transformation through the reconstruction of a partnership model that we believe, and hope, was the reality in many cultures and religions prior to the rise of patriarchy.

In examining the concept of energetic support, you might ask, "Who supports the guardian?" In the best of circumstances, it is her staff and another guardian facilitator. Guardian facilitators energetically connect to create a web that allows for energy flow between them. This connection allows for a constant conversation in the language of energy. Guardian facilitators are able to direct and boost energy where needed or support a guardian dealing with a shift in energy during ritual. As an example, if a participant broke the cast circle in the south, all the guardians would boost the energy to the south so the nearest guardian could repair the circle. Additionally, if a guardian facilitator needs to step away to attend to something happening outside of the ritual circle, the other guardians fill that energetic gap until she returns.

However, if serving as the only guardian, think of a soda straw with liquid passing through it. There's always some sweet stuff left over in the soda straw once the milkshake in the cup is empty. In doing her work, the guardian is like that soda straw. With all that energy passing through her during the ritual, she, too, is fed and supported.

To do her work safely and effectively, a guardian facilitator will have spent many hours consciously honing her abilities and skills. She can become fully present and centered at will. She must be able to shift her focus quickly and effectively so that she can respond to a need that arises at a moment's notice. She strives to keep an open heart and a clear mind. In ritual, she must be able to fully commit to the intention that is being embodied by the facilitator she is working in partnership with. She must also be able to support the intention of the ritual, the other facilitators and Priestesses, and the participants in tangible, demonstrable ways. This is no small task, and it requires ongoing practice. To do this work, a woman must have a commitment to spiritual service and the courage and clarity to face her own ego. Energetic support is not supportive if it comes with a personal agenda.

I asked Nicki, who is an ordained Priestess of the Guardian Path and has served in large community rituals for several years, about her experience of giving energetic support. She said,

> The experiences are innumerable, but the best experiences have been when I've worked with a woman who is comfortable accepting energetic support. The more specific the better, i.e., having that woman tell me exactly what they want. Do they want me to energetically connect so that they can feel me? Do they only want me to connect while they are invoking or, would they like an energetic connection throughout the entire ritual? And so, the first thing I have to do in my own process is to center myself and to completely feel my own energy level, so I can then sense that person's energy level and needs. Then I have to be as open and as wide as I can possibly be so that the interaction back and forth can happen. My most fabulous experiences

> have been when the woman I'm supporting and I have energetically connected together, and I've turned myself as wide open as can be. I was working in the South in this experience, and she had her own experience with the element of Fire, which she afterward said was in a way she had never before experienced. Personally, I was not attached to her experience; that was her experience with that Element, but I was the doorway to an awesome experience that makes me proud to serve the Goddess.

Guardians In The Craft

The word "guardian" is a familiar term used by practitioners of English traditional Craft, Stregheria (Italian Witchcraft), and the Western Mystery Tradition. Sometimes it is used to describe a mortal with shamanic skills. More often, however, it is used to speak of the stellar beings who guard the portals between this world and the astral realms.[210] In some Craft traditions, these guardians are also called the Watchers of the four directions. From their positions in the night sky, they turn the Wheel of the Year. In ancient times, as the seasons turned, the star Aldebaran, Watcher of the East, marked the Vernal Equinox. Regulus, Watcher of the South, marked the Summer Solstice. Antares, Watcher of the West, marked the Autumn Equinox; and Formalhaut, Watcher of the North, marked the Winter Solstice.[211]

Earlier in this book, you practiced building an elemental inventory; a cellular memory of elemental experiences to draw upon and embody when stepping forward to invoke the elemental powers in their associated directions. As part of her growth, every witch must also develop an intimate relationship with the elements and the Watcher who is associated

---

[210] Raven Grimassi , *Italian Witchcraft*, Llewellyn Publications, 2000, p. 68.
[211] Ibid.

with each elemental direction. It is the Guardian or Watcher of that elemental portal who hears our invocation and decides whether or not to open the portal into the astral realm. In his book, *Italian Witchcraft,* Raven Grimassi writes, "This is why certain gestures and signs of evocation, such as the pentagram, were designed, so as to 'announce' the presence of a trained practitioner to the presence of the Watchers (that is, one who had sworn not to misuse the arts). Once such signs and symbols are acknowledged by the Watchers, the portals to other realities open more readily."[212] Being Guardians of the Portals, they decide whether a magical working actually takes form or is dispelled.

In most books and traditions, the Watchers are assigned a gender, which is usually male. Not only that, but the Watchers are also often correlated with the Archangels, a form of spirit not recognized by old Craft practitioners but taken from Judeo-Christian tradition. No surprises there. So, in true Dianic style, I'd like to propose another perspective consistent with Dianic cosmology. To me, the Watchers represent the four quarters of our Mother Earth, the four quarters of our Mother galaxy, the four quarters of our Mother universe, and the four quarters of our sacred circles. The Watchers are the eyes of the Goddess. They have witnessed every circle gathered in Her name since time immemorial. When we step forward and ask the Watchers to lend us their support and come witness our rites, we are making a statement that everything we do in our rite is, and will be, in accordance with Her will. We are inviting the Watchers to witness what we do and to hold us accountable for our actions. The Goddess is everything, and everything is a variation of Her, including the Watchers.

The women who are called to the guardian path in the Dianic tradition have usually formed a deep relationship with the Watchers before their introduction to the Craft. Often their relationship to the Watchers begins in childhood. Many times I have heard women talking about

[212] Ibid, p. 72.

how as children they loved to call the wind or to make rain. They heard messages coming from stones and saw living creatures in campfires.

Falcon told me that the Watchers had introduced themselves to her when she was about three years old, telling her that they were called "The Watchers Who Wait". They taught her many skills of a magical nature, and their constant presence gave her great comfort throughout a rather difficult childhood. Decades later, she was shocked to pick up a book about Witchcraft and find a whole chapter devoted to the beings she had considered to be her own personal guides and guardians: The Watchers.

The women we train to serve in a guardian capacity for large ritual circles become the human counterpart on our side of the veil to the Watchers. We call these specialized guardians "gatekeepers"[213] because they stand in the four portals of our cast circle at the cardinal directions. When a ritual facilitator addresses an invocation to the spirit of air, fire, water, or earth and opens the portal on this side of the veil by scribing a pentacle, the guardian standing in the portal expands her energetic field, filling the portal and becoming a filter, a semi-permeable membrane. It is her job to make sure that only the invited energies, from any realm, and nothing else, may enter the cast circle. The partnership between the ritual facilitator and the woman serving as her gatekeeper must be a relationship based in mutual trust. Since they are working in partnership, the invoking ritual facilitator should inform the guardian facilitator in advance of who or what she will be inviting into the circle. Ideally, they will also have practiced together outside of ritual so that the invoking facilitator has confidence that her gatekeeper will provide the appropriate filter for the energy she invites. With training and practice, women serving in a guardian capacity can develop the ability to become "a bridge of living spirit, between the everyday world and the unseen realms."[214]

---

213 A term created by Falcon to describe those ritual guardians serving in the portals of the cast circle.

214 *Singing the Soul Back Home*, Caitlin Matthews, Element Books Ltd., 1995, pp. 1-2.

I asked Sara who has served as a guardian facilitator at Circle of Aradia, the Daughters of Diana Gathering in the Los Angeles area, to describe her experience when working in partnership with a ritual facilitator during invocation:

> Having conferred with the invoker before the ritual, I know what specific aspects of the element and Goddess she is calling into the circle. She may also have asked for specific personal support, such as help finding her words easily while she does her invocation. Drawing energy from my elemental allies, I embody the aspects of the element that are being invoked and create a well of support for the invoking woman to draw from. As she scribes the pentacle, I become a filter and gatekeeper, only allowing what has been invoked to enter the cast circle. My connection to the invoker remains, hopefully unobtrusive, throughout the ritual until the valedictions are complete and the circle is opened. (And this is all done while keeping a watchful eye on the parking lot outside, keeping the energetic spin of the cast circle going, and making sure the altar candles aren't burning dangerously close to anything!)

Nicki added:

> Sometimes at larger rituals the ritual facilitator and I have met and are very clear about the energetic being invited in her invocation, however, the participants in eagerness and excitement are calling in something different. One time I was in the South portal and the invoker was inviting very specific aspects of fire closer

> to candlelight or a warm hearth but participants were loudly hissing like a sizzling, crackling campfire. I felt a huge surge of heat at my back as the fire element showed up. I expanded my energetic field and did not allow anything through but what the invoker called for.

If a woman is used to serving in a guardian capacity, it can be a challenge to rejoin the circle as a participant again without automatically providing energetic support for the ritual's activities. Kathy, who has some training as a ritual guardian, recalled her experience of being a participant in a ritual, and finding herself offering energetic support to the women serving as guardian facilitators. She shared that when the circle participants were building energy through dance, "I found myself spiraling around the inner circle, and with their permission, offering energetic support to the guardians in the portals. The energy began to swirl in patterns that reminded me of a Van Gogh painting. The flow of energy was quite beautiful."

The Guardian Priestess Path

In her book, *Daughter of the Goddess: The Sacred Priestess*, Naomi Ozaniec writes,

> The term, 'priestess' has now appeared in contemporary feminist vocabulary, indeed the priestess has reappeared in person. It is simply assumed that current usage is identical with past meaning. The shamanic priestess, medium, and mediator are not identical in psychic function. The initiator into women's blood mysteries and the initiator into the transcendent mysteries are not identical either in function or intention. Yet both ministrants might be called priestesses.[215]

[215] *Daughter of the Goddess: The Sacred Priestess*, Naomi Ozaniec, The Aquarian Press, 1993, p. 12.

Although the training of a ritual facilitator and a guardian facilitator begin similarly and overlap in basic magical, energetic, and ritual-making skills, there is a point where the paths separate into specialized skills and bodies of knowledge in order to gain further expertise.

We can define the guardian Priestess as a woman who chooses to pursue a path of spiritual service primarily rooted in the knowledge, practice, and maintenance of energy. The requirements for a woman pursuing the guardian Priestess path, do not include physical size or prowess. It is a study of energy that is different from, and complementary to, the energy that the ritual Priestess works. The following sections are intended to give voice toward a definition of, and roles for women who wish to serve in community, in ritual, and as a vocational Priestess path.

Guardian Training

"Many hands make light work."

A woman with innate, intuitive abilities and talents will best develop into a guardian facilitator or Priestess with some form of specific magical training, especially in the arts of energetics. Human beings breathe intuitively: if we don't breathe, we die. However, just because we know how to breathe does not mean that we know how to use our breath to heal our bodies, to assist ourselves or another woman in giving birth, to project our voices to speak effectively or sing without damaging our vocal chords, or to extend our endurance during physical activity. It does not mean we know how to use our breath to relax, to take ourselves into a deep trance state, or to explore sexual or spiritual ecstasy. Learning how to use our breath for each of these various purposes takes training, guidance, and years of dedicated practice. The same can be said of women seeking to practice and serve on the guardian Priestess path.

The skill set needed for guardian work is extensive and demands the same disciplined practice as any other Priestess path. Activities and creative arts such as archery, martial art; the design, creation, and use of magical tools, and the creation of ritual garb all serve the same purpose: to hone the skills needed to integrate the body, mind, and spirit of the guardian facilitator. Community service, education in conflict transformation and communication skills and the balanced use of power, development of the personal will, and the ability to be "self-facing" are also essential. To be "self-facing" is the ability to critically examine your own motivations and issues and how they might be influencing your actions or attitudes for good or ill. It is important that women draw from their strengths and listen to their hearts while recognizing their limitations and understanding where they themselves may need the support of others.

The Community Guardian

Some women who feel a calling to the guardian path of service are not particularly interested in serving at women's rituals in a magical capacity. These women feel primarily called to offer service in community outside of the ritual circle. We have named this focus "community guardianship" to differentiate it from the ritual guardian facilitator focus. The calling to serve as a community guardian facilitator can be a path complete unto itself for those who choose to more deeply develop it over time.

Providing spiritual service through any conscious act of nurturing, intervention, or protection can be a profound way to experience the joys and challenges of supporting community. Women who serve as community guardian facilitators must learn the meaning of, and the difference between, selfless service and self-serving acts as they advance to deeper personal and community work.

Ways for community guardians to serve at gatherings, festivals, and rituals:

* Attend to the physical logistics, including setting up and tearing down.

* Help participants with personal or special needs.

* Assist with parking.

* Provide security. If the gathering is outdoors, these women may patrol the perimeter to keep the participants safe from any disturbances.

* Mediate conflicts or provide intervention and resolution.

* Watch for and assist women who may be emotionally disturbed or distressed.

Gatekeepers

"Gatekeepers" are women who, through the study and practice of psychic, energetic, magical, and shamanic skills such as weather-working, telepathy, glamory, shape-shifting, and journeying, are able to work between the world of the ritual container (the cast circle) and other realms. This focus of spiritual service can be a path unto itself, just as the community guardian facilitator's path can be. Many women who serve in a guardian capacity serve as both community guardians and gatekeepers.

Weather work is something every witch should have some skill in, especially if they are serving as guardian facilitators for an outdoor ritual. There is no way a woman can keep an advancing storm at bay so her community's ritual isn't rained out if she doesn't have a strong working relationship with the Watchers of East and West, and the elements of air and water. Even in the middle of winter, it is possible to bring warmth to the cast circle if you have a deep relationship with the Watchers of the North and South. With enough practice, a dedicated and skilled practitioner can draw upon the insulatory essence of earth and the heat of the element of fire to bring warmth to the cast circle.

Glamory is the psychic and energetic art of creating illusion. To provide security for an outdoor ritual where curious or ill-intended people could be disruptive, it is much easier to create, what in the martial art of Aikido is called a "re-direct." Better to send people on their way by making sure they don't even notice what is before their eyes, than having to behave like a nightclub bouncer. An energetic "re-direct" away from the ritual circle could be accomplished by imbedding an intention such as, "you really have to pee", or "it's too cold to stay here," into the outermost layer of the ritual container. Is this manipulation? Yes. We manipulate our environment constantly for various reasons. In this case, it is to ensure the safety and sanctity of the ritual and its participants as well as the safety of any intruder well-meaning, simply curious, or hostile.

The gatekeeper guardian path begins by learning how to work with the energetics of the ritual circle; how to create a container that holds a specific intention, and then maintain it for a specific length of time. In ritual, these guardian facilitators work to maintain the spherical form of the cast circle and to energetically support the ritual facilitators as they guide the ritual experience.

Gatekeepers work in partnership with ritual facilitators who invoke the elemental powers or the Goddess at center. Here is a description of one of my own experiences.

> The circle has been cast. The humming from the women in the circle is gently but powerfully, vibrating my body with overtones as I step forward to call the Goddess at the center of the circle. I pause for a moment in the delicious sound and breathe. As I prepare to invoke Her, I feel a flow of energy envelope me from the edge of the circle from the woman serving as my guardian. I know that I am alone, but I am not entirely alone. This energy is warm, supportive, loving, and whispers without sound, "Yes!" I can rest in that feeling and can easily summon my strength. I raise my arms to embody the chalice and open to Her. Like a fountain, my words pour out as I call Her into the circle from within and without.

Another Priestess calling that incorporates many of the skills of the gatekeeper, plus additional, specific skills, is working with people and animals who are in the process of dying: helping them prepare to make their transition from this life into the Summerland. Some Priestesses I have ordained have named this ministry "Priestess of the Veil." Most of these women have worked in hospice care as licensed nurses or volunteers. Others have applied their clairvoyant and energetic skills to animals that are ill or injured. These women have developed the ability to journey with the dead, accompanying the dead toward their next home, traveling with them as far as a living woman can safely go and still be able to return. Because of the difficulty and risks involved in this work, women who feel called to this practice should seek out an experienced teacher.

There are also many applications for gatekeeper skills among women involved as doulas and midwives who help women prepare for and birth their babies. The birth experience, especially the transition from the world of the womb, down the vaginal canal, into the world outside the womb, is a state of being between the worlds. Similarly, the same skills giving support to a woman in labor can assist a woman in her transition to death and beyond.

Suggestions for ritual guardian facilitators to serve in ritual:

* Purify the ritual space.
* Provide energetic support to specific facilitators or participants as needed.
* Cast the circle.
* Maintain the cast circle.
* "Cut a door" for women to exit or enter the cast circle if the need arises.
* Serve as gatekeepers in the portals between the elemental realm and

the ritual circle as energetic filters.

* Serve as ritual drummers.
* Deal with unforeseen logistical problems, conflicts, or emergencies that could arise.
* Provide psychological support.

Guardian Priestess of the Rite

A "guardian Priestess of the rite" is a term that we created to describe an ordained guardian Priestess who has gained extensive levels of expertise and experience as both a community guardian and a gatekeeper. A woman who is qualified to serve as guardian of the rite is a woman who has learned, through years of training and practice, to work in deep magical partnership with other ritual facilitators. She has honed her ability to focus her attention and energy around the circle, holding the form of the container while boosting any intention that the ritual facilitators at the center may have.

For example, a guardian of the rite would gather her sisters serving in a guardian capacity before the ritual begins and facilitates their coming into resonance together. They discuss any potential problems that could occur and how they might best handle them. Together they cast a huge energetic overlay container shortly before the ritual is about to begin that contains two intentions: 1) a glamour that will send away anyone who doesn't need to be there, and 2) be a beacon for anyone who is on her way and may be lost.

The guardian of the rite works in energetic partnership with the ritual facilitator or Priestess who is invoking the Goddess, providing energetic support to her when she steps forward to invoke, and at any other time that this woman is facilitating. She is also constantly monitoring the energy of the participants, and, with the help of the other ritual guardian facilitators, they maintain a deosil spin on the outer container of the circle itself for the duration of the rite. When the cone of power is about to be released, they open the top and bottom of the container to release the energy toward its goal and then close these openings once the release is complete.

If the ritual location is indoors, most, if not all, of our guardian facilitators work inside the cast circle because we cast the circle within the walls of the building. On the other hand, if the ritual location is outdoors in a public space or on private land, we prefer to have our community guardians and the guardian of the rite, working from beyond the cast circle for security reasons. At rituals held at larger outdoor gatherings, such as festivals and conferences, the guardians who work as gatekeepers of the elemental portals remain in their positions for the ritual's duration while the guardian of the rite, and any other women available to serve in a guardian capacity, patrol the perimeter.

The Staff: Tool of The Guardian

In Craft traditions, based on the dualism of the Goddess and the God, the staff is considered to be male, and a phallic symbol. In the Goddess-centered perspective of Dianic tradition, the wooden staff represents the Goddess in Her aspect as the World Tree, the source of all life and wisdom, past, present, and future in one perfect body.

As mentioned in Chapter 5, it is important that a staff be made from wood that was once part of the trunk of a tree, just as a wand should be made from that part of the tree which once waved in the breeze, the branch. Different trees have different magical properties, so the choice of which species of tree to use is a personal decision that should be made with thought to the staff's intended use. The proper measure of a staff is not agreed upon. Some traditions require that the staff be made to equal the height of the person plus the length of the distance between the inside of their elbow and their middle finger. In these traditions this measurement is considered to be the measure of one's full power.[216] Since Dianic tradition comes from a foundation of feminism and is dedicated to restoring balance in the world, we are not interested in "measuring our full power". We are committed instead, to transforming the dominator model of "power-over" culture that pervades our world, into a world of partnership, where power is shared compassionately and responsibly among all sentient beings. We propose that the ideal height for a woman's staff is that the top of the staff comes to rest at the woman's heart. It is from our hearts that our branches, our arms, must reach and spread to encircle our world and restore balance above and below.

Although all trees are sacred, oak is one of the best choices for a staff. In ancient mystic and folk traditions throughout Europe and the Mediterranean the oak is considered to be a doorway between this realm and the Otherworld. Just as your own mother was the portal through which you entered this world from the realm of spirit, the oak is considered to be a mother tree, associated with the Mother Goddess. In the beliefs of many ancient cultures, from Greece to northern Europe, trees give birth to the human race.[217] The old Irish/Gaelic name for oak is *duir,* meaning "door"[218]. The oak is the guardian tree of the door, the portal to the other realm, and is the door itself. It is no accident that front doors all over Europe and North America are traditionally made of oak. Magically, therefore, oak is the perfect choice of a staff for a woman who wishes to work in the portal of the cardinal directions or beyond the boundary of the cast circle.[219]

Most references to the oak speak of it as representing the Old God, as in the battle of the Oak King and the Holly King at Winter Solstice. But in early Greece, the oak was sacred to the Goddess Dione (Diana). Her sanctuary in a grove of massive oaks at Dodona, at the foot of Mount

---

216 *Encyclopedia of Wicca and Witchcraft,* p. 344.

217 *Tree Wisdom,* Jacqueline Memory Paterson, Thorsons, 1996, p.145.

218 Ibid, p. 189.

219 Falcon, Priestess of the Guardian Path.

Tomarus, was the most ancient and sacred sanctuary in ancient Greece.[220] For centuries people worshipped in the grove and sought prophecy from Her priestesses who could interpret Her voice in the rustling leaves and swaying branches. Eventually, Dodona went the way of many oracles and shrines in the ancient world with gods supplanting the Goddesses, just as "Zeus seized the oracle of Dodona from Dione and proclaimed it to be his."[221] Later, in central Italy, Iphigenia, a priestess of Diana, aided by her brother Orestes, established a sacred oak grove at Lake Nemi in honor of the Goddess Diana.[222]

Ritual guardian facilitators work in energetic partnership with their consecrated staffs, becoming and holding form as trees of life, recreating Her sacred grove. In practicing their skills as guardian facilitators, they must learn to become tree, forest, and grove, interweaving roots, trunk, and branches to provide shelter above, and below to support the cast circle, the other ritual facilitators, the ritual's participants, and each other. Standing together, they enable all of us to once again dance and worship safely and freely in Her sacred grove.

Oath of the Guardian

I hereby answer the call of the Goddess to her service as Guardian.
I vow to become and keep sound in body, mind, and soul,
so that She may best use me as one of Her sacred tools,
throughout all time, and throughout all worlds,
even unto death and beyond.
I vow to yield only unto Her,
knowing that She, who is Creatrix of all will lead me
to the path of honesty, integrity, honor, and courage.
You, who are wisdom, grant me wisdom.

---

[220] Paterson, *Tree Wisdom*, pp. 176-177.
[221] Ibid, p. 176.
[222] Raven Grimassi, *Hereditary Witchcraft*, Llewellyn Publications, 2001, p.11.

> ***You, who are pure, grant me pureness of heart.***
> ***You, who are radiance, light my way.***
> ***I, hereby answer the call of the Goddess and swear myself to Her service as Guardian.***[223]

Ordination

When a woman is ready for ordination as a Dianic Priestess, she knows it. However, this knowing does not come from a desire to be publicly named a Priestess. She has moved past that mystique and ego gratification and is simply doing the work she is here to do, without fanfare. In doing her work—in being challenged by it; in growing, integrating, and centering herself into the work, and the work into her—she *becomes* her service. It really no longer matters what she is called: she knows who she is because she has become the work, the hand of the Goddess is upon her, and others recognize her as living her work. At ordination, a woman begins a new cycle as Priestess. Ordination does not commemorate the end of her service but formally begins her work anew. She steps out as girl child again, in awe of the world, with gratitude that the Goddess has made it possible for her to serve as she has been called to do.

With ordination comes formal and public responsibility for her work, her interactions with others, the ways she conducts herself, and how she embodies the Goddess in the world on a daily basis. While you may remain a community member, you will forever be held to different standards, your actions and words will always be examined differently. You will be noticed and watched. Guardian Priestess, Falcon River says, "It won't get easier, but you will become more practiced dealing with it."

Core to the Priestess's service is assisting women in identifying their own needs and to support them in meeting those needs. A Priestess teaches women mostly through her example. To do this authentically, she must be motivated by a desire to serve life and to enhance life for all.

[223] Guardian priestess ordination vow of service by Falcon.

A Priestess presents opportunities for women to access their personal power and experience themselves as sacred, as the Goddess. In order to encourage my students to be honest, vulnerable, and open, I must do the same. In this way, power is equalized between student and teacher, while acknowledging differences with respect to experience and knowledge. To guide a student through deep transformational work, I must also have done my own inner work and must continue to do it.

A Priestess does not set herself apart from the community she serves but is deeply involved with its growth, with an open ear to feedback. She is especially open to constructive feedback, which equalizes power, encourages participation, and stimulates growth; and she works to create a feeling of partnership with the person giving her the feedback. This is very different than seeing the person with the criticism as an enemy or as being in opposition. Taking the initial position that both are working for the greatest good allows for real communication and for joint solutions to be made. Where there are very different positions being taken in a discussion, the Priestess must be strong enough to speak her truth, especially in the face of opposition or opinions she disagrees with, while still being able to listen to and consider other points of view. A Priestess must be open to the simple questions, the deep questions, and even the unspoken questions behind a question. She must learn to know when it is best to speak and when to keep silent and listen.

There is a difference between the call to service and the call to be ordained. In Western culture, most women are taught to serve others, but does that translate to an authentic call to serve the Goddess as a vocation? Because ordination often confers legal ministerial credentials, many women unconsciously revert to patriarchal-style thinking: "What are the guidelines and rules in order to get my 'stamp'?" Ordination is not a diploma for completed classwork. Being a Priestess is about what you are—what you become as a result of what you have done. *Who* you are can be a presentation. *What* you are is a totality of being. It is out of your *being* a Priestess that your spiritual service is sourced.

Ordination in the Dianic Tradition

In the Dianic tradition, a High Priestess can only be ordained by another High Priestess. This assures a continuity of lineage and some basic teachings, even though each High Priestess will take what she knows and teach the tradition through her own perspective. The women who have been ordained as High Priestesses by Z Budapest or by myself include women from diverse backgrounds and orientations. Most of them also have diverse backgrounds in their magical training. This diversity celebrates the evolution of the tradition and the gifts that diversity can bring. With a wide range of specialties, some of these High Priestesses focus on assisting women with individual spiritual development, while others work more often with groups and hold center in larger communities.

A Dianic Priestess, once ordained by either another Dianic Priestess or High Priestess, can ordain Priestesses at her responsibility and discretion. However, if a Priestess desires legal ministerial credentials, she may need to enroll in a Priestess training program that offers credentials or affiliate with a federally recognized Dianic or other Wiccan 501(c)(3) tax-exempt religious entity[224] can offer them. Ministerial credentials allow a Priestess to legally marry and bury, and they allow access to visit a sick, injured, or dying congregant in a hospital intensive-care ward without having to be immediate family. It may also allow her to offer healings and divination, and provide pastoral counseling to individuals. Priestesses can enroll in specialized courses for ministers to learn how to become a pastoral counselor. At this time, Temple of Diana, Inc. is the only federally recognized Dianic temple that offers a Priestess training program and legal ministerial credentials specifically for Dianic Priestesses as sourced from the 1971 birthplace of the Dianic tradition in Los Angeles, California.[225]

---

[224] In the language of the Internal Revenue Service who grants tax-exempt designations to religious groups, this is called "Church" status.

[225] Z Budapest facilitated the first Dianic ritual for Winter Solstice in 1971.

The traditional ceremony of Dianic ordination is intended to provide an energetic charge that empowers and nourishes the Priestess throughout her ministry. This "charge" is the very heart of the ordination ceremony as the ordaining Priestess transfers the lineage of our Tradition to the new Priestess. As the new Priestess is presented to the elemental Teachers, the ordaining Priestess transfers the lineage to her, invoking the blessings of the Goddess and these powers on her path of service. Lori, a Priestess I ordained who named her ministry "Priestess of the Singing Spirit," describes Dianic ordination this way:

> She (the Priestess) sources her spiritual foundation through her training that embodies the essential energetic context central to our tradition. This specific combination of Dianic education and the sacred rite of Dianic ordination ensures that every one of her Priestesses enters through the same doorway of service to the Goddess and Her women.

As an elder in my tradition and a High Priestess who as of Spring 2017 has ordained forty Priestesses and four[226] High Priestesses in the Dianic tradition, I am often asked about how I evaluate a prospective Priestess. What qualities do I look for in a candidate, and how do I identify those qualities? Things have changed a lot since the 1970s and 1980s, where more often than not, a woman was ordained as a Priestess based on her potential, not on an actualized, developed ministry. Today, when I consider ordaining a Dianic Priestess, I use the following questions and criteria, based on my own years of spiritual service: Is this woman definitely working her spiritual path? Can she clearly identify and articulate her focus? Can I easily observe that she is doing her work? What makes her Priestess work specifically Dianic, goddess and female-centered?

[226] I rescinded a High Priestess ordination in 2017, so only three HP ordinations are recognized.

A woman who fulfills that criteria excels in many areas but has a consistent, identifiable focus that is obvious to the women of her community. If a woman cannot name her ministry or clearly demonstrate the nature of her spiritual service, she is not yet ready for ordination. The work of a Priestess is not about potential but is actualized work in the world. *The being and the doing are one.* Is there a circle of women willing to accept this woman as a Priestess? If there is not, I would seriously question her readiness for ordination, at least within her chosen specialty. To ordain her without community recognition would be to put the cart before the horse.

When a woman is truly walking the Priestess path, she is passionate about her work; she is driven to do it and is also sustained by it. It is how she creates, and the work, however challenging, feeds her spirit. She wrestles with patriarchy and its limited concept of deity. She loves life and honors the Goddess by serving others, whether human, animal, or green ones. She knows how to craft energy, holds power responsibly, and values her own work. Such a woman demonstrates the ability and willingness to examine her own motivations and desires for service. She dares to dream. She dares to craft those dreams into reality. To endure and thrive on her path, she must be self-nurturing, self-sustaining, self-facing, and patient.

I look for strong women who will not be deterred, although they may struggle. Priestess work is not for those who are easily distracted or discouraged. I look for women who can take responsibility for their not-so-perfectly-evolved selves, and thus can be compassionate with others as they are compassionate with themselves. I look for women who aren't perfect. Frankly, I am a bit mistrusting of "perfect" women, because Priestesses are women who struggle in life like everybody else. They aren't afraid to be human and a part of the world. It is her humanity that gives a Priestess the ability to empathize and hold compassion for herself and those around her.

I look for a woman who is inspired by life and by other women's creativity and accomplishments. I look for a woman who is not afraid to be a beginner and to learn from others, especially the students who are there to learn from her. This woman refuses to stay on the pedestal others may try to place her upon. She also refuses to stay in the hole that others may try to push her off the pedestal into!

I look for a woman who is in it for the long haul. Although the nature of her service may change over time, she is doing her work with each breath because she has become a channel for the Goddess in the world. She is a Priestess because she is doing the work for the sake of the work. Being a Priestess is not a phase, a fad, or a cycle in her life that she is passing through. The Goddess is guiding her, even as she knows that the day-to-day reality of being in Her service is not always comfortable.

To live and work in spiritual service to women is to honor life's passages and transitions to the fullest. The path of the Priestess is to stand for the Goddess in the world, to speak for Her and to do Her work by being Her hands and heart. It requires courage, stamina, patience, a great love, and an enduring sense of humor. The function and role of the Priestess is needed again in the world as we return to creating and participating in women's rites. It is my hope that the role of the Priestess be restored anew, modeling power that comes from within, shared with her supportive sisters, helping to facilitate women's connection with themselves, each other, and the Goddess.

DRAWING DOWN THE GODDESS[227]

by Patricia Monaghan

She is the drum.
The skin on which life plays.
The pulse. The pounding heart.
Rhythm of starlight and blood.
The rap, the tap, the roll,
the clap, the rattle, the thunder.
Foot to ground, hand to hand.
Our hearts drum. And drum.
She is the drum.

Return to Her.
Return to yourself.

She is the voice.
Voice before words.
Cry of hunger. Cry of need.
Sob of fear. Hiss of pain.
Voice beyond words.
Satisfaction's murmur. Shouts of joy.
Panting urgency of sex.
Animals, birds, whales, women, men,
clanging and chiming, silvery and hoarse,
sweet and clear and loud and strong.
She is the voice.

---

[227] Used with permission from the estate of Patricia Monaghan. From *Seasons of the Witch – Poetry & Songs to the Goddess.*

The hour has arrived:
Invoke Her now.

She is the wind.
Tender breeze of spring
under a breathless moon.
Summer's great exhalation,
that warm green sigh.
Fall squalls, tempests of death
under a hunter moon.
The howling winter storm.
Fluting, piping, whistling wind
through our bodies, trumpeting,
bugling, wind through our bodies.
She is the wind.

Reach in and touch Her.
Call out and hear Her.

She is the dance.
Frenzy of hips and thighs,
hot desire oceans,
dark need and brightest joy.
Breasts pressing air.
Arms reaching, hands meeting,
heads swaying, eyes closing.
She is the dancer.
She is the dance.

Return to Her.
Return to yourself.

She is the drum, the voice,
the wind, the dance and
beyond words and time,
beyond knowing and the known,
beyond body and spirit moving through body,
beyond song and the singer,
beyond drums and the dancer,
beyond dance and dancer,
she is the silence.

The hour has arrived:
Invoke Her now.

Reach in and touch Her.
Call out and hear Her.

Return to Her.
Return to yourself.

appendix A

GODDESS-CENTERED RELIGION AND THE DIANIC TRADITION

On Winter Solstice 1971, in a small, smoky apartment in Hollywood, California, Hungarian-born Zsuszanna E. Budapest led the first Dianic ritual for the Los Angeles women's community. She was the first to blend feminism, contemporary Witchcraft, and goddess spirituality with the Eastern European folk magic traditions of her mother into what she coined "feminist spirituality," and is viewed largely as the mother of feminist Dianic Wiccan tradition.[228] On that Winter Solstice night, the small circle of women poured feminist values and goddess religion into the cauldron of change, and the Dianic feminist tradition was ignited, giving a life-quickening jolt of energy to the growth of what has become known as "feminist Witchcraft." At the same time, another tradition that also called itself Dianic began in the state of Texas. This tradition, however, was co-gender and largely Celtic in its lunar and seasonal rituals, and unlike the Dianic feminist tradition, much of the teachings were, and still are, kept secret, in contrast to the very public nature of the feminist Witchcraft tradition. To differentiate itself from Z Budapest's Dianic tradition, this branch now calls itself McFarland Dianic, after its founder, Morgan McFarland.

At the same time that Z's fledgling coven began, feminist scholars, activists, writers, artists, and musicians began to speak, publish, and create art, music, and song inspired by goddess iconography, mythology, feminist politics, and intuitive knowing. The works of "out" lesbians, straight feminists, and the artistic, musical, and written work of Shekhinah Mountainwater, Merlin Stone, Judy Chicago, Ruth and Jean Mountaingrove, the activist women of W.I.T.C.H., Mary Daly, and Kay Gardner inspired others and added to the growing tide of goddess

[228] Griffin, *Daughters of the Goddess*, 35, and Noonan, 153.

consciousness. Books such as *When God Was a Woman* by Merlin Stone, *The Great Cosmic Mother* by Monica Sjoo and Barbara Moor, *The Holy Book of Women's Mysteries* by Z Budapest, *The Spiral Dance* by Starhawk, *The Chalice and the Blade* by Riane Eisler, and *Beyond God the Father* by Mary Daly carried the women's spirituality movement into the bookstores of mainstream America. The work of archeologist Marija Gimbutas (1921-1994) provided an enormous academic contribution to the body of intuitive knowledge women held in their hearts. She argued that the original understanding and experience of what the dominant culture calls God was first worshipped as a goddess. Gimbutas authored many books on ancient civilizations that gave compelling evidence of the widespread existence of a Neolithic goddess-centered culture in pre-patriarchal Europe.[229] After decades of Gimbutas's research and findings being disputed and dismissed in some academic circles, by the end of 2017, her work has finally been vindicated. Due to new DNA evidence, Gimbutas's Kurgan theory on the widespread Indo-European expansion has been scientifically proven.[230] Practitioners of Dianic Witchcraft, goddess women, and goddess scholars interested in matriarchal studies continue to be thankful to Gimbutas for the inspiration and validation her pioneering work provided.

In the early 1970s, Dianic tradition spread as Z Budapest traveled across the U.S., bringing along her first book, *The Feminist Book of Lights and Shadows*. This early work was later incorporated into *The Holy Book of Women's Mysteries*, integrating feminist politics with goddess religion, Witchcraft, and ancient women's festivals from researcher Jane Harrison's books *Prolegomena to the Study of Greek Religion*, *Epilegomena & Themis*, and *Ancient Art and Ritual*. The wild fire Budapest started in California caught in many places, drawing many women to feminist and goddess-centered Witchcraft, spreading eventually to Great Britain, Australia, Canada, New Zealand, and other parts of Europe. Goddess spirituality organizations in the U.S.

---

229 Gimbutas, *The Gods and Goddesses of Old Europe*.
230 From "Marija Gimbutas Triumphant: Colin Renfrew Concedes" by Carol P. Christ, December 11, 2017.

like the Re-formed Congregation of the Goddess in Wisconsin helped women to network with other like-minded women for goddess-centered spiritual support.

In presenting my perspective of the Dianic tradition, I am well aware that the term "Dianic" has a much less clearly defined meaning in many communities throughout the United States and abroad than from its birthplace in Los Angeles, California. There are great numbers of women who either self-define as Dianic or who are defined by others as Dianic when describing a Witchcraft orientation that is female-and goddess-centered. Most often these women, either as solitaries or in groups, have little or no magical practice or ritual training in common with other Dianics, and while Dianics generally tend to be fairly eclectic in their practice, some groups are more eclectic than others. To this day, many of these self-identified Dianics do not affiliate with Budapest's lineage or have any knowledge that there is a herstory to their practice.

In some places, the term "Dianic" became synonymous with "lesbian witch." According to Z, from the earliest days of her coven, the Susan B. Anthony Coven #1, to the present, women of all sexual orientations were welcomed and participated and contributed to the Dianic tradition. Lesbian feminists were especially intrigued and drawn by the idea of women-only circles for female empowerment that combined political activism with a goddess-and female-centered spirituality. Over the years, different communities around the United States that embraced a Dianic or goddess spiritual focus drew a preponderance of lesbians, bisexual, or heterosexual women, or a fair combination of all. While the Dianic tradition was the first Witchcraft tradition in contemporary times to welcome and include lesbians, offering lesbian rites of passage and including same-sex union ceremonies, it was never Z's intention or vision that Dianic tradition be synonymous with lesbian religion. Her dream was to revive a Women's Mystery tradition for *all* women[231].

[231] *All* women" always referred to biological females from all sexual, racial, and ethnic orientations.

During my studies in folklore at the University of California, Santa Cruz, from 1974 to 1976, I sought information about the Goddess in the university library as I explored the Pagan roots of English and Celtic traditional folk ballads. At the same time, I studied goddess spirituality weekly with Shekhinah Mountainwater in her home, called the Moon Hut, in the redwoods of the Santa Cruz mountains with a small group of local women. By 1976, I was living in Los Angeles again, where I met Z, attended many of her seasonal rituals, and volunteered at bulk-mailing parties for the radical feminist, witchy newsletter called *Themis*. Z initiated many women in those early years, with minimal training, doing what she called "sowing seeds"—in her words, "You never know where it's going to take!" This was Z's philosophy in those days, and so, like many others, I was soon initiated into Z's coven, the Susan B. Anthony Coven #1. Four years later, and much to my surprise, Z asked me if I would consider ordination as a High Priestess since she planned to relocate to northern California. I was terrified. The responsibility was enormous and I felt so unprepared, in spite of my studies and experience up to that point as a committed ritualist and singer. After all, I was only twenty-five years old, with an infant daughter, and I wasn't even an ordained Priestess yet. Through my terror and insecurity I also saw my path, and eventually I said "yes."

On Halloween night in 1980, Z Budapest ordained me as a High Priestess. She charged me with continuing her ministry in Los Angeles through teaching classes and facilitating the seasonal rituals for the local women's community. Due to the dedicated service of countless women, I am proud to say that Dianic seasonal rituals for the Los Angeles women's community have continued to be provided since 1971. My first coven was named Moon Birch Grove, named for the month in which the coven formed, the Celtic tree month of birch, in January 1981. It was a time of enormous creativity fueled by women's awakening to feminism, goddess consciousness, lesbian identity for many, and Amazonian sovereignty for all. As information about the Goddess and Dianic Witchcraft became more available, greater numbers of heterosexual and bisexual women interested in the Dianic tradition and other goddess-centered and feminist circles increased. My own students and spiritual communities reflected this change as the years passed.

In 1985, I left Moon Birch Grove to teach Dianic Witchcraft full-time around the Los Angeles area and to give more energy to my work as a Pagan recording artist. To expand my spiritual work, in 1988, I co-founded Circle of Aradia,[232] which for decades was the largest Dianic community in the United States, and where often hundreds of women attended. Circle of Aradia eventually became a grove of Temple of Diana, and continues to offer open community seasonal rituals for the Los Angeles women's community.

While there were other Dianic groups and Dianic-inspired covens in Los Angeles in the 1970s - 2000, the Dianic tradition through Circle of Aradia maintained its continuity and identity through specific coursework, spellcraft, energetic awareness, and ritual traditions that I, and other community members, brought into our tradition. Ritual is the language that the community shared in common, trained from the same base to honor the Goddess. The Los Angeles Dianic community has rich traditions that are in their fourth decade now, and for me this has been a personal and unexpected harvest.

When I held center as High Priestess at Circle of Aradia, our rites included seasonal and lunar community rituals, initiations, and ordinations. Circle of Aradia was comprised of collectives of covens and solitaries that came together for the larger seasonal rituals, averaging between 125–225 women. Our community also provided "action circles," in which women would gather for political actions, honoring Women's Mysteries, facilitating public ritual, organizing community

[232] Circle of Aradia was co-founded by Ruth Barrett and Felicity Artemis Flowers. In 1993, Ruth incorporated Circle of Aradia as a religious nonprofit corporation in the state of California, followed by federal incorporation as a circle of The Re-Formed Congregation of the Goddess. In 2004, Circle of Aradia became federally affiliated as a grove of Temple of Diana, Inc.

events, working against racism, sobriety support (a Goddess-oriented "12-Step meeting), and providing service to women in our community experiencing crisis.

In 2000, I relocated to the state of Wisconsin with my life companion, Falcon River. To legally protect and support our tradition and graduates of our clergy training program wishing to start circles, we co-founded Temple of Diana, the only tax-exempt, federally recognized Dianic Temple for our Dianic tradition with affiliated groves (extensions of Temple of Diana in different geographic areas) throughout the United States. Temple of Diana groves offer a variety of ongoing local classes, lunar and seasonal community rituals, and a national training program for Dianic witches and clergy called The Spiral Door Women's Mystery School of Magick and Ritual Arts.

Feminism, Magical Traditions, and Religious Values

For over forty years, Dianic Wicca, the women's spirituality movement as a whole, and more specifically the goddess movement have evolved out of women's need to reaffirm the Goddess, the sacred female, in their lives and in the world. Women of all ages, races, cultures, religions, spiritual traditions, and walks of life have been creating rituals and ceremonies that specifically express and affirm their life experience as women and address the impact that patriarchal culture has had on their lives. Other women have revived family magical traditions, sometimes called "folk traditions," for both religious and secular holidays. These family traditions are believed to be surviving systems in which the Old Ways have been preserved and passed down through superstitions, practices, or folkways among the same bloodline.[233] Out of this need for a woman-honoring spiritual perspective that addresses contemporary issues, there has been a resurgence of women drawing inspiration from Witchcraft (the practice of magic and paganism primarily relating to pre-Christian

---

[233] Grimassi, *Italian Witchcraft*, 301.

European Paganism), ancient goddess religion, archeology, myth, and folklore. This has resulted in women inventing, rediscovering, renaming, recovering, adapting, creating, and celebrating original rituals that are meaningful to them and their loved ones. The result is an inspired and eclectic mix of information from many diverse sources, freeing women from the entrapment of patriarchal religions and limitations.

While there has been a wondrous burgeoning of spiritual creativity in recent years, the term "goddess spirituality," which includes the religion of contemporary Witchcraft as well as other revived and reconstructed Pagan spiritual traditions, has become interchangeably and incorrectly used to describe a smorgasbord of New Age, crystal, "anything goes" Christian and Eastern influences, cultural appropriation of Native American and other indigenous peoples' spiritual practices and religions, space alien worship, and personal cosmologies put forward in psycho-babble as The Universal Truth for everyone. This has only served to confuse the basic tenets of Wicca (the name for this new and old religion).

Being a "goddess woman" (a term that came into use in the 1990s) is not equivalent to being a witch. You can be a "goddess woman," who creates and celebrates rituals in honor of the Goddess and Her children, without practicing Witchcraft. However, a woman who practices Witchcraft is always a goddess woman because almost all Witches today practice, at its heart, a goddess-centered religion, even those who include male divinity in their practice. Note that I use the word *religion*. Wicca, or contemporary Witchcraft, as it is practiced in its current forms, is not only a personal spiritual path; there is a difference.

All religions function by fueling the psyche with symbols, images, cosmology, rituals, beliefs, philosophy, ethics, and codes of behavior. For better or worse, religion deeply affects the core of an individual, ultimately shaping their values and behavior. After all, this is part of the intention and purpose of religion. In addition, the beliefs and symbols within any given religion ideally reflect and support the personal values of the individuals who practice it. Therefore, feminist women seeking to create or reclaim female-centered religion must choose symbols that serve to empower their actions and move them in the direction they wish the future of humanity to go. Each woman's choices become an active and conscious part of changing "herstory" toward a gentler, more nature-respecting world.

A fundamental value that Dianic Wicca shares with other feminist Wiccan traditions, goddess-centered groups, and individuals is that all people must work to heal the personal and political imbalances caused by the various manifestations of patriarchy that have dominated Earth and humanity for the past 5,000 years. This value brings awareness that the spiritual and religious phenomenon of the return of the Goddess to human consciousness is both a new and ancient paradigm for living in balance with one another and the Earth.

If religious or spiritual values of a religious tradition focus primarily on an afterlife, the present life becomes less important. If the physical world has less value than spirit, there is less concern about what human beings do to the Earth in order to fulfill their needs and desires. Governmental institutions are guided or controlled by prevailing religious beliefs, whether they are openly declared or not. This is why religion is inherently political and always has been. This means that in order to change the political climate, one must change the accepted religious ideology about the way things are valued. Respected author bell hooks writes, "Whether we consciously explore the reasons we have a particular perspective or take a particular action there is also an underlying system shaping thought and practice."[234] This concept was the inspiration for the development of feminist theory and values, and feminist Witchcraft.

The elements that make up a religion include a set of beliefs regarding the form and nature of divinity, set holidays, symbols, a shared history, and an accepted set of ethics.[235] These criteria can be described as tribal,

---

234 bell hooks, *Feminism Is for Everybody*, 19.

235 The late folklorist Joseph Campbell gave a radio presentation where he discussed the criteria as to what differentiates a religion from personal spirituality. I do not have a program

the glue that binds people together and creates a community who shares common values, traditions, rites, and customs over time. Today, most branches of Wiccan religion and many other new goddess-focused traditions, regardless of the differences in deity names and variations in cosmology, share these criteria.[236] Any Christian traveling overseas near the holiday of Easter could expect to find a church service in any town where other Christians would be celebrating Easter. Likewise, a Wiccan traveling from America to Europe near one of the solstices, equinoxes, or cross-quarter days could, in theory, look up the local coven and expect to find a circle going on wherein she might participate. She could also assume that the theme and structure of the ritual celebration would be generally, though not specifically, familiar. It is precisely because Wicca is a religion that these common themes and practices exist.

On the other hand, individual spirituality is the internalized experience of deity that exists apart from any tribal agreement. It is the deeply personal relationship with the creative force in the universe that motivates an individual to act in accordance with the values of that relationship. While religion describes the beliefs of a specific community and the agreement to a common practice among the individuals who comprise that community, personal spirituality is about the truth that lives within the individual and is unique to each person.

A tradition is a body of teachings and practices that are intended, and are able, to be passed on to others. A living religious tradition is not something fixed or unchanging, but one that evolves over time from a foundation that is understood by those who evolve it. Learning and practicing within a specific Craft tradition is similar to the diversity of denominations within other religions. While there are similarities to be found between them all, having a tradition means there is a specific lineage of teachers,

---

title or broadcast date.

[236] The Old Religion, in its earliest form, was not a religion, as we understand it; it was more a way of living with intention than a formal expression of worship. Matthews, *The Western Way*, 27.

practices, tools, cosmology, ethics, and liturgy, a consistency that identifies each tradition as either Dianic, Reclaiming,[237] Faery, Gardnerian, Celtic, Alexandrian, Stregheria, a family tradition, etc.

Dianic witches are largely assumed to be entirely eclectic in their practice, with an aversion to anything that looks like imposed structure or "have-tos." While I would agree that some of this reputation is well deserved, the Dianic Craft is misunderstood. Like many other Wiccan denominations, Budapest's Dianic feminist tradition began as an eclectic compilation of women's folkways passed on through oral and written (collected) sources, personal and oracular revelations, with incorporated aspects from other Wiccan traditions and their respective origins. This inspired women's creativity to evolve the tradition. What makes a practice "Dianic" is not only the application or adaptation within a goddess-centered, female-centered, and female-exclusive context, but integrating a new practice into the foundation that already exists in continuity with our Dianic herstory.

There are many women and men who are feminist, goddess-centered, and clearly creative and inspired. Some of their work has contributed to the continued unfolding of Dianic practice. I personally acknowledge the inclusion of works and inspirational contributions of Shekhinah Mountainwater, Robert Graves, Janet and Stewart Farrar, Doreen Valiente, Marion Green, Caitlin Matthews, Carolyn Hillyer, and many others. From these contributors over the years, I incorporated what I found to work magically and applied these teachings either directly or in an altered form for a goddess- and female-centered practice. Nevertheless, these individuals are not Dianics.

Further, there are many groups of women who practice goddess spirituality in feminist, female-sovereign spaces who are not Dianic. Some groups form from study circles that become ongoing ritual circles. Sometimes women who practice within a denomination of the Craft that

---

237 While identifying as feminist Witchcraft (for at least a few decades), they specifically say their tradition is not Wicca.

practice female/male duality will gather separately on occasion to honor significant passages from women's life cycles. These rituals are highly individualized, and most often there are no magical or ritual practices in common by the participants or facilitators, and the groups have no connection to the herstory of Dianic practice. Others, after reading a few books such as Z's *Holy Book of Women's Mysteries*, believe themselves to be Dianic, yet share no magical training in common with others. Since all of these examples meet the basic definition and commonly held understanding of "Dianic," what is it that is missing?

Budapest's inspired activism, rituals, and writings, and the establishing of Circle of Aradia, et al., in Los Angeles, provided me a cauldron to create, develop, and teach a full Dianic curriculum toward initiation and beyond. Having a place to study, develop, and facilitate rituals in one locality for so many years allowed thousands of women to evolve a common magical practice together, a body of practice that endures and can be passed down to future generations. This kind of educational opportunity was, and is still, rare in most places around the United States, and thus, the Dianic tradition evolved differently elsewhere, more often with emphasis on personal spiritual development rather than on a cohesive group practice and a fully integrated magical system.

Many years ago, a third degree Gardnerian Priestess who also attended my community's rituals said to me that "No one raises power like Dianics, but once they have it, they don't know what to do with it." While I initially felt stung, I looked for the seed of truth in her words. Her comment challenged me to take a critical look at Dianic magical practice as it was and to take responsibility to do something about it. Training women for group practice became my passion ever since.

Although there are different ideas of what Dianic means, I believe that after forty-plus years it is our responsibility to weave together the diverse threads of Dianic tradition into a colorful and strong quilt we can pass on to our daughters and grand daughters. I believe in the power of women to create change in the world and in ourselves. Having a shared body of magical practice is not meant to replace personal spiritual development; both are equally important, complementary journeys. While we can do personal work on our own, the benefits of getting actual training in Dianic Witchcraft can teach us how to work together. It has been my consistent experience that when women share a cosmology, a language to understand and communicate about our magical experiences, tools to work with in common, and a common magical and ritual foundation by having similar training, we can work more powerfully together in community. This is a benefit of having religion.

The very word "religion" makes many feminist and goddess-centered women uncomfortable. They fled the religions of their childhood, having experienced those religions as oppressive and misogynist. However, the word "religion," from the Latin *religio*, means "re-linking or reunion." Taking this meaning to its truest sense, the term "female-centered religion" or "goddess religion" is appropriate as the Goddess and Her women are reunited, as they re-member goddess-honoring spiritual practices (by cellular memory or not) and intuitively reveal an emerging body of newborn/ancient ritual traditions. Although the term "female-centered" has many meanings, for Dianics it means knowing we are a reflection of the Goddess - that we embody Her, and She resides in us. It means understanding life through the paradigm of the Female of the species as the primary reference for life. I believe that this ancient perception for women was long associated with the Neolithic peoples of Old Europe that Marija Gimbutas brought into the spotlight of contemporary archeology in the mid-1970s.[238]

Dianic Cosmology

Dianic religion centers on a spiritual reclamation of the Goddess as Creator/Creation, and for some women this means a journey to uncovering the lost, forgotten, ignored, erased, and eradicated legacy of

[238] Gimbutas, *The Living Goddess*, xvii.

our foremothers from earliest times. An important part of reclaiming the Goddess is restoring an experience of sacredness about the female body as deserving of religious reverence. Although this may be heresy to many patriarchal doctrines, it is essential for women healing from centuries of lies, oppression, and violence. To see specifically female imagery on an altar, a place of religious reverence, is to begin reclaiming ourselves as sacred, born in Her divine image.

Central to the cosmology of Dianic tradition is the perception and experience that the source of life is symbolically, metaphorically, and literally female. This monist cosmology is sometimes misunderstood since it contrasts with most other Wiccan traditions in which the cosmology and religious practices are based on a dualism of the Goddess and the God. When Dianics say "the Goddess," we are saying that life is interdependent and whole. To say "the Goddess" is to affirm the existence of one interwoven web of life. Manifestation emanates from and is borne of Her; we live upon and are sustained by a female planet. The Goddess is all the seen and unseen forces, and like gravity, She holds us to Her in an eternal embrace. All things are birthed from Her and must return to Her.

The Goddess is metaphorically[239] understood as the Triple Goddess in Her aspects of Maiden, Mother, and Crone or She Who Creates, Sustains and Destroys; there is nothing that She is not. She is both creator and creation. She is an all-inclusive source, the one who is and contains all the parts. The Goddess doesn't *think* things into being, She *births* into being. She created Herself through the process of parthenogenesis: the process of impregnation and creation without sex (as humans have come to define it), thus emanating diverse life forms from the center of Her spiral self. Millennium later She created a variation of Herself, which we call "male," to add greater diversity of genetic material for the survival and evolution of Her many life forms. Propagandized over recent

239 The term "metaphor" as defined by Judy Grahn: A metaphor is a figure of speech using measurement, comparison, for the purpose of transferring power. *Blood, Bread & Roses*, 19.

millennium as separate from Her, He is a *variation* of Her: not "other," not the "opposite" sex, but a variation of the Goddess and Her creation. Simply put, females and males are both variations of the Goddess.

> *"There are only two kinds of people in the world, mothers and their children."*[240]

According to modern science, life starts out female. John P. Pinel, an expert in the field of biopsychology, writes that "maleness and femaleness are slight, multidimensional, and at times, ambiguous variations of each other."[241] All fetuses begin as female. The XX female is primary, and the XY male develops from that primary form as a variation of female.

> Sexual development unfolds according to an entirely different principal, one that many males, particularly those who still stubbornly adhere to notions of male preeminence, find unsettling. This principle is that we are all genetically programmed to develop female bodies. Genetic males develop male bodies only because their fundamentally female program of development is overruled.[242]

The universe and the smallest insect all have a mother source. She may lay eggs externally or within Her body to be birthed outside the womb. No matter what form of creature—be it winged, slithering, four- or two-legged, finned, or formless—She creates life through a variety of methods. Whether Her methods are primeval, as they were in the beginning of the earth, or a later evolution or variation, She creates all diversity from variations of Herself. The female is the Primal Matrix. To answer

---

240 Budapest, *The Holy Book of Women's Mysteries*, 163.
241 Pinel, *Biopsychology*, 293.
242 Ibid., 275.

the age-old question, "Which came first, the chicken or the egg?"—the chicken, of course! The chicken is primary, the egg is not. Where did you come from? For a daily reminder, just look at your belly button!

Our language cannot begin to describe the Goddess except through poetry and metaphor. "Deity is like colorless light which can be endlessly refracted through different prisms to create different colors."[243] The Goddess is simply too large for the written page and our limited human brains to fully comprehend, so we try to understand parts of Her in order to begin to fathom the whole of Her. She is, therefore, known by many names, which are attempts to describe aspects of a universal whole. There are many goddesses known throughout history (herstory) and the world. Each individual goddess is whole unto herself within her microcosm, yet each is a part of the Primal Mother, powerfully woven into Her web. We address and call Her by many names, knowing that each goddess embodies but a portion of Her, an aspect of the whole. Would one say that the planet Venus is the whole of the universe or that one flower is the whole of the garden? Each planet and each flower has its own attributes and energies unique to itself. One can focus on the qualities of a planet, yet that planet is not the universe, nor one flower the whole of the garden. Her many names throughout time are but facets of a brilliant diamond.

It has become popular and accepted in academic, therapeutic, and some goddess circles to call the Goddess "the Divine Feminine" or simply "the Feminine." Willow LaMonte, wrote[244]:

> That phrase always seems like an oxymoron to me, as well as a misnomer: in common usage "feminine" only describes certain women, not all. It is used to judge and divide us—as in "she's not feminine enough," which is a big flaw in a

---

243 Matthews, *The Western Way, Vol. I,* 111.

244 Willow LaMonte was Creatrix and editor of *Goddessing Regenerated*, an excellent international goddess journal for many years.

> patriarchal culture. Unlike many archaic English words, now used disparagingly for women but originally having important or sacred meanings, there isn't any reversed herstory here to reclaim with "the feminine." It's never been a word of power in English. I like to work with my Goddess as verb—that energy, juice, function, motion, action and activism that moves things in our lives and in the Universe, along with the still point, the inactive verbs of zest, essence, compassion. But to me "the feminine" is Goddess as adjective—the description and modifier of a noun. Might be some nice trappings, but where's the energy? If we merely use an adjective to explain what is sacred and divine and most valuable to us, aren't we going to take a really long time to ooze out of patriarchal consciousness?[245]

The Goddess is not simply an archetypal symbol—a safe, fashionable, and psychological term used to describe Her universality or appeal to modern sensibilities. The Jungian definition of archetype is

> irrepresentable in themselves, but their effects appear in consciousness as archetypal images and ideas. These are collective, universal patterns or motifs that come from the collective unconscious and are the basic content of religions, mythologies, legends, and fairy tales. They emerge in individuals through dreams and visions.[246]

For those who experience the reality of the Goddess in their spirituality or religion, She is not merely some disembodied, psychological construct or academic concept invented by Jungian scholars. She is very real, "as

---

[245] From an editorial by Willow LaMonte, *Goddessing Regenerated*, #18, 2003.

[246] Matthews, *The Western Way, Vol. I,* 111.

real as rock and river, wind and flame: as real, and as individual, as you and I."[247] To refer to Her solely as an archetypal symbol distances Her from us and only allows Her to live in our minds as a psychological construct instead of our entire being. Christians don't refer to their god as an archetype or "the divine masculine." He is assumed to be the real deal, the final product, even though a male god creating life without the mother has to be taken on faith, since nothing in nature substantiates such an absurdity. To Her ancient and contemporary worshipers, the Goddess lives and breathes through every poem, tree, stone, infant's breath, and the desire for freedom.

Celtic scholars Caitlin and John Matthews describe archetypes as collective, formalized energies that inhabit our psyches, and believe that there is

> a gradual image-building which grows in power and effect in relation to the visualization of the group-soul ... Deity or pure spirit has no form and for it to have any communication with humankind it must assume an acceptable form or symbol.[248]

The Matthews feel that there is some truth in all theories on how deity is formalized because it is normal and natural for every person to find their own metaphor for a condition that is understandably difficult to express in human terms: "There is no way any of us can escape the language of symbolism which lies, sometimes deeply hidden, within our cultural and genetic memory."[249] The use of the word "archetype" in this way recognizes the inherent existence and compassionate wisdom of the Goddess and Her consistent efforts to communicate with Her children over millennia.[250]

---

247 Matthews, *Sophia, Goddess of Wisdom*, 8.
248 Matthews, *The Western Way, Vol. I*, 110.
249 Ibid.
250 Ibid.

The Triple Goddess

The depiction of the Goddess in a trinity form is found in many cultures. This ancient triple form of deity was one of many concepts that Catholicism took from the earlier Pagan religions it encountered. The Goddess in Her triple aspect is a manifestation of the entire cycle of life: birth, maturation, and death. She has the power to bring forth life; nurture, protect, and sustain it; and then destroy it. This concept contains all of nature's continuum: from the sweet, gentle breezes to the typhoon; from lapping waves on a quiet pond to powerful tidal waves on the ocean. Since ancient times, the moon has symbolized this concept in her three phases of new, full, and dark, a constant and visible reminder of the natural law of change and transition. Dianics and other witches call these three phases of the Goddess the Maiden, the Mother, and the Crone. These three phases are general categories of age, and each has its respective characteristics and specific energies. They are life stations that every woman will go through in some form, should she live to maturity. These threefold phases of women's lives are marked by five life passages that comprise the core body of Women's Mysteries: the Nymph (birth and childhood), the Maiden (puberty), the Mother (creativity and sexuality), the Crone (elderhood and menopause), and the Hag (wisdom and death).

The Maiden

The Maiden aspect of the Goddess is symbolized by the new crescent moon in the sky. Her sacred color is white, and Her domain is the heavens. She is the breath of life that you take in when you inhale the fresh new buds and breezes of spring. She is virgin, meaning "an autonomous female who belongs to Herself."[251] She represents creativity, for the Maiden dares to explore and risk in the pursuit of experiences that will later bring Her knowledge. Like the image of the Fool in the tarot deck,

---

[251] Wilshire, *Virgin, Mother, Crone*, 20.

the Maiden has one foot on the edge of the cliff and the other stepping into the air, the unexplored realm of possibilities. Her wisdom is found in her curiosity and fearlessness. Her knowledge is more often learned from natural consequences and from direct experience of cause and effect. She is innocent and open. When one is older, one understands that "if I go down this road, this is likely to happen," but the Maiden's nature is to try things out of curiosity and natural wisdom; She has no prior experience to influence Her one way or another. Her motto is "Sure, why not?!" and "Let's do this and find out!" Her wisdom is in trusting in life's bounty and in exploring life's possibilities.

If a woman is biologically beyond her maiden years, she can still invoke the Maiden in ritual or magical workings. As a woman ages, the Maiden does not disappear; She still lives on within each woman as She transforms and ages into other aspects. When there is a new crossroads to be faced or a desired life change that feels fearful, work with the Maiden and Her ability to take risks, trusting your vision to manifest.

The Mother

The Mother aspect of the Goddess is symbolized by the full moon. The Mother's sacred color is red, not only for the womb-blood of life shed in birthing but also for passion and sexuality. She represents the fully sexual, passionate, and creative woman. Her domain is everything that is on the surface of the earth and that comes up from the soil. All the plants, animals, trees, oceans, deserts, forests, and mountains are the body of Mother Earth. The Mother, the Nurturer, is the one who nourishes and sustains life with Her own body's flesh and fluids.[252] She protects Her creations with the strength and passion of a mother lion protecting her cubs. The Mother is felt in the pause cycle of breath that is held in the fleeting moments between the inhale and the exhale, feeding our cells with oxygen.

[252] Ibid. 21.

The Mother phase of a woman's life may include the birthing and care of children, but this phased of life is not defined or confined to biological motherhood.

Archeologist Marija Gimbutas said that the Goddess as Creatrix in prehistoric times represented the powers of birth, death, and regeneration in all of life. She also spoke of the Goddess as Creatrix, the source of life.

> The reason the divine power was primarily portrayed as female by our ancestors is because their cultures valued women, the female body, and female wisdom. In the Paleolithic, woman the gatherer gave birth to and reared children as well as collecting fruits, nuts, and vegetables, preparing foods, and healing with herbal remedies. In the Neolithic, women were revered as the inventors of agriculture, pottery, and weaving. Each of these was a mystery of transformation: seeds planted and fruit and vegetables harvested, clay turned to fired pot, animal hair to thread and cloth. The secrets of these mysteries were held and passed on from mother to daughter. The mysteries of transformation in agriculture, pottery, and weaving were analogized to the mysteries of transformation in the female body, from which life emerges and is nurtured.[253]

A woman who makes a decision to not become a biological mother still participates in the Mother phase of her life, though she may claim another word for Mother, such as Creatrix or Maker. In this phase of life, women create songs, music, art, community, a career: any number of different things she may choose to bring into physical reality. In

---

[253] https://feminismandreligion.com/2018/02/05/great-goddess-mother-goddess-creatrix-source-of-life-by-carol-p-christ/ Gimbutas, *The Language of the Goddess* (Thames & Hudson, 2001).

the Mother phase of life, a woman not only creates and attends, but is willing to defend and protect her creations and what she loves as an Amazon. She may become "Mother" by tending her garden; taking care of animals; becoming a teacher, caregiver, healer, social worker, doctor, veterinarian, or a political and environmental activist. Being "Mother" is a biological and psychological state during which a woman becomes "queen" of her life. She decides what she wants to do from her inner sense of sovereignty. Decisions and choices are not made randomly now, but with care for the consequences gained from the experiences of the Maiden, now transformed into wisdom and skills.

The Crone

The Goddess as Crone is symbolized by the dark phase of the moon. She is the waning cycle of the moon that eventually renews Herself as the Maiden again. Her sacred color is black, and She rules the Underworld and everything that is under the earth. She is the Goddess as Destroyer; the cycle of life that literally and figuratively is about endings. We experience Her in the exhale of our breath before we automatically inhale again. The Crone is also known as "Death-Bringer"; She who reclaims all spent forms back into Her cauldron-womb where She recycles them, reshapes them, and transforms them into new possibilities which She then gives birth to.[254]

The Crone is the biological cycle of the mature woman who has completed menopause and who enters a new cycle of ever-deepening wisdom and psychic growth. As she grows older and closer to the veil of death and her final transition, her abilities to vision, dream, and see into the other world are enhanced. The Crone possesses the wisdom of long and wide perspective, to see and understand the bigger picture with uncanny peripheral vision. She has "been there and done that." Her perspective encompasses both the Mother and the Maiden. From

---

[254] Ibid.

this vantage point, She advises and is a resource to others who have not traveled so far. She is known as the Wise One. Because the Crone has this wider perspective, She rules the decision-making process. The Wise One exists within each woman now as an aspect of herself, even if the woman is not old in years. She exists in past, present, and future simultaneously, as do all the phases of the Goddess. If time is understood as a spiral, not as a linear progression, the Crone inside each of us already exists and is looking back at us at this moment. To access Her wisdom in the present, invoke She who is in your future. You can say to Her, "I need some guidance here. Which way do I go?"

In the Dianic Wiccan tradition, each phase of life, like the turning of the seasons, is honored in its time. Older women are valued, and there is a veneration of our ancestors similar to that of many other cultures in the world. This ethic is quite different from Western patriarchal cultures, where the elderly are routinely dumped and forgotten once they stop being productive, reproductive, or attractive according to American standards.

Developing a relationship with the Crone before you arrive at Her phase chronologically includes taking care of Her physical future by taking care of your physical health in the present. By living a healthy lifestyle, nourishing your body with real food, and living consciously, you are taking care of the old woman you will eventually become. Her quality of life depends on the choices you make as a Maiden and a Mother. If you plan on being a feisty old lady, making trouble all the way to the grave, taking care of your Crone-to-be in the present provides Her with a better chance to be a strong source of wisdom for you and for others long into the future.

Diana and Artemis

Diana, the Roman goddess of the hunt, represents the central mythic theme of Dianic cosmology, and it is She for whom the Dianic tradition was named. She was known as Artemis by the Greeks. Diana is a guardian and protector of women and the wild, untamed spirit of nature. While Diana does have a triple aspect, it is in Her aspect as Virgin Huntress that She guides Her daughters to wholeness. She is virgin in the ancient sense of "She Who Is Whole Unto Herself," from the ancient meaning of virgin as a woman who was unmarried, autonomous, and who belonged solely to herself. The original meaning of virgin was not attached to a sexual act with a man because Diana/Artemis did not associate or consort with men. She is often understood to be lesbian. The goddess Diana (*Dia Anna*, meaning "Nurturer Who Does Not Bear Young") was the name that women would call for in childbirth, since Artemis' mother, Leto, experienced an easy labor in childbirth. In the Homeric Hymns it is told that Artemis helped the Cretan goddess of childbirth, Eileithyia, to deliver Her twin brother Apollo. Dianic women understand Diana/Artemis as the spiritual warrior and call Her forth from within themselves in their personal magical practice. She is the Holy Archer, the one who can focus Her will and direct energy to Her goals. In the dawn of the feminist spirituality movement, the goddess Diana became a role model for personal autonomy and feminist activism, protecting and defending women's right to live without fear. Women identified with Her as a symbol of a strong, free, and capable woman walking in the world, whole and complete.

> We are Dianic because we model our lives on the actions of Diana, the goddess of free and wild nature. She is untamed and whole unto herself. She has a fiery personality and is aggressively active in the defense and well-being of women. Those pledged to her service are called to lead lives in the pursuit of women's rights and freedoms. Our rituals are for women only. We are Dianic because by definition our energy is derived from other women, the Earth, and our concept

> of the Goddess. Our bows and arrows are the magic of our poetry and art. Our tradition is a teaching tradition. Our commitment is to help women to see and experience the power of women's energy.[255]

Inspired by the nature and aspects of the goddesses Diana and Artemis as protectors of women and life, Dianic ritual work focuses on personal and global healing, environmental concerns, and a deep commitment to end patriarchal oppression of women and their children, both personally and globally. This work involves visioning and striving to create a world where the web of life is honored as the sacred creation of the Goddess. It is these values and practices of Dianic tradition that have so deeply influenced and inspired the contemporary goddess movement.

Artemis, Maiden Huntress

> *As the moon* streams silver through the trees, the Virgin Huntress, Artemis, walks the night. With sure-footed strength and the grace of a deer, Her naked body glows in this pale light. A quiver of arrows rides Her shoulder. With bow in hand, strong and proud, She belongs to this wild place. She wields Her sacred will through the arrows She lets fly. A crescent moon upon Her brow gleams sharp, cutting as truth, as piercing as Her arrows which fly to the heart of the matter. It is the will of Artemis that all women be free. Her arrows race through the air, focused and relentless, to hit their target with fierce certainty. The Maiden Huntress sees in the dark with wolf eyes, unblinking and waiting.

255 Roslund and Mills, "Why We Are Dianic," 9.

She is the Divine Virgin who cannot be taken or possessed. She is complete within Herself, needing none other than Herself to be whole. She is the Wild One, the woman who cannot be tamed, harnessed, caged, bridled, or muzzled. She cannot be taken, for She knows Herself fully. She is one with Her instincts and is comfortable in Her skin. Her presence moves with the certainty of earth, as flowing as water, quick as fire, smooth as air.

What can it mean to be whole and complete? This fractured world knows nothing of She who walks in the night with Her animals beside Her, unafraid and open to the night's darkness. She embodies the strength that is found in vulnerability, and embodies a vision for world peace - for every woman knows that real peace in the world is far more than the absence of war. Artemis reminds us that we will only have achieved true peace in the world when any woman or child can walk anywhere, day or night, and be safe from male violence. This is the freedom of mind, body, and spirit that Artemis personifies.

It is Artemis the Huntress who protects the pregnant animals and their young; thus human women call the name of Artemis from the bed of labor as the force of creation calls their own names. As the great mother bear bares her teeth and lifts her great paws to strike down anyone who would dare harm her cubs, Artemis will not tolerate transgressions made against women and children. There are no second chances, no plea bargaining with the Huntress. She will track the perpetrator down and wield death as easily as She gives life.

Hear the words of the Divine Virgin, Artemis, Lady of the Beasts:

"You are enough. Wholeness is your birthright, your natural state of being. Obey your instincts, and your true knowledge will lead you back to your wildness, your essential sacred self.

Be not afraid to remove your harness and step out of the cage. The cage door has never been locked, only untried.

Taste and drink of the freedom that is known to all creatures, and which you have lost.

Run with me and my nymphs through the forest, knowing the night as your lover, moving in and out of shadows, aglow with silver light.

Feel the wind on your bare body, and breathe in the ecstasy of a free woman.

To know me is to fully embrace your wild woman self, and from wildness comes all possibilities.

Let my spirit move in you like the running deer, without fear."

...

appendix B

DEFINING THE DIANIC WICCAN TRADITION

This appendix will address many of the questions asked of me over the years about what marks or distinguishes our Dianic tradition from other Wiccan traditions and goddess-centered spirituality forms. Much of this information has already been included throughout this book. The information presented here is a synthesis of my own experience and that of the thousands of women I have had the honor and pleasure of teaching, circling, sharing, and conspiring with. It is intended to provide you with topics to think about and discuss within your ritual circles.

What is presented here is a concise definition and explanation of Dianic tradition from the vantage point of a Dianic elder in the Z Budapest lineage who has perpetuated and evolved the tradition as it arose from its birthplace in Los Angeles in 1971. This timeframe spans the creation of Z's first coven, the Susan B. Anthony Coven #1, where I was initiated, to Moon Birch Grove, my first coven as a High Priestess, to Circle of Aradia, to its continuing evolution through Temple of Diana, Inc. and its affiliated groves. This means that the Dianic witches who are affiliated with this lineage have an identifiable and continuous tradition that spans over forty years, and thousands of women have greater or lesser degrees of training or exposure to the same herstory, cosmology, ethics, and magical and ritual practices. These Dianics use their creativity to design and facilitate rituals that are often repeated over the years as a stable liturgy while creating other rituals that change as often as the wind changes.

A wise woman once told me, "If you don't stand for something, you'll stand for anything." So it is here that I offer my stand, using the athame of my experience to discern and communicate the essence of the Dianic Wiccan tradition.

The Dianic Tradition

The Dianic tradition is a goddess, female-centered, and earth-centered, feminist denomination of the Wiccan religion that was revived and inspired by author and activist Zsuzsanna Budapest in the early 1970s. Dianic tradition is a vibrantly creative and evolving Women's Mystery tradition that is inclusive of all women and girls. Our practices include celebrating and honoring the numerous physical, emotional, and life-cycle passages that women and girls share by having been born a female human being. Contemporary Dianic tradition recognizes the greater or lesser effects and influences of the dominant culture on every aspect of women's lives. Since 1971, the Dianic movement has inspired and provided healing rituals to counter the effects of living in patriarchy, and has worked to understand, deconstruct, and heal from the dominant culture wherein we live and practice our faith. We define patriarchy as the use of "power-over" thinking and action to oppress others, both institutionally and within the personal sphere of our lives.[256]

The Dianic tradition is based on a goddess-centered cosmology and the primacy of She who is All and Whole Unto Herself.

Dianics spiritually reclaim the Goddess, both as the source of life and She to whom all will return in death. In seasonal, lunar, personal, and group rituals, our approach to the practice of magic and our liturgy, art, music, and personal perception lies outside of a male/female or Goddess/God dualism. The language and primary reference for life is female.

For many Dianics, the Goddess is not an entity but the web of life itself. We use female imagery as a metaphor to speak of this. This means that when we address the Goddess, we are addressing the whole web and acknowledging our part within the web at the same time. We do not pray in the usual sense; rather, we focus our conscious awareness on the web.

---

[256] The paragraph under "The Dianic Tradition" heading was validated by Z Budapest for accuracy in its definition of the feminist Dianic tradition.

We invoke Her by aligning our personal will with the energies we call to conscious awareness within and without. When we do magic, we try to focus our awareness and will on particular strands in the web.

Dianic tradition draws primary inspiration from the Amazon goddess, Artemis.

Predominantly inspired by the qualities and aspects of the Greek goddess Artemis, as embodiment of wild nature and as a protector of women. Dianic witches are committed to the fundamental values of 2nd Wave feminism: female sovereignty and agency, an end to violence against women and children, the healing and protection of the Earth Mother, equity and full human rights and liberation for women and all oppressed people. Dianics use magic and ritual as a tool for healing from patriarchal oppression within ourselves and in the world.

Dianic practices are inspired by the awareness that the Goddess has been known throughout time by many names and in numerous cultures worldwide.

Rather than a focus on one deity exclusively, Dianics honor the Goddess, who has been called by Her daughters throughout time in many places and by many names. While we honor all of Her names and faces, there is also an ongoing commitment to develop understanding and sensitivity where the lines of worship and cultural appropriation may cross. An ongoing commitment to examining and challenging racism is an integral part of the tradition.

Dianic rituals celebrate the mythic cycle of the Goddess within the earth's seasonal cycles of birth, death, and regeneration, and as Her cycle reflects women's own life-cycle transitions.

The Dianic wheel of the year celebrations of the solstices, equinoxes, and cross-quarter holidays are based on the ever-changing, cyclic, and eternal nature of the Goddess. Unlike other Wiccan traditions, Dianic seasonal rites do not focus on or celebrate the exclusively heterosexual fertility cycle of the Goddess and the God. Dianic rituals may be creatively altered in their design from year to year, even as the seasonal theme remains constant.

The Goddess is celebrated in Her triple aspect of Maiden, Mother, and Crone as a manifestation of the entire life cycle: birth, maturation, and death. The Goddess has the power to bring forth life, nurture life, protect life, sustain life, and destroy life. This concept contains nature's entire continuum.

Dianic tradition is a Women's Mysteries ritual tradition that celebrates female life-cycle events.

Dianic witches recognize that it is within our own power to restore meaning to our lives by honoring the rites of passage we call Women's Mysteries. We recognize that our human experience is filtered through and informed by our female bodies and our specifically female physiology. Dianics are committed to valuing equally all phases of women's lives, from childhood to becoming an elder. As with the turning of the seasons, each phase is honored in its time.

Women's Mysteries include the physical, emotional, and psychic passages that women universally share by having been born biologically female. The five blood mysteries, which are the core of our ritual work and spiritual ethic, are comprised of being born, menarche, giving birth/lactation, menopause, and death. These Mysteries acknowledge and honor women's ability to create life, sustain and protect life, and return our bodies to the Goddess in death. Whether or not a woman births children, all women pass through the Mother phase as they choose life paths that sustain and protect our species or other life forms.

Women's Mysteries rituals support and celebrate female bonding, honor other significant personal milestones and transitions in women's lives, and work to heal from the effects of the dominator culture, both personally and globally.

In the honoring of Women's Mysteries, we also recognize that "our biology makes us human females; our culture makes us women."[257] Dianic Witchcraft helps women to develop into full personhood, beyond limiting patriarchal gender stereotypes of what a girl or woman can be. Our vision is to empower women and girls and transform our global culture so that women and men live in true equality worldwide.

Dianic tradition is celebrated exclusively with girls and woman in female sovereign circles.

Dianics recognize that the God, and all that is specifically male in nature, is a variation of the Goddess, sourced from and contained within Her, as both males and females are created, contained within, and birthed from the wombs of women. Therefore, although the God is always present as one of Her sacred creations, He is not specifically invoked in Dianic ritual, and there are no specifically male images placed on a Dianic altar.

Being a Women's Mysteries tradition, Dianic religion is *for* women and girls, not *against* men and boys. We support the right of males to their exclusive celebrations of Men's Mysteries in recognition of their unique rites of passage and spiritual journey to the Goddess. Many Dianic circles welcome male infants and toddlers with their mothers, providing that the ritual itself is age-appropriate for any child to attend.

Dianics support all people in finding their path to the Goddess; however, since our tradition is based in embodiment necessitates actually *being* female. Therefore we do not include males in our circles or rites, or males who self-define as women.[258] Women's Mysteries cannot be experienced through a performance of stereotypical gendered behavior, and chemical or surgical alterations to a male body.

As women, we honor the ways that our lives and ability to work our

---

[257] From a personal conversation with Wendy Griffin, former professor of women's studies at California State Long Beach.

[258] This includes hormonally and/or surgically altered males who present as women (aka. transsexual or transgender).

power is informed by our female physiology and our cellular memory. Even if a woman has had her womb removed later in life, her body of wisdom has been informed by her physical experiences of girlhood and womanhood. She will continue to work power from the cauldron of her womb-space all her life. Because Dianic tradition focuses on rites to heal women from the effects of personal and global oppression, we deal with growing up female in female-hating cultures worldwide. The depth to which patriarchy has shaped and affected our lives as women cannot truly be understood unless one has experienced it from birth into adulthood.

Many other Wiccan traditions do not share this fundamental requirement, and are welcoming of males who self-identify as women as participants. Females who self-identify themselves as men, disavow their female biology, and live as men would, by their own definition, exclude themselves from Dianic circles. Those rare and true intersexed individuals who have been raised female in our culture have been welcomed in Dianic circles.

Dianics honor our foremother's voices, thoughts, and ideas.

Dianic tradition is committed to uncovering, examining, reclaiming, and ascribing contemporary meanings to the lost or forgotten legacies, traditions, and magical practices of our foremothers from earliest times, and to recovering our herstory. We recognize that women's practices of the past are time-and place-specific, and that it is up to us to ascribe and reconstruct new meanings for spiritual practices within today's cultural contexts.

We honor our ancestors and the wombs from which we sprang, understanding that without honoring our past, we have no present or future. We honor our foremothers whose courageous, pioneering efforts forged the way for us and made our path easier.

Power is sourced through our wombs.

Our wombs are literally and metaphorically our personal cauldrons of creation, our centers of creative power. Power, defined as the ability to do, comes from within and with, not from exercising power over another. We recognize that a woman's womb-space continues to be her energetic source of power, even if she has had a hysterectomy.

Dianics honor the female body as a manifestation of the Goddess.

Dianics believe that it is healing and joyous for a woman to have a personal and direct experience of herself as a sacred manifestation of the Goddess, not just intellectually, but on an ecstatic, cellular level. Dianic tradition promotes the spiritual, religious, and celebratory use of female imagery as one of the many manifestations of the Goddess, as we recognize ourselves, and all our children, as born in Her divine image.

Dianic ritual and magical practices honor women's creativity, intuition, and ability to improvise.

Rather than scripted or set liturgy as the consistent or expected norm, Dianics encourage improvisation (authentic creative expression in the moment) in the arts, dance, writing, inspired speech, music, movement, and song in ritual design and during the ritual itself. Beloved songs, chants, poetry, and invocations often become tradition when repeated over time and as they continue to provide meaningful ritual experiences for a group or a solitary practitioner.

Dianics recognize that women's magic is a sacred trust; therefore, Dianics do not teach their Women's Mysteries and magic to men.

"Until the equality between the sexes is a reality,"[259] Dianics are opposed to teaching women's magic and Mysteries to males for a couple of reasons. When this position was originally written in the early 1970s, it recognized

[259] Budapest, *The Holy Book of Women's Mysteries*, 3. From the manifesto of the Susan B. Anthony Coven #1.

that women and men don't yet live in a post-patriarchy, and males are still the primary perpetrators in our dominator society. Thus teaching males our female magic was thought to be akin to giving our secrets to "the enemy". Given that female magic and Mysteries are embodied from cradle to grave (and thus not accessible to males), and a post-patriarchy reality is not yet achieved, this position remains. However, sharing the personal ritual making process in this book can be useful for everyone, regardless of their sex, since every person brings their own needs to their ritual design process.

Most Dianics are pleased to discuss the Goddess with interested men or to refer men to books or other traditions that will encourage their own journey to the Goddess and address their life experiences and issues. Some women who practice in the Dianic tradition also share a different ritual practice with their male partners, family, friends, or sons.

Sexuality is sacred. When lovers meet in mutual love, trust, and equality, these expressions of love and pleasure are a gift to, and from, the Goddess.

Dianic tradition is committed to a feminist paradigm of true sexual liberation. We work to free ourselves from the effects of a patriarchal, female-hating culture that equates sexuality, sexual expression, and eroticism with sadism, masochism, pornography, dominance, and subordination. Sexual practices that dehumanize, and whose purpose it is to cause pain, humiliation, or suffering, whether consensual or not, are inconsistent with a new paradigm for an egalitarian, peaceful, and healed world where power shared means empowerment for all. We seek to eroticize *peace,* and support nothing less than a revolution from within and without, both in the world and in the temple of the bedroom.

Sacred play is a form of spiritual practice.

Finding ways to enjoy and appreciate the gifts of life offered by the Goddess daily is a way to worship Her. Partaking fully of these pleasurable moments counters despair and fuels our courage and activism.

Dianic tradition is a teaching tradition.

Women teaching, sharing, and passing down knowledge is an act of sharing power. Teaching the next generation will help to ensure that Dianic tradition will endure and that women's wisdom survives.

Adherence to the Wiccan Rede.

Dianic tradition is in accord with the Wiccan Rede, which states "An' it harm none, do what you will." We honor free will, with the intention that our magical actions be for the greater good of all.

This Wiccan guidepost supports full consciousness with regards to the use of power in magical workings and in daily life, and promotes critical, ethical examination of one's actions or inactions.

bibliography & resources

Adler, Patricia and Peter. *Membership Roles in Field Research*. Sage Publishing, 1987.

Alba, De Anna. *The Cauldron of Change*. Delphi Press, Inc., 1993.

Anderson, Raymond T. "The Essence of Air," in *Circle Network News*, vol. 20: no. 4.

——. "The Essence of Earth," in *Circle Network News*, Summer 1998.

Ashcroft-Nowicki, Dolores. *First Steps in Ritual*. The Aquarian Press, 1990.

Assagioli, Roberto, M.D. *The Act of Will*. Arkana, 1992.

Bly, Robert. *Iron John*. Addison-Wesley Publishing Company, 1990.

Brener, Anne. *Mourning & Mitzvah: A Guided Journal for Walking the Mourner's Path Through Grief to Healing*. Jewish Lights Publishing, 1993.

Brooks, Nan. *Ceremonies for Our Lives*. Spirit Magic Books, 1991.

Brown, Karen McCarthy. "Serving the Spirits: The Ritual Economy of Haitian Vodou," in *Sacred Arts of Haitian Vodou*, edited by Donald J. Cosentino. South Sea International Press, Ltd., 1995.

Budapest, Zsuzsanna. *The Feminist Book of Lights and Shadows.* Luna Publications, 1976.

——. *The Feminist Book of Lights and Shadows,* revised edition, 1980.

——. *The Holy Book of Women's Mysteries*, vol.1. Susan B. Anthony Coven #1, 1979.

——. *The Holy Book of Women's Mysteries*. Wingbow Press, 1989.

Christ, Carol P. "Embodied Thinking: Reflections on Feminist Theological Method," in *Journal of Feminist Studies in Religion*, vol. 5, no.1. Spring 1989.

Cohen, David, editor. *The Circle of Life: Rituals from the Human Family Album*. HarperSanFrancisco, 1991.

Cuhulain, Kerr. *Wiccan Warrior: Walking A Spiritual Path in a Sometimes Hostile World.* Llewellyn, 2000.

Daily Prayer Book. Jewish Reconstructionist Foundation, 1945.

Daly, Mary. *Beyond God the Father*. Beacon Press, 1973.

———. *Outercourse*. HarperSanFrancisco, 1992.

——— and Jane Caputi. *Webster's First New Intergalactic Wickedary of the English Language*. Beacon Press, 1987.

Danaher, Kevin. *The Year in Ireland*. The Mercier Press, 1972.

Davidson, H. R. Ellis. *Myths and Symbols in Pagan Europe*. Syracuse University Press, 1988.

Eisler, Riane. *Sacred Pleasure*. HarperSanFrancisco, 1996.

———. *The Chalice and the Blade*. Harper and Row Publishing, 1987.

Eller, Cynthia. *Living in the Lap of the Goddess: The Feminist Spirituality Movement in America*. Beacon Press, 1995.

———. "The Roots of Feminist Spirituality," in *Daughters of the Goddess*, W. Griffin, editor. AltaMira Press, 2000.

Ellwood, Robert, and Barbara McGraw. *Many Peoples, Many Faiths: Women and Men in the World Religions* (6th ed.) Prentice-Hall, 1999.

Farrar, Janet, and Stewart Farrar. *The Witches' Bible,* vol. 2. Magical Childe Publishing Inc., 1984.

———. *Eight Sabbats for Witches*. Phoenix Publishing, 1981.

Fisher, Robin. "The Priestess Path," in *The Beltane Papers, A Journal of Women's Mysteries*, Issue 2.

Frazer, James. *The Golden Bough*. MacMillan Publishing Company, 1922.

Gage, Matilda. *Woman, Church and State*, 1893. Reprinted by Persephone Press, 1980.

Geertz, Clifford. *The Interpretation of Symbols*. Basic Books, 1983.

Gimbutas, Marija. *The Gods and Goddesses of Old Europe: 7000 to 3500 BC: Myths, Legends and Cult Images*. University of California Press, 1974.

———. *The Language of the Goddess.* Harper & Row, 1989.

———. *The Civilization of the Goddess*. HarperSanFrancisco, 1991.

———. *The Living Goddess*, edited and supplemented by Miriam Robbins-Dexter. University of California Press, 1999.

Goldenberg, Naomi. *Changing of the Gods: Feminism and the End of Traditional Religions.* Beacon Press, 1979.

Goodrich, Norma Lorre. *Priestesses.* Harper Perennial, 1989.

Grahn, Judy. *Blood, Bread, and Roses: How Menstruation Created the World.* Beacon Press, 1993.

Graves, Robert. *The White Goddess.* Farrar, Straus and Giroux, 1948.

Green, Miriam. *The Path Through the Labyrinth.* Element Books, 1988.

———. *A Witch Alone.* The Aquarian Press, 1991.

———. *A Calendar of Festivals.* Element Books Inc., 1991.

———. *Natural Magic.* Element Books Limited, 1989.

Griffin, Susan. *Woman and Nature.* Harper & Row, 1978.

Griffin, Wendy, editor. *Daughters of the Goddess: Studies of Healing, Identity and Empowerment.* AltaMira Press, 2000.

Grimassi, Raven. *Italian Witchcraft, The Old Religion of Southern Europe.* Llewellyn, 2000.

———. *The Witches' Craft.* Llewellyn, 2000.

Hagan, Kay Leigh. *Fugitive Information.* Harper Collins, 1993.

———. *Women Respond to the Men's Movement.* HarperSanFrancisco, 1992.

Harrison, Jane. *Prolegomena to the Study of Greek Religion.* Merlin Press, 1962.

———. *Epilegomena & Themis.* University Books, 1962.

———. *Ancient Art and Ritual.* Oxford University Press, 1913, 1947.

Hart, Nett and Lee Lanning, editors. *Dreaming.* Word Weavers, 1983.

hooks, bell. *Feminism Is for Everybody.* South End Press, 2000.

Hope, Murry. *The Psychology of Ritual.* Element Books, 1988.

Hutton, Ronald. *The Triumph of the Moon.* Oxford University Press, 1999.

Jade. *To Know.* Delphi Press, 1991.

K, Amber. *Moonrise: Welcome to Dianic Wicca.* Re-Formed Congregation of the Goddess, 1992.

Kaplan, Mordecai. *Not So Random Thoughts.* Reconstructionist Press, 1966.

Kindred, Glennie. *The Earth's Cycle of Celebration.* Self-published. Appletree Cottage (Dale End, Brassington, NR Matlock, Derbyshire, England, DE4 4HA)

——. *Sacred Celebrations: A Sourcebook.* Gothic Image Publications, 2001.

Kirk, Robert, and R. J. Stewart. *Walker Between Worlds.* Element Books Limited, 1990.

Knightly, Charles. *The Customs and Ceremonies of Britain.* Thames and Hudson Ltd., 1986.

Lakoff, George and Johnson, Mark, *Metaphors We Live By,* The University of Chicago Press, 1980.

Lakoff, George and Turner, Mark, *More Than Cool Reason – A Field Guide to Poetic Metaphor,* The University of Chicago Press, 1989.

Legato, Marianne J. *Eve's Rib.* Harmony Books, New York, 2002.

Leland, Charles G. *Etruscan Roman Remains.* Phoenix Publishing Inc. Originally published in 1892.

Lerner, Gerta. *The Creation of Feminist Consciousness.* Oxford University Press Inc., 1993.

Levitt, Joy, and Michael Strassfeld, editors. *A Night of Questions: A Passover Haggadah.* The Reconstructionist Press, 2000.

Malinowski, Bronislaw. *Magic, Science, and Religion.* Waveland Press, 1982.

Markova, Dawna, Ph.D. *The Open Mind.* Conari Press, 1996.

Matthews, Caitlin. *Singing the Soul Back Home.* Element Books, Inc., 1995.

——. *Sophia, Goddess of Wisdom.* Mandala, 1991.

——. *The Celtic Spirit,* HarperSanFrancisco, 1999.

Matthews, John. *The Celtic Shaman.* Element Books, Inc., 1991.

Matthews, Caitlin and John. *The Encyclopedia of Celtic Wisdom.* Barnes & Noble Books, 1994.

——. *The Western Way,* volumes 1 and 2. Arkana/The Penquin Group, 1986.

Monaghan, Patricia. *Seasons of the Witch.* Llewellyn, 2002.

Mountainwater, Shekhinah. *Ariadne's Thread.* The Crossing Press, 1991.
Republished in June, 2018 by Echo Point Books & Media LLC, www.echopointbooks.com

Myss, Carolyn, PhD. *Energy Anatomy.* Sounds True Recordings, 1996.

Noble, Vicki. "Double Queens of the Amazons," in *The Beltane Papers*, Issue 18.

———. *The Double Goddess: Women Sharing Power*. Inner Traditions, 2003.

Noonan, Kerry. "May You Never Hunger: Religious Foodways in Dianic Witchcraft," in *Ethnologies*, vol. 20, no. 1–2, 1998.

Northrup, Christiane, M.D. *Women's Bodies, Women's Wisdom*. Bantam Books, 1998.

Orenstein, Deborah, ed. *Lifecycles: Jewish Women on Life Passages & Personal Milestones*, vol. I. Jewish Lights Publishing, 1994.

Oswald, Ramona Faith, editor. *Lesbian Rites: Symbolic Acts and the Power of Community*. Haworth Press, Inc, 2003.

Ozaniec, Naomi. *Daughter of the Goddess*. The Aquarian Press, 1993.

Paterson, Jacqueline Memory. *Tree Wisdom: The Definitive Guidebook to the Myth, Folklore, and Healing Power of Trees*. Thorsons, 1996.

Pearsall, Paul, PhD. *The Heart's Code*. Broadway Books, 1998.

Pinel, John. *Biopsychology*. Allyn & Bacon, 1997.

Redmond, Layne. *When the Drummers Were Women*. Three Rivers Press, 1997.

Rives, Cathy, M.D. "In Honor of Psychotherapy," in *Pacifica Newsletter*, 1998.

Roslund, Janet, and Mary Lou Mills. "Why We Are Dianic," in *The Best of Thesmophoria*, vol. 11, no. 1.

Sharma, Arvind, and Katherine K. Young, editors. *Her Voice, Her Faith: Women Speak on World Religions*. Westview Press, 2003 (particularly the article "Goddess Spirituality and Wicca").

Sjoo, Monica, and Barbara Mor. *The Great Cosmic Mother*. Harper and Row Publishers, 1987.

Skelton, Robin. *Spellcraft*. McClelland and Stewart, 1978.

Spence, Lewis. *The Magic Arts in Celtic Britain*. Dover Publications, 1999.

Starhawk. *The Spiral Dance*. HarperSanFrancisco, 1989.

Starhawk, Anne Hill, and Diane Baker. *Circle Round: Raising Children in Goddess Traditions*. Bantam Books, 1998.

Starhawk, M. Macha NightMare, and The Reclaiming Collective. *The Pagan Book of Living and Dying.* HarperSanFrancisco, 1997.

VanArsdall, Nancy. *Coming Full Circle.* Third Side Press, 1996.

Walker, Alice. *Possessing the Secret of Joy.* Harcourt Brace, 1992.

Walker, Alice, Pratibha Parmar, and Vicki Austin-Smith. *Warrior Marks: Female Genital Mutilation and the Sexual Binding of Women.* Harvest Books, 1996.

Walker, Barbara. *The Women's Encyclopedia of Myths and Secrets.* Harper & Row, 1983.

Ward, Edna M., editor. *Celebrating Ourselves: A Crone Ritual Book.* Astarte Shell Press, 1992.

West, Canon Edward N. *Outward Signs.* Walker & Co., 1989.

Wilshire, Donna. *Virgin, Mother, Crone.* Inner Traditions, 1994.

Wimberly, Lowry Charles. *Folklore in the English and Scottish Ballads.* Dover Publications, 1965.

Wolf, Naomi. *Promiscuities: The Secret Struggle for Womanhood.* The Ballantine Publishing Group, 1997.

We are blessed to live in a time where there is a wealth of resources for those interested in Pagan, Wiccan, and goddess education, music, and arts. Due to space limitations, I have listed only those Dianic organizations and programs with which I am either personally affiliated or specifically familiar with their work. The artists and musicians listed are but a few that I especially respect and enjoy.

Dianic Organizations/Educational Programs

Temple of Diana, Inc. (co-founded by Ruth Barrett and Falcon River)
www.templeofdiana.org

Dedicated to women's magic and mysteries. Rituals, classes, and workshops in the Dianic tradition, including The Spiral Door Women's Mystery School of Magick and Ritual Arts, a Dianic Priestess training program with Ruth Barrett and Falcon River. To find out where groves of Temple of Diana are located, please visit the website.

Daughters of the Goddess (contact: Leilani Birely, High Priestess)
San Francisco Bay area
email: leimermaid@aol.com
www.daughtersoftheGoddess.com
A Dianic temple dedicated in the spirit of Aloha, to the preservation and perpetuation of multicultural goddess culture, public ceremony, ritual, and Women's Mysteries.

Goddess-Centered Music

Ruth Barrett

CD Recordings by Ruth Barrett are available through Dancing Tree Music, Available through www.dancingtreemusic.com

Songs of the Otherworld (2011)
Garden of Mysteries (2008)
The Year Is a Dancing Woman: Seasonal Chants, Songs and Invocations for the Wheel of the Year, volumes I and II, (2003).
Parthenogenesis (1990).
Invocation to Free Women (1987), Ruth Barrett with Felicity Artemis Flowers and others.

Ruth Barrett and Cyntia Smith

The Early Years (1999) is a compilation of Ruth and Cyntia's first two recordings, *Aeolus* (1981) and *Music of the Rolling World* (1982).
Deepening (1984).
A Dulcimer Harvest (1991).
The Heart Is the Only Nation (1993).
Available through: www.dancingtreemusic.com

Kay Gardner

Ouroboros: Seasons of Life. (CD) An oratorio composed by Kay Gardner on Ladyslipper Records. Available through Goldenrod Distribution: www.goldenrod.com.

Carolyn Hillyer

Old Silverhead: Songs and Initiations of Womanhood. CD available through Seventh Wave Music, www.seventhwave.co.uk

Shekhinah Mountainwater

For CDs, WomanRunes, and a link to *Ariadne's Thread*
www.shekhinahmountainwater.com

Wendy Rule

www.wendyrule.com

Goddess-Centered Artists

Abby Willowroot, Goddess art, www.spiralgoddess.com

Ancient Visions, Artwork by artist/scholar ***Sid Reger.*** Stone Age Goddess figures, mandalas, masks, artworks, workshops on silent prehistoric goddesses. http://ancestralvisions.com/Goddess-Mandala/

Nancy Chien-Eriksen, Cover artist for this book, www.NancyArt.com

Joanne Powell Colbert, www.gaiantarot.com

Max Dashu, Goddess art and the best goddess and women slide show presentations you will ever see: www.supprssedhistories.net.

index

About the Author

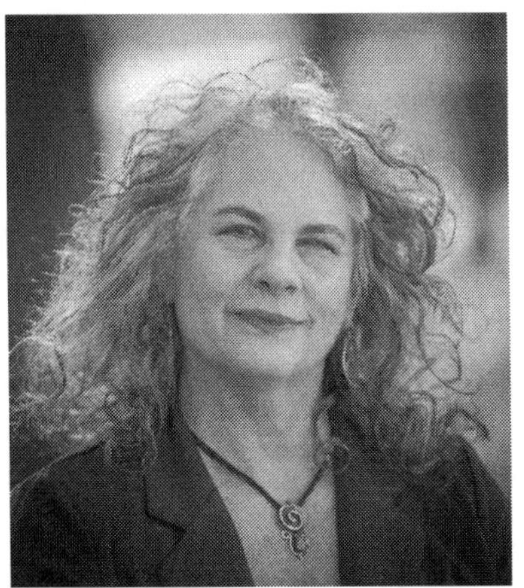

Ruth Barrett is an ordained Dianic High Priestess, seasoned ritualist, and award-winning recording artist. She inherited Z Budapest's Los Angeles ministry in 1980, and has taught Women's Mysteries, magic and ritual arts at women's festivals and conferences in the United States, Canada, and Great Britain. She co-founded and served the Los Angeles goddess community of Circle of Aradia for two decades before relocating to Wisconsin in 2000, where she and Priestess Falcon River, co-founded Temple of Diana, Inc., a national and federally recognized Dianic temple. Ruth received the 1997 L.A.C.E. award for community service at the Gay and Lesbian Center in Los Angeles. Her writings on women and ritual are included in several anthologies including, *Daughters of the Goddess* (Wendy Griffin, editor), *Stepping Into Ourselves: An Anthology of Writings of Priestesses*, (Anne Key and Candace Kant, editors), *Foremothers of the Women's Spirituality Movement: Elders and Visionaries* (Miriam Robbins Dexter and Vicki Nobel, editors). Ruth is the editor of *Female Erasure: What You Need to Know About Gender Politics' War on Women, The Female Sex and Human Rights*. Ruth directed the Candlelight Concert at the Michigan Womyn's Music Festival from 1992 – until the closure of the festival in 2015. Ruth resides in Michigan with her life companion, Falcon River. To contact Ruth:

* visit her website at www.guardiansofthegrove.org

* Photo © Ursula Hoppe Photography
  www.ursulahoppephotography.com

Manufactured by Amazon.ca
Bolton, ON

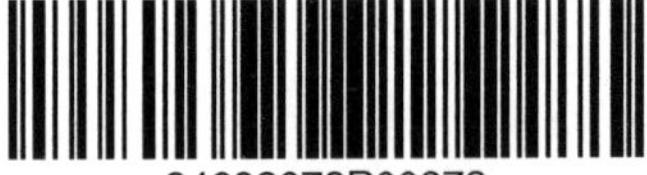